Affording Defense

Affording Defense

Investing in American Strength to Confront a More Dangerous World

Edited by
Mackenzie Eaglen

AEI PRESS

Publisher for the American Enterprise Institute
WASHINGTON, DC

ISBN-13: 978-0-8447-5094-1 (Paperback)

Library of Congress Cataloging in Publication data have been applied for.

Cover image: The Boeing MQ-25 T1 test plane transfers fuel to a Navy F/A-18 Super Hornet on June 4, 2021, marking the first time an unmanned aircraft has refueled another aircraft. Credit: Boeing/Kevin Flynn.

A꞊I PRESS

Publisher for the American Enterprise Institute
for Public Policy Research
1789 Massachusetts Avenue, NW
Washington, DC 20036
www.aei.org

Printed in the United States of America

Contents

1

On the Brink of Insolvency: Reversing Washington's 30-Year Strategy-Resource Mismatch for the US Armed Forces

MACKENZIE EAGLEN

For over three decades, the United States military has been expanding its mission while losing ground financially—even as its enemies and potential peer adversaries race ahead in meaningful technological and warfighting leaps. At the so-called "end of history" in 1991, the armed forces were forced to accept a procurement holiday on spending for weapons and new capabilities. This was followed by two decades of war. While money poured in, most of it was to make up for the shortfalls of the Clinton era and war-related consumables—a hollow and perishable spending spike.

Uncommon in our national history, Washington then began slashing military budgets with troops in harm's way when the era of fiscal restraint and the Tea Party began in 2010. The Budget Control Act (BCA), sequestration, and lasting reductions across the board followed. Even when new administrations swept into office with modest increases for defense above inflation, they were hardly enough to cover the potholes that grew out of this period. Restoring readiness became a priority while rebuilding combat power consistently slipped further to the right.

As the military's conventional and strategic deterrents eroded nearly simultaneously, the global threat environment grew only more vexing, interconnected, and expansive. The United States faces its most dangerous strategic environment since World War II—with more enemies, fewer resources, and growing risks of conflict on multiple fronts. We are facing a strategic landscape defined by the growing strength, aggression, and cooperation of US adversaries. China, Russia, Iran, and North Korea—once largely acting independently—are increasingly coordinating efforts to weaken American influence and successfully challenge and slowly reshape the norms of the international order.

At the same time, America's military is shrinking, aging, and over-committed, leaving it dangerously unprepared for modern warfare. This imbalance between expanding global commitments and a diminishing force structure has resulted in strategic insolvency.

Sound defense planning demands long-term thinking, considering not what changes—threats and technologies—but what stays the same: American interests and principles. Since 1945, international politics has been shaped by American military strength more than by anything else.

Restoring the nation's strategic credibility will require confronting this widening gap between national security ambitions and resources for hard power. Without significant investment in a modernized and capable military, the United States risks falling behind in its ability to deter threats and safeguard global leadership.

The Axis of Aggression: America's Multi-Theater Threats

America's adversaries are on the march. Revisionist powers around the world have escalated their respective efforts over the past decade to undermine US security, put the homeland at risk, and overturn the world order independently. These powers are increasingly working together to advance this goal across multiple theaters simultaneously.

China has aggressively sought to challenge US military might in the Indo-Pacific. At the same time, the Chinese Communist Party's military investment has increased rapidly, as its growing outputs demonstrate. According to the Pentagon, China is not only catching up to but exceeding the United States' military capabilities in several key areas.[1] China now fields the world's largest army, navy, and sub-strategic rocket force; possesses a steadily growing and technologically advanced air force; and aims to multiply the size of its nuclear arsenal.[2] Recent AEI research indicates that Beijing is investing up to three times its publicly reported military expenditures with an actual budget as large as ours. When considering that China is focused on changing the status quo in Asia, whereas the US military must always play an away game,

China's ability to generate force may be even greater than that of the US.[3]

Russia's invasion of a sovereign, democratic Ukraine stands at the center of its campaign to destabilize a continent and break an unprecedented generational alliance in NATO. To sustain its assault, Moscow has relied on support from Iran, which provides drones, tech know-how, and manufacturing capacity, and North Korea, which supplies weapons, manpower, and tunnel warfare expertise.[4] Yet this invasion has not fully occupied the Kremlin's attention. Russia continues to support Houthi efforts to disrupt Red Sea trade and bolster authoritarianism in the Middle East, illustrating Moscow's ongoing ambition to strengthen US adversaries and weaken US influence beyond Europe.

Emboldened by new ties with Russia and China, Iran has escalated its regional aggression, directly attacking Israel and US forces while enabling proxy campaigns across the Middle East.[5] Its proxies in Gaza and Lebanon have intensified strikes against Israel while ballistic missiles and drones have targeted US bases.[6] Tehran has also provided direct support to the Houthis, who have repeatedly engaged in monthslong shooting wars with the US Navy. Even after the incredible and successful strike to set back Iranian nuclear ambitions, the country's radical leaders continuously seek to further escalate tensions and destabilize the region.[7]

Interconnected threats across multiple theaters have left the US military stretched dangerously thin. Critical but scarce munitions must be divided between the competing needs of US allies and domestic stockpiles, and decisions on deploying missile defense systems pit the urgent demands of Ukraine, Israel, and Indo-Pacific bases and partners against one another.[8] Joint assets are constantly redeployed to cover gaps in one region, often creating vulnerabilities elsewhere—illustrating the fragile nature of the US military's current force structure.[9] If Russia escalated its aggression beyond Ukraine, China move on Taiwan, and Iran further embolden its proxies across the Middle East simultaneously, the United States military would be catastrophically overstretched, forcing impossible prioritization and leaving critical regions undefended.[10]

A One-War Military in a Three-Theater World

While military funding is typically flat or down from year to year, national ambitions and political habits change very little. That means they often only grow over time. The result is a military no longer sized or structured to fight and win in multiple theaters while Washington continues to assume it can. Successive National Defense Strategies under the Obama, Trump, and Biden administrations have emphasized global commitments and great-power competition, even as resources and force structure have declined.[11]

Historically, American defense strategy was built on the ability to fight and win two simultaneous wars, ensuring global stability and credible deterrence. This "two-war strategy" was key during the Cold War, allowing the US to engage in a major conflict while deterring the Soviet Union. However, after the Cold War, American leaders moved too aggressively to cut budgets even while strategic priorities grew as threats emerged and reemerged in the Indo-Pacific, the Middle East, and Europe.[12]

The 1997 Quadrennial Defense Review still reiterated that a "two-war" force was necessary, emphasizing the ability to "deter and defeat large-scale, cross-border aggression in two distant theaters in overlapping time frames, preferably in concert with regional allies," despite post–Cold War drawdowns in force size and strength.[13] The review also spelled out the danger of a one-war capacity, stating it would "risk undermining both deterrence and the credibility of US security commitments in key regions of the world."[14]

Despite these warnings, by the 2010s, shrinking defense budgets, reduced force structure, grinding long-term counterinsurgency operations, and evolving threats had further eroded this capability. More recent strategies have prioritized China while assuming the US can still manage risk in Europe and the Middle East—effectively accepting a one-war force. This has made the US military a one-war force lite. The 2024 National Defense Strategy Commission's report made this clear when it stated that the 2022 National Defense Strategy "does not sufficiently account for global competition or the very real threat of simultaneous conflict in more than one theater" and that the commission was "not confident that the US military would succeed in a regional conflict against China."[15]

America's Shrinking Defense Budget

The military's size and strength are correlated with the resources—primarily defense spending—available to it. While the defense topline has grown modestly overall since the post–Cold War lows, inflation-adjusted budgets have often failed to provide real growth, eroding purchasing power.[16] As a result, the armed forces have continued to shrink the active-duty force and delay the modernization of critical capabilities nearly across the board.[17] Recently, defense spending has declined in all three key metrics: as a percentage of gross domestic product (GDP), as a share of federal spending, and when adjusted for inflation.[18]

The most recent budgetary challenges can be traced to 2011's BCA. Designed to rein in federal spending, the BCA imposed stringent caps on discretionary spending, including on defense, triggering cuts via sequestration when Congress failed to reach broader deficit reduction agreements. This proved devastating for military readiness, modernization, and force structure, necessitating across-the-board reductions with little regard for strategic priorities.[19] The 2018 National Defense Strategy Commission estimated that these cuts amounted to $539 billion between fiscal years (FYs) 2012 and 2019.[20]

What made this era even more remarkable—and damaging—was that budget cuts accelerated while American troops remained deployed in combat zones. Unlike past drawdowns that occurred after wars ended, Congress slashed defense spending at the height of the Iraq and Afghanistan conflicts. This marked the first time since Vietnam that the US hollowed out its force while still involved in multiple theaters of conflict. Indeed, the reductions were so devastating that more US troops are now dying in peacetime accidents than in combat—even while meaningful force levels were still deployed in both Iraq and Afghanistan.[21]

Managed decline has led to deep cuts and outright cancellations of numerous necessary and already overdue weapons programs—regularly deferred after 1991. When defense budgets failed to provide real growth, policymakers often raided procurement and modernization accounts to cover immediate operational needs. Slowed procurement and modernization efforts resulted in a downsized military unable to do easily or quickly what it had for the generation prior.

Key programs like the *Seawolf*-class submarine, F-22 stealth fighter, and the Army's Future Combat Systems were either canceled outright or the Pentagon ended up buying fractions of the forecasted purchases at the time of program launch.[22] Today, as older platforms age out of service, the military faces a stark reality: There are no robust next-generation systems ready to replace them.[23]

That is, unless the once-in-a-generation reconciliation bill for the armed forces that was passed by Congress in July succeeds. This is a big question mark, but it is likely to inject a significant infusion of real money in a short amount of time to help scale research projects long overdue; update planned purchases for the warfighter in the face of tech that changes, in some cases, by the day or hour; and disrupt long-staid concepts of operations and force-planning assumptions. While it is a huge and welcome investment, it cannot become a fiscal cliff. Starting dozens or even hundreds of programs without a tail of investment to see them over the production finish line or sustain those weapons after they are fielded would be worse than waste; it would be a dereliction of duty for those in uniform who demand world-class capabilities.

The Cost of Doing More with Less

Though the US military remains the world's preeminent fighting force, its size and strength have eroded, compromising its ability to deter and operate effectively across multiple theaters. Consistently adapting to do more with less has come at a steep cost, undermining long-term readiness and credible deterrence. Incremental decisions to manage within annual budgetary limitations often established new baselines where deterrence degraded gradually and then suddenly.

The consequences of authoritarians on the march are increasingly tangible across key regions. In the Middle East, the Navy is consistently expending more munitions than it can replenish, setting the stage for significant munition shortages in a potential multiregional great-power war.[24] The Marine Corps, with its shrunken amphibious warship fleet, can no longer serve as the crisis response force and cannot meet combatant commanders' and allies' needs.[25] The Air Force no longer provides immediate or regional air superiority—resulting recently in the first US soldiers killed by an air threat since the end of the Korean War.[26]

The US Army active-duty force has seen a staggering decline until an uptick just recently. Though just a few years ago Army leaders sought to build up to around 550,000 troops, the Army saw little progress amid recruiting challenges and a lack of budgetary growth.[27] The most recent budget request puts the Army's end strength at just 442,000—100,000 short of that goal and the smallest it has been since before World War II.

Despite advances in technology and the deployment of new capabilities, the military's force structure has weakened drastically. While modern capabilities offer new advantages, sufficient capacity is necessary to sustain a globally deployed force. A single soldier, ship, or aircraft can still be in only one place at a time.[28] The US Navy, for example, is nearly half the size it was at the Cold War's height, yet the demand is the same or, more often, higher. In 1985, roughly 15 percent of the fleet—about 100 ships—was deployed at any given time, with typical deployments lasting six months. Today, the Navy forward deploys a similar number of ships but with a much smaller fleet, placing significantly more strain on each vessel and crew.[29]

In recent years, deployment length has effectively doubled while consuming 30 percent or more of the fleet since 2017.[30] Additionally, the Navy has failed to meet goals of having 75 mission-capable surface ships ready at any given time.[31] Fewer ships to spare means longer deployments, which, in turn, mean more hardship for service members and deferred maintenance on hardware, compounding growing costs on the shrinking fleet.

The US military is now too small and ill prepared to meet its full suite of global responsibilities. The persistent strain on platforms, people, and readiness is not a temporary challenge—it is a structural shortfall. When the force lacks sufficient capacity, it cannot sustain forward presence well, surge in crisis, or deter adversaries in multiple regions at once. This scarcity imposes hard trade-offs between the Indo-Pacific, Europe, the Middle East, and homeland defense and between current operations and long-term readiness.[32] Without additional capacity, the US will continue to fall short of its own strategy, undermining deterrence and increasing the risk that adversaries act while America is overstretched or absent.

Living Off the Reagan Buildup

The military buildup of the 1980s, which peaked under President Ronald Reagan, offers an important lesson for addressing today's challenges: Sustained investment and a clear strategic vision are essential to rebuilding military strength. Just as the United States faced heightened Soviet aggression following the post–Vietnam War drawdown, today's adversaries—China, Russia, Iran, North Korea, and their proxies—pose similarly coordinated and multifaceted threats. Reagan's approach to rebuilding the military contrasts sharply with modern efforts, which are marked by inconsistent funding and a lack of commitment to expanding combat power. Further, while Reagan oversaw the largest peacetime buildup of military forces in modern history, he also employed the armed forces with far less regularity than all of the presidents who would come after him who used it more but often funded it less.

First, the Reagan buildup devoted a much larger portion of national wealth to national defense. Though defense spending is nominally higher today than at the Reagan buildup's height (an inflation-adjusted $798 billion compared with $849 billion today), defense spending was much higher as a proportion of national wealth.[33] During the buildup, defense spending averaged around 5.9 percent of GDP. Today, it stands at just under 3 percent, the lowest it has been since the end of the Cold War (and lower than what the current administration is asking of NATO allies).[34] This means that defense spending received nearly twice as much economic commitment during the buildup as it does today.[35] If Washington allocated 6 percent of today's $27 trillion GDP to defense—the same percentage as during the Reagan buildup—the defense budget would be roughly $1.6 trillion, nearly twice its current size.[36]

Second, while the topline matters, how the budget is spent matters equally. Reagan's defense increases focused on purchasing substantial quantities of equipment and expanding the armed forces' capacity and end strength. From FY1983 to FY1987, the cumulative boost in current dollars in modernization spending—procurement and research and development (R&D) combined—amounted to $567 billion above the average of the preceding and following decades. This investment not only enhanced readiness but provided the foundation for a robust and well-equipped force that remains, in many ways, the backbone of today's military capabilities.

Modernization spending—research, development, test, and evaluation (RDT&E) and procurement—made up a larger share of the defense budget during the Reagan buildup.[37] In FY1985, it accounted for 42.9 percent of the budget, compared with just 36 percent in the FY2025 request. Reagan-era budgets also prioritized buying equipment over developing future systems, with $3.30 spent on procurement for every $1 on R&D. Today, that ratio has shrunk to $1.16.[38] While R&D spending is important to maintain a technological advantage, parity between procurement and R&D is a recipe for a smaller and weaker military.

In simple terms, mid-1980s defense budgets bought a whole lot of everything—airframes, ships, and armored vehicles. Take aircraft for instance: In FY1985, the US purchased a plethora of different fighter and attack aircraft, amounting to 338 aircraft, with 192 for the Air Force and 146 for the Navy.[39] This total doesn't even account for purchases of bombers, electronic warfare aircraft, and other planes.[40] Compare that with the FY2025 budget request, in which the administration is seeking to acquire only 86 fighter and attack aircraft, with 60 for the Air Force and 26 for the Navy.[41] This amounts to about 75 percent less than the same category of aircraft that the military purchased in 1985.

For the Army and Marine Corps, ground vehicle procurement offers a similarly sharp contrast. In 1985, the Army and Marine Corps acquired more than 2,000 tracked vehicles across multiple programs.[42] These large-scale buys built the core of the ground combat fleet in service today. In the FY2025 request, the combined total for new tracked vehicles is less than 250—including limited numbers of armored transport and amphibious vehicles and some modest upgrades to legacy platforms.[43] The gap between past and present output reflects the broader decline in the sustained procurement necessary to modernize the force at scale.

The Navy also saw significant expansion during the Reagan buildup, anchored by a clear strategic goal: a 600-ship fleet. The FY1985 shipbuilding plan included five submarines, three cruisers, one destroyer, and numerous auxiliary vessels, totaling 23 new ships.[44] In contrast, the FY2025 request calls for just six ships: one submarine, two destroyers, one frigate, one amphibious warfare ship, and one support vessel.

With planned retirements exceeding new construction, the Navy's fleet will decline from 287 to 283 ships—moving further away from stated force-level goals aspiring to a fleet of well over 300 ships.[45]

Military Modernization Bills Are Overdue, Mass Matters, and Our Tech Is Lagging

Recent administrations have tried to increase modernization spending, but persistent shortfalls remain given that defense increases often come after massive cuts. Spending spikes that are not sustained over time and above inflation therefore have little lasting impact. They are more like funding to fill potholes versus wholesale replacement of road for, say, high-speed rail. Procurement has not kept pace with the need to replace aging equipment on anything close to one-to-one or to close critical readiness gaps. The balance between procurement and RDT&E remains skewed, with insufficient investment in fielding new platforms at scale. As a result, modernization has lagged, creating a growing mismatch between current capabilities and future requirements.

In many ways, the US military is living off the fruits of the Reagan buildup. F-16 and F-15 fighters, which still form the backbone of the US Air Force's combat aircraft fleet, are on average over 30 years old.[46] Similarly, the Navy's *Ohio*-class ballistic missile submarines have an average age of approximately 35 years, while many of the Navy's destroyers are approaching or exceeding 30 years in service.[47] The US Army continues to rely on Abrams tanks and Bradley Fighting Vehicles, of which new procurement is limited and older variants are upgraded.[48]

Without replacements ready or politicians willing to risk leaping the acquisition "valley of death," the Pentagon has relied on increasingly expensive efforts to extend aging platforms' service lives. These extensions often lead to higher maintenance and operating costs with diminishing returns. Alternatively, some equipment is retired without replacement, shrinking the force and exacerbating readiness challenges.[49]

Even after the end of the BCA, budgets have done little to right the wrongs. The "Trump bump," which increased defense spending by $225 billion over previous plans, was not enough to change the trajectory of managed decline set in place by Barack Obama.[50] Much of this new funding was dedicated to personnel, operations, and maintenance accounts, which meant modest and inconsistent boosts to procurement hindering any wholesale replacement of aging equipment.[51]

While defense budgets increased under Joe Biden in nominal terms, they failed to offset inflation or meaningfully address the modernization backlog. The FY2025 request reflected a 1 percent increase over FY2024 to $849.8 billion and allocated just $170 billion to procurement—roughly 20 percent of the total budget and well below the share devoted to new equipment during the Reagan buildup. In real terms, this represented a decline from FY2024, highlighting the growing gap between strategic demands and available resources.[52]

Similarly, the FY2025 topline was $10 billion below the Pentagon's internal projections and fell short of inflation-adjusted requirements.[53] Much of the funding for new equipment has been deferred into the out-years, prompting former Secretary of Defense Lloyd Austin to acknowledge that "we'll need to have growth in a top line in the out-years to ensure that we can recapture some of the things that we weren't able to get into this budget." Without sustained real growth, that recapture looks increasingly unlikely.[54]

This overreliance on legacy systems has created a modernization backlog so severe that the US military is now firmly in the "Terrible 20s"—a decade in which equipment is aging out faster than it can be replaced.[55] It is also why the reconciliation bill for defense granting $150 billion in mandatory spending over the next several years is precisely what is needed for the US military at this moment. The Army, Navy, and Air Force are all facing simultaneous modernization demands, requiring urgent recapitalization to replace aging fleets, restore lost capacity, and adapt to the challenges of great-power competition—particularly with China.

A Fragile Posture in a Dangerous World

Winning wars does not solely demand capable forces, skilled leaders, smart planning, joint readiness, or exquisite and abundant weapons. Fundamentally, to win a war—and therefore deter one—demands (1) public support, (2) ample funding, and (3) a manufacturing and tech industrial base capable and large enough to crank out kit of sufficient quality to support a protracted war long after our high-end gear has run empty.

Unlike the Cold War, where a singular focus on deterring the Soviet Union defined strategy, today's threats are dynamic, sophisticated, and multilayered. Aligned adversaries pursue coordination that amplifies their ability to challenge the United States across domains, from economic and trade to cyber, space, and information warfare.[56]

This shift is likely to heighten demands on current US strategy, as simultaneous and interconnected threats require a level of agility and capacity that the current force struggles to meet. Today's military also faces additional challenges unique to modern warfare, including a largely transparent battle space, advanced precision weapons, anti-access and area-denial systems, and cyber capabilities that undermine traditional notions of deterrence and defense.

Compounding these challenges is the US industrial base, which decades of underinvestment have diminished.[57] Unlike the Cold War era, when the defense industry could rapidly scale production, today's constrained manufacturing capacity means the military lacks the surge potential to replenish equipment and adapt quickly to prolonged conflicts.[58] This bottleneck increases the risks of supply-chain disruptions and equipment shortages, further weakening the United States' ability to sustain prolonged operations.[59]

Ultimately, the interplay between these modern threats and declining US military strength leaves the force operating on a razor's edge. A significant escalation in one theater risks exposing critical vulnerabilities in another, creating openings for adversaries to exploit. China, Russia, and others understand that America lacks the depth to fight and sustain operations in multiple regions at once. This recognition increases the risk of opportunistic aggression, as adversaries may conclude that the current moment offers the best window to act. Addressing this precarious balance will require not only reinvestment in force structure but a deliberate effort to restore industrial capacity and adopt more innovative, resilient deterrence strategies.

The Path Forward: Resourcing to Match the Strategy

Rebuilding the US military to align with policymakers' aims, our global strategic commitments, and reality as it is versus what we wish it could be is essential to restoring global deterrence. Any effort to grow the military's size and strength must directly tackle the challenges of deferred modernization and insufficient funding.

As the US navigates the midpoint of the Terrible 20s, the consequences of decades of underinvestment and deferred modernization are becoming increasingly clear. Budget cuts, flat funding, and incremental increases are insufficient when the costs of maintaining a globally deployed, volunteer force continue to rise and adversaries rapidly modernize their capabilities. While toplines have grown nominally over the past five years, red-hot inflation has decreased the Pentagon's buying power. In fact, the average annual real rate of growth in the Pentagon's budget is –1 percent.[60] This is unsustainable as the costs of personnel, equipment, and operations continue to rise.

To reverse the military's current trajectory and meet the current strategy's demands, significant, sustained budgetary growth is required along the lines of the 2026 budget reconciliation for defense, at $150 billion over a half decade.

Both the 2018 and 2024 National Defense Strategy Commissions recommend an annual increase of 3–5 percent to offset inflation and provide the Pentagon with meaningful, sustained growth.[61] If the full 5 percent annual growth is achieved, the projected defense budget will grow by approximately $235 billion over the next five years. This level of investment would provide the necessary resources to address critical modernization needs, rebuild force capacity, and strengthen the defense industrial base, ensuring the military can support the sustained modernization and surge requirements necessary in great-power competition.[62]

Quite simply, trillion-dollar defense budgets should be here to stay.

New funding must focus on procurement at scale—acquiring the hardware needed to replace aging systems and expand the military's capacity. While R&D is essential for future innovation, it cannot address the immediate need to field cutting-edge equipment. Disproportionate spending on RDT&E has resulted in advanced systems being developed but not sufficiently procured, leaving the military reliant on outdated platforms.

It's not just about the dollars; it's about the outputs. While funding levels are key, the true measure of the resourcing's success is the delivery of tangible outcomes that favor America, our economy, and our way of life. That means fielding a force that is modern, capable, and able to deter America's adversaries effectively in multiple theaters at the same time.

Shipbuilding provides a clear example. Over the past few decades, the shipbuilding budget has seen real growth, yet the Navy remains trapped in a "doom loop" of aging platforms, limited new construction, and rising operational demands.[63] Despite this, shipbuilding continues to decline, as post–Cold War spending cuts have created an environment in which the industrial base is producing fewer ships each year and failing to meet the Navy's needs. As a result, costs have skyrocketed, productivity has plummeted, and the Navy's fleet goals remain out of reach.[64]

Consistent and predictable funding is a big part of breaking this cycle. Stable investments will enable shipyards to expand capacity, reduce inefficiencies, and deliver new platforms at scale, helping the Navy meet its readiness and force-structure goals. This approach must extend across all domains, ensuring that budgetary growth translates into a stronger, more capable military that can deter aggression in multiple theaters and safeguard US interests worldwide.

Investing in America's Future Defense

The United States stands at a strategic crossroads, facing a world that is more dangerous and complex than at any point since the Cold War. Yet the US military is shrinking, struggling to modernize, and operating with an increasingly strained industrial base. This decades-long strategy-resource mismatch risks enticing our allies to see America as a paper tiger, vulnerable to adversarial miscalculation and escalation. As this chapter has outlined, the problem lies in decades of inadequate defense budgets, insufficient modernization, and the absence of the sustained, strategic investments that once underpinned American military dominance.

History provides a clear example of what is needed. The Reagan-era defense buildup revitalized the military, expanded capacity, and restored deterrence by matching ambitious goals with consistent and robust funding. It focused on what can be bought at scale at the time versus promising scientific projects of tomorrow. By contrast, today's defense budgets, while nominally high, are insufficient in real terms to rebuild force structure, recapitalize aging systems, or invest in next-generation capabilities. Strategic insolvency is no longer a risk—it is the reality.

Without sustained real growth in defense spending after reconciliation works its way through the armed forces and industrial base, the US military will continue to be outpaced, outgunned, and outmaneuvered. The United States must recommit to sustained growth above inflation for defense year after year.

This introductory chapter has set the stage for understanding the depth of the challenges resulting from chronic underfunding of our national defense. The following book chapters will explore these issues in greater detail, examining the consequences of a shrinking force structure; the erosion of industrial capacity, supply chains, and workforces; the sharp rise in domestic entitlement spending, most notably in health care; and the risks of ongoing underinvestment in combat power. Together, they will win the argument that America can afford to defend itself.[65]

This book will show that the cost of a failure to adequately fund the armed forces at a steady state—commensurate with politicians' expectations of them—far outweighs the modest investments of deterrence against the overwhelming costs of war. It builds the case for bold action to restore America's strategic credibility and ensure our military is prepared today to meet the moment.

The first two chapters lay the strategic foundation for the volume. Hal Brands opens with a sweeping assessment of the global threat environment, tracing how the mismatch between American strategy and available resources has developed over time. He highlights how adversaries have grown more capable and coordinated just as US military power has stagnated or declined, and he outlines steps to close this dangerous gap. Dustin Walker follows with focused recommendations to reinvigorate a multi-theater military strategy, calling for a return to credible global deterrence through deliberate reforms of posture, readiness, and force.

The next series of chapters addresses the economic and fiscal foundations required to sustain a stronger defense. James C. Capretta argues that serious entitlement reform is essential to unlocking long-term budgetary flexibility—especially if defense is to be treated as a national priority. Michael R. Strain emphasizes the broader economic rationale for defense investment, contending that military strength underpins global economic stability and that the cost of deterrence failure far exceeds the price of preparedness. Todd Harrison considers the upper bounds of defense spending, offering a framework for evaluating how much is enough without succumbing to arbitrary limits. Elaine McCusker closes this section with a close look at the defense budget's mechanics, showing how erratic funding cycles and the diversion of defense dollars toward nondefense functions undercut long-term planning and readiness.

Dan Blumenthal and Zack Cooper then examine the Indo-Pacific, where they explore the operational challenges China's rise poses and lay out specific posture adjustments, capability investments, and alliance structures required to sustain US influence in the region.

The final set of chapters focus on force development and modernization. Kori Schake and James Mattis begin with an unflinching look at the recruitment and retention crisis plaguing the all-volunteer force, offering institutional reforms to build a larger and more capable military. Frederick W. Kagan draws on the war in Ukraine to illustrate how warfare is changing and how the United States must adapt by embracing flexibility and preparing for sustained, large-scale conflict. Domain-specific chapters from Giselle Donnelly (land), John G. Ferrari (sea), Rebecca Grant (air), and Harrison (space) assess the current state of US military forces and chart modernization paths that align with the demands of a multi-theater strategy. Finally, Kyle Balzer turns to the nuclear enterprise, making the case that a credible, modernized nuclear force remains essential.

Taken as a whole, this book provides a comprehensive plan for the current administration. Restoring American military strength is not a matter of rhetoric or marginal adjustments but of deliberate choices across strategy, spending, and force structure. The task ahead is not easy—but neither is it beyond reach. What is required is the political will to match America's ambitions with the resources and reforms needed to achieve them.[66]

Notes

1. US Department of Defense, *Military and Security Developments Involving the People's Republic of China*, 2023, https://media.defense.gov/2023/Oct/19/2003323409/-1/-1/1/2023-MILITARY-AND-SECURITY-DEVELOPMENTS-INVOLVING-THE-PEOPLES-REPUBLIC-OF-CHINA.PDF.

2. Mackenzie Eaglen, *10 Ways the US Is Falling Behind China in National Security*, American Enterprise Institute, August 9, 2023, https://www.aei.org/research-products/report/10-ways-the-us-is-falling-behind-china-in-national-security/.

3. Mackenzie Eaglen, *Keeping Up with the Pacing Threat: Unveiling the True Size of Beijing's Military Spending*, American Enterprise Institute, April 29, 2024, https://www.aei.org/research-products/report/keeping-up-with-the-pacing-threat-unveiling-the-true-size-of-beijings-military-spending/.

4. American Enterprise Institute, "Axis of Aggression: September 2024 Update," September 18, 2024, https://www.aei.org/research-products/one-pager/axis-of-aggression-september-2024/.

5. C. Todd Lopez, "U.S. Assets in Mediterranean Again Helped Defend Israel Against Iranian Missiles," US Department of Defense, October 1, 2024, https://www.defense.gov/News/News-Stories/Article/Article/3923123/us-assets-in-mediterranean-again-helped-defend-israel-against-iranian-missiles/.

6. C. Todd Lopez, "3 U.S. Service Members Killed, Others Injured in Jordan Following Drone Attack," US Department of Defense, January 29, 2024, https://www.defense.gov/News/News-Stories/Article/Article/3659809/3-us-service-members-killed-others-injured-in-jordan-following-drone-attack/.

7. Mackenzie Eaglen, "The U.S. Navy Doesn't Have Enough Air Defense Missiles," *The National Interest*, January 4, 2024, https://nationalinterest.org/blog/buzz/us-navy-doesnt-have-enough-air-defense-missiles-208353.

8. Brian Everstine, "Pacific Commander Raises Concerns over Depletion of Key Munitions," *Aviation Week*, November 19, 2024, https://aviationweek.com/defense/budget-policy-operations/pacific-commander-raises-concerns-over-depletion-key-munitions.

9. Greg Priddy, "U.S. Missile Defense Is Under Strain," *The National Interest*, October 17, 2024, https://nationalinterest.org/feature/us-missile-defense-under-strain-213274.

10. Mackenzie Eaglen, "America's One-War Military Is No Match for Reality," *National Security Journal*, August 7, 2024, https://nationalsecurityjournal.org/americas-one-war-military-is-no-match-for-reality/.

11. James Mattis, *Summary of the 2018 National Defense Strategy of the United States of America*, US Department of Defense, https://media.defense.gov/2020/May/18/2002302061/-1/-1/1/2018-NATIONAL-DEFENSE-STRATEGY-SUMMARY.PDF; and US Department of Defense, *2022 National Defense Strategy of the United States of America*, October 27, 2022, https://media.defense.gov/2022/Oct/27/2003103845/-1/-1/1/2022-NATIONAL-DEFENSE-STRATEGY-NPR-MDR.pdf.

12. American Enterprise Institute, Marilyn Ware Center for Security Studies, *To Rebuild America's Military*, October 2015, https://www.aei.org/wp-content/uploads/2015/10/To-Rebuild-Americas-Military.pdf.

13. US Department of Defense, *Report of the Quadrennial Defense Review*, May 1997, https://www.files.ethz.ch/isn/32542/qdr97.pdf.

14. US Department of Defense, *Report of the Quadrennial Defense Review*.

15. Commission on the National Defense Strategy, *Report of the Commission on the National Defense Strategy*, RAND Corporation, July 29, 2024, https://www.armed-services.senate.gov/imo/media/doc/nds_commission_final_report.pdf.

16. Mackenzie Eaglen, "The U.S. Military Needs More Capital for Capital Assets," *RealClearDefense*, May 22, 2023, https://www.realcleardefense.com/articles/2023/05/22/the_us_military_needs_more_capital_for_capital_assets_900836.html.

17. Mackenzie Eaglen and Hallie Coyne, *The 2020s Tri-Service Modernization Crunch*, American Enterprise Institute, March 23, 2021, https://www.aei.org/research-products/report/2020s-tri-service-modernization-crunch/.

18. Eaglen, "The U.S. Military Needs More Capital for Capital Assets."

19. United States Institute of Peace, *Providing for the Common Defense: The Assessment and Recommendations of the National Defense Strategy Commission*, September 2018, 67, https://www.usip.org/sites/default/files/2018-11/providing-for-the-common-defense.pdf.

20. United States Institute of Peace, *Providing for the Common Defense*.

21. Mackenzie Eaglen, "America's New Deadliest War Is Hiding in Plain Sight," *RealClearDefense*, September 7, 2017, https://www.realcleardefense.com/articles/2017/09/07/americas_new_deadliest_war_is_hiding_in_plain_sight_112244.html.

22. Harrison Kass, "China Would Have Gone into 'Meltdown': Navy Planned for 29 Seawolf-Class Submarines," *The National Interest*, October 19, 2024, https://nationalinterest.org/blog/buzz/china-would-have-gone-meltdown-navy-planned-29-seawolf-class-submarines-211779; Tyler Rogoway, "Retired General Says F-22 Production Was Killed So That a New Bomber Could Live," *TWZ*, February 6, 2019, https://www.twz.com/20472/retired-general-says-f-22-production-was-killed-so-that-a-new-bomber-could-live; and Sydney J. Freedberg Jr., "Total Cost to Close Out Cancelled Army FCS Could Top $1 Billion," *Breaking Defense*, June 19, 2012, https://breakingdefense.com/2012/06/total-cost-to-close-out-cancelled-army-fcs-could-top-1-billion/.

23. Eaglen and Coyne, *The 2020s Tri-Service Modernization Crunch*.

24. Mackenzie Eaglen, "Why Is the U.S. Navy Running Out of Tomahawk Cruise Missiles?," *The National Interest*, February 12, 2024, https://nationalinterest.org/blog/buzz/why-us-navy-running-out-tomahawk-cruise-missiles-209317.

25. Mackenzie Eaglen, "Give Marines the Sea-Going Tools They Need to Pack a Punch," *Defense & Aerospace Report*, February 5, 2024, https://www.aei.org/op-eds/give-marines-the-sea-going-tools-they-need-to-pack-a-punch/.

26. Lopez, "3 U.S. Service Members Killed, Others Injured in Jordan Following Drone Attack."

27. Michelle Tan, "Chief: 'The Army Needs to Get Bigger,'" *Army Times*, October 8, 2017, https://www.armytimes.com/news/your-army/2017/10/09/chief-the-army-needs-to-get-bigger/.

28. Mackenzie Eaglen, "The Bias for Capability over Capacity Has Created a Brittle Force," *War on the Rocks*, November 17, 2022, https://warontherocks.com/2022/11/the-bias-for-capability-over-capacity-has-created-a-brittle-force/.

29. Daniel Whiteneck et al., *The Navy at a Tipping Point: Maritime Dominance at Stake*, CNA, March 2010, https://www.cna.org/archive/CNA_Files/pdf/d0022262.a3.pdf.

30. US Naval Institute Staff, "USNI News Fleet and Marine Tracker: Dec. 2, 2024," US Naval Institute, December 2, 2024, https://news.usni.org/2024/12/02/usni-news-fleet-and-marine-tracker-dec-2-2024.

31. Megan Eckstein, "Seeking 75 Ships Ready for Combat, Navy Turns to New Readiness Orgs," *Defense News*, January 9, 2024, https://www.defensenews.com/naval/2024/01/09/seeking-75-ready-ships-navy-turns-to-new-readiness-orgs/.

32. See Eaglen and Coyne, *The 2020s Tri-Service Modernization Crunch*, Figure 2.

33. US Department of Defense, Office of the Under Secretary of Defense (Comptroller), *National Defense Budget Estimates for FY 2025*, April 2024, https://comptroller.defense.gov/Portals/45/Documents/defbudget/FY2025/fy25_Green_Book.pdf.

34. Dustin Walker and Mackenzie Eaglen, "Trump Wants NATO to Hit 3 Percent GDP on Defense. The US Could Fall Short," *Breaking Defense,* October 9, 2024, https://breakingdefense.com/2024/10/trump-wants-nato-to-hit-3-percent-gdp-on-defense-the-us-could-fall-short/; and Mackenzie Eaglen and Cole Spiller, *Behind NATO's 2 Percent: Measuring the True Scope of Alliance Defense Investments and the NATO Defense Deficit*, American Enterprise Institute, March 2025, https://www.aei.org/research-products/working-paper/behind-natos-2-percent-measuring-the-true-scope-of-alliance-defense-investments-and-the-nato-defense-deficit/.

35. Office of the Under Secretary of Defense, (Comptroller)/Chief Financial Officer, *Defense Budget Overview: Fiscal Year 2025 Budget Request*, April 4, 2024, https://comptroller.defense.gov/Portals/45/Documents/defbudget/FY2025/FY2025_Budget_Request_Overview_Book.pdf.

36. Abigail Tierney, "US Annual GDP 1990–2024," Statista, January 2025, https://www.statista.com/statistics/188105/annual-gdp-of-the-united-states-since-1990/.

37. See Eaglen and Coyne, *The 2020s Tri-Service Modernization Crunch*, Figure 16.

38. US Department of Defense, Office of the Under Secretary of Defense (Comptroller), *National Defense Budget Estimates for FY 2025*.

39. US Department of Defense, *Annual Report to the Congress, Fiscal Year 1987*, February 5, 1986, https://history.defense.gov/Portals/70/Documents/annual_reports/1987_DOD_AR.pdf.

40. US Department of Defense, *Annual Report to the Congress, Fiscal Year 1987*.

41. US Department of the Air Force, *Department of the Air Force Fiscal Year 2024 Budget Overview*, https://www.saffm.hq.af.mil/Portals/84/documents/FY24/Budget/FY24%20Budget%20Overview%20Book.pdf; and US Department of the Navy, Office of Budget, *Highlights of the Department of the Navy FY 2024 Budget*, 2023, https://media.defense.gov/2023/Mar/29/2003188749/-1/-1/0/HIGHLIGHTS_BOOK.PDF.

42. US Department of Defense, *Annual Report to the Congress, Fiscal Year 1987*.

43. US Department of the Army, *Fiscal Year (FY) 2025 Budget Estimates: Procurement of W&TCV, Army*, March 2024, https://www.asafm.army.mil/Portals/72/Documents/BudgetMaterial/2025/Base%20Budget/Procurement/Procurement-of-Weapons-and-Tracked-Combat-Vehicles.pdf.

44. US Department of Defense, *Annual Report to the Congress, Fiscal Year 1985*, February 1, 1984, https://history.defense.gov/Portals/70/Documents/annual_reports/1985_DoD_AR.pdf.

45. Office of the Chief of Naval Operations, *Report to Congress on the Annual Long-Range Plan for Construction of Naval Vessels for Fiscal Year 2025*, March 2024, https://s3.documentcloud.org/documents/24487775/rtc-pb25-shipbuilding_plan.pdf.

46. *Air & Space Forces Magazine*, "2024 USAF & USSF Almanac: Equipment," June 7, 2024, https://www.airandspaceforces.com/article/2024-usaf-ussf-almanac-equipment/.

47. Caitlin M. Kenney, "Navy to Keep Four Aging Destroyers Beyond Their Service Lives," *Defense One*, August 3, 2023, https://www.defenseone.com/policy/2023/08/navy-keep-four-aging-destroyers-beyond-their-service-lives/389087/; and Office of the Deputy Assistant Secretary of Defense for Nuclear Matters, *Nuclear Matters Handbook 2020 [Revised]*, 2020, https://www.acq.osd.mil/ncbdp/nm/NMHB2020rev/docs/NMHB2020rev_Ch3.pdf.

48. Jen Judson, "US Army Scraps Abrams Tank Upgrade, Unveils New Modernization Plan," *Defense News*, September 6, 2023, https://www.defensenews.com/land/2023/09/06/us-army-scraps-abrams-tank-upgrade-unveils-new-modernization-plan/.

49. US Navy, "SECNAV Announces Service Life Extensions for 12 Destroyers to 'Keep More Ready Players on the Field,'" press release, October 31, 2024, https://www.navy.mil/Press-Office/Press-Releases/display-pressreleases/Article/3952231/secnav-announces-service-life-extensions-for-12-destroyers-to-keep-more-ready-p/.

50. Editorial Board, "Trump Didn't Rebuild the Military," *The Wall Street Journal*, February 22, 2024, https://www.wsj.com/articles/donald-trump-defense-spending-u-s-military-joe-biden-b3af3ff2.

51. Mackenzie Eaglen, *Defense Budget Peaks in 2019, Underfunding the National Defense Strategy*, American Enterprise Institute, May 2018, https://www.aei.org/wp-content/uploads/2018/05/2019-Defense-Budget.pdf.

52. Eaglen, "The U.S. Military Needs More Capital for Capital Assets."

53. US Department of Defense, Office of the Under Secretary of Defense (Comptroller), *National Defense Budget Estimates for FY 2024*, May 2023, https://comptroller.defense.gov/Portals/45/Documents/defbudget/FY2024/FY24_Green_Book.pdf.

54. C. Todd Lopez, "Austin: FY 2025 Budget Includes 'Tough, but Responsible' Decisions," US Department of Defense, May 8, 2024, https://www.defense.gov/News/News-Stories/Article/Article/3769429/austin-fy-2025-budget-includes-tough-but-responsible-decisions/.

55. Eaglen and Coyne, *The 2020s Tri-Service Modernization Crunch*.

56. Mackenzie Eaglen and Todd Harrison, "How the U.S. Can Maintain Its Military Edge over China," *Time*, December 7, 2024, https://time.com/7199538/us-military-edge-china/.

57. US Department of Defense, *National Defense Industrial Strategy 2023*, November 16, 2023, https://www.businessdefense.gov/docs/ndis/2023-NDIS.pdf.

58. Army Science Board, *Surge Capacity in the Defense Munitions Industrial Base*, September 14, 2023, https://asb.army.mil/Portals/105/Reports/2020s/ASB%20FY%2023%20DMIB%20Report%20(E).pdf.

59. Mackenzie Eaglen, "If Ukraine Is Any Barometer of Expenditure Rates in Modern War, America Is Gonna Lose Taiwan," *19FortyFive*, August 1, 2023, https://www.19fortyfive.com/2023/08/if-ukraine-is-any-barometer-of-expenditure-rates-in-modern-war-america-is-gonna-lose-taiwan/.

60. The average is calculated from annual real growth as found in US Department of Defense, Office of the Under Secretary of Defense (Comptroller), *National Defense Budget Estimates for FY 2024*, Table 6–1.

61. United States Institute of Peace, "National Defense Strategy Commission Releases Its Review of 2018 National Defense Strategy," press release, November 13, 2018, https://www.usip.org/press/2018/11/national-defense-strategy-commission-releases-its-review-2018-national-defense; and Commission on the National Defense Strategy, *Report of the Commission on the National Defense Strategy*.

62. US Department of Defense, *2022 National Defense Strategy of the United States of America*.

63. Mackenzie Eaglen, "America's Incredible Shrinking Navy," *AEIdeas*, January 18, 2024, https://www.aei.org/foreign-and-defense-policy/americas-incredible-shrinking-navy/.

64. Mackenzie Eaglen, "How to Break the Navy's Shipbuilding Doom Loop," *National Review*, September 10, 2024, https://www.nationalreview.com/2024/09/how-to-break-the-navys-shipbuilding-doom-loop/.

65. James Mattis, "Statement of Hon. James N. Mattis, Secretary of Defense Written Statement for the Record Tuesday, February 6, 2018," testimony before the House Armed Services Committee, February 6, 2018, https://docs.house.gov/meetings/AS/AS00/20180206/106833/HHRG-115-AS00-Wstate-MattisJ-20180206.pdf.

66. Mackenzie Eaglen, "Funding the Fight: The Paradoxical Path to Reversing Defense Decline," Ronald Reagan Institute, June 25, 2024, https://www.reaganfoundation.org/reagan-institute/publications/funding-the-fight-the-paradoxical-path-to-reversing-defense-decline.

2

Our Prewar Era: America and the Dilemmas of Global Defense

HAL BRANDS

In a 1942 essay, George Orwell wrote of the folly of refusing to believe that the most terrifying geopolitical nightmares can come true:

> We in England underrate the danger of this kind of thing, because our traditions and our past security have given us a sentimental belief that it all comes right in the end and the thing you most fear never really happens. Nourished for hundreds of years on a literature in which Right invariably triumphs in the last chapter, we believe half-instinctively that evil always defeats itself in the long run.[1]

That conviction, the product of Britain's oceanic moat and Enlightenment traditions, had brought the country—and much of humanity—to the edge of the abyss in the worst moments of World War II. Were he alive, Orwell might see parallels in the American mindset today.

Most Americans alive now have known only a world structured, pacified, and made prosperous by unrivaled US power. For most Americans, then, it probably seems unthinkable that the international system could buckle under assault by revisionist states, much less that the next great-power war could end in a US defeat. That confidence is a testament to the world-altering success of US foreign policy since 1945. And it risks blinding Americans to their situation's precariousness.

In every key region of Eurasia, revisionist states are aggressively contesting the status quo. They are gathering into an autocratic bloc more cohesive than anything the United States has faced in generations. But even as our moment increasingly resembles a prewar era, America is trapped in a post–Cold War mentality that risks leaving the nation overstretched and under-armed if a graver crisis strikes.

As a result, an alarming gap has emerged between America's global commitments and ability to vindicate those commitments if they are tested. The world is becoming less stable. International affairs are becoming more violent. And the United States is running out of time to avoid its own geopolitical nightmare.[2]

* * * *

Throughout the modern era, struggles for global primacy have been struggles over Eurasia. That supercontinent is home to most of the world's population and economic resources. It is where the most powerful countries on earth, America excepted, are found. Three times in the 20th century—during World War I, World War II, and the Cold War—the international system was convulsed by clashes between autocratic powers that sought primacy in Eurasia and coalitions led by offshore democracies—first the United Kingdom, then the United States—that fought to hold them back. A fourth such contest is now underway, as a new group of autocracies challenges the security of each of Eurasia's vital regions.

In Europe, Russia's assault on Ukraine easily qualifies as the continent's most destructive conflict since World War II. The all-out Russian invasion in February 2022—merely the most intense phase of a struggle dating back to 2014—recalled the blatant land grabs and appalling atrocities that marked the worst parts of Europe's 20th century. As of this writing, Russia had failed to conquer or dominate Ukraine. But Kyiv and its backers had failed to decisively defeat the invasion and, with it, Vladimir Putin's project to overthrow the prevailing order in Europe and beyond.

Meanwhile, the war had produced global spillover, including violent Russian subversion in Europe, disruptions to world food and energy supplies, and geopolitical realignments from Scandinavia to northeast Asia. By late 2024, US observers from both parties were increasingly calling for a ceasefire.[3] But the end of the war won't end the threat from a hyper-revisionist, heavily militarized Russia with an epic grudge against the democratic world.

The Middle East is also a tinderbox. Hamas's attack on Israel in October 2023 touched off a long, grinding war in Gaza and fomented violent instability from Lebanon to the Gulf of Aden. In the year thereafter, Iran twice attacked Israel with ballistic missile barrages massive enough to rate among history's largest. The Houthis, with Tehran's sponsorship and Beijing and Moscow's complicity or encouragement, created the most sustained challenge to freedom of the seas since the 1980s.

To address these threats, Washington repeatedly rushed scarce resources—from missile defenses to aircraft carriers—back into a region it had spent the past decade trying to escape. Through resupply and other aid, it helped—sometimes grudgingly—Israel inflict sharp blows against Tehran and its proxies. But with Iran now a nuclear threshold state and even quasi-state actors like the Houthis having showcased a new level of capability, the crisis of Middle Eastern security is unlikely to be resolved anytime soon.[4]

East Asia isn't wracked by a major hot war, but amid multiple regional cold wars, no one can credibly say the peace is secure. North Korea is racing ahead with its nuclear and missile programs, raising the threat to the American homeland and testing the cohesion of the US–South Korea alliance. China is coercing the Philippines in the South China Sea and increasing the military pressure vis-à-vis Taiwan. It continues to push ahead with a record-smashing, quarter-century military buildup featuring many of the capabilities needed to subdue Taiwan while deterring or defeating American intervention.

Moreover, Beijing is now engaged in a rapid-fire nuclear buildup, which will make it a strategic peer of the United States by the 2030s, and developing a blue-water navy and other tools to project Chinese power around the world. "Whatever its actual intentions may be, I could not say," Secretary of the Air Force Frank Kendall warned in 2023, "but China is preparing for a war and specifically for a war with the United States."[5]

As the Biden administration wound down, then, serious military conflicts afflicted two of Eurasia's key theaters—the Middle East and Europe. In the third, maritime Asia, the danger of war was rising. Not since the early Cold War have instability and turmoil been so pervasive across the world's central landmass. Not since the run-up to World War II has the risk of violent conflict engulfing *all* of Eurasia's key theaters been so high. Even if there were *no* connections among the world's malign actors, this scenario would severely test defense and deterrence for America and its allies. Still worse, the Eurasian revisionists—united by their intense hostility to American power and liberal ideals—are locking arms.

Surging global tensions have nourished autocratic partnerships. Moscow and Tehran have established a flourishing, two-way military relationship that bolsters Putin's forces in Ukraine while arming and emboldening Iran in the Middle East. Russia and North Korea have signed a formal alliance that delivers vital arms and North Korean personnel to support Putin's military while aiding Pyongyang's advanced weapons programs and abetting its aggression.[6]

Russia and China unveiled their "no limits" strategic partnership just before Putin assaulted Ukraine. Since then, their economic and technological ties have expanded dramatically; their decades-old military relationship has become more substantive and, alarmingly, more secretive.[7] Other revisionist relationships, such as between China and Iran and between Russia and the Houthis, are emerging or evolving. This isn't a single, fully formed revisionist alliance. But it is an ever-denser network of ties connecting the world's most malign states.[8]

These ties' geopolitical effects are real, even if the details are sometimes hazy. Revisionist relationships hasten disruptive military innovation; for instance, China's buildup has been aided by Russian weapons and, now, increasingly sensitive Russian technology. Such relationships reduce the isolation and punishment aggressors might otherwise face: A thoroughly sanctioned Russia has kept fighting in Ukraine thanks to Iranian and North Korean arms and strategic trade with China.

These partnerships raise the likelihood of violent instability on some frontiers by dampening it on others. Warm relations between Moscow and Beijing allow Putin to deploy most of his army in Ukraine and Xi to push harder for an advantage in the western Pacific. They also enable pernicious military learning: Consider how Iran mimicked Russia's strike packages against Ukraine in its own drone and missile attack on Israel in April 2024.[9]

More profoundly, these relationships compound the chaos in today's world, as colluding revisionist powers assault the international order from multiple sides; they even suggest that one aggressive state might aid, whether kinetically or non-kinetically, another revisionist state locked in crisis or conflict with the United States.[10] Indeed, as relationships among America's adversaries link the tensions across several theaters, they raise the risk that a conflict in one place could spread contagiously into others.

If that happened, it wouldn't be the first time. Americans usually remember World War II as a global conflict. But it began as a set of regional crises—provoked by Germany's push to rule Europe, Japan's bid for conquest in China and then much of Asia, and Italy's aggrandizement in the Mediterranean and Africa—that eventually merged and climaxed. In the 1930s and early 1940s, aggression on one front encouraged it on others: Italy's invasion of Ethiopia encouraged Germany's revisionism in Europe, which eventually tempted Japan to surge into Southeast Asia to exploit the plight of desperate or defeated colonial powers. To support their radical expansion programs, the fascist powers banded together in a loose alliance, the Tripartite Pact, thereby polarizing international politics and setting the world on fire.

Yes, the United States faces regional military challenges more severe and numerous than any in decades. But the real geopolitical nightmare is the danger that escalating regional crises could, once again, converge into a global war.

* * * *

Many American national security elites know there is a problem. The bipartisan National Defense Strategy Commission warned, in July 2024, that "the threats the United States faces are the most serious and most challenging the nation has encountered since 1945."[11] Roger Wicker of the Senate Armed Services Committee likewise commented that "the United States is facing the most dangerous threat environment since World War II," because an "emerging 'axis of aggressors' is working to undermine U.S. interests around the world."[12]

On the campaign trail in fall 2024, the danger of "World War III" was a prominent theme.[13] Think tanks and US government officials have issued a litany of stark warnings about the rising danger of conflict in the western Pacific and beyond.[14] Yet the United States isn't remotely prepared for the world it now confronts.

This may seem absurd, since the US defense budget is creeping toward $1 trillion. But don't let the sticker price fool you. As a percentage of gross domestic product (GDP), US military spending is nearly as low as at any time since World War II.[15]

Per capita, the defense budget is roughly what it was in the mid-1950s, even though per capita income, adjusted for inflation, has skyrocketed since then.[16] And although the United States still has the biggest military budget in the world, that budget is stretched by the demands of deterring a multitude of rivals and has hardly kept pace with inflation in recent years. This creates glaring problems in America's global posture—not least its inability to cope with competing crises or conflicts.

This wasn't always the case. In World War II, the United States fought intensely in several theaters simultaneously. For most of the Cold War, American planners believed the United States should be able to check enemy thrusts in at least two regions, even if Europe was the top priority. Following the Cold War, the Pentagon preserved a two-war strategy so it could wage and win near-simultaneous conflicts against regional powers such as Iraq and North Korea.

The rationale was simple and persuasive: A country with worldwide commitments needs a two-war military, lest conflict in one theater leave it unable to respond to aggression in another. As one Pentagon report put it, the two-war strategy was "the *sine qua non* of a superpower."[17]

By the 2010s, however, America's two-war strategy was coming undone. Part of the problem was that the world had changed. It was one thing to fight two relatively weak rogue states when America was at the peak of its post–Cold War primacy. It was entirely another to confront the great-power adversaries that emerged—or reemerged—a generation later.

Another part of the problem was persistent disinvestment in defense. In hindsight, 1991 to 2016 was one long post–Cold War drawdown, interrupted temporarily by a post-9/11 splurge mostly on counterterrorism and counterinsurgency. Then, the Budget Control Act of 2011 and the deep cuts it triggered slashed US capabilities just as threats were becoming more severe. The military and financial math of a two-war strategy had become unworkable, resulting in a bipartisan shift—which began under Barack Obama and was consolidated under Donald Trump and Joe Biden—to the one-war strategy America has today.[18]

The one-war strategy is meant to focus the Pentagon on developing the capabilities and concepts needed to defeat one peer rival, namely

China, in a full-on conflict while deterring bad actors in other theaters—although how the US military will deter opportunistic aggression without the means to defeat it has never been adequately explained.[19] This shift is because a big war with China would consume most of America's global combat power and virtually all its strategic lift and logistics, likely straining the defense industrial base to the breaking point. That shift has forced the Pentagon to seriously consider how to project power into lethally contested environments, such as the first island chain, which runs from Japan to the Philippines. It has underpinned promising ideas, like the Replicator initiative, meant to marry mass and precision and thereby turn the western Pacific into a "hellscape" for Chinese forces.[20] Even so, the US military is beset by weaknesses that threaten its ability to win a single major war, let alone two.

Multiple studies have shown that the United States would quickly run short of long-range missiles, missile interceptors, and precision-guided munitions in a high-intensity conflict, with no good way of replenishing them.[21] The Navy is struggling to keep enough attack submarines—perhaps America's single greatest asset vis-à-vis China—at sea, let alone produce the desired quantity of new ones. The surface fleet is being run ragged because too few ships are trying to do too much across too many regions.[22] The effort to simply update the US nuclear arsenal is stumbling, even as China's buildup means Washington must soon deter two nuclear peers at once.

Things will get worse before they get better, since the Pentagon must retire many Reagan-era ships, submarines, and planes in the late 2020s, even though their replacements won't arrive, in many cases, until the 2030s. Broadly, the Pentagon faces two painful dilemmas—between conventional and nuclear modernization and between investing in future capabilities and procuring existing ones—because it doesn't have enough money to go around.[23] Many of those weaknesses, in turn, are rooted in the deep fragility of the defense industrial base, which limits America's ability to prepare for war and replace lost or used equipment once the shooting starts.

These problems' geopolitical effects are accumulating in real time. Through much of 2024, the Houthis created havoc in the Red Sea and mocked a superpower that supports freedom of navigation. Yet for months, the best Washington could do was a desultory tit for tat with the once-obscure extremists, because a more punishing, and potentially more decisive, campaign would consume America's limited stockpiles of key munitions and leave it unprepared for a bigger war in the Pacific. But even America's readiness for that one big war is increasingly questionable, as Washington's principal adversary races to prepare itself for a fight.

China is engaging in ever-more-menacing military exercises around Taiwan. It is hoarding food and energy and otherwise reducing its vulnerability to sanctions. Moreover, China's nuclear force doubled between 2020 and 2023, and its shipyards are churning out new vessels as its factories mass-produce missiles and bombs. As Seth Jones of the Center for Strategic and International Studies writes, "China now acquires weapons systems at a pace five to six times as fast as the United States."[24]

In a favorable scenario, the United States might still win a single war in the western Pacific, albeit at a horrifying price in lost planes, ships, and service members; the catastrophic disruption of key supply chains and trade routes; and serious risks of nuclear escalation.[25] But the balance of power is shifting so rapidly that America could well lose the next great-power war, and it would most likely be overwhelmed if it was forced to fight major wars—whether interrelated or not—in two or more regions at once.[26]

Such a defeat's geopolitical consequences could be momentous. It could well threaten the credibility and integrity of America's alliance structure. If the US military was battered in a high-intensity conflict, Washington might lose, if only for a time, the ability and will to continue leading global affairs.

Overall, the world would probably change in ways presently hard to enumerate or imagine. After all, major wars have historically set the terms of global order. If America loses the next great-power conflict, it might have to get used to a world where some other nation makes the rules.

* * * *

Of course, the United States wasn't ready for the biggest wars of the 20th century either. "Good Lord! You're not going to send soldiers over there, are you?" one senator exclaimed *after* the United States declared war on Germany in April 1917.[27] It was a fair question, since America's total land forces at the time numbered slightly more than 200,000. As World War II began, the US armed forces, which the retrenchment of the 1920s and 1930s had gutted, remained undersized, under-equipped, and under-trained. But America ultimately won that war, as it had won World War I, through an astounding, world-beating mobilization.

By the time the fighting ended in 1945, the United States had built more than 300,000 airplanes. In 1944 alone, American shipyards launched 2,247 naval vessels, a total that outstripped the rest of the world combined. American industry sustained the entire Grand Alliance: At Stalingrad on the eastern front and El Alamein in Africa, Soviet and British troops rode American tanks and trucks to victory.[28]

US forces weren't always the best on the battlefield, but their superiority in equipment and logistics was more than the Axis could overcome. "I cannot understand these Americans," one German commander remarked. "Each night we know that we have cut them to pieces, inflicted heavy casualties, mowed down their transport. But—in the morning, we are suddenly faced with fresh battalions, with complete replacements of men, machines, food, tools, and weapons."[29] This performance, as the great "arsenal of democracy," has lasting resonance for Americans. It may lead them to think that, if the world goes to pieces, America will mobilize and manage the same feat again.

Alas, it isn't so simple. One reason the United States mobilized so effectively in World War II was that it had a crucial head start: Its buildup began in earnest after the Munich crisis in 1938, a full three years before Pearl Harbor. US defense spending surged from well under 2 percent of GDP in 1938 and 1939 to over 5 percent in 1941.[30] In 1940 alone, the United States ordered nine battleships, 11 aircraft carriers, eight heavy cruisers, 31 light cruisers, and 181 destroyers—a fleet roughly the size of its entire navy today.[31] Moreover, the United States could surge production because its economic dominance was based on its manufacturing dominance and because the Great Depression had created lots of temporarily idle capacity that could be activated once the money began to flow.

Much has changed 80 years later. China is now the world's workshop, while America's industrial base is plagued by choke points and weaknesses. Those who believe America can wait for the fighting to start and then rapidly and decisively win the wartime mobilization race are living in another era.

Other shortcuts to strategic solvency are just as illusory. Some argue America can slash its global burdens by shifting them to allies. True, those allies have a tremendous stake in the present order, which can't be preserved unless they invest more in the common defense. But while some allies, such as Japan and Poland, are revolutionizing their defense strategies and military capabilities, too many others are still struggling to hit remedial spending targets or field forces remotely equal to the threats they face.[32] If defending the free world must be a collective endeavor, it will fail if America simply tries to substitute its allies' initiative for its own.

As officials from Tokyo to Canberra frankly acknowledge, no Indo-Pacific coalition can balance China unless the United States anchors it. Even in Europe and the Persian Gulf, where the material balance of power is more favorable, friendly countries would struggle to summon the capabilities and common purpose necessary to contain their enemies absent American leadership. Does anyone really believe, for instance, that the Europeans would have rallied to Ukraine's aid in February 2022 had the United States simply left the matter to them? Or, as seems far more likely, would a divided and demoralized continent simply have made its peace with another Russian conquest? An America that tries to slough off responsibility to allies won't enjoy greater security at lesser cost—it will find that its allies struggle to preserve a congenial global order if America itself is no longer committed to the task.

The same problem afflicts a final shortcut to solvency: focusing squarely on China and radically deprioritizing the rest of the world. It's true, as the Biden administration has often said, that China is "the only competitor with both the intent to reshape the international order and, increasingly, the economic, diplomatic, military, and technological power to advance that objective."[33] It's also true that losing a war in the western Pacific would be one of the worst things that could happen to the United States. But a China-only approach is no answer to America's global strategic dilemma.

For one thing, on the current trajectory, a few years from now, the United States might not be able to deter and, if necessary, defeat China even if it pulls back from other regions.[34] Thus, a China-only approach could provide a false comfort that undercuts any push for adequate defense spending—while still failing on its own terms in the end. Furthermore, such a strategy would come at a massive global cost.

In today's conditions, pulling back from Europe and the Middle East would exacerbate violent instability in those regions, raising the odds that America must return later and under worse conditions. And America *would* have to return, because those regions still matter greatly. Europe has real economic heft and still contains the world's largest concentration of liberal democracies; the Middle East commands vital energy resources, strategic geography, and the narrow waterways that connect Europe to Asia.

In the meantime, withdrawal from contested regions would raise grave questions—including in Asia—about America's commitment and staying power. It would also severely complicate the task of rallying recently abandoned countries in Europe and the Middle East to push back against China's worldwide influence. Even a global superpower must set priorities. But it can't choose to compete in one theater while excluding the rest.[35]

* * *

Addressing America's national security shortfall isn't just a matter of money. Even an infinite budget wouldn't relieve the United States of the need to fix a broken acquisitions process so the Pentagon can develop and field new capabilities more rapidly. Nor would it eliminate the need to develop operational concepts that allow the services to project power across vast distances and into crowded, deadly environments—nor the need to learn and incorporate the lessons from wars in Ukraine and the Middle East about the uses of uncrewed systems, the interaction between missiles and missile defenses, AI's role on the battlefield, and the prospects for massing and maneuvering in a world of ubiquitous overhead surveillance. Most critically, even greater abundance doesn't obviate the responsibility to make sound, sober decisions about how to deter and under what conditions to fight.

It bears restating that defending the international order is not solely an American responsibility. The United States and its allies must work toward higher spending thresholds and more ambitious capability targets in Europe and the Indo-Pacific. In the latter theater, especially, Washington must stitch various bilateral relationships together into a network that can more credibly promise and execute a collective defense.[36]

Integrating industrial bases is also essential: The best near-term option for offsetting a daunting US deficit in shipbuilding, for instance, is to work more closely with allies, such as Japan and South Korea, that have their own real capacity.[37] America's alliances are perhaps its greatest strategic advantage. More integration and collective effort among the democracies is the best response to the autocratic world's intensifying coercion and cooperation.

But those alliances, and the larger liberal order, rest on a foundation of hard power—specifically, American hard power—which urgently needs to be strengthened. The ins and outs of a more expansive US defense program are the subject of other chapters in this book. But generally, the United States needs a level of defense spending that eases trade-offs between the present and the future; addresses critical near-term shortages in munitions and other capabilities; pays to expand production lines and increase the defense industrial base's resilience; permits concurrent conventional and nuclear modernization; aids embattled friends, such as Ukraine and Taiwan, without unacceptable trade-offs for America's own capabilities; and, broadly, builds the capability and capacity necessary to reduce the gap between America's resources and the realities of a dangerous, disordered world.

The post–Cold War era is over. If America doesn't start acting like it faces a national security emergency, historians will likely look back on this moment as a prewar era.

The cost, no doubt, will be substantial. Serious observers' most aggressive proposals call for a defense budget equivalent to 5 percent of GDP (compared with slightly north of 3 percent today), with increases to be phased in over a few years so the Pentagon can effectively absorb new resources.[38] That's a lot of money—call it $1.5 trillion annually. But it's less, as a share of output, than the roughly 6 percent of GDP the United States spent at the height of the Reagan buildup; the 7.5 percent it spent, on average, over the entire Cold War; and the approximately 14 percent it spent at the peak of the emergency rearmament during the Korean War.[39]

America allocated vast sums to defense in prior crises. The view that spending a significantly smaller share of GDP on defense now is absurd or impossible shows how complacent Americans have become in a world they can't imagine falling apart.

During the Cold War, in fact, the United States often treated geopolitical shocks—like the outbreak of the Korean War and the Soviet invasion of Afghanistan—as opportunities to reinvest in defense. Washington could have done something similar after Russia's invasion of Ukraine. But despite everything the Biden administration did well in February 2022 and after—arming Ukraine, expanding NATO, and rallying a broad international coalition—it failed to pair support for Kyiv with a major US rearmament program.[40]

That decision was doubly unfortunate. It allowed critics to claim (somewhat misleadingly) that Ukraine aid was leeching capabilities from the US military.[41] And it let the energy that this century's greatest geopolitical crisis might have generated go to waste.

The politics of defense haven't subsequently become any easier. The economics are also difficult, mostly because runaway entitlement spending—and an allergy to taxation—has created spiraling deficits that not even the United States can forever ignore.[42] Yet it's ironic to suggest that fiscal rectitude requires holding the line on defense—but not on the issues that are truly wrecking America's national finances. It's also irresponsible, because if America waits to fund defense until it has fixed the deficit, it will have waited too long.

If America doesn't fix its defenses, it will ultimately pay the bill in lives, equipment, and influence lost and in the return of a world far less prosperous and secure than the one we know. The great lesson of the 20th century is that preserving global security is expensive. But it is far cheaper than rebuilding international peace and America's national security once they have been shattered.

Notes

1. George Orwell, "Looking Back on the Spanish War," Orwell Foundation, June 1943, https://www.orwellfoundation.com/the-orwell-foundation/orwell/essays-and-other-works/looking-back-on-the-spanish-war/.

2. Some of the ideas presented in this essay were first developed in other pieces, including Hal Brands, *The Eurasian Century: Hot Wars, Cold Wars, and the Making of the Modern World* (W. W. Norton, 2025); Hal Brands, "The Next Global War: How Today's Regional Conflicts Resemble the Ones That Produced World War II," *Foreign Affairs*, January 26, 2024, https://www.foreignaffairs.com/united-states/next-global-war; and Hal Brands, "Ukraine War Shows the US Military Isn't Ready for War with China," *Bloomberg Opinion*, September 18, 2022, https://www.bloomberg.

com/opinion/articles/2022-09-18/ukraine-war-shows-the-us-military-isn-t-ready-for-war-with-china.

3. Robert Kagan, "Are Americans Ready to Give Up on Ukraine?," *The Washington Post*, October 15, 2024, https://www.washingtonpost.com/opinions/2024/10/15/ukraine-stalemate-putin-pompeo-peacetalks-negotiations/.

4. Joby Warrick, "Nuclear Deal in Tatters, Iran Edges Close to Weapons Capability," *The Washington Post*, April 10, 2024, https://www.washingtonpost.com/national-security/2024/04/10/iran-nuclear-bomb-iaea-fordow/.

5. Frank Kendall, "Watch, Read: Secretary Kendall on 'Accelerating Readiness for Great Power Competition,'" *Air & Space Forces Magazine*, September 28, 2023, https://www.airandspaceforces.com/watch-read-secretary-kendall-great-power-competition/; and Noah Robertson, "China Leading 'Rapid Expansion' of Nuclear Arsenal, Pentagon Says," *Defense News*, October 24, 2024, https://www.defensenews.com/pentagon/2024/10/24/china-leading-rapid-expansion-of-nuclear-arsenal-pentagon-says/.

6. Lara Seligman and Michael R. Gordon, "U.S. Says North Korean Troops Heading to Russia's Kursk Region," *The Wall Street Journal*, October 25, 2024, https://www.wsj.com/world/u-s-says-north-korean-troops-heading-to-russias-kursk-region-f36312db.

7. Alexander Gabuev, "Putin and Xi's Unholy Alliance: Why the West Won't Be Able to Drive a Wedge Between Russia and China," *Foreign Affairs*, April 9, 2024, https://www.foreignaffairs.com/china/putin-and-xis-unholy-alliance.

8. This paragraph and the next draw on Hal Brands, "The New Autocratic Alliances: They Don't Look Like America's—but They're Still Dangerous," *Foreign Affairs*, March 29, 2024, https://www.foreignaffairs.com/united-states/new-autocratic-alliances.

9. Brian Carter and Frederick W. Kagan, *Iran's Attempt to Hit Israel with a Russian-Style Strike Package Failed . . . for Now*, Institute for the Study of War, April 14, 2024, https://www.understandingwar.org/backgrounder/iran%E2%80%99s-attempt-hit-israel-russian-style-strike-package-failedfor-now.

10. *Hearing to Receive Testimony on Worldwide Threats*, 118th Cong. 38–39 (2024) (statement of Avril Haines, Director of National Intelligence).

11. Commission on the National Defense Strategy, *Report of the Commission on the National Defense Strategy*, RAND Corporation, July 29, 2024, v, https://www.rand.org/nsrd/projects/NDS-commission.html.

12. Svetlana Shkolnikova, "Key Senator Proposes $55B Boost to Pentagon Budget to Counter 'Axis of Aggressors,'" *Stars and Stripes*, May 29, 2024, https://www.stripes.com/theaters/us/2024-05-29/senate-defense-budget-ndaa-wicker-russia-china-14019670.html.

13. Jared Gans, "Trump Claims Harris 'Guaranteed' to Get US into World War III," *The Hill*, October 26, 2024, https://thehill.com/homenews/campaign/4955539-donald-trump-kamala-harris-world-war-iii/; and *Roll Call*, "Remarks: Kamala Harris Holds a Campaign Roundtable in Royal Oak, Michigan—October 21, 2024," https://rollcall.com/factbase/harris/transcript/kamala-harris-remarks-campaign-event-royal-oak-michigan-october-21-2024/.

14. Michael Hirsh, "The Pentagon Is Freaking Out About a Potential War with China," *Politico*, June 9, 2023, https://www.politico.com/news/magazine/2023/06/09/america-weapons-china-00100373.

15. US Department of Defense, Office of the Under Secretary of Defense (Comptroller) and Chief Financial Officer, *Defense Budget Overview: United States Department of Defense Fiscal Year 2025 Budget Request*, April 4, 2024, 1–5, https://comptroller.defense.gov/Portals/45/Documents/defbudget/FY2025/FY2025_Budget_Request_Overview_Book.pdf.

16. Patrick Norrick, "Real Per Capita Defense Spending," unpublished PowerPoint presentation, American Enterprise Institute, October 22, 2024.

17. US Department of Defense, *Report of the Quadrennial Defense Review*, May 1997, 12, https://history.defense.gov/Portals/70/Documents/quadrennial/QDR1997.pdf.

18. Jim Mitre, "A Eulogy for the Two-War Construct," *The Washington Quarterly*, Winter 2019, https://www.tandfonline.com/doi/abs/10.1080/0163660X.2018.1557479. See also the analysis in Hal Brands, "The Overstretched Superpower: Does America Have More Rivals Than It Can Handle?," *Foreign Affairs*, January 18, 2022, https://www.foreignaffairs.com/articles/china/2022-01-18/overstretched-superpower.

19. US Department of Defense, *Summary of the 2018 National Defense Strategy of the United States of America: Sharpening the American Military's Competitive Edge*, 6, https://dod.defense.gov/portals/1/documents/pubs/2018-national-defense-strategy-summary.pdf.

20. Michael C. Horowitz, "Battles of Precise Mass: Technology Is Remaking War—and America Must Adapt," *Foreign Affairs*, October 22, 2024, https://www.foreignaffairs.com/world/battles-precise-mass-technology-war-horowitz; and Josh Rogin, "The U.S. Military Plans a 'Hellscape' to Deter China from Attacking Taiwan," *The Washington Post*, June 10, 2024, https://www.washingtonpost.com/opinions/2024/06/10/taiwan-china-hellscape-military-plan/.

21. Seth G. Jones, *Empty Bins in a Wartime Environment: The Challenge to the U.S. Defense Industrial Base*, Center for Strategic and International Studies, January 23, 2023, https://www.csis.org/analysis/empty-bins-wartime-environment-challenge-us-defense-industrial-base; and Nancy A. Youssef and Gordon Lubold, "Pentagon Runs Low on Air-Defense Missiles as Demand Surges," *The Wall Street Journal*, October 29, 2024, https://www.wsj.com/politics/national-security/pentagon-runs-low-on-air-defense-missiles-as-demand-surges-7fc9370c.

22. Anthony Capaccio, "Nearly 40% of US Attack Submarines Are out of Commission for Repairs," *Bloomberg*, July 11, 2023, https://www.bloomberg.com/news/articles/2023-07-11/us-navy-attack-submarine-readiness-almost-40-out-of-commission-for-repairs; and Ellie Cook, "US Navy Has a Maintenance Problem," *Newsweek*, November 24, 2023, https://www.newsweek.com/us-navy-maintenace-aircraft-carriers-russia-china-1846058.

23. Mackenzie Eaglen, *The 2020s Tri-Service Modernization Crunch*, American Enterprise Institute, March 23, 2021, https://www.aei.org/research-products/report/2020s-tri-service-modernization-crunch/.

24. Seth G. Jones, "China Is Ready for War: And Thanks to a Crumbling Defense Industrial Base, America Is Not," *Foreign Affairs*, October 2, 2024, https://www.

foreignaffairs.com/china/china-ready-war-america-is-not-seth-jones; and US Department of Defense, *Military and Security Developments Involving the People's Republic of China 2023*, October 19, 2023, viii, 103–13, https://media.defense.gov/2023/Oct/19/2003323409/-1/-1/1/2023-military-and-security-developments-involving-the-peoples-republic-of-china.pdf.

25. Mark F. Cancian et al., *The First Battle of the Next War: Wargaming a Chinese Invasion of Taiwan*, Center for Strategic and International Studies, January 9, 2023, https://www.csis.org/analysis/first-battle-next-war-wargaming-chinese-invasion-taiwan.

26. Hal Brands and Evan Braden Montgomery, "One War Is Not Enough: Strategy and Force Planning for Great-Power Competition," *Texas National Security Review* 3, no. 2 (2020): 80–92, https://tnsr.org/2020/03/one-war-is-not-enough-strategy-and-force-planning-for-great-power-competition/; and Eric Heginbotham et al., *The U.S.-China Military Scorecard: Forces, Geography, and the Evolving Balance of Power, 1996–2017*, RAND Corporation, September 14, 2015, https://www.rand.org/pubs/research_reports/RR392.html.

27. Robert Kagan, *The Ghost at the Feast: America and the Collapse of World Order, 1900–1941* (Knopf, 2023), 196.

28. Brands, *The Eurasian Century*, 109, 111.

29. Richard Overy, *Why the Allies Won* (W. W. Norton, 1997), 319.

30. Military Spending as a Share of GDP, Our World in Data, accessed October 30, 2024, https://ourworldindata.org/grapher/military-spending-as-a-share-of-gdp-gmsd.

31. Waldo Heinrichs, *Threshold of War: Franklin D. Roosevelt and American Entry into World War II* (Oxford University Press, 1990), 10.

32. See, for instance, Hana Kusumoto, "Japan's Defense Ministry Seeks Record $52.9 Billion for 2nd Year of Military Buildup," *Stars and Stripes*, August 31, 2023, https://www.stripes.com/theaters/asia_pacific/2023-08-31/japan-military-defense-budget-2024-11221680.html.

33. White House, *National Security Strategy*, October 12, 2022, 8, https://www.whitehouse.gov/wp-content/uploads/2022/10/Biden-Harris-Administrations-National-Security-Strategy-10.2022.pdf.

34. Heginbotham et al., *The U.S.-China Military Scorecard*.

35. This paragraph draws on Hal Brands, "Putting 'Asia First' Could Cost America the World," *Bloomberg Opinion*, August 25, 2024, https://www.bloomberg.com/opinion/features/2024-08-25/putting-asia-first-could-cost-america-the-world.

36. Michael J. Green, "Never Say Never to an Asian NATO," *Foreign Policy*, September 6, 2023, https://foreignpolicy.com/2023/09/06/asian-nato-security-alliance-china-us-quad-aukus-japan-australia-taiwan-military-biden/.

37. Ken Moriyasu, "U.S. Seeks to Revive Idled Shipyards with Help of Japan, South Korea," *Nikkei Asia*, March 4, 2024, https://asia.nikkei.com/Politics/Defense/U.S.-seeks-to-revive-idled-shipyards-with-help-of-Japan-South-Korea.

38. Roger Wicker, *21st Century Peace Through Strength: A Generational Investment in the U.S. Military*, Office of Senator Roger Wicker, May 29, 2024, 10, https://www.wicker.senate.gov/services/files/BC957888-0A93-432F-A49E-6202768A9CE0. See also Kori Schake, "America Must Spend More on Defense: How Biden Can Align Resources and

Strategy," *Foreign Affairs*, April 5, 2022, https://www.foreignaffairs.com/articles/united-states/2022-04-05/america-must-spend-more-defense.

39. John Lewis Gaddis, *Strategies of Containment: A Critical Appraisal of American National Security Policy During the Cold War* (Oxford University Press, 2005), 393–94; and Aaron L. Friedberg, *In the Shadow of the Garrison State: America's Anti-Statism and Its Cold War Grand Strategy* (Princeton University Press, 2000), 341.

40. In fairness, the administration worked to expand production of some key munitions, like 155-millimeter artillery ammunition. But these increases were targeted.

41. Most US military aid to Ukraine consists of delivering existing capabilities from American stockpiles—and appropriating funds to purchase new equipment for the US military. In other words, "aid to Ukraine" mostly allows the US armed forces to trade old equipment for newer equipment.

42. Amber Marcellino et al., *An Update to the Budget and Economic Outlook: 2024 to 2034*, Congressional Budget Office, June 18, 2024, 3, 9–11, https://www.cbo.gov/system/files/2024-06/60039-Outlook-2024.pdf.

3

US Defense Policy and Strategic Guidance for a Multi-Theater Military

DUSTIN WALKER

Today, the ambition of US grand strategy exceeds the US military's ability to support it.

The United States seeks to sustain deterrence and secure its interests across three key regions: Europe, the Indo-Pacific, and the Middle East. However, it seeks to do so without the margin of military, economic, or technological superiority it previously enjoyed. Despite the previous two administrations' efforts to set a new direction for US defense policy and strategy, the Department of Defense (DOD) has yet to effectively respond with the urgency, ambition, and imagination required. Congress has made the problem worse, saddling the US military with more than a decade of budgetary malpractice marked by continuing resolutions, sequestration, insufficient growth, and perpetual uncertainty.

The result is that the US military is in danger of becoming—if it hasn't already—a one-war military. Under plausible scenarios, that one war could be lost to China. At the same time, overlapping conflicts in Ukraine and the Middle East and the emergence of a nascent axis of aggressors have highlighted the risk of simultaneous conflicts in multiple theaters.

The United States needs to rebuild a multi-theater military—one that is capable of defending US interests across three key regions, prepared for simultaneous conflicts, and equipped with cutting-edge technologies fielded at scale. But how?

One thing a multi-theater military clearly needs is *more*. More capacity in key capability areas like munitions, long-range fires, integrated air and missile defense, contested logistics, undersea warfare, and persistent intelligence, surveillance, and reconnaissance (ISR). More production from the defense industrial base in peacetime and wartime. More people in the military and the defense industrial base with the right mix of education and skills. And more money, as DOD spending as a percentage of gross domestic product (GDP) is roughly half what it was during the major defense modernization 40 years ago.[1]

If only it were so simple. In reality, how to build a multi-theater military comes down to much more difficult issues, such as summoning political will to make tough and controversial decisions; organizing and managing one of the world's largest bureaucracies; developing feasible theories of victory against nuclear-armed adversaries; determining the proper mix of force structure for conflicts of uncertain scale, scope, and duration; sequencing investments over time; and prioritizing among theaters.

This chapter does not address all these issues in full. But it provides recommendations for US defense policy and strategy to move the joint force toward becoming a multi-theater military. These include changes in DOD force planning, contingency planning, concept development and force design, budget and force development, and posture and force employment.

The US military has real problems in an increasingly dangerous world. But it must rise to master these challenges without despair and without delay.

Alternatives to a Multi-Theater Military

Since the Cold War era, building and maintaining a US military capable of winning wars in multiple theaters has been an uncontroversial objective. No more. As the United States' adversaries have grown stronger, Washington's policy failures have allowed US military power to dangerously erode, leaving the joint force capable of fighting only one war at a time. Confronted with this difficult reality, some experts have asserted that a return to a multi-theater military would be too expensive, too slow, or downright impossible. According to this view, DOD should pursue one or more strategic alternatives for meeting its objectives.

The United States could prioritize by narrowing the objectives of its defense strategy and adopting a single-war force-planning construct. Proponents of this form of prioritization worry that attempts to pursue a multi-theater strategy despite material constraints will result in overstretch and neglect the pacing challenge China poses. This concern is not entirely without merit, particularly absent increased defense resources and more disciplined development and employment of the force.

That said, a one-war military is a problem to be solved, not a solution to be embraced.[2] A one-war military presumes certainty in a security environment in which uncertainty abounds. As the 1997 Quadrennial Defense Review observed,

> We can never know with certainty when or where the next major theater war will occur, who our next adversary will be, how an enemy will fight, who will join us in a coalition, or precisely what demands will be placed on U.S. forces. Indeed, history has repeatedly shown that we are often unable to predict such matters.[3]

A one-war military reduces the commander in chief to a gambler, "turning every decision to use military force into a catastrophically risky 'all or nothing' bet."[4] As one defense strategist once said, "A force that can only wage one conflict is effectively a zero-conflict force since employing it would require the president to preclude any other meaningful global engagement."[5] That's why DOD never had a one-war planning construct for the Soviet Union during the Cold War.[6]

Even the 2018 and 2022 National Defense Strategies (NDSs) were not meant to be strictly one-war constructs. Both strategies aimed to deter opportunistic aggression while fighting a major war, though they were unspecific as to what forces would be required to do so. As Jim Mitre wrote of the 2018 NDS force-planning construct,

> U.S. forces must be able to succeed across a broader range of scenarios and conditions reflecting the breadth and sophistication of adversary abilities.
>
> To say that the NDS prioritizes force planning for war against a potential great power adversary does not remove the necessity to deter an opportunistic aggressor.[7]

He went on to say that "force sufficiency for narrowly prescribed scenarios can no longer be the DOD's primary metric for decision."[8]

Though DOD can and should prioritize China, building toward a multi-theater military is a hedge against uncertainty. Force planners must do their best to estimate the scale, scope, and duration of a conflict with China. However, should those calculations be wrong, force structure originally fielded for other theaters or a second conflict could be applied as a reserve.

Another set of alternatives would still have DOD commit to deterring or winning a second war but through means other than standing conventional forces: nuclear escalation, wartime mobilization, and burden sharing.

DOD could rely more on its nuclear arsenal to deter opportunistic aggression in a second theater, a modern version of the Eisenhower-era policy of massive retaliation. Such a radical shift in DOD's approach to warfighting is neither likely nor tenable. US adversaries, especially nuclear-armed adversaries like China and Russia, are likely to doubt the credibility of threats of nuclear escalation in response to conventional aggression against a US ally or partner (e.g., Israel, NATO, or Taiwan). Indeed, many US allies and partners would oppose such a policy.

The United States should remain focused on maintaining strategic deterrence against its two nuclear peers in Russia and China and modernizing its arsenal of strategic and theater nuclear weapons to achieve this objective. That's why the Congressional Commission on the Strategic Posture of the United States recommended that DOD field sufficient conventional forces to win simultaneous conflicts and avoid increased reliance on nuclear weapons.[9]

Rather than build standing conventional forces capable of fighting two conflicts, DOD could rely on wartime mobilization to rapidly surge manpower and industrial capacity to win a second conflict. This, too, would be problematic. Put simply, it's already evident that the United States must undertake a massive revitalization of its defense industrial base to build standing conventional forces sufficient for credible deterrence and support US allies and partners. Surge production capacity in excess of present DOD and international demand, especially for major capital systems, is unlikely to materialize in the foreseeable future. Moreover, DOD faces persistent challenges with recruitment and retention. Any significant expansion of end strength in wartime would likely require a compulsory draft, which is a heavy burden on the national leadership's political will.

Given current industrial and personnel limitations, the best-case scenario is that the joint force replaces personnel and matériel losses during a conflict of limited duration. Force planners should not rely on wartime mobilization to significantly and rapidly produce new force structure sufficient for a second conflict.

Another often-posed alternative to a multi-theater military is to rely more on US allies and partners and entrust them with the primary responsibility for security in theaters such as Europe and the Middle East.

Greater contributions from US allies and partners are not just welcome or fair. Given the scope and scale of the challenges our adversaries pose in Europe, the Indo-Pacific, and the Middle East, such contributions are a necessary complement to a US multi-theater military. Therefore, the question is not whether the United States should ask more of its allies and partners. It should. Rather, the question is how best to ensure that greater contributions from allies and partners actually materialize and do so in a manner that supports US strategic interests; aligns with US force design, development, and employment priorities; and enhances the credibility of deterrence against shared adversaries.

While a comprehensive answer to this question is beyond the scope of this chapter, there are some key observations salient for a US multi-theater military.

Greater allied and partner contributions will not remove the need for US leadership. US interests in theaters like Europe and the Middle East are too important to simply delegate and hope things turn out for the best. The United States and its frontline allies are not better off outsourcing Russia policy to France or Germany or likewise entrusting Iran policy to Saudi Arabia or the United Arab Emirates. That's why the United States should seek to preserve its political and military leadership of (formal and informal) coalitions to deter and defend against Russia and Iran—leadership that is underwritten by a sustained (though perhaps reduced) US military commitment in each theater.

Greater allied and partner contributions will not materialize quickly or alleviate the demand for US forces in key theaters. Just as in the United States, allied and partner investments in expanding force structure and rejuvenating the defense industrial base will take many years to show results. Indeed, many allies and partners are starting from a weaker position than the US. US force planners should not make assumptions about any significant increase in allied and partner capability or capacity in the near to medium term.

Achieving greater allied and partner contributions will require resolute US leadership, deft US diplomacy, and uncharacteristic US patience. And the US must find ways of holding nations accountable for meeting their commitments. That said, political threats, acts of retribution, and the sudden withdrawal of US troops from allied nations risk political backlash, splintered alliances, or—worse—driving friendly nations into making accommodations with US adversaries.

Europe and South Korea are the most likely places where the US could gradually reduce its overall military commitment while remaining confident in the political strength of each alliance and the long-term trajectory of allied capability and credible deterrence. NATO allies can take, should take, and are taking on a larger role in providing for their own defense. Going forward, capability targets apportioned to European allies through the NATO defense planning process should be intentionally selected to reduce overreliance on the United States for key capabilities enablers, as recommended by the Commission on the National Defense Strategy.[10] New European defense investments spurred by Russia's invasion of Ukraine should focus on delivering on those capability targets. Likewise, South Korea's military has the will and capability to lead deterrence and defense against North Korea. Its impressive industrial base will continue to bolster its military modernization.

Finally, not all burden-sharing contributions are measured in defense spending as a percentage of GDP. The United States needs more from its allies and partners than bigger budgets. It needs expanded posture access in the Indo-Pacific. It needs partners in Africa, Latin America, and the Middle East to reject Chinese and Russian military presence. It needs allies like Australia, Japan, and the Philippines to agree to arrangements for combined contingency planning and command and control. And it needs allies and partners to overcome parochial political opposition to expanded defense industrial cooperation. All these are critical for a multi-theater military but don't necessarily come with a price tag.

A New Force-Planning Construct

Determining what a multi-theater military would look like starts with a force-planning construct. It is policymakers' answer to the question, "What do you want the US military to be able to do?" With a set of fundamental missions, scenarios, and specified time frames, a force-planning construct guides defense planners and budgeteers on the size and shape of the military they should build and the budget required to do so. In this respect, a force-planning construct is a normative statement about the military we should have in the future rather than a strictly objective statement about the military we have at present.

The most recent National Defense Strategy, published in 2022, did not provide a force-planning construct for a multi-theater military. Recognizing increasing global challenges but opposed to increased defense spending, the Biden administration sought to achieve ambitious strategic ends with little to no change in the means (force structure, budget, etc.). To bridge this ends-means gap, the Biden administration sought to change the "ways" of US defense strategy with the concept of "integrated deterrence."[11] This strategy produced a force-planning construct that sized and shaped the force to prevail in one conflict while deterring opportunistic aggression elsewhere with few compelling specifics as to how that would be accomplished. It seemed more like an estimate of what the current force could do than a statement of what the future force must do. In short, the Biden administration adopted—rather than adapted to—the limitations of the joint force.

Going forward, the next National Defense Strategy, due in 2026, should articulate a force-planning construct for a multi-theater military with certain key attributes.

A force-planning construct must be selective, prioritized, and resource informed. As the Commission on the National Defense Strategy stated, DOD force planning "must be prioritized to effectively and efficiently allocate finite resources, address threats of varying scope and scale, and ensure a mix of US instruments of national power that are tailored to specific strategic objectives."[12] Even with a multi-theater military, the United States cannot defend every one of its interests with equal vigor simultaneously. Overly ambitious force-planning constructs along these lines "have typically led to force structure estimates twice as large as more-realistic, budget-informed planning approaches."[13]

A corollary proposition is that force-planning constructs must be based on not only plausible scenarios but military responses that are feasible within reasonable political and financial constraints. The Kennedy and Johnson administrations based their "2 ½ war" construct on a scenario involving a conflict with the Soviet Union in Europe, a war in Asia, and a potential "brushfire" in the Western Hemisphere.[14] While rooted in plausible scenarios during this tense period of the Cold War, this force-planning construct proved unaffordable and impossible, especially given the costs of the Vietnam War. Consequently, it ceased to meaningfully influence the direction of force development.

A new force-planning construct must carefully distinguish among adversaries and conflicts. Force-planning shorthand can often confuse more than it clarifies. The post–Cold War "two-war" planning construct referred to two "major regional contingencies" of similar scale against similar adversaries (e.g., Iraq and North Korea) engaged in similar forms of aggression (e.g., an "armor-heavy, combined-arms offensive against the outnumbered forces of a neighboring state") requiring a similar US response (e.g., rapidly deploying forces into the region, halting the invasion, and defeating the aggressor).[15] A force-planning construct for a multi-theater military would not be a return to two-war construct for the simple reason that there are no two wars the United States might fight against its potential adversaries that are likely to be of similar scope, scale, intensity, and duration. A war with China is not the same as a NATO-Russia war. Neither of those is the same as an operation to take out Iran's nuclear program. Simply labeling all three as "wars" misses the point.

Finally, a new force-planning construct must make realistic assumptions about international force contributions accounting for differences in the nature of US alliances and partnerships in key theaters. Consider the contrast between US alliances in Europe and the Indo-Pacific. In Europe, the United States enjoys a highly institutionalized, multilateral alliance committed to coalition warfare and deeply ingrained in DOD's doctrine, organization, training, matériel, leadership and education, personnel, and facilities (DOTMLPF). NATO engages in detailed planning for collective defense, including preassigning forces to specific plans to be maintained at high readiness and made available to the alliance on an assured basis.[16] In the Indo-Pacific, the United States has a hub-and-spoke network of bilateral alliances of varying degrees of maturity. In a conflict with China involving a Taiwan scenario, allied contributions are not guaranteed, let alone specified in advance. Thus, DOD force planners should make conservative and differentiated assumptions about the contributions of allies and partners.

With these factors in mind, DOD should adopt a force-planning construct that sizes and shapes the joint force to simultaneously do the following:

- Defend the homeland;

- Maintain strategic deterrence;

- Deter and, if necessary, defeat Chinese aggression in the Indo-Pacific in a major, potentially protracted conflict;

- Deter and, if necessary, defeat Russian aggression against the NATO alliance as part of a US-led but predominantly European combined force; and

- Conduct targeted military operations in the Middle East, including with regional partners, to counter and dissuade Iranian malign activities and prevent mass-casualty terrorist attacks.

To be clear, the US military is not currently sized and shaped for such a force-planning construct. Over the long term, defense budgets should be designed to build a force capable of defending against an axis of aggressors on multiple fronts. Until we can build that force, prioritization in force design, development, and employment will be critical. In each of these areas, China should remain the highest priority.

Changes to Contingency Planning

A new force-planning construct must be complemented by changes in DOD contingency planning to effectively shape the department's strategic direction. DOD contingency plans shape not only the employment of the current force but also the design and development of the future force. The secretary of defense's *Defense Planning Guidance*, *Contingency Planning Guidance*, and specific campaign and contingency plans are key inputs into joint and service concept development and requirements-generation processes.

Congress assigned the role of global integrator to the chairman of the Joint Chiefs of Staff in the National Defense Authorization Act for Fiscal Year 2017.[17] Since then, DOD has increased focus on the conduct of integrated contingency planning across combatant command areas of responsibility, functions, and domains and on managing the reallocation or reassignment of forces globally. For example, DOD has made progress in ensuring that operation plans are developed with realistic assumptions about the availability of forces in functional areas such as transportation, the cyber domain, space, strategic deterrence, and homeland defense.[18]

However, despite these improvements, DOD's contingency planning is not optimized for a multi-theater military. Going forward, DOD contingency planning must account for multiple simultaneous conflicts, the possibility of protracted conflict, and the defense industrial base support required for successful execution of the conflicts.

Generally speaking, DOD does not plan for simultaneous contingencies. Instead, it develops "integrated contingency plans" that coordinate "the activities of multiple [combatant commands] in time and space to respond to *a single contingency*" (emphasis added) across geographic boundaries and functional responsibilities.[19] Consequently, any two contingency plans executed simultaneously would risk making overlapping or conflicting claims on the same forces, functional support, and resources. Contingency plans involving combat operations at significant scale would be at the highest risk.

Instead of regular contingency planning, DOD treats "multiple crises" that "concurrently impact two or more" combatant commanders as a situation to be handled by "planning in a crisis," which often takes place on condensed timelines in direct response to events.[20] DOD regularly conducts crisis planning, refining or adapting existing plans into executable operation orders or developing them from scratch in unforeseen circumstances.

Multiple simultaneous conflicts would not be an out-of-the-blue scenario, and planning for this should not be deferred to crisis planning. Such a scenario is all too plausible and its consequences for national security too grave to be planned on the verge or in the midst of calamity. Planning for simultaneous conflicts in multiple theaters should be part of DOD's regular contingency planning.

Likewise, DOD contingency planning does not sufficiently account for the possibility of a protracted conflict. Since the end of the Cold War, DOD has generally assumed "that technology-fuelled advances in combat velocity will automatically lead to great-power wars that are shorter, sharper, and more localised."[21] This assumption is no longer valid. Great-power adversaries will not necessarily terminate their aggression due to an initial failure to achieve their objectives rapidly. Indeed, as Russia has done in Ukraine, an adversary may persist in its aggression, calculating that it can outlast the political will and material capacity of the United States and its allies and partners. Indeed, experts warn that a conflict with China "could morph into . . . a protracted struggle that also evolves into a gruelling war of attrition, spanning multiple theatres and drawing on all dimensions of national power."[22]

Furthermore, bureaucratic incentives tend to bias DOD toward planning for shorter wars. As Evan Montgomery and Julian Ouellet assess, "Planning scenarios used for strategy are often simultaneously used for constraining service budgets—all else being equal, shorter wars should be cheaper than longer wars." Shorter wars are also easier to plan, focusing on "quantifiable and easy-to-measure issues such as force flows, exchange ratios, and attrition rates" rather than "qualitative and hard-to-measure[] topics such as adversary will and resolve," on which longer wars may turn.[23]

Planning for protraction is essential not just because such a scenario is plausible. Short and long wars are fundamentally different—even opposite—in their theory of victory, concepts of operations, and time-phased force requirements. Moreover, failing to account for protraction in a conflict in one theater may render the joint force unable to respond to crisis or conflict in another theater.

DOD contingency planning also needs better integration with defense industrial planning. The Commission on the National Defense Strategy observed that DOD contingency plans do not sufficiently consider needs specific to the industrial base relevant to the execution of operational plans, leading to an "operational-industrial gap."[24] DOD should incorporate the defense industrial base directly into its contingency plans, specifically issues such as war reserve matériel requirements, prioritized wartime surge production needs, anticipated Defense Production Act (DPA) Title I actions in wartime, and alignment of DPA Title III actions with contingency plan requirements.

Fortunately, Congress has recognized the need to update DOD contingency planning practices and processes. In section 1074 of the Servicemember Quality of Life Improvement and National Defense Authorization Act for Fiscal Year 2025, Congress instructed DOD to assess and report on its operational plans, specifically its planning assumptions for simultaneous and protracted conflicts. This is a welcome intervention of congressional oversight.[25]

The next secretary of defense should go further and issue contingency planning guidance to account for multiple simultaneous conflicts, protracted conflict, and the defense industrial support required for successful execution. At a minimum, the secretary should direct the development of contingency plans detailing how the joint force would respond to Russian or Iranian aggression when already engaged in an all-domain conflict with China.

DOD may assess plans developed for simultaneous or protracted conflict to be impossible to execute given limitations on the forces assumed or projected to be available. Likewise, execution risk might result from defense industrial base limitations. But that is exactly why this detailed planning and analysis must take place now: to give DOD and congressional leaders an authoritative account of the capability and capacity gaps that must be addressed for the United States to build a multi-theater military.

Concept Development and Force Design

With the 2018 National Defense Strategy, DOD acknowledged that assumptions underpinning the traditional "American way of war" no longer hold. DOD cannot count on an expeditionary force projection model in which the joint force can use uncontested logistics to deploy large numbers of forces thousands of miles from its homeland sanctuary to largely invulnerable bases near the theater of operations, build up over a lengthy period, and then commence offensive operations at a time of its choosing with ample intelligence support and the overwhelming technical advantage to establish all-domain superiority and degrade enemy forces such that US forces can achieve operational objectives with minimal casualties.[26] DOD recognized it needed a new model for operating a multi-theater military. And it's been searching for one ever since.

Over the past several years, the Joint Staff and the services have developed a variety of new warfighting concepts and pursued new force design initiatives to address threats from advanced adversaries like China and Russia. These include the Joint Warfighting Concept, the Army's multi-domain operations, the Air Force's Future Operating Concept, the Marine Corps's Force Design 2030 and suite of supporting concepts, and the Navy's Navigation Plan and Distributed Maritime Operations concept. To varying degrees, these efforts have focused on similar force attributes and capabilities: integrated command and control; dispersal, distribution, and expanded maneuver; resilient logistics; long-range fires; persistent ISR; force protection; and air and missile defense.

However, major questions remain as to how DOD intends to assemble this hodgepodge of concepts and force designs into a coherent joint concept with a feasible theory of victory. Moreover, with the exception of the Marine Corps, these force design and concept development efforts have had a limited impact on the joint force's overall trajectory.

The Navy and Air Force in particular seem unable to achieve internal consensus sufficient to initiate and sustain decisive changes in force design and future force structure. Both services are mired in interminable debates on interrelated questions about the proper mix of near-, medium-, and long-term investments; manned and unmanned systems; survivable and attritable platforms; stand-in and standoff forces; service-retained forces in the continental United States; forward-stationed assigned forces; and more. Critical decisions and the concepts and force design necessary to move the joint force toward a multi-theater military are being deferred, with risk-averse service leaders unable or unwilling to resolve these issues.

For the two most capital-intensive services, the longer these debates rage on, the slower or more expensive their options become, if they don't disappear entirely. The lack of sufficient, timely, and predictable defense budgets makes this problem worse. Budget uncertainty prolongs debate and instills pessimism that renders creative, bold solutions as unaffordable luxuries. This strategic paralysis leaves both services trapped in a death spiral: perpetually shrinking, divesting force structure due to budget constraints despite unyielding operational tempo, and investing more dollars in smaller numbers of exquisite platforms that are slow to arrive (if they ever do).

Meanwhile, the Army appears to have a relatively stable force design and conceptual approach. The real question is whether the Army is big enough to fulfill its own vision. Dwindling end strength is harming Army readiness and risks leaving the service too small to carry out its broad set of roles and missions. It recently announced the elimination of 32,000 billets to free up space for personnel aligned to key modernization capabilities.[27] An ever-shrinking Army will struggle to provide the land power backbone in Europe and South Korea, serve as the "linchpin service" in the Indo-Pacific, and maintain responsibility for joint capabilities already under strain, like integrated air and missile defense.[28]

The challenges of the Navy, Air Force, and Army to decisively establish and effectively implement consistent force design and warfighting concepts directly impede a multi-theater military. These struggles cut right to the heart of being able to field the right mix of capabilities at sufficient capacity and readiness to operate across multiple theaters.

Decisive political leadership and budget certainty are two critical aspects of the solution. The secretary of defense, deputy secretary of defense, and secretaries and undersecretaries of the service departments must personally drive decision-making processes to definitive conclusions and enforce strict adherence to defense planning and budgetary guidance. We need decision-makers that actually make decisions and stick to them, not risk-averse officeholders who prefer no decision to the wrong decision. Time has run out for that. Meanwhile, Congress must appropriate sufficient, timely, and predictable funding that provides financial space for bold solutions and a sufficient time horizon to carry force design and concept development initiatives to fruition.

When it comes to concepts, the secretary and deputy secretary of defense must push for a true joint operating concept that drives service concept development (rather than the other way around) and directly influences service force design and development priorities.

DOD should place increased emphasis on concepts of denial, particularly for China and Russia. Rather than focusing on how to overcome enemy anti-access and area-denial capabilities to enable US force projection with existing force structure, future concepts should emphasize preventing adversaries from projecting force and defending the territory of allies and partners using asymmetric capabilities. Ukraine's successful sea-denial campaign against Russia in the Black Sea shows the promise of this concept.[29] The US Indo-Pacific Command's recently announced "hellscape" concept suggests DOD is also beginning to move in this direction.[30] These defensively oriented concepts, which do not assume or require superiority or dominance in a particular domain, would also be more easily adopted by allies and partners.

Future concepts also need to more fully consider the long game and the endgame, particularly for China and Russia. As previously mentioned regarding contingency plans, DOD's operational concepts tend to emphasize conflicts of limited duration. DOD needs to focus more on concepts for protraction. This is less about industrial considerations of what to build in the event of protracted conflict. Rather, it is about how the joint force, in concert with other elements of national power, presses US advantage between major operations. DOD also needs to place greater emphasis on concepts for war termination, particularly in conflicts with China and Russia, nuclear adversaries against whom total victory is unlikely if not impossible.

Closely aligned with concept development, leaders in the Office of the Secretary of Defense and the service should advance force design initiatives that fully embrace broad and deep adoption of autonomous systems, lower-cost weapons, and the software-defined networks and command and control systems that power them. Combatant commands should be given a strengthened hand in influencing force designs to ensure these new technologies are tailored for multi-theater application.

Budgets and Force Development

A multi-theater military requires a variety of capabilities for specific operational challenges. But more fundamentally, it requires additional capacity. A multi-theater military needs affordable mass that demonstrates to adversaries that the joint force can operate flexibly across multiple theaters simultaneously, absorb attrition, and generate sustained combat power in a protracted conflict.

Business as usual will not produce affordable mass. DOD must confront the harsh reality that any strategy that seeks to restore US military superiority "solely by growing today's munitions stocks and force structure is doomed to fail."[31] The atrophy of the defense industrial base and the sclerosis of the acquisition system mean that rapid growth of traditional force structure is no longer possible.

That is why DOD needs to embark on an ambitious and transformative shift of procurement dollars over the near and medium term to scale production of lower-cost, mass-producible, all-domain autonomous systems. The time for decade-long research and development projects and innovation theater is over. The systems should be procured in large quantities and fully integrated into joint and service DOTMLPF to complement existing force structure. Rather than the smaller, tactical, shorter-range systems employed in Ukraine, DOD should focus on establishing programs centered on larger autonomous vehicles that have sufficient range, power, payload, and survivability to be relevant in the geographically expansive, operationally stressing environment of the Indo-Pacific. These systems would also be valuable in projecting power over greater distances in the air and maritime domains against Russia and Iran.

DOD would likely need to procure these capabilities outside the traditional acquisition system to ensure speed and avoid burdensome, industrial-age requirements processes ill-suited to this technology. Likewise, DOD should lean heavily into the commercial sector, which has advanced the foundational technologies behind autonomous systems to build a new, alternative defense industrial base to produce these systems at scale.

At the same time, DOD should prioritize ease of exportability as it develops and fields autonomous systems, forming the basis of a new class of cooperative programs with allies and partners. Autonomous systems could be a new frontier of defense industrial cooperation delivering a diplomatic, military, and economic force multiplier.

A multi-theater military also requires a substantial increase in munitions stockpiling and production. DOD should expand the use of modular kits to turn dumb bombs into precision weapons, as well as glide kits[32] and other add-ons that extend the range of existing precision weapons. Most importantly, DOD needs to move beyond efforts to increase the production of existing weapons and accelerate the development and production of new weapons types.

In particular, DOD should prioritize modular weapons that can be more easily manufactured at a lower cost by a wider variety of producers making greater use of commercial supply chains.[33] Rather than focus on piling as many exquisite and expensive capabilities as possible onto one missile, modular weapons would allow DOD to build heterogeneous salvos that would be more survivable and cost-effective. This approach would provide the military services with the acquisition flexibility to buy more modular weapons ahead of need rather than waiting to procure systems that meet a precise operational requirement. Likewise, it would provide operational flexibility for warfighters in multiple theaters to tailor sensors and payloads by the minute in accordance with their needs.

In addition to autonomous systems and lower-cost weapons, other DOD budget and force development priorities should include resilient, all-domain sensing networks; integrated air and missile defense; long-range fires; and contested logistics, including expanding the Combat Logistics Force.

To be clear, the United States can and should make some long-term investments in the traditional defense industrial base, especially shipbuilding. Critical programs such as the *Virginia*-class submarine must be kept on track to preserve critical US advantages. And programs such as the B-21 bomber should be expanded to ensure long-term capacity in key capability areas. However, these investments alone will be insufficient without focus on the affordable mass delivered by autonomous systems and low-cost weapons.

Posture and Force Employment

One of the fundamental challenges for a multi-theater military is how the joint force is postured and employed during competition and crisis.

Lack of capacity is clearly a major problem, routinely forcing high-demand, low-density assets to be shifted between theaters in response to events largely outside US control. DOD cannot operate a multi-theater military if global force management is reduced to a game of Whac-a-Mole across three theaters.

Most obviously, it harms military readiness. The US military is too small to handle unexpected deployments of any sustained duration. The counter-ISIS campaign caused a "readiness crisis" and depleted munitions inventories.[34] Immediately following defense budget increases to repair readiness, the "maximum pressure" campaign against Iran wore out the US Navy and led to consecutive record-long aircraft carrier deployments.[35]

Furthermore, an approach of robbing Peter to pay Paul produces a toxic boom-bust cycle in global force management in which forces are taken from one theater (raising questions about US commitment), sent to another theater (raising expectations about US commitment), eventually withdrawn (leading to disappointment), and finally returned to the theater from which they came (where their impermanence undermines their deterrent value).

But a lack of capacity is not the only issue that must be addressed to operate a multi-theater military. DOD needs to take a deeper look at the relationship between global force management and deterrence, particularly the rationale behind shifting allocated forces between theaters.

Broadly speaking, the United States has accustomed itself, its allies and partners, and its adversaries to a language of deterrence in which the deployment of forces into a given theater is the vocabulary of choice. While force deployments can send a powerful deterrent message, overreliance on them is problematic.

First, there is the obvious capacity issue. When there are too few forces to go around, force deployments tax military readiness and increase risk in other theaters. Second, there is the risk that policymakers become less intentional and discerning in their decisions to deploy forces and instead treat such deployments as a knee-jerk response to any international tension. Likewise, a third risk is that force deployments become too focused on activity rather than outcomes. Policymakers may come to value the political message that force deployments send at home, for example, rather than the actual effect they have on adversaries' behavior. Fourth, frequent force deployments increase the risk that adversaries view any reduction in operational tempo as a signal of reduced US commitment.

Rather than attempting to dynamically shift forces between theaters, DOD should aim to build a multi-theater military composed of more capable, self-sufficient assigned forces stationed forward in key theaters. The aim should be to enable combatant commanders to more sustainably manage competition and crisis and respond more rapidly and effectively in conflict.

In this model, combatant commanders would have greater resources and accountability for managing their assigned missions with their assigned forces, including in periods of increased tension. Reducing their reliance on additional allocated forces, combatant commanders would make greater use of a broader portfolio of flexible deterrence options. Alternative actions might include increasing the readiness posture of forces already in theater, upgrading alert status, conducting show-of-force actions, increasing and expanding ISR collection, conducting increased or short-notice training and exercise activities, and increasing active and passive protection measures.

Greater emphasis on forward-stationed assigned forces would have other benefits as well. Enduring command relationships with a combatant command would enable service-provided units to build deeper theater-specific expertise and relationships, increase readiness for specific contingencies through focused planning, and expand participation in joint planning and training. More assigned forces might also narrow the gap between the needs of warfighters in the combatant commands and the planning and budget of the services responsible for manning, training, and equipping the force. Units would be in a better position to advise their services on theater-specific requirements. Meanwhile, assigned forces would provide combatant commanders a longer planning horizon than allocated forces and increase their insight and influence in the planning, programming, budgeting, and execution process.

Increased assigned forces would also enable combatant commanders to respond more rapidly and effectively to adversarial aggression. China and Russia in particular may seek to use speed and local geographic advantages to rapidly achieve military objectives before the United States can mount an effective response and to use the threat of further escalation to coerce war termination on favorable terms. To defeat this theory of victory, forward-stationed assigned forces would be sized and shaped to deny early adversarial gains with minimal early warning and without major reinforcements, buying time for a larger-scale US response. These forces would be first in line to receive asymmetric capabilities such as lethal and attritable autonomous systems. They would require increased forward stocks of munitions and fuel. And they would need more capability to survive and operate in the face of sustained attack through emphasis on mobility, hardening, dispersal, deception, and active and passive defenses.

The Indo-Pacific should be the first priority for posture improvements and additional assigned forces. DOD continues to move slowly to realize the more capable, distributed, and resilient posture it professes as its goal. As Zack Cooper lays out in his chapter, the United States will have to pursue multiple lines of effort simultaneously. These include vigorous defense diplomacy to expand US access to more operating locations. To the greatest extent possible, the United States should press to expand combined basing with allies like Australia, Japan, and the Philippines to complicate China's strategic and operational calculus. DOD will have to field more systems capable of operating from austere locations with minimal infrastructure support, including mobile missile launchers, autonomous aircraft, and unmanned surface and undersea vessels. At the same time, DOD will have to continue investing in long-range projection platforms as a complement to its forces operating forward.

As it continues to allow more resource-efficient approaches in other theaters, DOD should consider managing forces in Europe and the Middle East more closely together. Over many years of instability and conflict, the United States has routinely moved ground, air, and naval forces on rapid timelines from Europe to the Middle East to defend its interests there.[36] Building on this, DOD should consider building the eastern Mediterranean into a strategic hub to defend US interests in Europe and the Middle East. This would entail increasing US force presence in countries like Greece and Romania. At the same time, overall assigned forces in the Middle East would decline even as DOD maintained a constellation of small distributed bases in the region. In this way, the US could reinforce NATO's eastern and southern flanks, retain forces close to the Middle

East for crisis and contingency response, and improve US capability and capacity for the defense of Israel.

Conclusion

More than any specific policy recommendation made in this chapter, the most important resource for building a multi-theater military is political will. This moment of crisis and decision requires active political leadership from the president, the secretary of defense, and senior DOD officials. Building a multi-theater military will pose organizational, conceptual, technical, and financial conundrums. But none of these are beyond the United States' ability to solve. Fundamentally, we face a test of statesmanship, and the stakes could not be higher. We must not squander what opportunity remains to fundamentally change the course of US defense policy in time to prevent a war rather than fight one.

Notes

1. US Department of Defense, Office of the Under Secretary of Defense (Comptroller) and Chief Financial Officer, *Defense Budget Overview: United States Department of Defense Fiscal Year 2025 Budget Request*, April 4, 2024, 1–5, https://comptroller.defense.gov/Portals/45/Documents/defbudget/FY2025/FY2025_Budget_Request_Overview_Book.pdf.

2. Roger Zakheim and Dustin Walker, "Defense 'Prioritization' Is Not Enough," *National Review*, September 17, 2024, https://www.nationalreview.com/2024/09/defense-prioritization-is-not-enough/.

3. William S. Cohen, *Report of the Quadrennial Defense Review*, US Department of Defense, May 1997, 12, https://apps.dtic.mil/sti/pdfs/ADA326554.pdf.

4. Zakheim and Walker, "Defense 'Prioritization' Is Not Enough."

5. Mara Karlin, testimony before the Senate Committee on Armed Services, November 30, 2017, https://www.armed-services.senate.gov/imo/media/doc/Karlin_11-30-17.pdf.

6. Eric V. Larson, *Force Planning Scenarios, 1945–2016: Their Origins and Use in Defense Strategic Planning*, RAND Corporation, 2019, https://www.rand.org/pubs/research_reports/RR2173z1.html.

7. Jim Mitre, "A Eulogy for the Two-War Construct," *The Washington Quarterly*, Winter 2019, 26, https://www.tandfonline.com/doi/full/10.1080/0163660X.2018.1557479.

8. Mitre, "A Eulogy for the Two-War Construct," 27.

9. *America's Strategic Posture: The Final Report of the Congressional Commission on the Strategic Posture of the United States*, Congressional Commission on the Strategic Posture of the United States, October 2023, https://www.usip.org/sites/default/files/America's_Strategic_Posture_Auth_Ed.pdf.

10. Commission on the National Defense Strategy, *Report of the Commission on the 2022 National Defense Strategy*, RAND Corporation, July 29, 2024, 13, https://www.rand.org/nsrd/projects/NDS-commission.html.

11. US Department of Defense, *2022 National Defense Strategy of the United States of America*, https://media.defense.gov/2022/Oct/27/2003103845/-1/-1/1/2022-NATIONAL-DEFENSE-STRATEGY-NPR-MDR.pdf.

12. Commission on the National Defense Strategy, *Commission on the National Defense Strategy*, July 2024, 38, https://www.rand.org/nsrd/projects/NDS-commission.html.

13. Larson, *Force Planning Scenarios, 1945–2016*, back cover.

14. Larson, *Force Planning Scenarios, 1945–2016*, 51.

15. Daniel Goure, *The Measure of a Superpower: A Two Major Regional Contingency Military for the 21st Century*, Heritage Foundation, January 12, 2013, https://static.heritage.org/2013/pdf/SR128.pdf.

16. North Atlantic Treaty Organization, "New NATO Force Model," https://www.nato.int/nato_static_fl2014/assets/pdf/2022/6/pdf/220629-infographic-new-nato-force-model.pdf.

17. National Defense Authorization Act for Fiscal Year 2017, Pub. L. No. 114-328.

18. Joint Staff, *Management and Review of Campaign and Contingency Plans*, January 31, 2019, https://www.jcs.mil/Portals/36/Documents/Library/Instructions/CJCSI%203141.01F.pdf.

19. Joint Chiefs of Staff, *Joint Planning*, 2020, I-10, https://irp.fas.org/doddir/dod/jp5_0.pdf.

20. Joint Chiefs of Staff, *Joint Planning*, I-12–I-13.

21. Iskander Rehman, *Planning for Protraction: A Historically Informed Approach to Great-Power War and Sino-US Competition* (International Institute for Strategic Studies, 2023), 12.

22. Rehman, *Planning for Protraction*, 12.

23. Evan Montgomery and Julian Ouellet, "American Defense Planning in the Shadow of Protracted War," *War on the Rocks*, November 18, 2024, https://warontherocks.com/2024/11/american-defense-planning-in-the-shadow-of-protracted-war/.

24. Commission on the National Defense Strategy, *Commission on the National Defense Strategy*, 36.

25. Servicemember Quality of Life Improvement and National Defense Authorization Act for Fiscal Year 2025, Pub. L. No. 118-159.

26. Chris Dougherty, "Why America Needs a New Way of War," Center for a New American Security, June 12, 2019, https://www.cnas.org/publications/reports/anawow.

27. Lauren C. Williams, "Army Aims to Cut 32,000 Billets over Five Years, Including 3,000 in Special Operations," *Defense One*, February 27, 2024, https://www.defenseone.com/policy/2024/02/army-aims-cut-32000-billets-over-five-years-including-3000-special-operations/394517/.

28. Andrew Eversden, "Wormuth: Here's the Army's Role in a Pacific Fight," *Breaking Defense*, December 1, 2021, https://breakingdefense.com/2021/12/heres-what-the-army-would-do-in-a-pacific-fight-wormuth/.

29. Christopher Mahoney, "Four Lessons on Sea Denial from the Black and Red Seas," *Defense News*, June 18, 2024, https://www.defensenews.com/opinion/2024/06/18/four-lessons-on-sea-denial-from-the-black-and-red-seas/.

30. Josh Rogin, "The U.S. Military Plans a 'Hellscape' to Deter China from Attacking Taiwan," *The Washington Post*, June 10, 2024, https://www.washingtonpost.com/opinions/2024/06/10/taiwan-china-hellscape-military-plan/.

31. Bryan Clark and Dan Patt, *Campaigning to Dissuade: Applying Emerging Technologies to Engage and Succeed in the Information Age Security Competition*, Hudson Institute, July 2023, 9, https://s3.amazonaws.com/media.hudson.org/051623_Clark_Campaigning_to_Dissuade_Report_v2.pdf.

32. Richard R. Burgess, "Navy Orders Quickstrike Glide Kits for Sea Mines," *Seapower*, July 23, 2021, https://seapowermagazine.org/navy-orders-quickstrike-extended-range-glide-kits-for-sea-mines/.

33. Christopher S. Lofts, *Modular Missile Technologies (MMT): A Modular Open Architecture Approach for Guided Missiles*, US Army, Research, Development and Engineering Command, Aviation and Missile Research, Development and Engineering Center, April 2015, https://apps.dtic.mil/sti/pdfs/ADA622336.pdf.

34. Brian W. Everstine, "Security on the Brink," *Air & Space Forces Magazine*, October 9, 2017, https://www.airandspaceforces.com/article/security-on-the-brink/.

35. David B. Larter, "With Iran Tensions High, a US Military Command Pushes a Dubious Carrier Strategy," *Defense News*, March 24, 2020, https://www.defensenews.com/naval/2020/03/24/with-iran-tensions-high-centcom-pushes-a-dubious-carrier-strategy/; and Meghann Myers, "As Nimitz Heads Home, Questions Arise About Carrier Presence in Middle East," *Military Times*, February 3, 2021, https://www.militarytimes.com/news/your-military/2021/02/03/as-nimitz-heads-home-questions-arise-about-carrier-presence-in-middle-east/.

36. Nancy Montgomery, "173rd Airborne Brigade Troops to Deploy to Middle East," *Stars and Stripes*, January 6, 2020, https://www.stripes.com/theaters/europe/173rd-airborne-brigade-troops-to-deploy-to-middle-east-1.613712; Chris Gordon, "Air Force F-16s from Germany Deploy to Middle East," *Air & Space Forces Magazine*, October 27, 2024, https://www.airandspaceforces.com/air-force-f-16s-germany-deploy-middle-east/; and C. Todd Lopez, "U.S. Assets in Mediterranean Again Helped Defend Israel Against Iranian Missiles," US Department of Defense, October 1, 2024, https://www.defense.gov/News/News-Stories/Article/Article/3923123/us-assets-in-mediterranean-again-helped-defend-israel-against-iranian-missiles/.

4

Reconciling More Spending on Defense with Long-Term Fiscal Stability

JAMES C. CAPRETTA

A disruptive national election in the United States has opened the door to a new course for fiscal and defense policy. It is an opportunity that leaders from both parties should seize, as the nation's long-term vitality and strength depend on sustaining a stronger commitment to hard military power and consolidating finances elsewhere.

Upon initial inspection, the separate objectives of less debt and more defense appear contradictory. And of course, if nothing else changed, higher expenditures for military accounts would push up federal borrowing even more rapidly than would be the case under current laws and policies. But the reason defense has been squeezed in the post–Cold War period and yet federal debt is still rising is because there are other powerful forces overwhelming all other budgetary concerns.

Specifically, as Congress has approved and expanded large benefit programs that support individual Americans and their families, spending on them has escalated rapidly and without a permanent and growing hike in federal taxes. As pressure has grown, elected leaders have struggled to sustain these programs, fund defense adequately, and keep deficits manageable. By default, Congress has chosen to protect all benefit commitments and sacrifice defense and fiscal stability.

The long-term fiscal deterioration caused by growing entitlement spending, which was already visible in the 1990s, has been further complicated by two global economic emergencies in the past two decades. When times were good, Congress did not provide a budgetary cushion that would accommodate the fiscal expansion needed to mitigate the consequences of the financial crisis during 2007–09 and the COVID-19 pandemic, which began in 2020. All the support Congress approved was thus added to already wide annual budget deficits, with a resulting step-up in total borrowing and net interest costs that have pushed federal debt near to record levels relative to the size of the nation's economy.

While these successive global crises substantially exacerbated the debt problem, the core fiscal challenge of relentless entitlement spending growth was not unforeseen; it has been building for decades due to population aging and health care cost growth at rates above those of the economy's expansion. The strong political opposition that has prevented benefit program reform to this point clearly indicates that, if and when policymakers ever approve changes, they will need to be phased in gradually for voters to see them as fair.

That should not be a problem, assuming Congress moves relatively soon. The fiscal challenge is not due to the borrowing needs in any given year. The problem is that there is no clear prospect of annual borrowing requirements lessening over the medium and long term. Indeed, population aging and health care cost pressures are expected to make the problem much worse in the coming years and decades. The risk is that financial markets will conclude at some point that it will be impossible for the US government to meet its debt obligations in an orderly manner— that is, without using inflation to effectively diminish it. At that point, the ensuing economic disruption would hit the real economy hard.

It need not come to that. A phased-in debt-stabilization plan would provide relief relative to current projections that would compound over time and thus create ever-growing space for other priorities. That means it should be possible to move quickly on reinvesting in defense as part of a longer-term reform that makes room for that investment even as it brings total debt down to a sustainable level.

How the US Got Here

The federal budget has undergone an important transformation in the postwar era.

Before the New Deal, creating and managing large programs that provide benefits directly to individual citizens were not seen as major, population-wide federal responsibilities. With the creation of Social Security, unemployment compensation, and aid for poor women and their children in the mid-1930s, the federal government opened the door to a new era. After World War II, Congress vastly expanded direct benefit support to individuals through a series of law changes that lasted until the 1970s.

In this way, the US was moving in tandem with other Western industrialized countries. Just before and after World War II, the governments of these nations were active in building social welfare protection systems, covering health, retirement, unemployment, and income security as a way of buffering the risks and burdens of their evolving economies. It was an inevitable and welcome development.

While a change in the government's program portfolio was to be expected, it did not follow that a new era of fiscal distress was also unavoidable. The deterioration in federal finances occurred only after many years of programmatic evolution and was a direct result of elected leaders' choices when building and amending the key programs.

All Western democracies are suffering from the fiscal pressure associated with population aging, but the US has two additional factors that complicate its budgetary outlook.

First, the US became the West's most powerful democracy in the aftermath of World War II. In the years that followed, as the Cold War era dawned, there was a bipartisan consensus that it was in the national interest for the US to take a decisive leadership role in global affairs. That role has involved investment in an expansive military presence that entailed much higher spending relative to the size of the economy than has been the case in allied countries.

Second, the US has not adopted a fully nationalized health system. Instead, it has put in place four main programs to support enrollment in health insurance: Medicare (for the elderly), Medicaid (for lower-income individuals), tax support of employer-based coverage for working-age persons and their families, and direct premium subsidies, authorized by the Affordable Care Act, for modest-income households not eligible for employer-sponsored plans.

While this patchwork system of insurance has led to most Americans having protection against large medical expenses, the US has not put in place a systematic cost-control mechanism that resembles the budgetary and regulatory restraints seen in other countries. The result is a far higher national bill for health. The Organisation for Economic Co-operation and Development estimates the US devoted 16.7 percent of gross domestic product (GDP) to health expenditures, which was about 40 percent above what Germany spent in the same year (11.8 percent of GDP).[1]

The combination of increasingly expansive eligibility rules, the aging population, and substantial upward pressure on health spending per person has pushed federal obligations for the major benefit programs—especially Social Security, Medicare, and Medicaid—to ever-higher percentages of GDP, as shown in Table 1. In 1962, before Congress passed the 1965 law creating Medicare and Medicaid, spending on Social Security was just 2.4 percent of GDP. By 1980, with the major health programs expanding rapidly, total spending on the three largest entitlements had reached 5.9 percent of GDP. In 2023, it was 11.0 percent of GDP, and by 2054, the Congressional Budget Office (CBO) projects it will reach 15.1 percent (assuming that Medicaid, which is not separately projected by CBO, remains relatively stable during this period). It is the growth of these programs, which now dominate the federal budget, that squeezed the fiscal space available for defense appropriations. It also led to significant borrowing.

The US fiscal outlook temporarily improved in the 1990s, when the Soviet Union's collapse led to a substantial downsizing of certain aspects of Cold War deterrence policy. In the ensuing years, Congress gradually captured this "peace dividend" by appropriating less for military accounts, until defense had fallen to just 2.9 percent of GDP in 2000, down from 5.1 percent in 1990.[2] Without this budgetary relief, the fiscal pressures from entitlement spending growth would have become acute during those years. As it turned out, the US was able to run a surplus during the later years of the Clinton presidency. (The surplus reached 2.3 percent of GDP in 2000.)

From there, however, the budget outlook has been in a state of continuous and sometimes rapid deterioration. The outlook was already expected to become extremely challenging as the baby-boomer generation headed into retirement, but then the twin shocks of the financial crisis and the COVID-19 pandemic led to substantial increases in emergency borrowing. There has never been the political will to pair this borrowing with renewed fiscal discipline once the crises abated.

Table 1. Budget Aggregates, Historical and Long-Term Projections

	Percentage of GDP				
	1962	**1980**	**2000**	**2023**	**CBO Estimate 2054**
Defense Discretionary	9.0	4.8	2.9	3.0	2.5*
Nondefense Discretionary	3.3	5.1	3.2	3.4	2.4*
Total Discretionary	**12.3**	**9.9**	**6.1**	**6.4**	**4.9**
Social Security, Medicare, Medicaid, and Other Health	2.4	5.8	7.1	10.8	14.1*
Other Mandatory	2.3	3.6	2.3	3.1	2.0
Total Mandatory	**4.8**	**9.4**	**9.4**	**13.9**	**16.2**
Net Interest	**1.2**	**1.9**	**2.2**	**2.4**	**6.3**
Total Outlays	**18.2**	**21.2**	**17.7**	**22.7**	**27.3**
Total Revenues	**17.0**	**18.5**	**20.0**	**16.5**	**18.8**
Annual Deficit or Surplus	−1.2	−2.6	2.3	−6.3	−8.5
Debt Held by the Public	42.3	25.5	33.7	97.3	166.2

Source: Congressional Budget Office, *The Long-Term Budget Outlook: 2024 to 2054*, March 2024, https://www.cbo.gov/system/files/2024-03/59711-Long-Term-Outlook-2024.pdf; and Congressional Budget Office, "Budget and Economic Data," February 2024, https://www.cbo.gov/data/budget-economic-data#1.
Note: * CBO did not project this line item to 2054. The figure represents the author's forecast based on current trends. Totals have been rounded.

The Building Blocks of a Major Fiscal Reset

The federal government is a vast enterprise with hundreds of functions, budgetary programs, and revenue sources, and the electorate expects and deserves careful political scrutiny of every corner of it. No dollar should be wasted.

But stabilizing the fiscal outlook in a way that will make sufficient room for what is required for military strength and deterrence will not come about from closer looks at scores of small- or even medium-sized accounts. Most of these programs are funded through annually approved domestic appropriation bills, which are not the principal sources of today's fiscal deterioration. Moreover, even with the savings possible from eliminating low-value expenditures, the sum would be minimal relative to the depth of the fiscal hole.

What is required is a concentrated focus on the most financially conse-quential policies—the major entitlement programs, the defense budget, and taxes—to better align those critical budgetary forces with the objec-tives of sustained military strength and a long-term decline in federal debt relative to the size of the national economy.

Despite ongoing political paralysis around the budget, there are actu-ally numerous public plans available that would address the first prob-lem, regarding spiraling debt. Indeed, the Peter G. Peterson Foundation has periodically commissioned the development of competing plans from politically diverse research organizations to demonstrate that there are multiple pathways toward a solution. That is an important service, as whatever is done in the end will almost certainly be a compromise that borrows from various ideological starting points. Neither Republicans nor Democrats have demonstrated sufficient political determination to pur-sue a solution to this problem on their own.

But before a compromise is even possible, it is important to present and defend concepts built on a set of principles that are internally consis-tent and compatible. The plan produced for the Peterson Solutions Ini-tiative in 2024 by American Enterprise Institute scholars (including this chapter's author) provides a sensible starting point for considering how to right this ship.[3] The AEI plan was one of only two that committed more to defense as part of a debt-stabilization program.[4]

The AEI offering was built on three main principles. First, the plan starts from the perspective that the US must sustain a dynamic and growing economy to have any hope of stabilizing its debt while maintaining its role as global leader of Western democracies. That means the reforms selected must emphasize business formation and investment, free-market competition to promote innovation and productivity growth, and strong incentives for an ever-expanding supply of skilled labor.

Second, as noted above, the plan takes as its most important objective the need to seriously reform the major entitlement spending programs, to prevent spiraling debt and make room for pro-growth tax policy and a higher commitment to defense. Those reforms center on health care and Social Security.

Third, the presumed path for defense spending should be well above what is forecast in today's baseline, which is a declining commitment relative to the size of the national economy. For all other discretionary spending, there should be no presumption of large-scale savings, as there are just as many legitimate claims for increases as there are opportunities for savings from eliminating waste and low-value expenditures.

These principles were translated into the following specific policy recommendations.

Tax Reform. In 2017, during the first year of President Donald Trump's first term, Congress approved a major tax cut, called the Tax Cuts and Jobs Act (TCJA), which included many provisions that will expire at the end of 2025. There is now a push to make these tax cuts permanent or extend them into the future as far as politically feasible, without finding offsetting spending reductions or tax hikes. That would be a mistake. At this point, it is plain that the priority should be fiscal consolidation with a tax reform plan that is pro-growth. That means paying for whatever tax plan is assembled rather than continuing tax cuts.

Consistent with that perspective, the AEI plan proposed a tax reform that would produce revenue in the future equivalent to today's current-law baseline—that is, the baseline that assumes expiration of many TCJA provisions will occur as scheduled at the end of 2025. But the reform would be far more pro-growth than pre-TCJA law because it would eliminate scores of tax expenditures to finance the lowest possible rates to taxable income, for both businesses and individuals.

The most significant reforms in the plan are as follows:

- The exclusions and deductions from taxation of interest on municipal bonds, interest paid on home mortgages, state and local taxes, medical expenses above a threshold, and a variety of business preferences would be fully repealed or substantially modified.

- The estate and gift tax would be repealed, but unrealized capital gains (above a threshold amount) would be taxed at death.

- A carbon tax would be adopted to replace the Clean Power Plan and other climate-related regulations.

- The gasoline tax rate would be increased.

- The exclusion of employer-paid premiums for health coverage would be capped.

These provisions would pay for lowering the tax rates applicable under TCJA by another 5 percentage points in each tax bracket.

Health Care. The major focus in health care must be to bring more cost discipline to the provision of services. In the AEI plan, that would be accomplished through several channels.

In Medicare, private plans and the traditional, government-managed benefit implicitly compete with each other, but only imperfectly, as the rules make comparisons difficult. The AEI plan recommends changing these rules based on the premium-support model. This would require the plans offering coverage to Medicare beneficiaries to compete more vigorously based on the premiums they charge for standardized coverage, which would include annual out-of-pocket protection for all beneficiaries and a single deductible across all three parts of the insurance benefit (A, B, and D). Beneficiaries would lower their costs by gravitating to the most efficient plans. The rules for Medigap insurance, which wraps around the traditional program, would be modified, too, to promote competition and lower overall costs.

Medicare spending would be reduced further by raising the general premium rate from 25 to 30 percent, tightening the reimbursement rules for hospital-affiliated clinics ("site neutral" payments), and gradually raising the eligibility age for the program so that it conforms to current law under Social Security (to age 67).

In Medicaid, the emphasis would be on straightening out the federal and state governments' financial responsibilities. Instead of today's matching system, which leads to program-integrity problems, the federal government would provide states with a fixed amount per Medicaid enrollee (sorted by eligibility categories). In addition, the permissive rules governing the use of provider taxes to satisfy the state-matching requirement would be substantially tightened.

Social Security. The plan proposes a sweeping overhaul of Social Security to move the program toward more secure old-age protection for low-wage earners and a less generous benefit for upper-middle-class households. The plan, based in part on the successful model adopted in Australia, has the following elements:

- Over a long transition, new entrants to the system would receive a flat dollar benefit based on a universal formula, not tied to workers' individual earnings records. The benefit would assure all participants of an income in retirement above the elderly poverty threshold. The flat amount would grow each year with increases in the national average wage.

- All workers would be automatically enrolled in fully portable employer-managed retirement accounts, with a minimum contribution of 3 percent of earnings. These accounts would fund supplements to the flat benefit.

- To encourage workers to stay employed as long as possible, the payroll tax would be eliminated for earnings starting at age 62.

- The early eligibility age for benefits would be phased up from age 62 to 65.

- For disability benefits, employers would pay an experience-rated tax based on the number of workers they employ who become disabled and qualify for benefit payments.

Defense. The plan did not attempt to support a specific program of improved military readiness and resilience. Instead, its budget forecast assumed a steady increase in annual defense appropriations of 10 percent through 2030, after which the funding boost would be steadily eliminated. This increase remains well below what is likely required for rebuilding an effective deterrence against multiple emerging national security risks.

Nondefense Discretionary Appropriations. The plan assumes no savings in the sliver of the budget devoted to domestic appropriations, as the opportunities for reductions are matched by legitimate claims on more resources among programs that perform well but receive inadequate budgets for their missions.

The Plan's Effects. When this plan is pulled together in a comprehensive projection of budget totals, the results, reflected in Table 2, are encouraging.

The plan's major emphasis is a substantial moderation in long-term spending on the major entitlement programs. The reforms aimed at these major line items ease fiscal pressure sufficiently to begin reducing debt even as federal revenue is held to baseline levels. The plan also benefits from a boost in expected economic growth from tax reforms that incentivize business investment and an expansion of the labor force.

When all the various policies are pulled together, the effect on federal borrowing is substantial and positive. As shown in Figure 1, under current law, federal debt is projected to reach 166 percent of GDP in 2054. By contrast, under the AEI proposal, debt would rise modestly in the coming decade and then begin a gradual decline until it reached 85 percent of GDP in 2054—a level not seen since 2019.

Providing Additional Fiscal Space for Defense

The plan submitted by the AEI team to the Peterson Solutions Initiative was written to demonstrate that serious entitlement reform combined with a pro-growth tax plan could boost economic growth and stabilize federal borrowing at levels that would lessen the risk of a debt-induced economic rupture. The plan included an acknowledgment that the allocation

Table 2. Budget Aggregates, Current Law vs. AEI Proposal (Peterson Initiative)

| | Percentage of GDP | | | |
| | 2034 | | 2054 | |
	Current Law	Proposal	Current Law	Proposal
Defense Discretionary	2.5*	2.6**	2.5*	2.5**
Nondefense Discretionary	2.5*	2.5**	2.4*	2.2**
Total Discretionary	**5.0**	**5.1**	**4.9**	**4.7**
Social Security, Medicare, Medicaid, and Other Health	12.6	11.2	14.1	10.0
Other Mandatory	2.5	2.5	2.0	2.0
Total Mandatory	**15.1**	**13.7**	**16.2**	**12.0**
Net Interest	**3.9**	**3.5**	**6.3**	**2.7**
Total Outlays	**24.3**	**22.3**	**27.1**	**19.4**
Total Revenues	**17.9**	**17.9**	**18.8**	**18.8**
Annual Deficit or Surplus	**−6.1**	**−4.4**	**−8.5**	**−0.6**
Debt Held by the Public	116	106	166	85

Source: Congressional Budget Office, *The Long-Term Budget Outlook: 2024 to 2054*, March 2024, https://www.cbo.gov/system/files/2024-03/59711-Long-Term-Outlook-2024.pdf; and Joseph Antos et al., "A Balanced Plan for Fiscal Stability and Economic Growth," in *Solutions Initiative 2024: Charting a Brighter Future*, July 2024, Peter G. Peterson Foundation, https://solutions2024.pgpf.org/plans/aei/.
Note: * CBO did not project this line item to 2054. The figure represents the author's forecast based on current trends. ** The AEI plan did not separately project defense and nondefense in presented data for these years. The figures represent the author's estimates based on trends. Totals have been rounded.

Figure 1. Debt Held by the Public, CBO Baseline vs. AEI Proposal (Percentage of GDP)

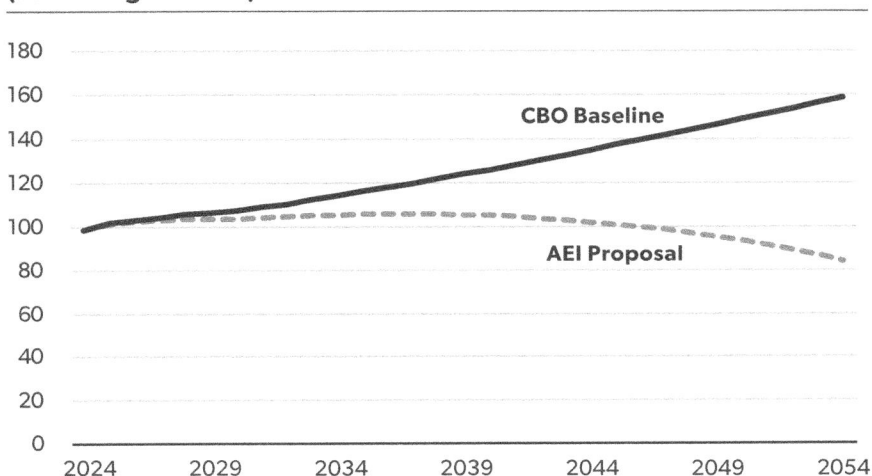

Source: Congressional Budget Office, *The Long-Term Budget Outlook: 2024 to 2054*, March 2024, https://www.cbo.gov/system/files/2024-03/59711-Long-Term-Outlook-2024.pdf; and Joseph Antos et al., "A Balanced Plan for Fiscal Stability and Economic Growth," in *Solutions Initiative 2024: Charting a Brighter Future*, July 2024, Peter G. Peterson Foundation, https://solutions2024.pgpf.org/plans/aei/.

to defense in current projections is inadequate and therefore requires a boost, but the amounts provided in the plan were small compared to what national security experts are now stating is required to build an effective deterrence against multiple security threats.

To provide more space for a sustained defense-funding boost over a longer time span (such as two decades), incoming leaders should consider budget reforms that go beyond what AEI's plan contains. Given the size of the current hole in military funding, leaders may choose to push the commitment in the coming years by 1 to 2 percentage points of GDP above what is contained in the plan described in the previous section. That could mean annual defense funding reaching, and staying at, somewhere between 4 and 5 percent of GDP each year.

Given the already substantial reforms recommended for the major entitlements in the AEI plan included in the Peterson report, there is little room there for recommending additional restraint. That plan, however, did not call for a net tax increase, which means more revenue is a realistic option.

There are many options for raising revenue, but two stand out because of the compelling need to shift from current practice.

A Carbon Tax with Slightly Higher Individual Rates for Upper-Income Households. In the plan AEI scholars submitted to the Peterson effort, a new tax on carbon emissions was advanced as one line item that would allow for pushing individual tax rates down as much as possible (with a top bracket set at 35 percent). To generate more revenue, this tax, which was set in the plan at $25 per metric ton of CO_2 equivalent in 2025 and then indexed to inflation plus 2 percentage points annually, could generate higher overall revenue instead of paying for a revenue-neutral reform. It could also be adjusted as needed to generate even more revenue than is assumed in the current AEI plan.

The potential for a boost in tax receipts is substantial. According to the International Monetary Fund, carbon taxes could generate revenue equal to about 1 to 2 percent of national GDP.[5] The tax can also be designed to apply fairly to the pricing attached to imports and exports (as the AEI plan called for).

A carbon tax has a further additional benefit in that it is consistent with a climate strategy built on apolitical oversight of the energy market. That is much less possible with mitigation predicated on the allocation of subsidies to relevant industries and stricter energy regulations. With a carbon tax, market participants will have strong incentives to balance all the objectives they must weigh when trying to maximize their profit, including the price effects of tax on carbon emissions. There would be no need for excessive political interference in such decisions, which invite favoritism and corruption.

Higher Payroll Tax Revenue for Medicare. An important and largely unnoticed factor in the past few decades' fiscal deterioration has been the steady rise in the burden Medicare imposes on the Treasury's general fund. Parts B, for physician and outpatient services, and D, for outpatient prescription drug coverage, are heavily subsidized by annual transfers from this fund. When the government is running large overall deficits, as it is today, these transfers effectively force the Treasury to borrow more in public markets than it would otherwise.[6]

This dependence on Treasury subsidies runs contrary to how Medicare was originally presented to the public: as a program that would not become a fiscal burden because it would be financed largely from new payroll taxes (like Social Security). That turned out to be only partially true and, as the years passed, less and less of an accurate depiction of the program's financial effects. In 1980, the general fund transfer to Medicare totaled only 0.4 percent of GDP. By 2023, it had reached 1.6 percent, and the Medicare trustees expect it to reach 2.8 percent of GDP in 2050.[7]

As part of a significant fiscal reset, policymakers should consider lessening Medicare's dependence on the general fund by financing more of the program from traditional payroll tax receipts. The shift in program financing could be calibrated to meet fiscal goals associated with making more room in the federal budget for defense spending. One goal might be to limit the general fund commitment to Medicare in future years to what it was in 2023—1.6 percent of GDP. That implies increasing taxes to provide about 1 percentage point of GDP to the program as a replacement source of revenue. While it would be most straightforward to simply increase today's Medicare payroll tax rate of 2.9 percent of taxable wages, Congress could choose instead to place more of the burden on high-wage workers to avoid placing new financial burdens on lower-wage households.

There are of course many more ways besides these two options for raising revenue. However, these two were selected because they have compelling policy rationales beyond the need to increase revenue for defense funding. Medicare's financing model is now outdated and should be modernized, and Congress will need to settle soon on a long-term strategy for climate change mitigation. Raising more revenue with the changes described here would therefore satisfy multiple public policy objectives.

Budgeting as Deterrence

America's most powerful adversaries have converged on a public narrative that Western dominance of global affairs is either in terminal decline or a paper tiger, owing to its internal contradictions. This assessment has them emboldened to take more consequential risks than in the recent past. One obvious factor is the unwillingness or inability of the primary Western powers, especially the US, to provide the resources necessary for an effective deterrence strategy. The current fiscal outlook provides these adversaries with all the evidence they need to argue that they are ascendant and their adversaries are not.

When viewed this way, it is possible to see that an exercise focused on increasing military power through allocating more resources to that purpose must also demonstrate that this is an affordable proposition over the medium and long term and not something that will be reversed because there is insufficient room in the national budget. Thus, getting serious about rebuilding the hard-power foundation of US global leadership requires embedding this commitment within a larger fiscal plan that is sustainable over the long run.

In recent years, leaders both in and out of the military have noted that rapidly escalating federal debt is a national security concern. Their contention is accurate on two levels.[8] On its own, runaway debt poses a substantial risk to sustained economic prosperity because at some point creditors will doubt the country's wherewithal to pay it all back. In addition, that the budget is today badly out of balance and expected to remain so indefinitely makes it hard for elected leaders to commit to a long-term military rebuilding plan. Indeed, rising federal debt is one reason Congress has been unwilling, or perhaps unable, to provide more robust increases for defense in recent years, even as global security threats have mounted.

There are of course reasons to doubt the US can break from this defeatist pattern. Since the turn of the century, elected leaders have failed to put together a fiscal framework that would prevent debt from escalating to dangerous levels, as the politics of consolidation are challenging. The two parties have widely diverging priorities that are hard to reconcile in a plan intended to guide policy over multiple years and even decades.

But that is not a reason for abandoning the mission. This problem will appear almost insurmountable until the relevant leaders get to work on a realistic and pragmatic plan to change course. It is not an impossible assignment, as the United States' resilient economy provides sufficient resources to sustain a strong global leadership role and provide its citizens with a secure and generous system of social support. There just needs to be a long-overdue rebalancing reflecting the changed circumstances of the current century. It is time to get to work.

Notes

1. Organisation for Economic Co-operation and Development, "OECD Data Explorer," https://data-explorer.oecd.org.

2. US Department of Defense, Office of the Under Secretary of Defense (Comptroller)/Chief Financial Officer, *Defense Budget Overview: United States Department of Defense Fiscal Year 2025 Budget Request*, April 4, 2024, 1-5, Figure 1.3, https://comptroller.defense.gov/Portals/45/Documents/defbudget/FY2025/FY2025_Budget_Request_Overview_Book.pdf.

3. The four AEI authors of the plan are Joseph Antos, Andrew G. Biggs, Alex Brill, and James C. Capretta. See Joseph Antos et al., "A Balanced Plan for Fiscal Stability and Economic Growth," in *Solutions Initiative 2024: Charting a Brighter Future*, Peter G. Peterson Foundation, July 2024, https://solutions2024.pgpf.org/plans/aei/.

4. In addition to the AEI submission, the American Action Forum plan also recommended a defense increase. See Douglas Holtz-Eakin, "Unbalanced," in *Solutions Initiative 2024*.

5. Ian Parry, *Putting a Price on Pollution*, International Monetary Fund, December 2019, https://www.imf.org/en/Publications/fandd/issues/2019/12/the-case-for-carbon-taxation-and-putting-a-price-on-pollution-parry.

6. For a description of the history of the Medicare trust funds, see James C. Capretta, "Medicare's Trust Funds: Background and the Need for Reform," American Enterprise Institute, January 24, 2024, https://www.aei.org/research-products/report/medicares-trust-funds-background-and-the-need-for-reform/.

7. Centers for Medicare & Medicaid Services, "2024 Expanded and Supplementary Tables and Figures," May 2024, https://www.cms.gov/data-research/statistics-trends-and-reports/trustees-report-trust-funds.

8. Kate Brannen, "Mullen Focuses on Debt as Threat," *Politico*, December 6, 2012, https://www.politico.com/story/2012/12/mike-mullen-focuses-on-debt-as-security-threat-084648.

5

The US Military Makes America and the World Safe for Commerce

MICHAEL R. STRAIN

When considering the benefits of a strong United States military, it is natural to think of the military's crucial role in protecting Americans from foreign adversaries and providing security and stability around the world. But safeguarding America's interests at home and abroad offers the nation substantial economic advantages as well. Properly understood, the US military offers direct and tangible economic benefits to American businesses, workers, and households.

This chapter discusses some of these benefits. First, I give an overview of some of the ways a strong US military provides support for the structure of the economy by reducing the costs facing businesses, providing a foundation on which global commerce can occur, lowering borrowing costs, and increasing the productivity of private firms and the consumption of households through technological innovation. In certain situations, military spending can also support US businesses and households by smoothing the business cycle. Second, I discuss some conceptual challenges with characterizing the optimal amount of military spending. Though many analysts believe the US should increase defense spending, formulating this need in a rigorous way is difficult. Finally, I discuss the threats to increased defense spending presented by rising interest rates, the deteriorating US fiscal outlook, and weakened—and weakening—international security alliances.

Structural Benefits

A strong and capable military offers many structural features that advance the long-term prosperity of American households and businesses. A comprehensive treatment of those features is beyond the scope of this chapter. Instead, I will focus on four: reductions in costs associated with military protection, the economic benefits of security alliances, the funding advantages enjoyed by military hegemons, and the positive spillovers from investments in military technologies.

Cost Reductions. A strong military reduces the costs facing US businesses, increasing their competitiveness. This can easily be seen by considering naval protection of shipping lanes, which can be viewed as a form of economic technology. Thanks to the protection offered by the US Navy, the costs for private firms to transport goods are much lower than they would be if all shipping convoys had to pay for their own security.

The 2024 Red Sea military conflict illustrates how lawlessness on the high seas can increase the costs facing private businesses. In 2024, the Iran-aligned Houthis damaged more than 40 vessels and targeted nearly five times that number. Attacks continue at the time of this writing (February 2025). The Houthis partly control what cargo enters the Suez Canal, through which 12 percent of global trade flows.[1]

Higher freight rates and longer shipping journeys added substantial sums to global shipping costs. In fact, the Red Sea attacks appear to have reversed a downward trend in freight rates. The Asia-Mediterranean prices for 40-foot container units were 176 percent higher in January 2024 than five years earlier.[2] The price of shipping a container from Shanghai to Rotterdam in July 2024 was five times as high as the average price in 2023.[3] Rather than facing the risk of a Houthi attack, many commercial ships avoided the Red Sea altogether and took the longer route around South Africa's Cape Peninsula, increasing costs.

Insurance premiums for shipments increased as a consequence of the attacks. As of January 2024, roughly two months after the Houthis began attacking merchant vessels, war risk premiums had increased from 0.7 percent of the value of a ship to 1 percent of its value, adding hundreds of thousands of dollars of additional costs for shippers.[4]

To be clear, I am not asserting a direct link between the US Navy's capabilities and the Houthi attacks. But this episode is instructive for several reasons. The economic theory of crime argues that the level of criminal behavior increases as the probability of getting away with criminal behavior increases.[5] If naval power diminishes, economic theory predicts that more incidents like the Houthi attacks will occur. In addition, the suddenness of the attacks provides a helpful illustration of how quickly and substantially private-sector costs can rise when lawlessness increases. Furthermore, because many of those costs will be passed on to consumers, this episode shows how a strong military can reduce the costs facing households.

Of course, this illustrative example extends beyond naval power. Land-based military strength plays a similar role in providing a foundation on which commerce can take place at relatively lower costs to businesses and households.

Security Alliances. Most of the discussion of political and military alliances like NATO focuses on their diplomatic and security implications. But these alliances have significant economic implications as well. And the strength of NATO is proportional to the strength of the US military. NATO can't be strong without a strong US military—strengthening NATO is another way in which a strong military advances the economic interests of US businesses and households.

US alliances and forward military presence advance economic outcomes in several ways. They prevent conflict to which the US would be a party. By lowering the odds of US military involvement in a war, they advance the economic interests of American businesses and households. They also deter US adversaries from attacking US allies and deter US allies from instigating military conflict.[6] In this way, security alliances and a strong global US military presence help prevent conflicts in other parts of the world that would negatively affect US economic activity.

The degree of economic integration across the world means that US businesses and households are exposed to economic risk from military and security disruptions abroad caused by conflict that does not directly involve America. War abroad can reduce the supply of commodities, increasing their global price. It can hurt US exporters by restricting market access. It can create a chilling effect on US business investment. It can disrupt trade flows and global supply chains, raising costs to US businesses and consumers. And as discussed above, it can increase shipping costs.

By reducing the risk of war and strengthening ties between nations, a strong US military—along with the strong international alliances that a strong US military enables—increases international flows of goods and capital, which boosts American workers' productivity and wages and US businesses' competitiveness.[7]

Trade between the United States and the European Union represents around one-third of global economic output and 30 percent of global trade. Moreover, either the EU or the US is the largest trade and investment partner of nearly every other country in the world.[8] Bilateral trade and investment between the EU and US supports 9.4 million jobs (and indirectly supports as many as 16 million jobs). For scale, the number of jobs supported by economic integration is larger than the number of people who live in Switzerland or Virginia.[9]

European Union companies invest heavily in America. In 2022, they invested €2.7 trillion in the United States.[10] These investments increase the stocks of technical knowledge and capital in the US, raising workers' productivity. Workers that are more productive are more valuable to firms, which go on to compete more aggressively for them in competitive labor markets. This heightened competition puts upward pressure on workers' wages, increasing household income and potentially increasing employment opportunities and economic output.

Examples from history also help to illustrate this point. A strong US military helped to facilitate Japan's rapid economic development after the Second World War. Today, Japan is one of America's strongest economic partners. Japan is a major source of foreign investment in the US and holds more US Treasury securities than any other foreign nation. In 2023, US exports to Japan totaled $121 billion ($77 billion in goods, $44 billion in services). US imports totaled $184 billion, with goods accounting for the majority ($149 billion). In 2021, US-based affiliates of Japanese firms employed nearly one million US workers.[11]

The United States' forward military presence has been a major factor contributing to South Korea's rapid economic development as well. Today, South Korea is one of the largest sources of foreign investment in the United States, with $77 billion of investment in 2023. And US entities find South Korea to be an attractive place to invest. In 2023, the US invested $36 billion in South Korea, which purchased $91 billion of US exports.[12]

Funding Advantage. Military hegemons enjoy a funding advantage in global debt markets. Investors consider the risk of a hegemon defaulting to be much lower than that of other nations. This credibility with lenders manifests itself in lower interest rates.

The lower interest rates on government debt that exist due to US military hegemony make government borrowing relatively less costly to US taxpayers. Lower rates make it relatively less expensive for businesses to expand operations using debt financing and for households to finance home and auto purchases.

To demonstrate the funding advantage of military hegemons, economists Carolin Pflueger and Pierre Yared study the interest rates on government debt around the time of hegemonic transitions. Specifically, they study the transition in hegemonic regimes from Great Britain to the United States in the period spanning the First and Second World Wars and the transition at the end of the 18th century from the Netherlands to Great Britain.[13]

As Figure 1, Panel A shows, before World War I, Britain was able to borrow at cheaper rates than the US was. This reversed after that war. Following World War II, the United States' funding advantage was solidified. Similarly, the Dutch navy was dominant in the 16th through 18th centuries. But the Netherlands was invaded by the Napoleonic armies in 1795, after which it lost its funding advantage over Britain (Figure 1, Panel B).

Pflueger and Yared also find that the funding advantage enjoyed by a hegemon increases as the risk of military conflict increases. Moreover, the hegemon's funding advantage may increase even if the conflict does not directly involve the hegemon. In Figure 2, Pflueger and Yared demonstrate that the United States' funding advantage relative to both Russia and Ukraine increased following Russia's invasion of Ukraine in February 2022.

Technology Spillovers. Military technology can have important spillovers into the private sector, generating economic value for US businesses and households.

The Defense Advanced Research Projects Agency (DARPA) is the best example of this. Following the 1957 launch of Sputnik, DARPA was created by President Dwight D. Eisenhower to ensure US military superiority in

Figure 1. Changing Military Dominance and Bond Yields

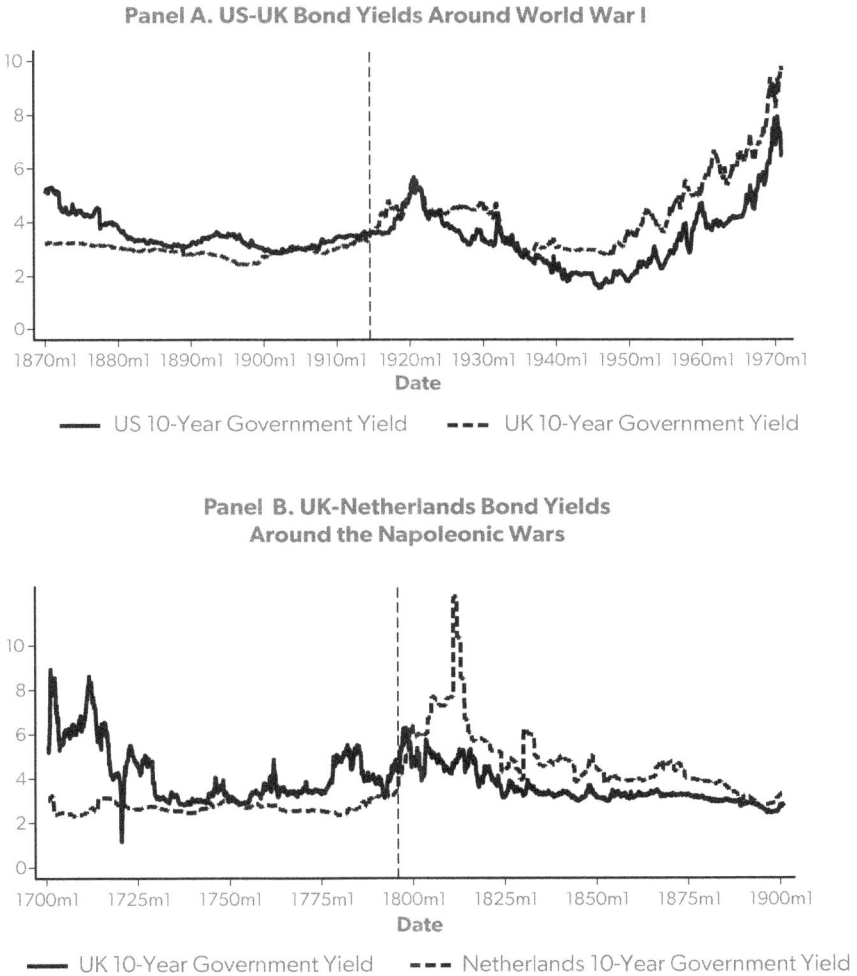

Panel A. US-UK Bond Yields Around World War I

— US 10-Year Government Yield   - - - UK 10-Year Government Yield

Panel B. UK-Netherlands Bond Yields
Around the Napoleonic Wars

— UK 10-Year Government Yield   - - - Netherlands 10-Year Government Yield

Source: Carolin Pflueger and Pierre Yared, "Global Hegemony and Exorbitant Privilege," Working Paper No. 32775 (National Bureau of Economic Research, August 2024), 7, https://www.nber.org/system/files/working_papers/w32775/w32775.pdf.

Figure 2. Bond Prices Around Russia's Invasion of Ukraine

Ukraine/US Bond Price   Russia/US Bond Price

Source: Carolin Pflueger and Pierre Yared, "Global Hegemony and Exorbitant Privilege," Working Paper No. 32775 (National Bureau of Economic Research, August 2024), 9, https://www.nber.org/system/files/working_papers/w32775/w32775.pdf.

America's competition with the Soviet Union. DARPA awards research and development (R&D) grants to researchers at universities and private companies. Scientists insulated from politics make the grant decisions, with the goal of funding high-risk, high-reward projects.

DARPA has made material contributions to a large number of technological breakthroughs in recent decades, including weather satellites, materials science, the computer mouse, the internet, miniaturized GPS receivers, high-definition TV, wafer-scale semiconductor integration, and autonomous vehicles, among many others.[14]

To be sure, following a 1973 amendment to its mission, the purpose of DARPA is not to create commercial technology. But, as the list above demonstrates, its military projects have commercial spillovers.

A potential concern may be that an expansion of government-funded R&D might crowd out private R&D. This might happen if the supply of research inputs in an economy is limited and nonresponsive to an increase in research resources (e.g., if there are only so many scientists in a particular industry).[15] In this case, government R&D funding merely shifts research activity away from projects prioritized by the private sector and toward projects prioritized by the government.

At the same time, it is also possible that public-funded R&D might crowd in private R&D (i.e., that an increase in government funding for research might stimulate additional private-sector research). Public research might fund large fixed costs (e.g., labs and human capital accumulation), which might make private projects feasible on the margin. Technological and human capital spillovers across firms are another reason to suspect that crowding in could occur.[16]

In a recent paper, economists Enrico Moretti, Claudia Steinwender, and John Van Reenen use a country-industry-year-level dataset for Organisation for Economic Co-operation and Development countries and a firm-year-level dataset for France to study this question. They focus on defense-related R&D spending.[17]

They find strong evidence of crowding in. In their preferred estimates, a 10 percent increase in defense R&D translates into a 5 percent increase in privately funded R&D. In 2002, government-funded aerospace R&D was $3 billion. According to their estimates, this generated an additional $1.9 billion in privately funded aerospace R&D. Their results imply that government R&D spending generates twice as much private-sector R&D spending as R&D tax credits. They also find that defense R&D increases overall productivity growth and economic growth, albeit modestly.[18]

The US should not fund defense research with the goal of creating commercial spillovers. But when such spillovers occur, they can create wealth for US households that can be well in excess of the level of their congressional appropriation.

Short-Term Economic Benefits

In the previous section, I discussed some of the long-term, structural benefits of a strong US military for the nation's economy, businesses, and households. There may be short-term benefits as well. This is particularly true during economic downturns, when consumers and businesses pull back on spending. In a recession, there is a compelling case for increased government spending to offset those private-sector declines.

Proponents of this sort of Keynesian response to recessions often overstate their case. Government spending can stabilize overall economic output during a recession, but it cannot permanently increase output. It boosts output today, but it has future offsetting effects from the economic drag of additional debt, consequent inflationary pressures, the response of monetary policy, or other factors. (If this weren't the case, then policymakers should stimulate the economy at all times.)

These considerations have important implications for the design of economic stimulus—namely, that the timing and composition of the government stimulus spending matters.

Defense outlays are attractive due to the ability of policymakers to time them appropriately. Stimulus spending that relies on infrastructure investment often gets the timing wrong because there are not many "shovel-ready jobs" when the economy is contracting and the permitting process for such projects is onerous and long. Similarly, stimulus in the form of temporary tax cuts or direct checks to households suffers from a timing problem because policymakers are not able to control when households actually spend the money they receive. But Congress can quickly increase appropriations for the Department of Defense, which can in turn quickly spend appropriated funds.

Regarding composition, defense spending is an attractive option for stimulus because, unlike make-work infrastructure projects with low social value or stimulus checks to high-income households, it is not wasteful. The Department of Defense should spend on items during the recession that it would eventually have to purchase in the future, essentially pulling forward future spending into the period of economic slack.

That spending should include an increase in outlays for procurement, research, and operations and maintenance, which would boost the economy when private spending is falling. In a severe recession with rising long-term unemployment, the spending could potentially include an increase in recruitment as well.

Of course, even during a severe recession, it is important for Congress to scale the size of any stimulus package to the underlying economic need. The importance of this observation—well-grounded in economic theory and evidence—was apparent in the aftermath of the American Rescue Plan of 2021. According to my calculations, by stimulating demand well in excess of the economy's underlying productive capacity, the American Rescue Plan contributed 3 percentage points to underlying inflation in 2021.[19]

In a mild economic downturn, it is typically prudent to leave business cycle management to the Federal Reserve. That is true for several reasons, including that it is difficult to temporarily increase military spending (and hiring). The basic idea is to pull future spending into the present—an idea that is prudently applied only to severe downturns that are relatively long-lived. But in such a severe recession—like the US experienced following the 2008 global financial crisis—there is a clear role for fiscal policy. Temporary increases in defense spending offer a particularly attractive form of economic stimulus.[20]

Optimal Defense Spending

Economists might naturally wish to characterize the optimal level of defense spending. This is a challenging exercise.

Marginal Analysis and Insurance. In determining the optimal level of defense spending, economists might naturally reach for a notion of costs and benefits, arguing that the optimal amount of defense spending is the amount at which the marginal benefit of the last dollar of defense outlays equals its marginal cost. The basic intuition: If the benefit of additional spending is greater than the cost, then the government should increase spending, and if the benefit of additional spending is less than the cost, then the government should reduce spending; therefore, the optimum occurs at the spending level when the benefit and cost of the marginal dollar of expenditure are equal.

The challenge with this approach is that, while the costs of defense outlays are clearly defined, the benefits are not. How to quantify the economic benefit of a major war that never happened?

Economists might also consider defense spending as a form of insurance. To see this intuition, consider a simple descriptive illustration. Suppose there are two states of the world, one in which the US has a strong military and one in which the US has a weak military. Think of defense spending as insurance against a major economic contraction brought on by military conflict that directly involves either the US or a US trading partner.[21] Unlike a typical insurance policy, national defense cannot be turned on and off on an annual basis, so in this descriptive illustration defense spending happens in all periods.

To fully insure, the US should spend on defense an amount equal to the product of the probability of a major contraction caused by conflict, the amount of national income lost in such an event, and the frequency of such events. Assume that, with a weak military, the odds in any given year of such a conflict are 10 percent. In this case, relative to current defense outlays, the US is underinvesting in defense when the fourth such event occurs. Assume that, with a strong military, the odds are 2 percent. In this case—again, relative to current defense outlays—the US is underinvesting in defense when the 19th such event occurs.[22]

And, of course, viewed as a form of insurance, defense outlays mitigate risk from not just disasters but also a host of economic disruptions, such as those discussed in the structural benefits section above.

Share of Gross Domestic Product Target. Many foreign policy scholars and advocates of increased defense spending argue for spending a certain share of national income on defense (e.g., 5 percent). A target of 5 percent of gross domestic product (GDP) is a useful framework in the current policy debate because it implies a substantial but politically and economically achievable increase in defense outlays.

However, a share-of-GDP framework would imply that defense spending should fall when the economy contracts. As I argued previously, if anything, defense spending should increase in a recession.

Moreover, it is likely the case that—over a sufficiently long time horizon—national income and the nation's defense needs do not increase one for one. A 10 percent increase in national income does not necessarily imply that the US needs 10 percent more aircraft carriers or soldiers. Historically, surplus income gains have flown disproportionately away from necessities. For example, as the US became wealthier, the share of national income spent on food fell from 15.7 percent in 1929 to 10 percent in 1970 to 5.3 percent in 2012.[23]

Figure 3. Defense Spending

Source: Federal Reserve Bank of St. Louis, Federal Government: National Defense Consumption Expenditures and Gross Investment, January 30, 2025, https://fred.stlouisfed.org/series/FDEFX.
Note: Shaded areas mark recessions.

Strategic Competition. As shown in Figure 3, President Ronald Reagan increased defense spending by 57 percent between 1981 and 1985 in order to win the arms race with the Soviet Union. Analogously, the US might characterize its optimal defense spending as a target relative to China's defense spending—say, 180 percent of Chinese spending,[24] or the growth rate of China's spending plus a markup.

Three Challenges to Increasing Military Spending

There are at least three major challenges advocates of increased defense spending need to address: a higher neutral rate of interest, the US fiscal outlook, and President Donald Trump's efforts to weaken international security alliances.

Rising Neutral Interest Rate. Higher interest rates are a major challenge for defense spending when that spending is financed by government borrowing because the level of interest payments on the debt rises with borrowing rates. It appears that higher interest rates will be a feature of the US economy, at least over the medium term, making their challenge to the goal of increasing defense outlays greater.

Interest rates started increasing in the early months of 2022, as the Federal Reserve began its efforts to control rapidly rising consumer prices. But the inflation of 2021 is not the only reason interest rates are increasing.

The principal determinant of interest rates is the balance between the demand for investment and the supply of savings. In recent years, many factors affecting investment and savings have led to considerable upward pressure on interest rates. Elevated geopolitical tensions are leading to rising military spending, which, along with a greater reliance on deficit financing, is pushing up debt levels. Elevated tensions are also leading some supply chains to reorganize. So-called resiliency investments are becoming more common. Investment demand is elevated due to the energy transition and the prospect that advances in artificial intelligence will increase productivity growth and the profitability of certain businesses.

The neutral rate of interest is the rate that prevails when the economy is at full employment and inflation is at the Federal Reserve's target. Since the end of 2019, the median view among voting members of the Fed's policy-setting committee was that the neutral overnight interest rate was 2.5 percent. Last year, this view began to shift upward. In December 2024, the median Fed member thought this neutral rate was 3 percent.[25] In my view, the actual neutral rate is at least 4 percent.

Accordingly, longer-term interest rates—which matter most for investment decisions—are rising. The yield on a 10-year Treasury bond was around 2 percent before the pandemic. At the time of this writing (February 2025), it is 4.6 percent.

Economists debate whether interest rates—particularly longer-term rates—will remain high over the coming years.[26] To the extent that they do, they present a challenge to efforts to increase defense spending.

Fiscal Outlook. Similarly, the US fiscal outlook will make it challenging for Congress to increase military outlays.

Over the half century from 1975 to 2024, the average annual federal budget deficit was 3.8 percent of GDP. The deficit in 2024 pulled up that average: It was an eye-popping $1.9 trillion, or 6.6 percent of GDP. In 2035, the nonpartisan Congressional Budget Office expects the deficit to be 6.1 percent of that year's economic output. Moreover, in 2025, Congress is likely to change federal tax law in a way that will increase deficits above these projections.

Over the next decade, the Congressional Budget Office expects three categories of spending to increase: Social Security, Medicare, and interest payments on the national debt. Other government spending (e.g., defense, education, law enforcement, disaster relief, and national parks) is projected to fall as a share of annual economic output.[27]

Rising spending on these programs crowds out fiscal and political space to increase defense spending. Congress and Trump would do well to consider the warning issued in 2011 by Admiral Michael Mullen, then chairman of the Joint Chiefs of Staff:

> I believe that our debt is the greatest threat to our national security. If we as a country do not address our fiscal imbalances in the near-term, our national power will erode. Our ability to respond to crises and to maintain and sustain influence will diminish.[28]

The national debt's share of GDP has increased by 61 percent since Admiral Mullen's warning.

Weakening Security Alliances. Throughout the past eight years, Trump has shown considerably less support for NATO than his predecessors did. This has been true with respect to Trump's rhetoric, but also his actions.

In his first term, Trump increased tariff barriers on imported goods from key security allies, including European nations and Canada. Joe Biden followed suit, with industrial subsidies that tilted the playing field toward the US so dramatically that they led to French President Emmanuel Macron warning they could "fragment the West."[29] And since taking office for his second term, Trump has again threatened Europe with additional tariffs and increased tariff rates on Canada (along with Mexico and

China). Moreover, at the time of this writing (February 2025), Trump and senior members of his administration have actively sought to distance the US from European allies with respect to the war in Ukraine, the threat to Europe posed by Russia, and the rise of extremist political parties in some European nations.

One of the ways a strong US military increases the prosperity of American businesses and households is strengthening the security alliances that have been a bedrock of prosperity since the end of the Second World War. By weakening those alliances, Trump is weakening the economic return on taxpayer dollars invested in defense outlays.

In January 2025, Ursula von der Leyen, the president of the European Commission, warned that the world economy has "started fracturing along new lines" after Trump threatened to increase tariffs. She warned that it was in "no-one's interest, to break the bonds in the global economy."[30]

Scholars and advocates usually, and correctly, think of the domestic economic benefits from international alliances as being downstream from the security benefits. But stronger economic benefits with allied nations can increase the value of alliances. And weaker economic relationships make such alliances less valuable.

Conclusion

A strong military costs money. At a time of rising deficits and growing debt, it is tempting to consider reducing defense outlays. I am an economist, not an expert in defense or foreign affairs—but just as you don't need to be a meteorologist to know it's raining, it is apparent that land wars in Europe and the Middle East and rising geopolitical tensions in the south Pacific require a stronger US military. From a security perspective, now is not the time to cut defense spending. Military outlays should increase above current levels.

As this chapter has demonstrated, a stronger military will also advance long-term prosperity, strengthening the economic outcomes of businesses, workers, and households. Taxpayers spend large sums on defense. But they get a high return on their tax dollars.

Notes

1. Andres B. Schwarzenberg, *Red Sea Shipping Disruptions: Estimating Economic Effects*, Congressional Research Service, May 8, 2024, https://crsreports.congress.gov/product/pdf/IF/IF12657.

2. World Trade Organization, *Global Trade Outlook and Statistics*, April 2024, https://www.wto-ilibrary.org/content/books/9789287076335/read.

3. *The Economist*, "Inside the Houthis' Moneymaking Machine," January 18, 2025, https://www.economist.com/interactive/international/2025/01/18/inside-the-houthis-moneymaking-machine.

4. Jonathan Saul, "Red Sea War Insurance Rises with More Ships in Firing Line," Reuters, January 16, 2024, https://www.reuters.com/business/finance/red-sea-war-insurance-rises-with-more-ships-firing-line-2024-01-16/.

5. See, for example, Gary S. Becker, "Crime and Punishment: An Economic Approach," *Journal of Political Economy* 76, no. 2 (1968): 169–217, https://www.journals.uchicago.edu/doi/10.1086/259394.

6. Hal Brands and Peter D. Feaver, "What Are America's Alliances Good For?," *Parameters* 47, no. 2 (2017): 15–30, https://press.armywarcollege.edu/cgi/viewcontent.cgi?article=2928&context=parameters.

7. See, for example, Vincenzo Bove et al., "US Security Strategy and the Gains from Bilateral Trade," *Review of International Economics* 22, no. 5 (2014): 863–85, https://onlinelibrary.wiley.com/doi/10.1111/roie.12141.

8. European Commission, "EU Position in World Trade," https://policy.trade.ec.europa.eu/eu-trade-relationships-country-and-region/eu-position-world-trade_en; Central Intelligence Agency, "The World Factbook: Field Listing—Imports—Partners," https://www.cia.gov/the-world-factbook/field/imports-partners/; and Central Intelligence Agency, "The World Factbook: Field Listing—Exports—Partners," https://www.cia.gov/the-world-factbook/field/exports-partners/.

9. European Commission, "EU Trade Relations with the United States. Facts, Figures and Latest Developments.," https://policy.trade.ec.europa.eu/eu-trade-relationships-country-and-region/countries-and-regions/united-states_en.

10. European Commission, "EU Trade Relations with the United States."

11. Cathleen D. Cimino-Isaacs and Kyla H. Kitamura, *U.S.-Japan Trade Agreements and Negotiations*, Congressional Research Service, April 3, 2024, https://crsreports.congress.gov/product/pdf/IF/IF11120.

12. Liana Wong and Mark E. Manyin, *U.S.-South Korea (KORUS) FTA and Bilateral Trade Relations*, Congressional Research Service, November 19, 2024, https://crsreports.congress.gov/product/pdf/IF/IF10733.

13. Carolin Pflueger and Pierre Yared, "Global Hegemony and Exorbitant Privilege," Working Paper No. 32775 (National Bureau of Economic Research, August 2024), https://www.nber.org/system/files/working_papers/w32775/w32775.pdf.

14. Michael R. Strain, "Protectionism Is Failing and Wrongheaded: An Evaluation of the Post-2017 Shift Toward Trade Wars and Industrial Policy," in *Strengthening America's Economic Dynamism*, ed. Melissa S. Kearney and Luke Pardue (Aspen Institute,

2024), https://www.economicstrategygroup.org/wp-content/uploads/2024/10/Strain-AESG-2024.pdf.

15. Austan Goolsbee, "Does Government R&D Policy Mainly Benefit Scientists and Engineers?," Working Paper No. 6532 (National Bureau of Economic Research, April 1998), https://papers.ssrn.com/sol3/papers.cfm?abstract_id=226269.

16. Enrico Moretti, "Workers' Education, Spillovers, and Productivity: Evidence from Plant-Level Production Functions," *American Economic Review* 94, no. 3 (2004): 656–90, https://www.aeaweb.org/articles?id=10.1257/0002828041464623.

17. Enrico Moretti et al., "The Intellectual Spoils of War? Defense R&D, Productivity, and International Spillovers," *Review of Economics and Statistics* 107, no. 1 (2025): 14–27, https://eml.berkeley.edu/~moretti/military.pdf.

18. Moretti et al., "The Intellectual Spoils of War?"

19. Michael R. Strain, "Yes, the Biden Stimulus Made Inflation Worse," *National Review*, February 10, 2022, https://www.nationalreview.com/corner/yes-the-biden-stimulus-made-inflation-worse/; and Michael R. Strain, "The American Rescue Plan: Some Good, Some Bad and Too Large," testimony before the House Committee on Financial Services, February 4, 2021, https://www.aei.org/wp-content/uploads/2021/02/2021.02.04_biden.stimulus.testimony.pdf?x85095.

20. Some economists believe government spending is relatively more stimulative when the unemployment rate is high or when policy interest rates are very low and relatively less stimulative in the presence of high government debt. For a review of this literature and discussion of these issues, see Valerie A. Ramey, "Ten Years After the Financial Crisis: What Have We Learned from the Renaissance in Fiscal Research?," *Journal of Economic Perspectives* 33, no. 2 (2019): 89–114, https://pubs.aeaweb.org/doi/pdfplus/10.1257/jep.33.2.89.

21. Such events do happen, and not just due to war. Studying 36 countries with data beginning between 1870 and 1914 and ending in 2006, economists Robert J. Barro and Tao Jin calculate that the probability of a macroeconomic disaster in which GDP contracts by at least 10 percent is 0.04, that the US experienced five such disasters in the first half of the 20th century, and that the average magnitude of a disaster is the loss of 20 percent of GDP. See Robert J. Barro and Tao Jin, "On the Size Distribution of Macroeconomic Disasters," *Econometrica* 79, no. 5 (2011): 1567–89, https://www.jstor.org/stable/pdf/41237785.pdf.

22. Unlike a typical insurance setting, a nation can't buy and cancel the existence of a military in the same way a person can buy and cancel an insurance policy. So in this illustration, military spending occurs every year. Now, I'll define some terms. Defense spending (defined here as outlays as a share of annual GDP) is d. The probability of a catastrophe is p. The loss in the event of a catastrophe is L. The number of catastrophes is n. In this simple illustration, the US is underinvesting in defense spending if $d < p \times L \times n$, which implies that the US is underinvesting when $n > d / (p \times L)$. At the time of this writing, $d = 0.037$. We are assuming that a catastrophe results in GDP contracting by 10 percent, or $L = 0.1$. With a probability of catastrophe of 0.1, the US is underinvesting when the fourth catastrophe occurs; with $p = 0.02$, when the 19th event occurs.

23. For more discussion of this issue, see Michael R. Strain and Alan D. Viard, "Six Long-Run Tax and Budget Realities," *Tax Notes* 139, no. 13 (2013), https://papers.ssrn.com/sol3/papers.cfm?abstract_id=2233953.

24. The precise amount China spends on its military is hard to determine. Mackenzie Eaglen argues that in 2022, China spent roughly the same as the US. Using Eaglen's numbers, if the US had spent 5 percent of GDP on defense in 2022, it would have spent 180 percent more than China on defense. Mackenzie Eaglen, *Keeping Up with the Pacing Threat: Unveiling the True Size of Beijing's Military Spending*, American Enterprise Institute, April 29, 2024, https://www.aei.org/research-products/report/keeping-up-with-the-pacing-threat-unveiling-the-true-size-of-beijings-military-spending/.

25. Federal Reserve, Federal Open Market Committee, "Meeting Calendars, Statements, and Minutes (2020–2026)," https://www.federalreserve.gov/monetarypolicy/fomccalendars.htm.

26. See, for example, Olivier Blanchard, "Secular Stagnation Is Not Over," Peterson Institute for International Economics, January 24, 2023, https://www.piie.com/blogs/realtime-economics/2023/secular-stagnation-not-over.

27. Congressional Budget Office, *The Budget and Economic Outlook: 2025 to 2035*, January 2025, https://www.cbo.gov/publication/61172.

28. Michael G. Mullen, testimony before the Senate Committee on Appropriations, Subcommittee on Defense, June 15, 2011, https://ogc.osd.mil/Portals/99/testMullen06152011.pdf.

29. Yasmeen Abutaleb et al., "Biden Says He Might Meet with Putin—but Not Now," *The Washington Post*, December 1, 2022, https://www.washingtonpost.com/politics/2022/12/01/macron-biden-warning-western-alliance/.

30. Ursula von der Leyen, "Davos 2025: Special Address by Ursula von der Leyen, President of the European Commission," January 21, 2025, https://www.weforum.org/stories/2025/01/davos-2025-special-address-by-ursela-von-der-leyen-president-of-the-european-commission/.

6

How Much Is Too Much?

TODD HARRISON

A constant concern in national security is the alignment between strategy and budget—whether the resources available are necessary and sufficient to support the force structure and capabilities the strategy demands. This concern is especially relevant in the current fiscal environment. The overall federal budget deficit is projected to exceed $1.9 trillion in fiscal year (FY) 2025 and grow to more than $2.8 trillion by FY2033. The debt held by the public now exceeds the size of the economy, and the nation spends more on interest payments than national defense.[1]

The deteriorating global security environment makes the situation even more alarming. A revanchist Russia is at war in Europe, an increasingly coercive China is attempting to shift the balance of power in the Indo-Pacific region, the rogue states of Iran and North Korea are more emboldened and enabled through their ties with Russia and China, and terrorist organizations, such as Hamas and Hezbollah, are waging proxy wars on behalf of their sponsors.

The tension between fiscal and security concerns is not new. In the early years of the Cold War, the nation faced the dual dilemmas of rising deficits and growing threats. In National Security Council (NSC) policy paper 162/2, the Eisenhower administration acknowledged this tension, noting that "it is vital that the support of defense expenditures should not seriously impair the basic soundness of the U.S. economy."[2] The strategist Bernard Brodie observed in 1959 that "today we are spending far more on security than we have ever spent before in peacetime, but we are fated to remain far less secure." He went on to write that the nation's security needs are "essentially limitless," while the resources available for defense are "definitely limited."[3] Defense could always benefit from more funding because the nation can never be too secure, but the nation does not have an unlimited ability to spend.

When Robert McNamara took over the Pentagon in the 1960s, the "Whiz Kids" he brought into government reframed the problem with a deceptively simple question: How much is enough?[4] Their concerns were primarily about sufficiency and efficiency: How much is necessary to meet the threats the nation faces at an acceptable level of risk? Implicit in this question is the assumption that a sufficient level of defense spending—a budgetary floor for what is necessary—is also an affordable and prudent level of spending.

The threat environment today is arguably more complex than it was during the Cold War, and the decline of the nation's overall fiscal health further complicates the situation. These factors have morphed the debate over defense spending into a debate over affordability. Is defense spending harming the nation's fiscal health and economic security? Is defense spending on an unsustainable trajectory? What can the nation really afford to spend on defense? These questions imply a theoretical maximum level of spending—a budgetary ceiling for what is affordable and sustainable. Rather than asking how much is enough, policymakers are increasingly asking, How much is too much?

The fear is that the two trend lines—how much is enough and how much is too much—have crossed and the nation can no longer afford to execute its current strategy. If this is true, critics argue, a new and more restrained strategy is required—one that reduces America's role in the world and the military's role in US foreign policy.[5] The economic and security consequences of such a shift in strategy would be profound.

Rather than assuming the worst, this chapter seeks to answer the question of how much is too much by looking at quantitative trends in the budget, the economy, and other nations' defense spending to determine what characteristics are associated with an unaffordable and unsustainable level of US defense spending. It explores trends in defense spending adjusted for inflation, as a share of the federal budget, compared with other nations, and as a percentage of gross domestic product (GDP). It concludes with an assessment of what each of these indicators suggests about the affordability of current and proposed levels of defense spending.

Defense Spending in Inflation-Adjusted Dollars

From the founding of the nation through the end of World War II, US defense spending followed a predictable pattern. In times of peace, the United States maintained a minimal military force with minimal funding. When war approached, the nation quickly mobilized forces and increased spending. And each time war subsided, it demobilized forces and returned to a minimal state of funding.[6] The advantage of this approach is that it required much less funding during peacetime. The disadvantage, however, was that the nation often found itself unprepared at the outset of conflict with insufficient time to mobilize. While the United States arguably won every war during this period, it was not without false starts and unnecessary loss of life.[7]

This pattern of rapid mobilization and demobilization ended with the start of the Cold War. A new trend emerged that was less a strategic choice than a consequence of changes in the conduct of war. The combination of nuclear weapons, long-range missiles and bombers, and a long-term strategic competition with the Soviet Union meant the US military could no longer rely on its ability to mobilize. Intercontinental-range weapons negated the US geographic advantage of having large oceans to its east and west and compliant neighbors to its north and south. The nation could find itself at war with little warning, and the military had to be ready to fight at a moment's notice.

Figure 1 shows total defense outlays (adjusted for inflation) versus active end strength (i.e., the number of people in the active-duty military at the end of each fiscal year). After World War II, the two trend lines diverged at a pace not previously seen. While the overall budget continued to rise and fall in cycles corresponding to the Korean War, Vietnam War, military buildup of the 1980s, and wars in Afghanistan and Iraq, the gap between defense spending and force size continued to grow. The trend is similar with other measures of force size, such as the number of ships in the Navy or combat aircraft in the Air Force.[8]

These trends highlight a core structural issue in the defense budget. Since FY1950, the total cost per person (including compensation, operations, equipment, basing, and all other costs) has grown at a compound annual rate of 2.7 percent above inflation, a rate that is remarkably similar

Figure 1. Defense Outlays and Active End Strength, 1791–2023

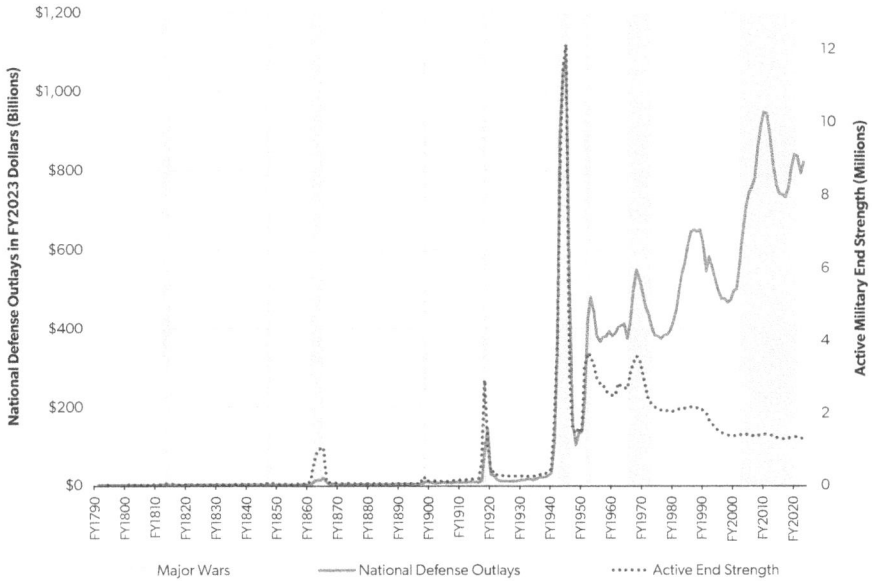

Source: National defense outlays and active end strength data for 1791–1947 are from US Department of Commerce, *Historical Statistics of the United States from Colonial Times to 1970*, part 2, 1975, 1114–15, 1141–43, https://www2.census.gov/library/publications/1975/compendia/hist_stats_colonial-1970/hist_stats_colonial-1970p2-chY.pdf. National defense outlays and active end strength data for FY1947–2023 are from US Department of Defense, Office of the Under Secretary of Defense (Comptroller), *National Defense Budget Estimates for FY 2025*, Table 6-13, Table 7-1, and Table 7-5, https://comptroller.defense.gov/Portals/45/Documents/defbudget/FY2025/fy25_Green_Book.pdf. Outlays are adjusted for inflation using the GDP Chained Price Index from Samuel H. Williamson, "What Was the U.S. GDP Then?," MeasuringWorth, 2024, http://www.measuringworth.org/usgdp/.

to what military and civilian leaders have called for in recent years. For example, in a 2017 congressional testimony, General Joseph Dunford, then chairman of the Joint Chiefs of Staff, stated, "We know now that continued growth of the base budget of at least 3 percent above inflation is the floor necessary to preserve today's relative competitive advantage."[9]

Growth in the cost per person above inflation is due to three main factors. First, the Department of Defense's labor costs—particularly the

costs of military compensation and benefits, including health care—
have grown faster than inflation. This trend accelerated during the
2000s, but in recent years it has moderated.[10] The costs of operating
and maintaining major weapons systems, such as aircraft, ships, and
ground vehicles, have also grown as these platforms have aged. And as
these legacy systems are replaced, the latest generation of weapons systems often cost even more to operate and maintain.[11] Finally, the threats
our military faces and the pace of innovation required to meet these
threats is accelerating, requiring higher levels of research and development just to keep pace with threats and progressively higher unit costs
to procure more advanced weapons.[12] These trends suggest, as General
Dunford and others have asserted, that to sustain the same size force
at roughly the current level of readiness with modernization programs
that merely keep pace with threats will require a budget that grows at
about 2.7 percent above inflation.

Growth in the cost per person above inflation is concerning, but it
appears to be largely unavoidable, notwithstanding a significant reduction in threats or a change in the political constraints placed on how
defense funding is allocated.[13] Whether this trend is affordable in the
long term depends on whether the cost per person grows faster than the
economy. Over time, this would mean that either the size of the military must get progressively smaller or the nation will need to devote a
progressively larger share of the economy to defense. While this could
be tolerated in the short term, in the long term it would eventually be
unsustainable because either the military would become too small to do
anything meaningful or its budget would consume an ever-increasing
share of the economy.

Thankfully, this is not the situation the United States finds itself in
today. From 1950 through 2023, the US economy grew at a compound
annual rate of 3.1 percent in real terms.[14] While the economy has its ups
and downs, as long as the long-term rate of growth in the defense budget's
cost per person remains below the long-term rate of economic growth,
the current trajectory is sustainable. Despite claims to the contrary, the
mere fact that total defense spending and the cost per person are growing
faster than inflation does not mean the current trajectory is unaffordable
or unsustainable.[15]

Figure 2. Defense, Interest, and Veterans' Benefits as a Share of the Federal Budget, 1791–2023

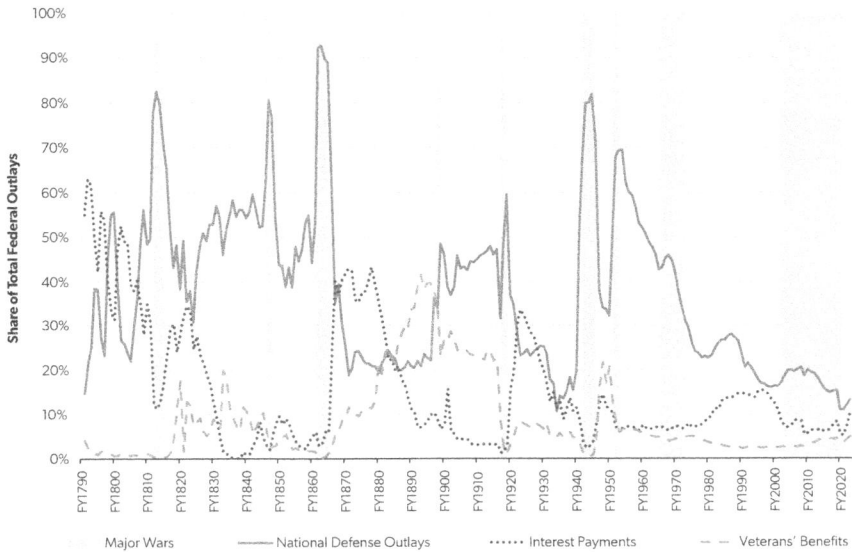

Source: Outlays data for FY1791–1947 are from US Department of Commerce, *Historical Statistics of the United States from Colonial Times to 1970*, part 2, 1975, 1114–15, https://www2.census.gov/library/publications/1975/compendia/hist_stats_colonial-1970/hist_stats_colonial-1970p2-chY.pdf. Outlays data for FY1947–2023 are from US Department of Defense, Office of the Under Secretary of Defense (Comptroller), *National Defense Budget Estimates for FY 2025*, Table 7-1, https://comptroller.defense.gov/Portals/45/Documents/defbudget/FY2025/fy25_Green_Book.pdf.

Defense Spending as a Share of the Federal Budget

Another metric often cited in debates over affordability is the share of the overall federal budget used for defense. As shown in Figure 2, the share of the budget allocated for defense has varied considerably over time, particularly during times of war. From 1791 to just before the Civil War (1860), defense consumed an average of 45 percent of the federal budget (excluding the War of 1812 and the Mexican-American War). In contrast, from the post–Civil War era to just before the Spanish-American War (1867–97), defense consumed just 24 percent of the overall budget. This decrease was due in part to higher levels of spending in other parts of the government, particularly interest payments on the public debt and the cost of veterans' benefits. In FY1871, for example, the nation spent $126 million on interest and $34 million for veterans' benefits, compared to $36 million for the Army and $19 million for the Navy. For nearly every year from 1791 through 1930, these three areas of the federal budget (i.e., defense, veterans' benefits, and interest) together consumed more than half the federal budget.

In the 1930s, the composition of the federal budget began to change in significant ways, and defense fell as a share of overall federal spending. President Franklin D. Roosevelt's New Deal led to a sharp increase in non-defense spending for new programs, such as Social Security, and efforts to pull the country out of the Great Depression. These trends temporarily reversed during World War II, with defense surging to more than 80 percent of the overall federal budget, as it had during the War of 1812, Civil War, and Mexican-American War. After the war, however, the increases in nondefense spending that began under Roosevelt continued.

On the surface, the trends in Figures 1 and 2 may seem in conflict with one another because Figure 1 shows a general increase in defense over the past seven decades, while Figure 2 shows a general decline. Both are true because they measure different things. Since the end of World War II, defense spending grew faster than inflation, but nondefense spending grew at an even faster rate, causing defense as a share of the overall budget to decline.

This suggests that the United States could spend a much greater share of its budget on defense, as it has in the past. The nation spends a smaller share on defense because other forms of spending have taken priority. This is a policy choice, but it is not a fiscal constraint.

US Defense Spending Compared with Other Nations

The debate over the level of defense spending often references how much the United States spends on defense relative to other nations. Such a comparison, however, is difficult to make because we do not always know with accuracy what other nations spend on defense, labor and material

Figure 3. Defense Spending by Nation in 2023

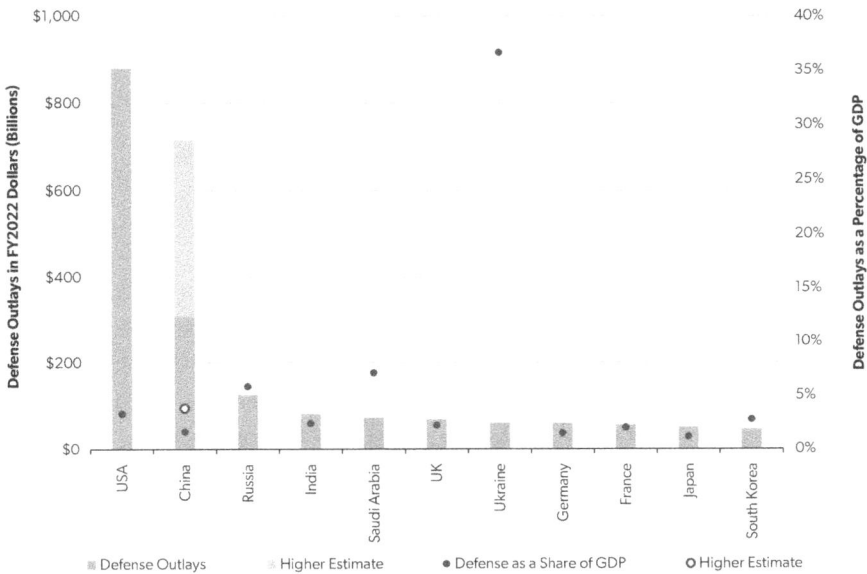

Source: Defense outlays and outlays as a share of GDP are from Stockholm International Peace Research Institute, "Military Expenditure by Region in Constant US Dollars," 2023, https://www.sipri.org/databases/milex. The higher estimate for Chinese defense spending is from Mackenzie Eaglen, *Keeping Up with the Pacing Threat: Unveiling the True Size of Beijing's Military Spending*, American Enterprise Institute, April 29, 2024, https://www.aei.org/research-products/report/keeping-up-with-the-pacing-threat-unveiling-the-true-size-of-beijings-military-spending/.

costs vary significantly among nations, and the way countries categorize defense and nondefense spending varies. As shown in Figure 3, estimates for China's defense spending range from $309 billion to $711 billion (in 2022 US dollars).[16] Although China is quickly catching up, the United States still spends more than any other nation on defense. As a share of GDP, though, the United States spends less than many other nations—Ukraine, Russia, Saudi Arabia, Israel, and others devote much more of their economy to defense.

These comparisons do little to shed light on whether the United States is spending too much. The United States spends more than other nations because it has more security commitments around the world—it is the primary defender of the global economic system and the free flow of commerce that enables our modern way of life. While this may not seem fair, and allied nations could certainly spend more, the United States spends the most because it has the most at stake. This does not mean the United States is spending too much or more than it can afford—it merely means it is spending more than others.

Defense Spending as a Share of GDP

Defense spending as a share of GDP is a measure commonly used to argue that the nation can or should spend more on defense. Some proponents of higher spending point to the general decline over the past seven decades, shown in Figure 4, as evidence that defense spending is on the decline. However, as Figure 1 made clear, defense spending has not actually declined—it is near a post–World War II high in inflation-adjusted dollars. This common misunderstanding stems from the fact that defense spending as a share of GDP (Figure 4) is the ratio between two weakly correlated values: defense outlays in the numerator and the size of the overall economy (GDP) in the denominator. These values are weakly correlated because they can move in opposite directions. When the economy contracts during a recession, defense spending can increase; when the economy is expanding, defense spending can decline.

Defense spending as a share of GDP is different from defense spending. Defense spending as a share of GDP measures the economic burden of defense—how much of the nation's economy is used each year to provide for the common defense. Because it is a ratio of two values, it rises and falls in response to changes in both the numerator and the denominator, which can be counterintuitive. If defense spending grows and GDP grows even faster, the ratio becomes smaller. Likewise, if defense spending declines and GDP declines even faster, the ratio becomes larger. In 2020, for example, Japanese defense spending fell by 1.2 percent (or 0.9 percent adjusting for inflation) from the prior year, but defense spending as a percentage of GDP grew from 0.99 percent to 1.02 percent. Japan spent less on defense, but because its economy contracted by even more, defense as a percentage of GDP went up.[17]

Figure 4. The Economic and Demographic Burden of Defense

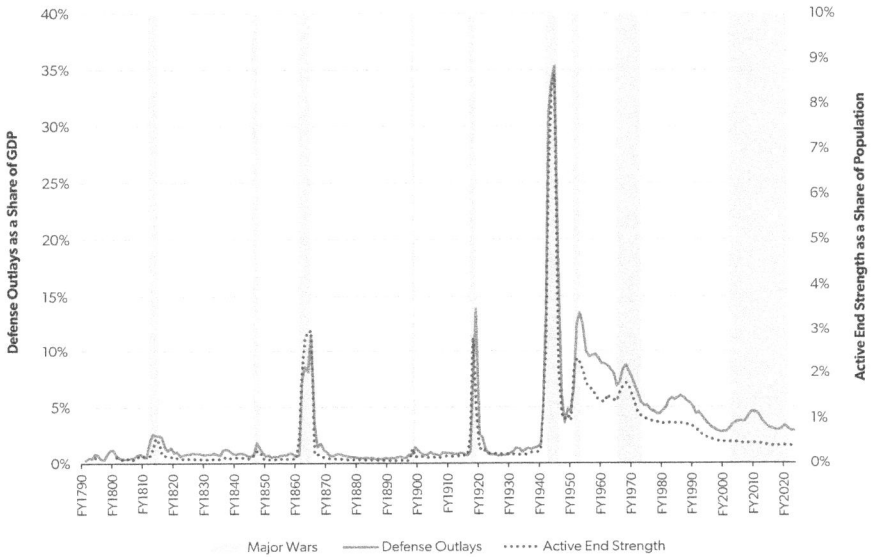

Source: National defense outlays and active end strength data for 1791–1947 are from US Department of Commerce, *Historical Statistics of the United States from Colonial Times to 1970*, part 2, 1975, 1114–15, 1141–43, https://www2.census.gov/library/publications/1975/compendia/hist_stats_colonial-1970/hist_stats_colonial-1970p2-chY.pdf. National defense outlays and active end strength data for FY1947–2023 are from US Department of Defense, Office of the Under Secretary of Defense (Comptroller), *National Defense Budget Estimates for FY 2025*, Table 6-13, Table 7-1, Table 7-5, https://comptroller.defense.gov/Portals/45/Documents/defbudget/FY2025/fy25_Green_Book.pdf. GDP data are from Samuel H. Williamson, "What Was the U.S. GDP Then?," MeasuringWorth, 2024, http://www.measuringworth.org/usgdp/. US population data for 1790–1960 are from US Department of Commerce, *Historical Statistics of the United States from Colonial Times to 1970*, part 1, 1975, https://www2.census.gov/library/publications/1975/compendia/hist_stats_colonial-1970/hist_stats_colonial-1970p1-chA.pdf. US population data for 1960–2023 are from World Bank, "Population, Total for United States," Federal Reserve Bank of St. Louis, July 2, 2024, https://fred.stlouisfed.org/series/POPTOTUSA647NWDB.

Attempting to peg the defense budget to a certain share of the economy or use the percentage of GDP as a floor for defense spending is fundamentally unsound. In the case of Japan in 2020, holding defense as a share of GDP steady would have meant even deeper cuts in defense spending. The United States has never stayed at a relatively stable level of defense spending, either in inflation-adjusted dollars or as a share of the economy, because world events have a way of intervening. It stands to reason that defense spending should rise and fall based on changes in strategy and threats. Defense spending should not be dictated by economic activity or the whims of the business cycle that drive GDP growth. Setting spending at a fixed level of GDP lets the budget drive the strategy rather than letting strategy drive the budget; it is based on the nation's ability to spend rather than what it needs to spend.

While the economic burden of defense is not a useful indicator of whether the nation is spending enough on defense, it is perhaps an ideal measure of whether the nation is spending *too much*. Defense as a share of GDP is best used as a ceiling for defense spending rather than a floor. If the economic burden of defense is too high, it could hamper economic growth and lead to a downward and self-reinforcing economic spiral, as the Eisenhower administration warned about in NSC 162/2. There is no such economic risk from having too low of a defense burden, but there is surely a security risk from having too low of an absolute level of defense spending (regardless of GDP).

History serves as a useful guide for how large a defense burden the economy can support—a theoretical ceiling. The United States has only spent more than 10 percent of GDP on defense four times in its history, and each time was relatively short in duration and in support of major wars. Some Middle Eastern nations, such as Israel, Jordan, Oman, and Saudi Arabia, have spent well above 10 percent of GDP for many years consecutively. Israel, for example, spent more than 20 percent of GDP on defense from 1970 through 1978—a period in which it faced significant security challenges.[18] Ukraine currently spends more than 30 percent of GDP on defense, similar to the United States during World War II. As a general rule of thumb, however, spending more than about 10 percent of GDP on defense should be reserved for the direst circumstances.

In peacetime, one expects that the threshold would be lower. From the end of the Korean War through the end of the Cold War (FY1954–90), the United States averaged spending 6.6 percent of GDP on defense, and during this time the economy grew at a compound annual rate of 3.5 percent above inflation. From FY1991 through FY2023, the nation spent an average of 3.2 percent of GDP on defense, and the economy grew at a

Figure 5. Revenues and Outlays as a Share of GDP

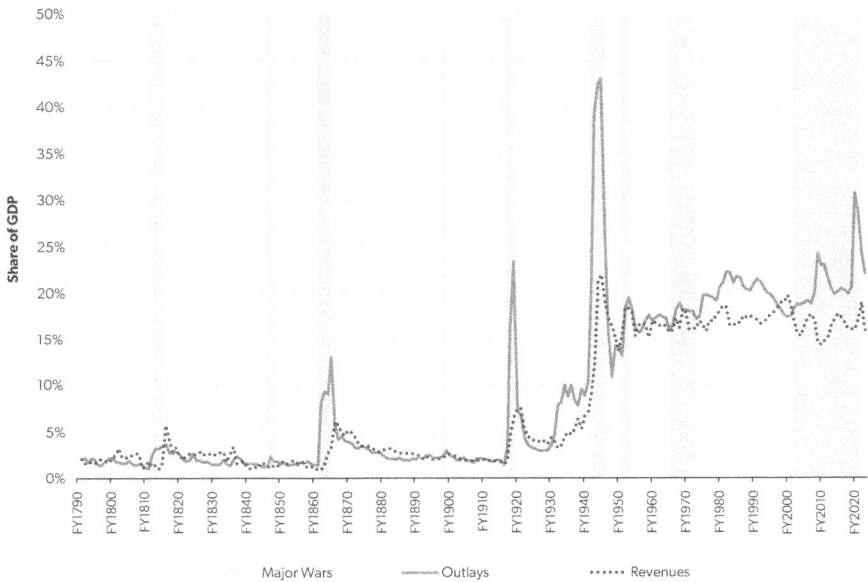

Source: Outlays and revenues data for 1791–1961 are from US Department of Commerce, *Historical Statistics of the United States from Colonial Times to 1970*, part 2, 1975, 1105–6, 1114–15, https://www2.census.gov/library/publications/1975/compendia/hist_stats_colonial-1970/hist_stats_colonial-1970p2-chY.pdf. Outlays and revenues data for FY1962–2023 are from Congressional Budget Office, Historical Budget Data, February 2024, https://www.cbo.gov/data/budget-economic-data.

compound annual rate of 2.6 percent above inflation.[19] To be clear, this correlation does not necessarily mean that higher defense spending *causes* higher economic growth, but it does suggest that spending more than 6 percent of GDP on defense did not harm the economy in the past.

For the United States in its current fiscal condition, the situation is complicated by two additional factors. As shown in Figure 5, total federal outlays as a share of GDP are at a high level by historical standards—they have only been higher during World War II, the COVID-19 pandemic, and the Great Recession. Moreover, as outlays have generally trended higher as a share of GDP for the past seven decades, revenues have not grown in proportion. This is an unsustainable trend leading to policy choices that could affect defense spending. Any changes in fiscal policy that widen the deficit, such as tax cuts or increases in nondefense spending, make the situation worse and put long-term downward pressure on the defense budget.

This review of historical data suggests that the current economic burden of defense at 3 percent of GDP is not more than the economy can bear. The nation could spend double what it does on defense without causing serious economic harm, provided it is willing to make the necessary spending and revenue choices to keep the annual deficit at a sustainable level. While the United States has the ability to spend more on defense, it may lack the political will to do so.

Conclusion

Determining how much defense spending is too much is not a simple matter of finding an absolute level that is unaffordable. As this chapter has shown, the affordability and sustainability of defense spending depends more on relative growth rates than on absolute levels. Norman Augustine famously projected in 1967 that if growth in the unit cost of tactical aircraft continued increasing at its current pace, by 2054 the entire defense budget would be needed to procure just one aircraft. His observation was based on simple math: If two trend lines are growing at different rates, the one that is growing faster will eventually overtake the other. When the trend lines are nonlinear, such as compounding growth, the results can be surprising.

A similar set of laws governs the affordability of defense. If the cost per person grows faster than the economy, at some point the nation's entire GDP will be needed to pay for just one soldier (or, more likely by the time this happens, one guardian). Likewise, if the overall size of the defense budget grows faster than the economy, the defense budget will eventually consume the entire economy. Well before either of these extreme conditions occurs, the nation would begin to encounter serious economic and security consequences. Exactly when those consequences become too much to bear is a matter of politics and risk tolerance.

History suggests that spending as much as 6 percent of GDP on defense can be sustained over time without causing economic harm, but spending more than 10 percent of GDP should be reserved for periods of crisis. A more conservative and forward-looking approach, however, is to monitor the long-term growth rates in defense outlays per person and total defense outlays to ensure the nation stays on a sustainable trajectory and never risks venturing into dangerous fiscal territory during peacetime.

By each of these measures, US defense spending is on a sustainable trajectory with ample room for growth. The economic burden of defense is less than half what it averaged during the Cold War and slightly below the post–Cold War average. Moreover, the cost per person has grown at 2.2 percent above inflation over the past 10 years (excluding costs related to the wars in Iraq and Afghanistan), which is below the 2.7 percent growth rate experienced since 1950 and the 3.1 percent growth rate in the economy.[20]

While the United States spends more than any other nation on defense, this gap is closing quickly as China grows and modernizes its military. Interest payments are projected to exceed defense outlays for the foreseeable future, but both figures remain at a relatively small share of the budget by historical standards. A more concerning trend is that overall federal spending has grown, while revenues have not kept pace. This has led to higher deficits, a larger public debt, and rising interest payments.

Defense spending at its current level is affordable, even if the overall federal budget is on an unsustainable trajectory. The Commission on the National Defense Strategy recommended in 2018 that the defense budget grow at an annual rate of 3–5 percent above inflation, and the commission reiterated this recommendation in its 2022 report.[21] While 3 percent real growth should be sustainable, 5 percent real growth could only be sustained for a finite time—a catch-up period. More recently, Senator Roger Wicker, now chair of the Senate Armed Services Committee, recommended that the defense budget gradually increase to 5 percent of GDP.[22] While this would mean growing the defense budget by roughly 70 percent above its current level, history suggests that the nation would be able to devote 5 percent of its economy to defense indefinitely— provided it makes the necessary choices to raise taxes or reduce other spending. But pegging the budget to an arbitrary share of GDP is the antithesis of strategy.

At current and proposed levels of defense spending, it is not a question of affordability but rather priority. Policymakers must decide if defense should be afforded a higher priority than nondefense programs and activities, and they must be willing to pay for their decisions. Many of the chapters in this book make the case that more resources are needed for defense, and in aggregate these increases are still well within the range of what the nation can afford. This does not mean the nation should increase the defense budget without adequate scrutiny or strategic guidance, nor does it mean the United States should spend more just because it can. How much the nation spends on defense is important, but how the nation spends those precious resources is even more important.

Notes

1. See Congressional Budget Office, "10-Year Budget Projections," https://www.cbo.gov/data/budget-economic-data#3; and Congressional Budget Office, *An Update to the Budget and Economic Outlook: 2024 to 2034*, June 18, 2024, https://www.cbo.gov/publication/60039.

2. Executive Secretary on Basic National Security Policy, *A Report to the National Security Council*, October 30, 1953, 23, https://irp.fas.org/offdocs/nsc-hst/nsc-162-2.pdf.

3. Bernard Brodie, *Strategy in the Missile Age* (RAND Corporation, 1959), 359, 364.

4. See Alain C. Enthoven and K. Wayne Smith, *How Much Is Enough? Shaping the Defense Program, 1961–1969* (Harper & Row, 1971).

5. See, for example, William D. Hartung, *More Money, Less Security: Pentagon Spending and Strategy in the Biden Administration*, Quincy Institute, June 2023, https://quincyinst.s3.amazonaws.com/wp-content/uploads/2023/06/17212841/QUINCY-PAPER-NO.-12-HARTUNG.pdf.

6. Richard K. Betts, *Military Readiness: Concepts, Choices, Consequences* (Brookings Institution Press, 1995), 5–6.

7. Brodie, *Strategy in the Missile Age*, 358.

8. Todd Harrison and Seamus Daniels, *Analysis of the FY 2018 Defense Budget*, Center for Strategic and International Studies, December 2017, 7–11, https://csis-website-prod.s3.amazonaws.com/s3fs-public/publication/171208_Defense_Budget_Analysis.pdf.

9. Jim Garamone, "Dunford Urges Congress to Protect U.S. Competitive Advantage," *DoD News*, June 12, 2017, https://www.jcs.mil/Media/News/News-Display/Article/1211862/dunford-urges-congress-to-protect-us-competitive-advantage/.

10. American Enterprise Institute, "Defense Budget Navigator," 8, https://defensebudget.aei.org/.

11. Todd Harrison and Seamus P. Daniels, *Analysis of the FY 2019 Defense Budget*, Center for Strategic and International Studies, 16–17, https://csis-website-prod.s3.amazonaws.com/s3fs-public/publication/180917_Harrison_DefenseBudget2019.pdf.

12. Todd Harrison, *Building an Enduring Advantage in the Third Space Age*, American Enterprise Institute, May 8, 2024, 26, https://www.aei.org/research-products/report/building-an-enduring-advantage-in-the-third-space-age/.

13. For example, much of the true inefficiency in the defense budget is due to political constraints placed on the Department of Defense's ability to close bases, consolidate functions, and retire equipment it no longer needs.

14. Samuel H. Williamson, "What Was the U.S. GDP Then?," MeasuringWorth, 2024, http://www.measuringworth.org/usgdp/.

15. See Dan Grazier et al., "Current Defense Plans Require Unsustainable Future Spending," Stimson Center, July 16, 2024, https://www.stimson.org/2024/current-defense-plans-require-unsustainable-future-spending/.

16. Data are from Stockholm International Peace Research Institute, "Military Expenditure by Region in Constant US Dollars," 2023; and Mackenzie Eaglen, *Keeping Up with the Pacing Threat: Unveiling the True Size of Beijing's Military Spending*, American Enterprise Institute, April 29, 2024, https://www.aei.org/research-products/report/keeping-up-with-the-pacing-threat-unveiling-the-true-size-of-beijings-military-spending/.

17. Stockholm International Peace Research Institute, "Military Expenditure by Region in Constant US Dollars."

18. Stockholm International Peace Research Institute, "Military Expenditure by Region in Constant US Dollars."

19. National defense outlays and active end strength data for 1791–1947 are from US Department of Commerce, *Historical Statistics of the United States from Colonial Times to 1970*, part 2, 1975, 1114–15, 1141–43, https://www2.census.gov/library/publications/1975/compendia/hist_stats_colonial-1970/hist_stats_colonial-1970p2-chY.pdf. National defense outlays and active end strength data for FY1947–2023 are from US Department of Defense, Office of the Under Secretary of Defense (Comptroller), *National Defense Budget Estimates for FY 2025*, Table 6-13, Table 7-1, Table 7-5, https://comptroller.defense.gov/Portals/45/Documents/defbudget/FY2025/fy25_Green_Book.pdf. GDP data are from Williamson, "What Was the U.S. GDP Then?"

20. US Department of Defense, Office of the Under Secretary of Defense (Comptroller), *National Defense Budget Estimates for FY 2025*, Table 6-13, Table 7-1, Table 7-5; and Williamson, "What Was the U.S. GDP Then?"

21. Jane Harman et al., *Commission on the National Defense Strategy*, RAND Corporation, July 2024, https://www.rand.org/content/dam/rand/pubs/misc/MSA3057-4/RAND_MSA3057-4.pdf.

22. Roger Wicker, *21st Century Peace Through Strength: A Generational Investment in the U.S. Military*, https://www.wicker.senate.gov/services/files/BC957888-0A93-432F-A49E-6202768A9CE0.

7

Affordable American Security

ELAINE MCCUSKER

D efense should not be *a* priority for the federal government but *the* priority. Yet America is not spending as much as people think on defense. Meanwhile, taxpayer funds are being wasted by the billions each year under temporary funding measures.

How much can America afford to spend on national security? How do we know how much our security really costs? And how can we get the most bang for our defense buck? To bluntly answer these questions, we need more transparency and predictability in the federal budget than we currently have.

Most Americans support increases in military spending, but as the defense budget approaches $900 billion a year, we should understand our priorities for that budget, what is really in it, and how to get the most from what we spend.[1]

And we need to start with the basics.

The Declaration of Independence asserts that the government's first duty is securing the self-evident and unalienable rights to life, liberty, and the pursuit of happiness. A strong national defense is foundational to all three of these rights. In addition, the United States Constitution makes clear that national defense is the only mandatory function—and exclusively the responsibility—of the national government.[2]

There are a number of metrics used to evaluate the adequacy of defense spending for America's needs over time. Some are useful barometers, including defense spending as a percentage of gross domestic product (GDP), which can help the nation understand how its economic growth and vitality are connected to its spending on security. Some are not useful, such as the ratio of defense spending to nondefense spending, which often accompanies the theory that there should be parity between the two. Federal budgets should reflect national priorities and requirements, not some arbitrary notion of equally divided spending.

The best way to measure the adequacy of the defense budget, however, is not its parity with other costs or its percentage of the GDP but its sufficiency in meeting the military requirements necessary to execute national security and defense strategies and associated missions. On this front, multiple bipartisan commissions have found that the budget—and the defense strategy itself—falls short of what America needs.

For example, according to the most recent assessment of the Commission on the National Defense Strategy, "The threats the United States faces are the most serious and most challenging the nation has encountered since 1945 and include the potential for near-term major war." Yet the commission found that "in many ways, China is *outpacing* the United States and has largely negated the U.S. military advantage in the Western Pacific through two decades of focused military investment."[3] (Emphasis in original.) Interestingly, the commission also noted,

> The U.S. public are largely unaware of the dangers the United States faces or the costs (financial and otherwise) required to adequately prepare. . . . They have not internalized the costs of the United States losing its position as a world superpower.[4]

To address resource shortfalls, the commission rightly recommended that Congress immediately provide supplemental funding for a multi-year investment in the national security and innovation industrial bases, focusing particularly on shipbuilding and munitions.

The Strategic Posture Commission made complementary observations regarding the strategic environment, stating,

> Today the United States is on the cusp of having not one, but two nuclear peer adversaries, each with ambitions to change the international status quo, by force, if necessary: a situation which the United States did not anticipate and for which it is not prepared.[5]

In the increasingly violent and chaotic world that these commissions describe, it has never been more important that Americans and their leaders know what the United States defense budget is, how it works, and

Figure 1. Defense Budget Transparency and Predictability Save Money

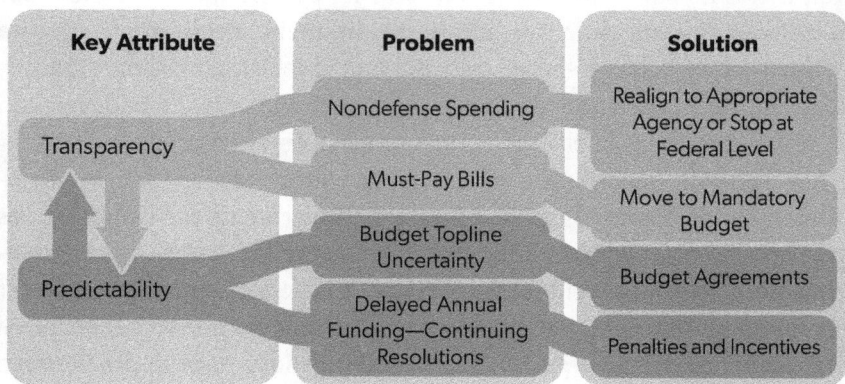

Source: Author.

what it buys. Two key attributes provide the clarity needed to make smart decisions about defense spending and guarantee returns on our security investments: transparency and predictability.

Transparency in the defense budget is inhibited by two things: (1) programs and activities that do not produce military capability and (2) must-pay bills, which give the illusion of flexibility. Both of these affect performance of core functions and fiscal decisions.

Predictability depends on two conditions: (1) the timely passage of annual appropriations and (2) budget agreements that set funding toplines far enough in advance to matter. Without these conditions being met, American military competitiveness is wasted.

The key attributes of transparency and predictability are interrelated, and the challenges that impede them have solutions (Figure 1).

Transparency

Nondefense and Mandatory Spending in the Defense Budget. Budget transparency matters for three key reasons. First, Americans should understand what their security costs and carefully consider the implications of distracting the Pentagon from the missions only it can do. Second, we should be aware of the government-wide reverberations of diverting resources from other agencies' core missions to defense (known as "mission creep"). And third, if political leaders continue to insist on parity between defense and nondefense spending, we should have accurate data for those discussions and for any spending comparisons between the United States' spending and that of our allies and adversaries.

Many people know the current Pentagon budget is about $850 billion, so they understandably think that is the cost of the military. It is not. The defense budget is loaded with resources for programs and activities that do nothing to produce military capability. It also contains many annual must-pay bills, which are essentially entitlement spending and mask the real cost of modernizing the military we have into the one we need.

The notion of core functions is crucial to budget transparency. Core functions are the things the Department of Defense (DOD) is expected to do and that only it can do, such as building a Navy, Army, Air Force, Marine Corps, Space Force, and cyber proficiency capable of competing with China; sustaining and modernizing air, maritime, ground, and special operations forces with power-projection competence; and maintaining America's nuclear capabilities.

Using a simple methodology to examine the defense budget, Table 1 groups the fiscal year (FY) 2025 request into three categories: (1) military capability and operations, (2) must-pay bills (such as compensation and health care), (3) and missions of other agencies and departments. Even a generous allocation of programs and activities into Category 1 for any efforts that are not clearly defined results in nearly 60 percent of defense spending ($487 billion) falling into Category 2. There, it is consumed by what is essentially mandatory spending, meaning expenses that are tied to previous decisions such as compensation and base operating support, which are not easily changed on an annual basis. More than $15 billion falls into Category 3 and should not be performed by DOD at all. This means that only roughly 40 percent of the annual defense budget is actually discretionary spending that is producing military capability and modernizing the force.

One key reason the military performs so many noncore functions is that the definition of national security has expanded to include numerous

Table 1. Defense Budget Categorical Spending

Appropriation Title	FY2025 President's Budget Request	Category 1: Military Capability	Category 2: Compensation and Personnel	Category 3: Nondefense Programs and Activities
Military Construction	$17,545	$11,974	$4,117	$1,454
Military Personnel	$181,881	$0	$181,656	$225
Operations and Maintenance	$337,921	$28,015	$298,528	$11,378
Procurement	$167,546	$167,135	$359	$52
Research and Development	$143,157	$140,512	$2,029	$615
Revolving and Management Fund	$1,721	$30	$118	$1,572
Total	$849,771	$347,667	$486,808	$15,296

Source: Author's analysis of materials in US Department of Defense, Office of the Under Secretary of Defense (Comptroller), "Defense Budget Materials—FY2025," https://comptroller.defense.gov/Budget-Materials/Budget2025/.
Note: Numbers may not add due to rounding. Dollar amounts are in millions.

other federal responsibilities. Some such activities assigned to the military may seem small in the scheme of the overall budget. Many are worthy efforts. However, they artificially inflate the defense budget and distract from true defense priorities.

A second and related reason is the military's immense capabilities—particularly in planning, logistics, and emergency response—which lead to an understandable tendency to rely on the armed forces for things beyond their core purpose. When a natural disaster strikes—domestically or internationally—the military is called on to respond. When the southwest border is overrun by those seeking refuge from political persecution or economic hardship—or by criminals trafficking drugs, people, and violence—the National Guard is called to support Customs and Border Protection. When domestic police forces face violent protests, the military may be called for backup.

Table 2. Defense Funding for Other Department and Agency Missions

Category 3: Nondefense Programs and Activities	FY2025 President's Budget Request
Education	$4,774
Security Assistance, Humanitarian and Disaster Response, and Other Civil and Domestic Missions	$3,390
Environment	$1,414
Commissaries	$1,570
Medical and Health Care	$4,149
Total	**$15,296**

Source: Author's analysis of materials in US Department of Defense, Office of the Under Secretary of Defense (Comptroller), "Defense Budget Materials—FY2025," https://comptroller.defense.gov/Budget-Materials/Budget2025/.
Note: Numbers may not add due to rounding. Dollar amounts are in millions.

The military's exceptional planning and operational capabilities further diffuse its missions. When people seek security, stability, and safety, they look to the military. But the military is a warfighting organization with training and equipment for this mission—not for domestic tasks. Such expansion of the military's mission brings consequences, financial and otherwise.[6] This is particularly true for a military that is already underfunded to meet the expectations of the National Defense Strategy, which is itself outdated.[7]

Looking closely at Category 3 (Table 2) reveals more than $15 billion in programs and activities that are completely outside the defense mission and should be closely examined for either termination or transferal to a more appropriate agency budget. The entire federal government, including domestic departments and agencies, should contribute to the nation's security through its assigned missions in homeland security, education, energy, the environment, and health care. Those missions should not be assigned to the Pentagon.

For example, if the nation needs a workforce skilled in engineering, advanced manufacturing, artificial intelligence, and data analytics (and it does), the Department of Education should focus on educating and producing such experts. Yet the Pentagon runs a global school system, educating more than 45,000 students in 106 schools located in 11 countries. These are excellent schools, but running them requires devoting resources to buildings, teachers, and family assistance.

In addition, the defense budget contains set-asides for education research, grants, tuition assistance, and general skill development programs. While these programs may deserve support, they are certainly not a core defense mission. Should funding for them really be considered under defense in budget discussions? And should the Pentagon maintain infrastructure to oversee this activity, thereby distracting it from its primary purpose and the military missions that only the DOD can carry out?

Security assistance, overseas humanitarian disaster and civic aid, foreign economic assistance, and other civil programs are within the purview of the State Department and other civilian agencies. Yet the defense budget has resources for each of these missions—and not just a few million dollars to support the defense contribution to these activities but billions of dollars. These accounts include funding for regional security studies, international legal studies, border security, coalition support, and large investments in security assistance that are typically funded through the State Department as foreign military financing or sales programs. Including funding for these activities in the defense budget artificially inflates the public's perception of what national security costs, requires manpower to manage them, and pulls resources from the Pentagon's primary mission.

The Environmental Protection Agency has the specific mission, designated expertise, and accountability for environmental cleanup and restoration, climate change mitigation, and related research. Yet ensconced in the DOD's operations and maintenance account are environmental restoration programs, each costing hundreds of millions of dollars. Other DOD efforts examine the social science of environmental security and support broad applied research in these areas.[8] Again, managing these programs distracts the military from its core function.

Arguably, the military departments should clean up their activities' environmental effects and contribute to addressing climate change. But the military services are primarily warfighting organizations, charged with developing, deploying, and operating lethal capabilities to protect the nation and its citizens. Though the DOD can and should be a good partner to those charged with these responsibilities, it is important to know how much money is in the budget to lead these efforts.

Note that many of the DOD's non-mission-critical defense programs and activities that overlap with or duplicate those of other federal departments are funded by defense-wide appropriations accounts. These centralized accounts are not part of the military departments.

Defense-Wide Programs. As efforts are made to save money, reduce redundancy, and improve coordination, the pendulum swings between centralized and decentralized approaches to managing and executing joint functions.

When centralized, shared, or joint functions roll into defense-wide accounts, the accounts are sometimes called the "fourth estate" or—officially—the defense agencies and field activities (DAFA). These defense-wide accounts, totaling $53 billion in operational spending in 2024 alone, are not one thing.[9] They are more than 25 different things. Since they involve agencies that are heavily populated by civilian personnel, they tend to be categorized as overhead and targeted for cuts.

But that is a dangerously simple view. These accounts include Special Operations Command, Cyber Command, the Missile Defense Agency, the Defense Logistics Agency, the Defense Contract Management Agency, the Defense Information Systems Agency, and numerous classified accounts. These can't simply be eliminated. But they can and should be examined to determine what their relevance is to the core military mission, whether centralized management still makes sense, and whether the required functions are best performed by the government at all.

For example, hidden in DAFA is an annual appropriation of close to $1.6 billion for commissaries.[10] Tracing their history back to 1825, the commissaries—now run by the Defense Commissary Agency—were set up to provide convenience and support to military families in austere locations. Now seen as an earned benefit for military members, their families, and veterans, the commissaries should deliver the best possible service and savings to patrons while maintaining budget-neutral operations for the taxpayer.[11]

But according to numerous reviews, studies, and assessments over the past decade, the commissaries are falling short and costing more. While the cost to the taxpayer rises, performance and utility steadily decline.[12] Yet the Pentagon has been unwilling to even fairly test alternative management structures. This is a prime example of a taxpayer-funded, non-core military activity that provides subpar service to deserving Americans and that could—and should—be better run to provide improved service in a self-sustaining manner.

In another instance, the National Institutes of Health is charged with performing fundamental research to improve health and reduce illness, so it leads basic and applied medical research on cancer and autism, among other things. Yet DOD also spends billions each year on these efforts. For example, the $40 billion Defense Health Program (DHP) provides medical and dental services to active forces and other eligible populations while training medical personnel. The DHP includes $900 million for research to address some military—but many nonmilitary—challenges. The DHP's budget request includes almost $63 million for research on breast cancer, gynecological cancer, and similar nondefense efforts, which would be more appropriately funded by other agencies whose mission is to tackle these challenges.[13]

Moreover, Congress routinely adds billions in nondefense spending to the budget—money that, in a zero-sum fiscal situation, often comes from the accounts the Pentagon uses to buy weapons or sustain force readiness. For example, every year, over $1 billion is added for medical research, $85 million for various education programs and grants, $50 million for the National Guard Youth Challenge Program, $53 million for DOD Starbase (a STEM education program for grade school children), and $25 million for natural resource management.[14] These efforts may be worthwhile, but it would be hard to argue that this spending is more important to military capability than addressing the numerous warfighting shortfalls in unfunded priorities that the nation's senior military leaders list each year.

Assigning all these responsibilities to DOD inflates perceptions of the nation's security spending and diverts attention from military capabilities. Every time a new mission is assigned to DOD, it must manage, plan, execute, assess, and report on the activity. This draws time and resources from the core defense mission: preparing for, fighting, and winning America's wars.

It remains crucial for agencies with complementary missions—such as the Departments of Defense, Energy, Homeland Security, and State—to work closely together. And though some of these separate missions and agencies could arguably be consolidated, this should not be done by putting the budget for one agency with distinct responsibilities—and accountabilities—into another agency's budget and organizational structure.

There is also a second-order corrosive effect of deferring to defense planning, management, and response expertise. Assigning nondefense missions to the Pentagon has ramifications for civilian-military relations. As the military is asked to perform nonmilitary activities, the lines between military and civilian roles and responsibilities blur, which risks damaging the military's historical, appropriate place in society as the nation's warfighting force.

Making Spending on Military Capability More Transparent. Solving the defense budget transparency and misalignment problems is straightforward, involving two basic steps. But it is not easy, as it will require cooperation by DOD, the Office of Management and Budget, and Congress.

First, we need to clear out the noncore-mission programs and activities that have complicated the budget structure and pulled resources and attention from core defense programs. We should align environmental, energy, education, security assistance, and civilian medical research programs with their relevant organizations. If such programs are deemed lower priority, we should terminate them, at least at the federal level. If, like the commissaries, they can be better run while improving service, we should not hesitate to test and make changes. We should then move entitlement-like spending that is embedded in the defense budget—for things like health care, compensation and benefits, military and civilian pay, and operational support—to a separate mandatory budget for management and execution.[15]

Once those two things are done (which, with sufficient support, could be accomplished in a few budget cycles), we will have a clearer picture of the $348 billion in actual defense discretionary spending. We should then restructure the budget to support the most effective program management and to easily—and automatically—answer key management and oversight questions. This effort falls under budget reform and will be easier once the first two steps are taken.

Even the most productive and successful defense budgeting modernization effort for speed, agility, responsiveness, and transparency won't matter without budget agreements that enable timely enactment of annual appropriations. This brings us to the second main attribute necessary for getting the most out of each defense dollar—predictability.

Predictability

The Waste and Consequences of Delayed Funding and Unpredictable Budgets. The second key driver of defense budgeting waste and confusion is the dual failure of the annual federal budget and appropriations processes.

In 2011, the country was faced with such increasingly high deficits (some of which were created by these processes) that, under the Budget Control Act, the Joint Select Committee on Deficit Reduction was formed to fix it. As an incentive, the act specified that if the commission failed to reduce the deficit, draconian and arbitrary cuts known as "sequestration" would be made.

No one expected the commission to fail, but it did, and in January 2013, sequestration began. Starting in December 2013, Congress reached a series of two-year bipartisan budget agreements to set funding caps above the Budget Control Act's limits. These agreements demonstrated that setting discretionary budget caps in advance of the budget year is actually possible. Such multiyear budget agreements should happen regularly to establish discretionary funding targets without incurring damage like that caused by the Budget Control Act, from which defense readiness and modernization are still recovering today.

Continuing Resolutions. The second and related key expression of federal fiscal failure is the annual appropriations process. When Congress fails to pass 12 separate pieces of funding legislation, it resorts to temporary stopgap funding measures known as continuing resolutions (CRs), which extend the previous year's funding and priorities into the new fiscal year and restrict new spending. Otherwise, the federal government experiences a lapse in appropriations and shuts down.

The consequences of delayed funding and CRs can be dire—including significant and unnecessary costs to taxpayers, lost lives, poor living conditions for United States service members, and delayed contracts necessary to procure and manufacture the defense equipment and technology we need.

The nation has lost five of the past 15 years to avoidable and wasteful CRs.[16] During this time, defense programs, activities, contracts, innovation, and personnel have stagnated when the nation could—and should—have been advancing military competitiveness. Without funding for new priorities, the Pentagon must incrementally fund what it needs, driving up the costs of goods and services and burning time we can't afford to lose. In fact, the taxpayer has lost nearly $68 billion in buying power under CRs in the past two years alone. This does not include the increased costs of incrementally funding contracts or the widespread impact on anyone who works on or for military bases across the country.[17]

In 2023 alone, 33 service members were killed in training-related accidents. Nine soldiers perished when two HH-60 Black Hawk helicopters crashed during a nighttime training accident in Kentucky.[18] Eight Air Force special operators were killed in a CV-22 Osprey crash in Japan during a training mission.[19] Similar stories account for the other deaths during air refueling, parachute, and other training missions.[20]

Military training accidents can have many causes, but it is clear that delayed and unpredictable funding disrupts training schedules and, as a result, affects the safety of our service members. Consistent training and meticulous care of equipment are cornerstones of an effective, professional, and safe military. These standards are more difficult to uphold when funding is uncertain or indefinitely delayed.

Further piling onto the avoidable problems attributed to budgetary unpredictability is the impact on the maintenance of facilities where our uniformed personnel live and work. The restrictions on new funding under CRs mean that no new military construction projects are awarded until regular appropriations are enacted. This affects family housing, which is already widely known to have many serious problems, including safety risks, sewage overflows, inoperable fire systems, broken windows, bug infestations, cold showers, inadequate heating or cooling, and mold. The Pentagon is trying to make improvements, but insufficient, inconsistent, delayed funding for this fundamental and fixable need undermines force readiness, harming America's security.

The impacts of budget uncertainty and delays in annual appropriations cascade into the industrial base and supply chain, since unpredictable— or missing—demand signals and incremental contracting result in acquisition strategies that must hedge against various budget topline scenarios. Alliances and partnerships also suffer from budget uncertainty, which delays exercises and forces foreign militaries to hedge their bets on sales we may be unable to fulfill on time. Without annual funding, the Pentagon can't award contracts. As a result, industry, the workforce, and the supply chain wait, and the health and resilience of the entire system withers. Meanwhile, America's military equipment ages, becoming more expensive to maintain.

A CR's customary resolution is an omnibus appropriations bill covering all (or large portions of) federal spending. Such legislation—which typically contains thousands of pages and awards trillions of dollars of funding—forces members of Congress to vote with little knowledge of its contents. This leaves the public largely in the dark as to how national security is funded and what it costs.

It is hard to imagine a way to inflict more expensive, avoidable harm to the American economy and military competitiveness than what we see each year during the annual appropriations process. Imagine running a race and spending one-third of it looking for your shoes. What are your chances of winning?

Budget Agreements and Defense Planning, Programming, Budgeting, and Execution. Planning and programming without a budget often result in strategy-resource mismatches and contingency planning, which waste time and inhibit good decision-making.

In turning strategic direction into military capability, the military starts planning and programming years before the budget request is actually submitted to Congress. This advance planning is necessary, but it would be more effective if budget agreements set topline discretionary funding levels, even if those caps are modified during the process. Instead, when the DOD begins planning its budget, it often faces three years of uncertainty before the budget even reaches Congress. For example, as the Pentagon plans programs that will be in the FY2027 budget request, it is operating under a CR for FY2025 and is in the budgeting phase of programs for FY2026, which has an unknown topline (Figure 2). This makes such planning a shot in the dark at a near-fictional budget future.

This mismatch leads to numerous hedging and contingency strategies in budgeting and acquisition that spread uncertainty, and therefore inefficiency, throughout the system. Innovation, manufacturing, construction, and even education and training are all subject to best-guess planning, which increases costs and reduces responsiveness. If we wonder why the federal government—and the Pentagon in particular—can't make smarter decisions, this is a key reason. Consistent, predictable budget agreements and funding would yield more informed decision-making and better contract negotiations.

Budgeting—particularly any Future Years Defense Program projections that the Pentagon is required to produce—is also inhibited by delayed annual funding and general budget uncertainty. For example, it is now common for agencies to operate under temporary funding measures, as mentioned above, while making decisions for the next budget year and building programs for the next five years. Programs are unlikely to be executed as envisioned while they wait for defense appropriations, yet the ability to execute them is being used to evaluate program performance and inform future budget estimates.

The Pentagon cannot get the best deals if it does not know how much it will be buying or even whether Congress will approve what it proposes to buy. Acquisition strategies rely on contracts that are unlikely to even be awarded within the first two quarters of the fiscal year (thanks to CRs). As a result, opportunities for accelerating innovation are lost, the technological "valley of death" between developing and implementing promising solutions to evolving military problems—like counter-drone warfare—widens, and the department is forced into incrementally funded, year-by-year procurement deals. This inflates unit costs due to uncertain or

Figure 2. The Impact of Budget Uncertainty on Defense Planning, Programming, Budgeting, and Execution

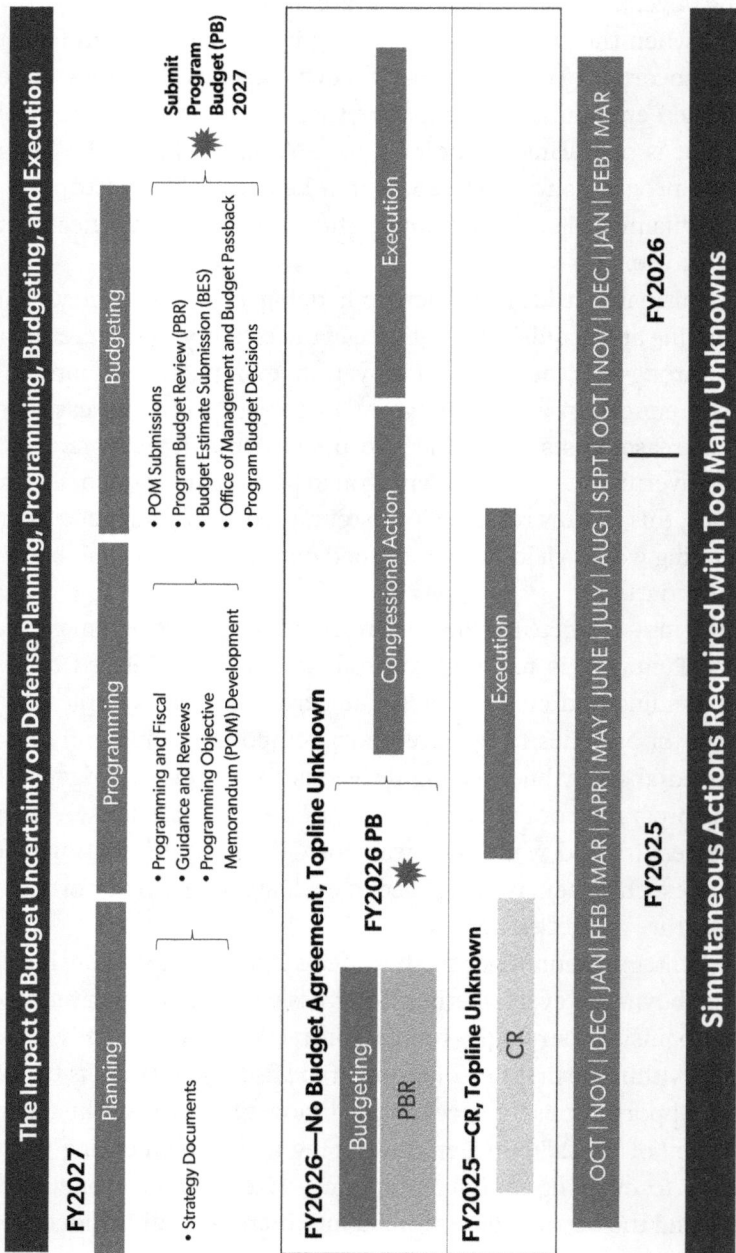

The Impact of Budget Uncertainty on Defense Planning, Programming, Budgeting, and Execution

FY2027

Planning | Programming | Budgeting

Submit Program Budget (PB) 2027

- Strategy Documents

- Programming and Fiscal Guidance and Reviews
- Programming Objective Memorandum (POM) Development

- POM Submissions
- Program Budget Review (PBR)
- Budget Estimate Submission (BES)
- Office of Management and Budget Passback
- Program Budget Decisions

FY2026—No Budget Agreement, Topline Unknown

Budgeting | FY2026 PB
PBR

Congressional Action | Execution

FY2025—CR, Topline Unknown

CR | Execution

OCT | NOV | DEC | JAN| FEB | MAR | APR | MAY | JUNE | JULY | AUG | SEPT | OCT | NOV | DEC | JAN | FEB | MAR

FY2025 | FY2026

Simultaneous Actions Required with Too Many Unknowns

Source: Author.

truncated orders, which is not exactly a recipe for a good return on what should be strong buying power.

In the end, the self-inflicted wound of uncertain and delayed budgets results in a less ready, less modern, and less resilient force; a more vulnerable and costly industrial base; and a public that does not have the visibility and security it deserves. All this is funded by a budget loaded with tangential missions and must-pay bills that are financed in the least cost-efficient manner.

Fixing the Budget Uncertainty Problem. Similar to improving budget transparency and responsiveness, solving the budget uncertainty problem to get the best return on the defense investment requires close partnership with—and action from—Congress.

To support effective planning by defense program and budget experts and the industrial base, we must know what the budget is, and it must be enacted on time. This requires the right incentives in the right places.

The penalty for not reaching budget agreements or passing annual appropriations on time should be directed at those with the power to make the change and the responsibility to do so. Our elected officials seem to recognize the importance of regularly developing and approving annual government spending legislation. For instance, the Fiscal Responsibility Act, which was enacted in 2023 to raise the debt limit and set budget caps for 2024 and 2025, included a penalty for failing to enact regular appropriations bills by the start of the calendar year.[21] But though this nod to the importance of finishing work on time was admirable, it did not prove valuable. In fact, the penalty for failure—further reductions to an already insufficient defense budget—was imposed on the nation's security and not on the elected officials in a position to do something about it.[22]

However, creating penalties and incentives was the right tactic. If Congress agrees it should avoid CRs, it should make governing this way so toxic that it stops happening. There are three complementary ways to get serious about this approach.

First, suggestions that Congress should not pay itself if it does not perform its fundamental duty on time have been ignored. But they are key to breaking the current pattern. Congressional pay should be linked to completing appropriations on time. For each week of delay after the start of the fiscal year, Congress should impose a 10 percent pay cut on itself until it enacts final appropriations.

Second, term limits should be linked to job performance—meaning accomplishing the fundamental duty of passing annual federal funding legislation on time each year. One way to do this is to connect running for reelection to some minimum successful outcome on behalf of the American taxpayer. Elected representatives and senators should agree that if they miss budget deadlines in any three years of a six-year cycle, they will not run for office in the next election.

Third, after the new fiscal year starts on October 1, if annual appropriations are not done, then all other congressional priorities should halt until they are. Congress could include this directive in a budget reconciliation measure—making clear that until annual appropriations are enacted, there will be no action on other legislation. During this time, the DOD will not be required to submit any congressional reports or provide witnesses for hearings. And no government-supported congressional or senior leader travel will be conducted.

Implementing these three incentives would clarify the importance of Congress fulfilling its most fundamental job on time, involve every member of Congress (not just those in leadership or on appropriations committees), and save taxpayers billions that is lost annually under CRs.

Conclusion

Solving the lack of budget transparency and predictability that obscure the affordability of American national security and waste money require fearless leadership and close partnership among the Pentagon, the White House, and Congress to prioritize America's defense.

Transparency and predictability can save money and improve Americans' understanding of what our military costs. To achieve these two interconnected attributes, policymakers should take four actions. First, stop loading the defense budget with items that do not produce military capability. Second, treat must-pay defense bills as what they are, mandatory spending. Third, de-link defense spending from nonsensical discussions about parity, and routinely and consistently pass budget agreements that set discretionary spending toplines. Fourth, create tangible incentives and penalties for causing uncertain and delayed budgets, thus eliminating huge, delayed omnibus spending measures. In summary, put America's security first, and get the best price for what the country buys.

Notes

1. Beacon Research, "US National Survey of Foreign Policy Attitudes on Behalf of the Ronald Reagan Institute," November 14, 2024, https://www.reaganfoundation. org/reagan-institute/centers/freedom-democracy/survey/reagan-institute-summer-survey-2024.

2. US Const. art. IV, § 4; and US Const. art. I, § 10.

3. Jane Harman et al., *Commission on the National Defense Strategy*, RAND Corporation, July 29, 2024, v, https://www.rand.org/nsrd/projects/NDS-commission.html.

4. Harman et al., *Commission on the National Defense Strategy*, viii.

5. Madelyn R. Creedon et al., *America's Strategic Posture: The Final Report of the Congressional Commission on the Strategic Posture of the United States*, Institute for Defense Analyses, October 2023, v, https://www.ida.org/research-and-publications/publications/all/a/am/americas-strategic-posture.

6. Elaine McCusker, "The Potential National Security Consequences of Unplanned Domestic Military Missions," *Lawfare*, September 26, 2024, https://www.lawfaremedia. org/article/the-potential-national-security-consequences-of-unplanned-domestic-military-missions.

7. Elaine McCusker, "2025 Defense Budget Request—Substance v. Spin," *AEIdeas*, March 12, 2024, https://www.aei.org/foreign-and-defense-policy/2025-defense-budget-request-substance-v-spin/; and US Department of Defense, *2022 National Defense Strategy of the United States of America*, October 27, 2022, https://media.defense.gov/2022/Oct/27/2003103845/-1/-1/1/2022-NATIONAL-DEFENSE-STRATEGY-NPR-MDR.PDF.

8. US Department of Defense, Office of the Under Secretary of Defense (Comptroller), "Defense Wide Budget Documentation—FY2025," https://comptroller. defense.gov/Budget-Materials/Budget2025/.

9. US Department of Defense, Under Secretary of Defense (Comptroller), *Department of Defense Operation and Maintenance, Defense-Wide Fiscal Year (FY) 2025 Budget Estimates: Summary by Agency*, https://comptroller.defense.gov/Portals/45/Documents/defbudget/FY2025/budget_justification/pdfs/01_Operation_and_Maintenance/O_M_VOL_1_PART_1/Summary_by_Agency_(Part_1).pdf.

10. US Department of Defense, Defense Commissary Agency, *Operating and Capital Budget: Fiscal Year (FY) 2025 Budget Estimates*, February 2024, https://comptroller. defense.gov/Portals/45/Documents/defbudget/FY2025/budget_justification/pdfs/06_Defense_Working_Capital_Fund/DeCA_PB25_J-Book.pdf.

11. Elaine McCusker, "Should Military Commissaries Be Privatized? Yes . . . ," Ripon Forum, November 2024, https://www.aei.org/op-eds/appreciating-servicemembers-and-veterans-through-a-better-commissary-benefit/.

12. Elaine McCusker, "It's Past Time to Unleash the Defense Commissaries," *Military Times*, July 26, 2023, https://www.militarytimes.com/opinion/2023/07/26/its-past-time-to-unleash-the-defense-commissaries/.

13. US Department of Defense, Office of Prepublication and Security Review, *Defense Health Program: Fiscal Year (FY) 2025 President's Budget, Operation and Maintenance Procurement, Research, Development, Test and Evaluation*, March 2024, https://comptroller.defense.gov/Portals/45/Documents/defbudget/FY2025/budget_justification/pdfs/09_Defense_Health_Program/00-DHP_Vols_I_and_II_PB25.pdf.

14. H.R. 9747, 118th Cong. (2025).

15. Mackenzie Eaglen, "For Better Defense Spending, Split the Pentagon's Budget into Two," *The Hill*, February 15, 2023, https://thehill.com/opinion/national-security/3859140-for-better-defense-spending-split-the-pentagons-budget-into-two/.

16. Elaine McCusker, "Are We Paying for Performance," *AEIdeas*, September 24, 2024, https://www.aei.org/foreign-and-defense-policy/are-we-paying-for-performance/.

17. Elaine McCusker, *2024 Continuing Resolution: Defense Losing $300 Million per Day in Buying Power*, American Enterprise Institute, January 25, 2024, https://www.aei.org/wp-content/uploads/2024/01/McCusker-Buying-Power-One-Pager-Final.pdf.

18. Sharon Johnson et al., "9 Killed in Army Black Hawk Helicopter Crash in Kentucky," Associated Press, March 30, 2023, https://apnews.com/article/us-military-helicopters-crash-kentucky-89c9dbcd035b3cc7c637c2b1f0a037a2.

19. Courtney Mabeus-Brown, "Air Force Ends Effort to Recover Final Member of Downed Osprey's Crew," *Air Force Times*, January 11, 2024, https://www.airforcetimes.com/news/your-air-force/2024/01/12/air-force-ends-effort-to-recover-final-member-of-downed-ospreys-crew/.

20. Lolita C. Baldor, "US Military Aircraft Crashes over Eastern Mediterranean Sea," Associated Press, November 11, 2023, https://apnews.com/article/military-aircraft-crash-mediterranean-50b45d9fc4956ede96076a7d21f42eb4; Gidget Fuentes, "Parachuting Accident Claims Life of Navy SEAL," US Naval Institute, February 22, 2023, https://news.usni.org/2023/02/22/parachuting-accident-claims-life-of-navy-seal; Jessica Edwards and Davis Winkie, "Three Dead After Two Apache Helicopters Collide in Alaska," *Army Times*, April 27, 2023, https://www.armytimes.com/news/your-army/2023/04/28/two-apache-helicopters-crash-in-alaska/; and US Marine Corps, "15th MEU Identifies Marine Killed in Rollover at Camp Pendleton," press release, December 14, 2023, https://www.15thmeu.marines.mil/News/Press-Releases/Announcement/Article/3617925/15th-meu-identifies-marine-killed-in-rollover-at-camp-pendleton/.

21. Fiscal Responsibility Act of 2023, Pub. L. No. 118-5.

22. Elaine McCusker and John G. Ferrari, "Budget Endgame Scenarios: From Acceptable to Apocalypse," *Breaking Defense*, August 28, 2023, https://breakingdefense.com/2023/08/budget-endgame-scenarios-from-acceptable-to-apocalypse/.

8

Toward a Western Pacific Defense Concept

DAN BLUMENTHAL

The People's Republic of China's (PRC's) military buildup, the largest and most comprehensive military modernization program since World War II, is well into its third decade. It is arguably the single most important driver of the epochal change in international politics that has ended US military predominance. China has shifted the military balance in its favor in the western Pacific, which is, together with Europe, the world's most vital region.

The PRC does not hide its grand ambitions to remake the world order or its perception that the United States is the one country that stands in its way. Indeed, Chinese Communist Party (CCP) General Secretary Xi Jinping has emphasized to his cadre that the current period is one of "protracted struggle" as the US slowly wakes from its slumber regarding China's rise and resists China's growing power and influence.[1] In March 2023, Xi told delegates to the Chinese People's Political Consultative Conference that "Western countries led by the United States have implemented comprehensive containment, encirclement, and suppression against us, bringing unprecedented severe challenges to our country's development."[2]

The PRC's strategy is to overcome this perceived containment and build its sphere of influence by harnessing and accumulating national power and coercive leverage. Beijing already uses coercive force to advance its interests but may escalate its low-intensity conflicts into an all-out war for primacy in the Pacific. The US and its allies need a defense strategy that deters China from intensifying its aggression by moving from its ongoing campaigns of coercion into a full-scale war to break the US alliance system.

This chapter builds on the work of Andrew Krepinevich and the Center for Strategic and Budgetary Assessments to develop an operational concept for a coalition of US alliances and partners to defend the western

Pacific.[3] Such a concept can help policy leaders in Congress and the executive branch focus their diplomatic and economic statecraft efforts and properly resource national defense.[4] The diplomatic tasks of stitching together a global coalition to deter a major Chinese attack are immense. But such efforts can be enhanced when diplomats know more specifically what each potential coalition partner needs and when the US and others are willing to pay the economic and other costs of forming a coalition. While Australia, Japan, and the US must form the core of the coalition, many other countries are needed to effectively defend the western Pacific from Chinese hegemony.

Breaking alliances and replacing them with security partnerships that place China at the center of geopolitics is an oft-stated Chinese grand-strategic goal. Indeed, Chinese aspirations for hegemony cannot be achieved if the US alliance system is still operable. That is why alliance-breaking goals were central to Xi's announcement of a "new era" of geopolitics in 2017.[5]

Beijing has two options to break the alliance system. It can continue to pursue its current strategy, which includes supporting Russia's attempts to fracture NATO while China coerces and pressures its own neighbors into obeisance, or it can go to war against the US and its allies and win decisively. Beijing may start such a war against Taiwan, the Philippines, or even Japan.[6] But Taiwan is the most likely place China would attack to start a war that breaks the alliances. And as this chapter demonstrates, China cannot successfully invade and occupy Taiwan without committing acts of war against US allies.[7] Thus, a Chinese attack on the democratic island is not just a contingency, as CCP propagandists would have it; rather, it would be a major attack on the US alliance system. Indeed, this is likely why China has not yet gone to war.

Unless China achieves the short, sharp victory it is planning, this war will likely become protracted, and the US will need a strategy of exhaustion supplemented by attrition to win it.[8] This will require not only attriting Chinese forces and denying them the ability to invade and occupy Taiwan or other territory but also degrading and depleting China's means of fighting and will to endure. A global coalition will likely be needed to fight a protracted war of exhaustion and attrition based on a Western Pacific Defense Concept (WPDC).

As this chapter shows, the WPDC is not a call for global economic warfare. The WPDC would require the coalition to disrupt, delay, and defeat invasion forces. But in the likelihood that China will not stop fighting after the war's first phases, the WPDC would have to also include blockades of key Chinese sea lines of communication (SLOCs). Indonesia and India, now nonaligned, and Singapore, a wary US military partner, would need to join the coalition. To fight a war of exhaustion, the coalition would have to garner support from China's key commodity suppliers to restrict exports to China and from China's major trade and investment partners to cut commercial relations in wartime.[9] Washington must approach its coalition diplomacy with a sense of urgency, convincing skeptical countries that such preparations need to be put in place now to persuade China not to start a war.

Some might argue that developing a coalition around a warfighting concept puts the operational cart before the strategic horse. However, an effective and realistic alliance operational concept would add immeasurably to the United States' grand-strategic goal of frustrating China's strategic designs and strengthen the US position in Asia. When Admiral Phil Davidson, a former head of the US Indo-Pacific Command, pushed for an Indo-Pacific warfighting concept to stabilize regional deterrence, he said any "new warfighting concept must deliver a similar sense of assurance to our allies and partners today that AirLand Battle provided to NATO member states in Europe in the 70s and 80s."[10] Put another way, while cautious US partners may initially resist a coalition warfighting concept, over time it will reassure them that Washington has a plan to stabilize deterrence. The alternative is a hegemonic China.

Strategic Impediments

Washington is hindered in these efforts for strategic and political reasons beyond the US military's power to resolve. First, there is not necessarily broad agreement in the would-be coalition that China seeks to build a Greater China—incorporating Taiwan; the South China Sea, including islands belonging to Indonesia, Malaysia, the Philippines, Taiwan, and Vietnam; Japan's Senkaku Islands and possibly the Ryukyus; and parts of

Nepal and India[11]—or that China is preparing to fight. The US and the core of the coalition, Japan and Australia, should redouble their diplomatic efforts to persuade their allies that China is preparing to fight a war that will damage all of them. The core partners need only remind their allies of China's strategic history. Contrary to Beijing's propagandistic campaigns to persuade its neighbors that it does not seek forceful hegemony, China's strategic culture evinces a strong belief in the efficacy of using force to achieve strategic goals.

China has a long military history that includes conquests of great masses of territory that it still holds today, including Xinjiang and Tibet. Moreover, after the collapse of dynastic China, the CCP ascended to power through a long and bloody civil war. It then fought wars against the US and South Koreans in Korea, against India, and against Vietnam. Since its 1979 war with Vietnam, China has continuously used force to expand its territory and coerce other countries to submit to its will. Thus, China's post-1993 military modernization program is a continuation of its long military history. Australian, Japanese, and US persuasion efforts must situate China's daily use of coercive power as part of a well-thought-out and deliberate move to Finlandize the western Pacific out to the second island chain.[12]

Second, at a grand-strategic level, the hub-and-spoke bilateral alliance system that emerged after World War II falls short of a collective defense system that can pool allied strength. In contrast to a multilateral defense arrangement like NATO, the hub-and-spoke model is characterized by a dominant, security guarantor "hub" (the United States), which projects power through a series of bilateral alliance "spokes" (US treaty allies and partners). This alliance structure means that even countries aligned with the US about the nature of the threat, such as Australia, Japan, the Philippines, and Taiwan, are not obligated to fight for each other. Other countries, such as Indonesia, Singapore, South Korea, and Vietnam, are more conflicted about their approaches to China and the US. Potential coalition partners that rarely exercise together and hardly engage in combined strategic and operational planning will be ill prepared to fight side by side.

All Indo-Pacific countries also face unrelenting Chinese economic and political influence campaigns to break their will to join a coalition. Even in the Philippines, which is aligning with the US on security, China dominates many key sectors of the economy and can influence politics. This dynamic is even sharper in Indonesia, Malaysia, and Thailand—countries that do not yet see eye to eye with the US on the threat China poses. To truly contain China's expansionism, US grand strategy must not only persuade the broader coalition of China's threat but also form a more collective alliance system. Only by doing so could the US adequately expand and diversify its military posture, be assured that key countries would join a coalition in a major war, and help allies build militaries additive to deterrence.

Third, the US has under-resourced its military power for decades, a problem that must be solved at the political level. The US defense industrial base is in crisis, stretched to the breaking point as it supports allies in Europe and the Middle East in a global conflict while deterring PRC aggression. Defense under-resourcing has been well documented. For example, Senate Armed Services Committee Chairman Roger Wicker released a report that found the US is on track to spend just 3 percent of its gross domestic product on defense, a low not seen since the end of the Cold War. The report states,

> Of all the categories of federal spending defense has actually grown most slowly since 2000. 2024 will be the first time in U.S. history that we will spend more financing the debt than we spend on defense. In 2018, after a lost decade of defense cuts under the Budget Control Act, Congress reset the defense budget, but since then, the defense budget has largely grown with inflation.[13]

The result is a "death spiral" for the Pentagon's buying power, even as the demand for US military power has grown. The report puts it bluntly:

> In short, the overall mission tasking assigned to the U.S. military has grown significantly since the early 1980s, but the capacity of the armed forces has shrunk precipitously. The clearest examples of this phenomenon are in the U.S. Navy fleet and the U.S. Air Force aircraft fleets.[14]

The US nuclear submarine fleet, which is, together with the long-range bomber fleet, the most important capability in the western Pacific, is retiring faster than it can be recapitalized. The mix of tremendous Chinese firepower, China's top-tier battle network and associated surveillance and reconnaissance, and the distances US military assets need to travel from relatively safe zones to the center of the fight mean coalition bombers and attack submarines will be the workhorses of a coalition warfighting strategy. But due to inadequate recapitalization, "one third of the navy's attack submarines are idle at depot maintenance shipyards."[15] Similarly, due to maintenance problems, a large portion of the bomber fleet is not mission capable. Nor are these two services buying sufficient munitions to support their missions. US military and weapons stockpiles shrank after the Cold War, with the government purchasing smaller stockpiles supplemented by just-in-time production.

This has resulted in a boom-and-bust cycle of procurement that sees a ramp-up in purchases when needed during conflicts to a quick de-prioritization following the conflict's conclusion.[16] Stop-and-go weapons procurement has resulted in another death spiral of acquisitions, as a lack of purchasing stability has disincentivized the industry from "investing in facilities, modernization, or advanced manufacturing capabilities." Due to this, the industrial base is now unable to surge production when needed.[17]

Finally, Taiwan, the most likely place China would start a conflict, is not part of a regional security architecture or US alliance system. The US cooperates with Taiwan based on the Taiwan Relations Act, which authorizes de facto diplomatic relations and security assistance.[18] The United States' official policy on Taiwan's defense is "strategic ambiguity," meaning its security commitment to the island is highly contingent. The lack of a formal treaty with Taiwan or ironclad commitment to its defense against aggression, combined with the absence of commitments even similar to the Taiwan Relations Act from any other nation, are substantial obstacles to helping Taipei improve its deterrent posture.[19] Potential coalition partners such as Australia and Japan have almost no security cooperation with the island. The gap between the strategic stakes of a successful defense of Taiwan and the limits on coalition defense cooperation with the island is dangerously wide.

These four problems have stood in the way of the US forming an alliance-centered operational concept similar to what it developed during the Cold War to deter and contain the Soviet Union. Strategically, the US needs to weave together a cohesive warfighting coalition that can deter conflict, properly resource its military, and tie Taiwan into a more cohesive alliance structure. Operationally, the US must think and plan as if it is the late 1970s and early 1980s, after the loss of the Vietnam War. Back then, as now, the US faced the operational challenge of deterring a technologically sophisticated, numerically superior enemy preparing to fight a high-intensity conflict close to its homeland, and a demoralized US military still managed to develop alliance warfighting concepts that resolved what seemed like insurmountable operational challenges.

Like the Chinese today, the Soviets had strategic depth and could operate along interior lines of communication. Through many years of trial and error, the US military developed AirLand Battle and the Follow-On Forces Attack concepts. The basic idea was that smaller frontline allied forces would block and blunt the first wave of Soviet forces while so-called deep-strike forces made of combat aircraft, missiles, and artillery would reinforce frontline forces and defeat the second and third waves of Soviet forces. The US Navy developed a distinct maritime strategy that would secure SLOCs across the Atlantic Ocean to help the US reinforce the front line.

These warfighting concepts helped focus US diplomacy and defense strategy and helped Department of Defense managers develop specific defense programs. Diplomats and statesmen knew what type of access agreements to negotiate and could focus diplomatic efforts on keeping European partners aligned around a very forward-leaning concept of deterrence. Civilian defense officials could prioritize the procurement and training that would support the alliance's operational concept. In that era, the Department of Defense and the defense industry developed the Army Tactical Missile System, Apaches, and advanced sensors like Global Hawk, among other breakthroughs, all of which are still in use today. All these systems served the warfighting concept. It was the beginning of the American formation of its precision reconnaissance strike complex that it used to great effect in subsequent wars. This was the result of the US military solving dangerous operational challenges in the Cold War's central front. The US can rise to the occasion again.

How China Wants to Fight: Across Domains; Short and Sharp.
Designing a coalition warfighting concept requires an understanding of
how China wants to fight an alliance-breaking war. China plans on fighting
a short, sharp war that delivers a rapid knockout blow to its enemies. It
is practicing multi-domain operations to leverage surprise, using its home
court advantage to fight on interior lines, and taking advantage of US allies'
lack of strategic depth. The allies have only a relatively small forward-
deployed force in the first island chain, far away from reinforcements.[20]

Chinese military doctrine emphasizes the need to strike first to surprise the enemy, set the operational tempo, and achieve victory before
suffering heavy losses.[21] The People's Liberation Army (PLA) has developed an operational concept, translated as the "Joint Island Landing
Campaign," to project decisive power in the first island chain. This strategic plan requires mutually reinforcing operations that dominate the
information, electromagnetic, air, and maritime domains to support the
projection and sustainment of combat forces that will seize and control
territory.[22] Absent the ability to seize and control territory, the PLA is
unlikely to succeed.[23]

Given the aforementioned massive modernization program, the PLA
can now amass enormous combat power in the first island chain. According to Robert Haddick, retired Rear Admiral Mark Montgomery, and Isaac
"Ike" Harris, the PLA now has more warships than any navy in the world,
the most airpower in Asia, and the greatest inventory of missile power in
the Indo-Pacific.[24] It has developed the sophisticated reconnaissance and
command and control systems necessary for high-tech and high-intensity
military operations. According to the authors,

> The result is a region spanning battle network, combining sen-
> sors and long-range missiles, that is specifically designed to
> destroy US naval forces underway out to Guam and the Second
> Island Chain and to devastate the US military's air and naval
> bases in the Western Pacific.[25]

The authors estimate that the PLA Air Force can launch 1,400 precision-
guided land attack and anti-ship missiles per day, "day after day," at allied
bases and warships up to 3,000 kilometers from the Chinese coast—

a distance that encompasses the second island chain. In addition, in 2023, the Department of Defense estimated that the PLA has up to 2,800 land-based surface-to-surface ballistic and cruise missiles, some of which are capable of precision attacks against Guam. The PLA Navy has an equally large number of cruise missiles in its arsenal.[26] This amounts to massive firepower knitted together by a very sophisticated battle network.

Should China decide that control of Taiwan is its first and main target, it would need to establish sea control across the Taiwan Strait by fighting in and dominating multiple domains. As Krepinevich has outlined, local sea control would require not only warships and submarines but also space, cyber, and electromagnetic capabilities to jam communications, corrupt data, interfere with logistics systems, and blind satellites.[27] Early in a conflict, the PLA would attempt to cripple the coalition's central nervous system—its battle network. The PLA would likely attack forward-deployed coalition forces, including air and naval bases, missile bases, aircraft carriers, and large warships. It would seek to suppress and destroy allied integrated air and missile defense systems. If the PLA crippled coalition forces in the first island chain, it would set the conditions for a massive invasion force to get across the strait and decisively defeat coalition forces on Taiwan.

The Five Ds of Success: Deter, Delay, Disrupt, Defend, and Defeat. To defeat this likely war plan, the US-allied warfighting concept should organize, train, and equip to *deter*, *delay*, and *disrupt* PLA forces before counterattacking to *defend* and *defeat*.[28] Although the coalition should make every effort to *deter* Chinese aggression in the region, the following strategy assumes that deterrence has failed and coalition forces must therefore implement strategies focused on the remaining four Ds.

Coalition forces on the front lines of a Chinese conflict—those in Japan, the Philippines, and Taiwan—must *delay* and *disrupt* invasion forces. US doctrine defines delaying actions as operations "under pressure [that trade] space for time by slowing down the enemy's momentum and inflicting maximum damage on enemy forces without becoming decisively engaged."[29] During these initial operations, frontline delaying and disrupting forces do not need decisive victories. Rather, they need to buy time for air and sea power to engage decisively from safer zones originating from Guam, other Pacific territories, Australia, Hawaii, and the continental United States.[30]

Delaying and disrupting actions buys the coalition time to *defend* and ultimately *defeat* Chinese invasion forces. In the initial phases of a conflict, coalition forces must create the conditions for reinforcing forces to move to a counteroffensive that attrits Chinese forces and exhausts China's means of continuing to fight.

Phase I: Delay and Disrupt—a Strategy to Buy Time

To buy time for a counteroffensive, coalition "delay and disrupt" forces must be trained and equipped to contest Chinese attempts at air superiority, sea control, and information dominance and to disrupt attempts to come ashore and establish a lodgment.[31] As they conduct these operations, the coalition forces can begin to mass air and naval forces outside this Chinese kill zone where they enjoy some sanctuary from Chinese missile ranges.

Therefore, the coalition must increase the quantity of US and allied ground forces equipped with cruise and ballistic missiles. Lethal, dispersed mobile and networked allied ground forces along the first island chain should be backed by naval, air, and electronic forces that can maximally disrupt a Chinese invasion force.[32] A new alliance warfighting concept would transform islands in the first island chain into defensive strongpoints that can withstand Chinese assaults.[33] This force structure would also begin to incorporate an emerging tactical reconnaissance strike complex (TRSC) used to great effect by Ukraine and Russia. A term coined by Frederick W. Kagan of the American Enterprise Institute and Kimberly Kagan of the Institute for the Study of War, the TRSC is

> the combination of pervasive tactical reconnaissance, primarily by drone; drone-corrected precision artillery fire; precision munitions delivered by fixed- and/or rotary-wing aircraft; drone-launched precision munitions; and large numbers of FPV [first-person view] loitering munitions with support from extensive offensive and defensive electronic warfare systems and operational and strategic reconnaissance assets.[34]

This TRSC—which has highly developed, layered integrated air and missile defense systems—has reduced the effectiveness of mass air and missile strikes in a cost-effective manner. It has also reduced the effectiveness of operational-level maneuver.[35] This development could be promising for defense against amphibious forces. While the millions of aerial drones buzzing around the battlefields of Ukraine have not been used at scale to sink ships, properly repurposed, they could wreak havoc on a maritime invasion force, potentially achieving many mission kills in the maritime domain.

Frontline forces must build up sea-denial capabilities that degrade Chinese maritime forces so they cannot successfully land invasion forces on allied territory. Frontline forces also must prevent a maritime break-out that allows the PLA Navy to cut off the SLOCs for reinforcing forces. Diplomats must keep working toward tighter coordination among Japan, Taiwan, and Southeast Asia to limit PRC entry into the Pacific and Indian Oceans.

Fundamentally, the WPDC requires allied forces to use East Asia's geography to US and allied advantage and exploit China's geography as a vulnerability. China's one, long coastline, which faces US allies, potentially limits its routes into the Pacific and Indian Oceans. Denying this access is key to the success of allied defeat and defend missions. In initial phases, the coalition must keep its own SLOCs open so reinforcements can flow to the front lines. Right now, the coalition is in a disadvantageous position, as China's ongoing hybrid warfare has militarized the South China Sea islands, removing strategic depth while extending the range of Chinese fires.

Ground forces are critical not just in denying air and sea control to Chinese forces. Frontline ground forces from the Philippines and Taiwan (and possibly Vietnam), where China may seek to grab territory, should also be trained in irregular warfare so they resist occupying forces, a prospect that concerns China's strategic planners. Such forces, augmented by US and coalition special forces, could field what is known in military parlance as advanced precision-guided rockets, artillery, mortars, and missiles. They can use similar tactics to what Hezbollah used against Israel in the 2006 Lebanon war. Hezbollah employed guerrilla and conventional methods, combining irregular and scattered rocket units, a ground force trained to delay Israeli attempts to grab and hold territory and neutralize targets, and a hardened network of tunnels and command bunkers. Hezbollah proved that well-trained and disciplined irregular cells can deny the objectives of a stronger, conventional force that controls the air and the sea and is equipped with heavy armor.[36]

Phase II: Defend and Defeat—a Strategy of Exhaustion

It is safe to assume that if coalition forces succeeded in the first phases of fighting, both sides would continue fighting. The coalition would then move from a strategy of delay and disrupt to a strategy of defend and defeat. Most likely, this would require not only sinking much of the Chinese invasion fleet and destroying its invasion forces but also depleting China's means of offsetting losses and continuing to fight. This strategy would require attriting Chinese forces outside China and, to a limited extent, on the mainland. It also would require economic warfare to degrade China's means to continue to fight.

A new WPDC would thus take advantage of China's position as the world's largest importer of raw materials. Its seaborne imports traverse three straits in East Asia—Lombok, Malacca, and Sunda. Here again, coalition forces could adopt an irregular warfare mindset and make China's massive merchant shipping fleet a vulnerability. Land-based forces could intercept ships heading to China, similar to Houthi tactics in the Red Sea. The Houthis have targeted a key maritime choke point—the Bab al Mandeb strait—with missiles, drones, and unmanned vessels, resulting in disrupted trade and immense pressure on regional powers. Coalition forces could similarly conduct maritime interdiction operations against Chinese vessels at strategic maritime choke points. Indonesia and Singapore are key to such a strategy, and India could support these efforts from the Andaman and Nicobar Islands.[37]

The WPDC would attempt to exploit other Chinese vulnerabilities as well. China has land borders that span 14,000 miles. Its air defenses are heavily focused along its coast, but China cannot discount India's involvement in a major war and would need to dedicate some assets to protecting against such a scenario. If India joined a coalition and continued to focus investment on long-range strikes, China would have to move more of its defensive forces to its west, exhausting more of China's forces. Over time, the WPDC should work to disallow China's complacency over the security of its land borders. A longer-term task for US diplomats is to improve relations with Central Asian states bordering China to get China to divide its finite defense resources. But China is way ahead in this dimension of the competition, as its alliance with Russia is driven in part to secure cooperation on pacifying its land borders.

There is a robust academic debate about whether the US should pursue "deterrence by punishment" or "deterrence by denial."[38] The former would demonstrate to China that it will suffer punishing costs if it starts a war while the latter would demonstrate to China that it cannot achieve its military objectives. The notional WPDC stays clear of the debate. Rather, it recognizes that denying China its initial war aims will not necessarily defeat China's war plans. Exhausting China's means of continuing to fight while attriting its forces without massively targeting the mainland should be the basis of sound strategy. If the Chinese war machine can offset Chinese losses, the war will continue. The WPDC acknowledges that securing cooperation from the nonaligned Indonesia and the wary Singapore will be the most challenging diplomatic tasks.

The Criticality of Japan and Australia. Simply put, without Japan and Australia, there can be no alliance warfighting concept and deterrence in the western Pacific will fail. Japan is critical to every phase of a potential conflict: from providing frontline forces that can delay and disrupt a Chinese invasion to serving as a logistics and sustainment hub for reinforcing forces. To this end, the US and Japan must continue their efforts to diversify basing arrangements and force structure. Fortunately, Japan's defense posture is changing fundamentally. It has been improving defenses along the Ryukyu Islands, which run parallel to China's coast. Forces along this island chain will be equipped with surface-to-air missiles and anti-ship cruise missiles, and Tokyo is extending the ranges of these systems.[39]

Japan has also begun developing longer strike capabilities that can hold Chinese assets operating in the East China Sea at risk. They are also able to hit key military and economic targets along much of China's northern coast. In 2022, Japan changed its policy to allow the Japan Self-Defense Forces to strike enemy bases that are preparing to launch attacks. To this end, Japan's Ministry of Defense is considering developing several types of missiles, including hypersonic missiles, that its forces can launch from land, sea, and air.

In addition, allied use of Australia as a launch point for longer-range attacks, logistics, and sustainment is key. If the SLOCs from forward positions back to the continental US are kept open, the allies can reinforce the front line from bases in Australia, Guam, and other Pacific nations and territories. Australia is a key staging area for long-range forces outside the most lethal parts of the PRC battle network. Long-range bombers and nuclear submarines are key for the initial delay-and-disrupt missions and the counterattack that defeats Chinese invasion forces. A successful Australia-UK-US Agreement program would provide Australia with *Virginia*-class submarines and their equivalent, which the Royal Australian Navy can use to help defend the frontline states in the first island chain and secure SLOCs between the US and Australia. Canberra should also be encouraged to extend its long-range strike capability and provide more firepower to the delay and degrade missions.

Conclusion

The PRC is pursuing a grand strategy that amasses comprehensive power, bending the international governance system to its will, supporting Russia in attempting to fracture NATO, and pursuing alliance breaking in Asia through coercion. Meanwhile it is training and equipping its military for a major war. The US has no chance of winning a war against China without a strong coalition willing to leverage its geography for strategic advantage. Such a coalition must forge an operational concept that survives a massive conventional first strike against frontline states and forces, delays and disrupts Chinese invasion forces, and buys time to organize a decisive defeat. Given China's system-upending grand-strategic goals, it is very unlikely that China would stop fighting if it did not achieve its initial war aims. A fully mobilized PRC would likely continue to fight until it advanced at least some of its strategic objectives.

Thus, after successfully delaying and disrupting Chinese invasion forces, the coalition must be prepared to shift its strategy to one of exhaustion of Chinese means to fight. This would require economic warfare and extended attrition of Chinese forces. While Australia, Japan, and Taiwan are key to the coalition's success, India, Indonesia, the Philippines, Singapore, and Vietnam will also be important in the latter stages of fighting. US security assistance policy should focus on helping Vietnam and the Philippines build their own anti-access and area-denial capabilities to turn the South China Sea into a vulnerability and work with Indonesia and Singapore to deny China the use of key straits for merchant shipping.

The trend lines on building an alliance warfighting concept are mixed. China's influence in many parts of Southeast Asia is growing in strategic locales such as Bangladesh, Cambodia, Myanmar, and Pakistan. It has significant influence in Singapore and Indonesia as well. It has funded the expansion of the Ream Naval Base in Cambodia on the Gulf of Thailand and is expanding a Cambodian airport as well. It is exercising and equipping Thai forces. China is clearly looking for alternative routes into the open oceans. Meanwhile, its success in controlling and militarizing part of the South China Sea has expanded Chinese power while dealing a blow to US prestige. It is also growing its influence in the south Pacific through malign economic influence by providing police and other internal security forces.

A WPDC will not solve all of Washington's challenges in East Asia. But it can give allies a sense of reassurance that China can be defeated in a major war and thus stabilize that deterrence. This will require deft diplomacy, a properly resourced US military, and reshaped and focused security assistance efforts.

Notes

1. Party School of the Central Committee of the Communist Party of China (National Academy of Administration), trans. China Aerospace Studies Institute, *Xijinping xin shidai zhongguo tese shehui zhuyi sixiang jiben wenti* [Basic Issues of Xi Jinping Thought on Socialism with Chinese Characteristics for a New Era], 2023, https://www.airuniversity.af.edu/Portals/10/CASI/documents/Translations/2023-10-30%20ITOW%20Xi%20Jinping%20Thought%20on%20Socialism%20with%20Chinese%20Characteristics%20for%20a%20New%20Era.pdf.

2. *People's Daily*, "Zhèngquè yǐndǎo mínyíng jīngjì jiànkāng fāzhǎn gāo zhìliàng fāzhǎn" [Correctly Guide the Healthy and High-Quality Development of the Private Economy], March 7, 2023, http://paper.people.com.cn/rmrb/html/2023-03/07/nw.D110000renmrb_20230307_1-01.htm.

3. Andrew F. Krepinevich, *Preserving the Balance: A U.S. Eurasia Defense Strategy*, Center for Strategic and Budgetary Assessments, January 19, 2017, https://csbaonline.org/research/publications/preserving-the-balance-a-u.s.-eurasia-defense-strategy/publication/1; and Andrew F. Krepinevich, *Archipelagic Defense 2.0*, Hudson Institute, September 14, 2023, https://s3.amazonaws.com/media.hudson.org/Archipelagic+Defense+2.0+-+Andrew+F.+Krepinevich+Jr+-+September+2023.pdf.

4. To be sure, US military and defense leaders are developing new operational concepts. But a truly alliance-centered defense concept requires efforts by diplomats and economic officials as well.

5. Chinese State Council, "Xijinping jiejian 2017 niandu zhu wai shijie gongzuo huiyi yuhui shijie bing fabiao zhongyao jianghua" [Xi Jinping Meets with Envoys Attending the 2017 Annual Work Conference and Delivers an Important Speech], December 28, 2017, https://www.gov.cn/xinwen/2017-12/28/content_5251251.htm.

6. There are scenarios in which China attacks Vietnam to keep it from growing closer to the US, as it did in 1979, when Vietnam was allying with the Soviets. China also could take advantage of a North Korean attack on South Korea to break that alliance.

7. China cannot succeed in invading Taiwan without a massive attack on Japan, including blockading part of its territory. See Dan Blumenthal, "Is China Preparing to Attack Japan?," *The Hill*, September 20, 2024, https://thehill.com/opinion/4890957-china-japan-missile-attack/.

8. Krepinevich describes the Union strategy of exhaustion in the Civil War in a way that usefully illustrates what would be needed to defeat the PLA. The North, he writes, "gravitated to the view that a war of attrition would be necessary to secure victory—but not sufficient. So it, too, adopted a strategy of exhaustion." Citing Herman Hattaway and Archer Jones, Krepinevich writes that the Union sought

> to exhaust the rebels by occupying territory and gradually depriving them of the resources and recruits for maintaining their armies. Thus, the strategy that ultimately won the war for the North was a version of the Anaconda Plan, which called for the Union to blockade Confederate ports, seize control of the Mississippi River to preclude mutual support between the eastern and western parts of the Confederacy, and destroy the South's transportation infrastructure and arsenals. The strategy, combining exhaustion and direct attrition of the rebel forces through sustained engagement, succeeded in denying the South the ability to offset its combat losses while also convincing the Southern people that they could not achieve their goal of secession.

Krepinevich, *Archipelagic Defense 2.0*, 72. See Herman Hattaway and Archer Jones, *How the North Won: A Military History of the Civil War* (University of Illinois Press, 1991), 19.

9. More research and study are needed on how to degrade China's potential war economy. Such planning would have the added benefit of speeding up efforts on targeted decoupling and building resiliency in peacetime.

10. Quoted in Paul McLeary, "Indo-Pacom Presses All Domain Ops; Sends Plan to Hill Soon," *Breaking Defense*, March 24, 2020, http://breakingdefense.com/2020/03/indo-pacom-presses-all-domain-ops-sends-plan-to-hill-soon/.

11. Krepinevich, *Preserving the Balance*, 21; Michael Bristow, "China Encroaching Along Nepal Border—Report," BBC, February 8, 2022, https://www.bbc.com/news/world-asia-60288007; and Orange Wang, "China Asserts Claim to Indian-Held Arunachal Pradesh in Latest List of Place Names," *South China Morning Post*, March 31, 2024, https://www.scmp.com/news/china/diplomacy/article/3257387/china-asserts-claim-indian-held-arunachal-pradesh-latest-list-place-names.

12. This "chain" of islands includes Japan's Bonin and Volcano Islands southeast of Tokyo; the Mariana Islands, including Guam; and the Caroline Islands, including Palau.

13. Roger Wicker, *21st Century Peace Through Strength: A Generational Investment in the U.S. Military*, May 29, 2024, 8–9, https://www.wicker.senate.gov/services/files/BC957888-0A93-432F-A49E-6202768A9CE0.

14. Wicker, *21st Century Peace Through Strength*, 9.

15. Robert Haddick et al., "Sink China's Navy," in *The Boiling Moat: Urgent Steps to Defend Taiwan*, ed. Matt Pottinger (Hoover Institution Press, 2024), 140.

16. Stacie Pettyjohn and Hannah Dennis, "The Pentagon Isn't Buying Enough Ammo," *Foreign Affairs*, May 21, 2024, https://foreignpolicy.com/2024/05/21/united-states-defense-pentagon-military-industrial-base-ammunition/.

17. Mackenzie Eaglen, "The Pentagon Is a Terrible Customer to Its Industry Partners," *AEIdeas*, October 23, 2024, https://www.aei.org/foreign-and-defense-policy/the-pentagon-is-a-terrible-customer-to-its-industry-partners/.

18. Taiwan Relations Act, 22 U.S.C. § 3301 (1979).

19. Regarding debates for and against strategic ambiguity, see Richard Haass and David Sacks, "American Support for Taiwan Must Be Unambiguous," *Foreign Affairs*, September 24, 2020, https://www.foreignaffairs.com/articles/united-states/american-support-taiwan-must-be-unambiguous; Ivan Kanapathy, "Taiwan Doesn't Need a Formal U.S. Security Guarantee," *Foreign Policy*, April 26, 2022, https://foreignpolicy.com/2022/04/26/taiwan-us-security-guarantee-defense-china-ukraine-war/; and Raymond Kuo, "'Strategic Ambiguity' Has the U.S. and Taiwan Trapped," *Foreign Policy*, January 18, 2023, https://foreignpolicy.com/2023/01/18/taiwan-us-china-strategic-ambiguity-military-strategy-asymmetric-defense-invasion/.

20. The first island chain stretches from the Kamchatka Peninsula in the northeast to the Malay Peninsula in the southwest. It includes the Kuril Islands, the Japanese archipelago, the Ryukyu Islands, Taiwan, and the Philippines.

21. Toshi Yoshihara, "Chinese Missile Strategy and the U.S. Naval Presence in Japan," *Naval War College Review* 63, no. 3 (2010): 39–62, https://digital-commons.usnwc.edu/nwc-review/vol63/iss3/4.

22. US Department of Defense, *Military and Security Developments Involving the People's Republic of China*, 2022, 126–27, https://media.defense.gov/2022/Nov/29/2003122279/-1/-1/1/2022-MILITARY-AND-SECURITY-DEVELOPMENTS-INVOLVING-THE-PEOPLES-REPUBLIC-OF-CHINA.PDF. Thus,

the traditional mentality that land outweighs sea must be abandoned, and great importance has to be attached to managing the seas and oceans and protecting maritime rights and interests. It is necessary for China to develop a modern maritime military force structure commensurate with its national security and development interests, safeguard its national sovereignty and maritime rights and interests, protect the security of strategic SLOCs and overseas interests, and participate in international maritime cooperation, so as to provide strategic support for building itself into a maritime power.

Chinese State Council Information Office, "China's Military Strategy," Xinhua News Agency, May 27, 2015, 137, http://eng.mod.gov.cn/Database/WhitePapers/index.htm; and Dean Cheng, "How China's Thinking About the Next War," *Breaking Defense*, May 19, 2021, http://breakingdefense.com/2021/05/how-chinas-thinking-about-the-next-war/.

23. Short of seizing and occupying territory, China could inflict sufficient coercive pain against US allies to compel them to accept unfavorable peace. But seizing and annexing territory is likely needed to complete the Chinese strategic objectives in an alliance-breaking war.

24. Haddick et al., "Sink China's Navy," 130.

25. Haddick et al., "Sink China's Navy," 132.

26. US Department of Defense, *Military and Security Developments Involving the People's Republic of China*, 2023, https://media.defense.gov/2023/Oct/19/2003323409/-1/-1/1/2023-MILITARY-AND-SECURITY-DEVELOPMENTS-INVOLVING-THE-PEOPLES-REPUBLIC-OF-CHINA.PDF.

27. Krepinevich, *Preserving the Balance*; and Krepinevich, *Archipelagic Defense*, 127.

28. The US military has doctrinal definitions for each of the five Ds. US Department of the Army, *Tactics*, 2023, Glossary-8–Glossary-9, https://armypubs.army.mil/epubs/DR_pubs/DR_a/ARN38160-FM_3-90-000-WEB-1.pdf.

29. US Department of the Army, *Tactics*, Glossary-8.

30. US doctrine states that the delay and disruption of an attack "is appropriate when policy, resource, or risk limitations prevent friendly forces from inflicting greater costs on an enemy or adversary." Joint Chiefs of Staff, *Joint Planning*, 2020, IV-42, https://irp.fas.org/doddir/dod/jp5_0.pdf.

31. Krepinevich, *Archipelagic Defense 2.0*, 106.

32. Thomas G. Mahnken et al., *Tightening the Chain: Implementing a Strategy of Maritime Pressure in the Western Pacific*, Center for Strategic and Budgetary Assessments, 2019, https://csbaonline.org/uploads/documents/Tightening_the_Chain_web_Final.pdf.

33. To be sure, the US Armed Forces are already moving in this direction. See, for example, the concept of Marine Corps "Stand-In Forces." Andrew Feickert, *U.S. Ground Forces in the Indo-Pacific: Background and Issues for Congress*, Congressional Research Service, August 30, 2022, https://crsreports.congress.gov/product/pdf/R/R47096.

34. Riley Bailey and Frederick W. Kagan, *A Defense of Taiwan with Ukrainian Characteristics: Lessons from the War in Ukraine for the Western Pacific*, Institute for the Study of War, October 30, 2024, 10, https://www.understandingwar.org/sites/default/files/A%20

Defense%20of%20Taiwan%20with%20Ukrainian%20Characteristics_0.pdf. See also Frederick W. Kagan and Kimberly Kagan, *Ukraine and the Problem of Restoring Maneuver in Contemporary War*, August 12, 2024, https://www.understandingwar.org/sites/default/files/Ukraine%20and%20the%20Problem%20of%20Restoring%20Maneuver%20in%20Contemporary%20War_final.pdf.

35. Bailey and Kagan, *A Defense of Taiwan with Ukrainian Characteristics*, 3–4.

36. Matt M. Matthews, *We Were Caught Unprepared: The 2006 Hezbollah-Israeli War* (Combat Studies Institute Press, 2008), https://www.armyupress.army.mil/Portals/7/combat-studies-institute/csi-books/we-were-caught-unprepared.pdf. See also Lumpy Lumbaca, "Taiwan: Insurgents Needed," *Small Wars Journal*, May 2, 2024, https://smallwarsjournal.com/2024/05/02/taiwan-insurgents-needed/.

37. Krepinevich, *Archipelagic Defense 2.0*, 134.

38. Both sides' positions in this debate can be explored in Erica D. Borghard et al., "Elevating 'Deterrence by Denial' in US Defense Strategy," Atlantic Council, February 4, 2021, https://www.atlanticcouncil.org/content-series/seizing-the-advantage/elevating-deterrence-by-denial-in-us-defense-strategy/; Jim Derleth and Jeff Pickler, "21st Century Threats Require 21st Century Deterrence," Irregular Warfare Center, September 23, 2024, https://irregularwarfarecenter.org/publications/insights/21st-century-threats-require-21st-century-deterrence/; and Michael J. Mazzar, "Understanding Deterrence," RAND Corporation, 2018, https://www.rand.org/content/dam/rand/pubs/perspectives/PE200/PE295/RAND_PE295.pdf.

39. Krepinevich, *Archipelagic Defense 2.0*, 95.

9

America First in the Indo-Pacific?

ZACK COOPER

To maintain deterrence vis-à-vis China, American defense policy must undergo a fundamental shift in the years ahead. Legacy US investments—fighter aircraft, aircraft carriers, stealth bombers, surface ships, and attack submarines—will be vital to stabilize the military balance in East Asia. But alongside these traditional capabilities, the United States will have to field a new set of systems with which it has much less experience. Long-range missiles, combat-capable autonomous aircraft, and uncrewed undersea vehicles will have to be developed and fielded in large numbers if the United States is to counter China's rapid military modernization. The mix of these large and expensive legacy platforms with cheaper and more expendable systems will be vital to stabilizing the military balance in the region.

Unfortunately, the United States has thus far avoided many of the hard decisions this would require. Trade-offs between readiness, modernization, and force structure are unavoidable unless the United States significantly increases defense budgets. Since US defense spending has remained stagnant when adjusted for inflation, this has not been sufficient to fund both the existing force structure and the development of these new capabilities. The result has been decreases in readiness and delays in modernization while the US force has shrunk. During this period, China has built the world's largest navy and deployed an increasingly advanced set of air and naval capabilities.[1] In short, Beijing has modernized while Washington has muddled through. If deterrence in the western Pacific is to hold, this atrophy cannot continue.

The Hard Realities of the Iron Triangle

The iron triangle of defense choices—force size, modernization, and readiness—dictates that investments in modernization require either additional funding or substantial cuts to force size or readiness. The number of platforms deployed by the US Navy and Air Force has indeed shrunk in recent years, and the readiness of the US military has generally deteriorated.[2] Yet force modernization has progressed only slowly. In short, Washington has adopted a strategy that is the worst of all worlds. It has allowed its legacy forces to shrink and undercut their readiness but has not deployed new forces with the degree of urgency required.

Ten or 20 years ago, the United States might have had the opportunity to make these modernization investments without the threat of an imminent challenge from a near-peer competitor. But today, Russia is fighting the biggest land war in Europe since World War II, and China is posturing the People's Liberation Army to credibly threaten the use of military force against Taiwan within this decade.[3] As a result, the United States cannot afford a decrement in the readiness of its forces. One leg of the iron triangle must therefore be locked in place.

Nor can the United States shrink its force structure dramatically, since it will take time to deploy any newly developed systems. A shift from large, heavy, and expensive units to more nimble ground, naval, and air forces might be in the offing, but until this change happens, legacy forces will remain vital for both deterrence of adversaries and assurance of allies and partners.[4] The US Marine Corps has made rapid changes to its force structure to adapt to this new reality, but as this experience has demonstrated, shifting the mix of forces in a military service usually requires investments in new systems that can be costly to produce.[5]

Some, myself included, have argued that a greater focus on China would necessitate a shift not across the iron triangle but among the US military's services and combatant commands. The needs of the Navy and Air Force might be prioritized in accordance with the more maritime-oriented requirements of the Indo-Pacific Command. But without increased funding, this would mandate major cuts to ground forces, particularly the Army, as well as a number of geographic combatant commands, likely including both European Command and Central Command.

Despite the Army's efforts to demonstrate its value in a China contingency, it is more likely to be a supporting service than a supported service. The US will not contemplate a land invasion of China, given the People's Republic of China's huge population and geographic advantages. Army units may be critical for logistics and some cross-domain capabilities, but these are less central in a US-China conflict than they would be in a ground war.[6] Yet cutting Army force structure while Iran, North Korea, and Russia are cooperating more closely than ever will be a hard sell in Washington.

If US forces are less capable of prevailing over Iran in the Middle East, North Korea on the peninsula, or Russia in Eastern Europe, then US allies and partners will have to pick up more of the burden themselves, and quickly. This is basic math—the United States has few forces in Southern Command and Africa Command, so unless it stops doing certain missions currently addressed by European Command, Central Command, and perhaps even US Forces Korea, it will not be able to make major cuts across its geographic combatant commands. Although there is some discussion today of prioritization, few missions have thus far been jettisoned. Hard choices have not been made, but they remain unavoidable.

Embracing Technological Change

Today, most experts acknowledge that there are two major military shifts occurring simultaneously—one regional and another global. The regional shift (discussed in greater detail below) is that the Chinese People's Liberation Army has rapidly caught up to the militaries of the United States and its allies and partners in the Indo-Pacific. Although differences of opinion remain on whether Beijing is yet capable of defeating US forces in an actual conflict, the margin between the two sides has shrunk dramatically.

At the same time, a global shift has occurred that has called into question the cost-effectiveness of existing US power projection platforms. As the world has witnessed in Afghanistan, Ukraine, Yemen, and elsewhere, it is now possible for countries and even nonstate actors to field expendable unmanned systems that can hold at risk surface ships and forward bases. Many observers have noted that the combination of these two trends means that China is catching up to the United States just as America's legacy forces are more vulnerable and less cost-effective than they have been in decades.

There is, however, a more optimistic take. It is true that China's military modernization creates challenges for the United States and that legacy American forces are more at risk today than they have been for decades. But two factors could work in Washington's favor—if US leaders can recognize and embrace them. First, China is now investing in the same type of power projection platforms—aircraft carriers, forward bases, and so on—that are increasingly vulnerable to cheaper and more expendable systems. Second, the United States is a status quo power, while China's military aims would require it to eject American forces from the region through the use of force or coercion. If China and the United States are both unable to project power effectively and the result is a no-man's-land, then Beijing will not be able to alter the territorial or maritime status quo. These two factors are too often overlooked in Washington's debate about China's rise.

The changes in military technology occurring today have been poorly understood in part because experts have often equated advances in missiles, drones, and other uncrewed systems with advances in technologies that enable offense. If this were correct, then anti-access systems would give revisionist powers an edge and undermine the interests of the United States and other status quo countries. But this is wrong. Advances in autonomy, robotics, and miniaturization do not make it easier to take and hold territory. Rather, they make it easier to deny an opponent the ability to exert control over land or maritime zones. Therefore, the fact that expendable systems are cheaper and more effective today advantages neither offensive nor defensive strategies but rather denial strategies over control strategies.

Consider the lessons from Ukraine. Russia has been able to conduct attacks deep into Ukrainian territory using long-range missiles. This has done tremendous damage. But it has not enabled Russia to rapidly take and hold territory without great risk to its manned forces, which are necessary to sustain a military presence. Moscow's advances in recent years have come at tremendous cost, in part due to the effectiveness of Ukraine's own unmanned systems in denying Russia the ability to generate mass without creating major vulnerabilities. The same was true of US operations in Iraq and Afghanistan. Although US forces had a tremendous edge in many domains, nonstate groups were still able to make it highly costly for American units attempting to control territory. In both cases, denying forces the ability to cheaply occupy territory has become easier due to recent technological advances.

There has long been a debate about whether military technologies advantage the offense or defense. This has typically been framed as the ratio of funding or forces required for the offense to prevail over the defense and has become known as the offense-defense balance. But what has been overlooked is the control-denial balance. This is the ratio of funding or forces required to exert control over territory and maritime zones as compared to those required to deny that control. Recent technological advantages have shifted this control-denial balance by helping the latter at the cost of the former.

In short, one might consider four types of capabilities based on these two balances: offensive control, defensive control, defensive denial, and offensive denial. Offensive control requires sustainable mobility—effectively power projection forces such as aircraft carriers and mobile ground units. Defensive control is most cost-effective with sustainable but immobile systems that can conduct garrison fortification—examples include large, fixed bases and related infrastructure. Defensive denial, on the other hand, can be done through immobile and expendable systems, such as land and sea mines or short-range missiles or drones. Finally, offensive denial necessitates expendable yet mobile systems—longer-range missiles, more advanced drones, and uncrewed naval systems typically associated with anti-access capabilities. Because offensive control through traditional power projection has become more costly, many have assumed that defense has become easier. But the reality is that both offensive and defensive denial are cheaper today than ever before. In other words, technology is advantaging denial, not offense or defense.

This is critical because the United States needs not take new territory. For China to take Taiwan, it must be able to project and sustain power at least 100 miles from its coast. Denial capabilities may be useful for this mission, but they are not sufficient unless Taiwanese leaders capitulate under coercive pressure. If the Communist Party is to take Taiwan by force, it cannot fight to a draw in the Taiwan Strait; it must be able to exert control both on and around the island. Yet the same technological forces that made the People's Liberation Army's anti-access capabilities so fearsome in recent years also allow the United States and its allies and partners to flip the script on Beijing. By embracing smaller, cheaper, and more expendable systems, it might be possible to put China on the wrong side of a cost-imposition strategy and use technological change to America's advantage.

China's Military Modernization

The reason the United States finds itself having to consider a new strategy is that China has moved quickly in recent years, while America has been distracted elsewhere. Since 2008, China has moved decisively toward investments in power projection platforms while still fielding additional anti-access systems.[7] The result is an overlapping mix of capabilities designed to hold at risk US forces in the western Pacific while increasingly exercising control within the first island chain, which runs from Japan to Indonesia. In other words, Beijing has constructed a large anti-access and area-denial bubble stretching from the Chinese mainland over Japan, Guam, and much of Southeast Asia. Inside this area is a smaller bubble in which China will be able to more confidently project power, unless the United States moves expeditiously to hold these forces at risk.

The anti-access bubble was first imagined in the 1990s, after China watched the United States dramatically defeat the Iraqi military in the first Gulf War and then deploy two carrier strike groups to the waters around Taiwan in the 1995–96 Taiwan Strait Crisis.[8] In response, the People's Liberation Army developed a range of new capabilities, headlined by long-range conventional missiles, designed to neutralize US bases in Japan, the Philippines, and Guam before US forces are able to use them as jumping-off points.[9] Maritime strike versions of these ballistic and cruise missiles were also fielded in large numbers to push US aircraft carriers and surface combatants farther from Chinese so-called "near seas" in a conflict's opening days and weeks.[10] If successful, these systems might force the United States to keep many of its most effective air and maritime strike systems far away from the locus of conflict at the outset of combat.

Fighting back through these layered Chinese defenses would be no easy task, but it is made significantly more difficult by the fact that the People's Liberation Army is also fielding new forces designed to project power within this larger bubble. Just a decade ago, the People's Liberation Army Navy would have had difficulty keeping ships on station far from China's shores. Now it is surging forces far from China's coast, with more regular patrols by Chinese aircraft and ships. Perhaps most notable has been Beijing's acquisition of three aircraft carriers, with more on the way, including a more advanced, nuclear-powered version. Meanwhile, China has demonstrated a series of new aircraft, many of which appear to be modeled on existing US aircraft. Combined, these platforms could start to create a power projection bubble inside the western Pacific, particularly if they were operating within China's larger anti-access and area-denial zone.

Finally, the United States increasingly finds itself encountering a Chinese military presence far from China itself. Recent Pentagon reports have suggested that alongside Chinese military basing in Djibouti, there is the prospect of the People's Liberation Army having access to foreign facilities in Cambodia, Pakistan, Peru, Sri Lanka, and the Solomon Islands, to name a few locations. If this comes to pass, then the United States will find itself needing to monitor the Chinese military presence across much of the globe. Washington might still have an edge for several decades globally, given its deep network of alliances and partnerships, but Beijing's ability to field more platforms and offer substantial economic incentives for cooperation could pose a real challenge in the long term.

Thus far, China's growing capabilities and capacity have not been matched by a similar set of American investments. Instead, the United States has actually shrunk key elements of its force in size, as well as decreasing readiness and modernization funds. These trends are not sustainable if the United States is to maintain the military balance in the region and around the world. A new American approach will be necessary.

America's Response Options

The United States has a straightforward, but hard to solve, challenge in the western Pacific: how to offset China's strategic depth and ability to rely on hundreds of regional bases when the United States has only a handful of major bases and a limited network of other access points. There are three potential answers. First, the United States could expand access by persuading current hosts to allow access to new facilities and convincing new countries to open new locations to US forces. Second, the United States could field more systems, such as mobile missile launchers, that can operate from austere locations without long runways or large ports. Third, the United States could try to become less reliant on forward bases by relying more on long-range power projection systems such as aircraft carriers.

Recent US administrations have focused primarily on the first option. Going back to the Obama administration, policymakers in Washington have worked closely with Australia to create new operating locations for some ground, air, and naval forces.[11] US marines now deploy rotationally through Darwin, in northern Australia, while US Navy vessels will operate from Perth, in Western Australia, and US Air Force assets will routinely visit bare bases across the region. In the Trump and Biden administrations, there was progress in deepening discussions with Pacific Islands countries about deploying US forces to some new locations in the Pacific. Most notably, the governments of the Republic of Palau, the Marshall Islands, and the Federated States of Micronesia have all agreed to new compacts of free association with the United States.[12] The United States has entered into arrangements to periodically deploy US forces into some of Japan's southwest islands that have not previously had a US presence. These features—Yonaguni, Ishigaki, Miyako, and others—could provide critical alternatives to bases in Okinawa and other major US facilities in Japan's main islands.[13]

The Biden administration has also made some progress in efforts to field new systems and adopt new operational concepts that are less reliant on large forward bases. Most notably, the US Marine Corps has reoriented itself around Force Design 2030, which will use Marine Littoral Regiments to operate in contested environments via expeditionary advanced base operations.[14] Meanwhile, the US Army is pursuing what it calls the Multi-Domain Battle concept, the US Air Force is implementing the Agile Combat Employment concept, and the US Navy is attempting to implement its Distributed Maritime Operations concept. All four of these concepts are designed to decrease the services' reliance on fixed forward bases and ensure greater resilience. Meanwhile, the Department of Defense more broadly has started to acquire some capabilities that could be cheaper and more expendable. Most notable in this regard is the Replicator initiative, which promises to field thousands of autonomous systems to add to the capabilities of legacy forces, which will remain the dominant elements of the force for the foreseeable future.[15]

The third option, which is to rely more on long-distance power projection systems that are independent of bases, has received less attention. The United States could opt to buy more long-range ships and aircraft (long-range bombers, nuclear-powered attack submarines, or aircraft carriers, for example), but these systems are expensive, and recent administrations have generally opted to keep procurement of these systems as planned, rather than adding to them. The Trump administration could, however, opt to purchase more B-21 bombers and invest in the submarine industrial base through a new Ships Act, which could increase the numbers of long-range platforms that are less reliant on bases near an adversary's territory.

These options are not mutually exclusive. Indeed, the United States will likely have to combine all three options to build the capabilities in the near term that would be needed to maintain a balance during China's rapid military buildup. New operating locations will have to be brought online to decrease US vulnerability to a first-strike attack. Meanwhile, new systems will have to be developed and fielded to increase the firepower that the United States can wield in the opening hours, days, and weeks of a conflict. And Washington will have to simultaneously invest in legacy forces that can be put into the theater quickly but that are less dependent on large forward bases. Together, this mix could stem the declining military balance in East Asia, if not reverse it altogether.

Spurring Allied Differentiation

One heretofore unexamined implication of these challenges is that the United States will want to ask its allies and partners to differentiate their forces more from those fielded by the US military. Washington does not have the luxury of keeping its forces in one location—it must be able to shift between regions and within regions, since it faces multiple challenges around the globe simultaneously. For this purpose, legacy power projection forces will remain critical. Yet because military bureaucracies often prize large and expensive power projection systems and seek to imitate the most advanced military in the world—that of the United States—US allies often attempt to build forces that look like America's. This is understandable and was tolerable in the post–Cold War world, when the United States and its allies and partners retained a substantial edge over any potential military challenger. Today, however, US allies and partners need to differentiate their forces and fill in the gaps that Washington cannot address on its own. Power projection may be a mission that the United States must continue to conduct, but that does not mean that allies and partners should also follow this pathway.

Although it is common for Americans to complain about needing allies and partners to step up, the current situation is in no small measure the fault of US policymakers. Allies and partners must be given clear guidance about the roles, missions, and capabilities that US forces will not be able to conduct on their own. This happens all too infrequently. Indeed, there are incentives for US leaders to push allies and partners to acquire American-made systems to ease interoperability challenges and simplify combined operations. At the same time, allies and partners must have substantial confidence in the United States to show up when needed, or else they will try to duplicate existing US capabilities rather than build forces designed to fill in those capability gaps. This has also been a frequent challenge for policymakers in Washington, who all too often appear to shift their thinking and thereby undermine allied confidence in existing security guarantees.

If these challenges could be overcome, then there would be space for key allies and partners to invest rapidly in a range of denial-focused capabilities. Japan, the Philippines, and Taiwan, in particular, could build out their own anti-access and area-denial capabilities and therefore increase the risk to Chinese forces attempting to operate in and around the first island chain. In other words, while Beijing is busy building capabilities to create a power projection bubble within a larger anti-access bubble in the East Asia littoral, leaders in Washington and friendly capitals could start to divide these roles between the United States and its allies and partners.

No military fields only one type of system. Friendly forces will retain some power projection capabilities just as the United States increases its own denial capabilities. But by dividing missions to a greater degree, the United States and its allies and partners would allocate capabilities more efficiently and be better prepared for a variety of challenges.

There is, however, one major and unavoidable downside to this necessary division of labor: Allies and partners will find themselves more reliant on the United States in some gray-zone situations. Since denial capabilities such as anti-ship missiles are usually expended when used, it is difficult to use them for signaling without escalating a crisis or conflict. Beijing has been highly effective in using its newly constructed power projection platforms—particularly navy, coast guard, and maritime militia vessels—to coerce other countries. If US allies and partners have fewer of their own power projection systems, then they will have to rely more on those of the United States. This would require a change of mindset in both Washington and allied capitals. Rather than allowing Beijing to press its advantage in the gray zone against less capable regional states, US leaders would have to demonstrate a willingness to become more involved at lower levels of escalation. This would be a reversal of current practices, in which US forces largely wait until a certain threshold has been crossed to become involved. This is not an insurmountable challenge, but it would require closer cooperation between the United States and its allies and partners to develop combined strategies and operational concepts to deter China's gray-zone coercion.

Implications for the Next Administration

As is evident from this discussion, there is no silver bullet to America's worsening strategic situation in East Asia. More resources are needed. Existing funds could be used more efficiently, of course, but simply shifting more forces to East Asia will not solve the operational problems that the United States faces today. Allies and partners will need to step up. But they will not be able to match Beijing's military modernization without a major shift in approach from Washington. US leaders will have to find ways to rebuild readiness while they increase the size of America's air and maritime forces and simultaneously modernize key portions of the force to keep up with technological change.

Additional resources must be part of the equation, given that recent efforts at sequestration and prioritization have yielded only limited financial savings. Yet more funding will not solve the problem alone, since part of China's advantage is that the United States has underinvested in a whole suite of capabilities—long-range, conventionally armed missiles, for example—that are critical today. If the US defense enterprise were allocated more resources, there is a danger this would allow the defense community to avoid hard choices and continue to muddle through—that is no longer an option. Administration leaders will have to direct major changes to how the United States builds, maintains, and operates its military. Washington will also have to have related discussions with allies and partners about aligning their own reform efforts with those of the United States. This will be politically challenging and require deep institutional knowledge from American policymakers. These reforms are possible, but US leaders will have to make a clean break with several decades of distraction and dithering. There is no time to waste.

Notes

1. Alexander Palmer et al., "Unpacking China's Naval Buildup," Center for Strategic and International Studies, June 5, 2024, https://www.csis.org/analysis/unpacking-chinas-naval-buildup.

2. Mackenzie Eaglen, "America's Incredible Shrinking Navy," *AEIdeas*, January 18, 2024, https://www.aei.org/foreign-and-defense-policy/americas-incredible-shrinking-navy/.

3. US Department of Defense, Office of the Secretary of Defense, *Military and Security Developments Involving the People's Republic of China 2023*, October 19, 2023, https://media.defense.gov/2023/Oct/19/2003323409/-1/-1/1/2023-MILITARY-AND-SECURITY-DEVELOPMENTS-INVOLVING-THE-PEOPLES-REPUBLIC-OF-CHINA.PDF#page=10.

4. Mackenzie Eaglen, *The 2020s Tri-Service Modernization Crunch*, American Enterprise Institute, March 23, 2021, https://www.aei.org/research-products/report/2020s-tri-service-modernization-crunch/.

5. Bruce Stubbs, *Ten Challenges to Implementing Force Design 2030*, Atlantic Council, November 25, 2023, https://www.atlanticcouncil.org/in-depth-research-reports/report/ten-challenges-to-implementing-force-design-2030/.

6. Wilson Beaver, *The Army's Role in the Indo-Pacific*, Heritage Foundation, March 12, 2024, https://www.heritage.org/defense/report/the-armys-role-the-indo-pacific.

7. Dan Blumenthal, "The Power Projection Balance in Asia," in *Competitive Strategies for the 21st Century: Theory, History, and Practice*, ed. Thomas Mahnken (Stanford University Press, 2012), https://www.aei.org/research-products/working-paper/the-power-projection-balance-in-asia/.

8. Lindsay Maizland, *China's Modernizing Military*, Council on Foreign Relations, February 5, 2020, https://www.cfr.org/backgrounder/chinas-modernizing-military.

9. Eric Heginbotham et al., *The U.S.-China Military Scorecard: Forces, Geography, and the Evolving Balance of Power 1996–2017*, RAND Corporation, September 14, 2015, https://www.rand.org/paf/projects/us-china-scorecard.html#chinese-air-base.

10. Dennis M. Gormley et al., *A Low-Visibility Force Multiplier: Assessing China's Cruise Missile Ambitions*, Institute for National Strategic Studies, April 1, 2014, https://inss.ndu.edu/Media/News/Article/699509/a-low-visibility-force-multiplier-assessing-chinas-cruise-missile-ambitions/.

11. Michael E. Miller, "Australia Offers U.S. a Vast New Military Launchpad in China Conflict," *The Washington Post*, August 24, 2024, https://www.washingtonpost.com/world/2024/08/24/us-military-base-australia-china/.

12. Derek Grossman, "Chinese Strategy in the Freely Associated States and American Territories in the Pacific: Implications for the United States," testimony before the House Committee on Natural Resources, Subcommittee on Indian and Insular Affairs, May 16, 2023, https://www.rand.org/pubs/testimonies/CTA2768-1.html.

13. Hal Brands and Zack Cooper, *Dilemmas of Deterrence: The United States' Smart New Strategy Has Six Daunting Trade-Offs*, Center for Strategic and International Studies, March 12, 2024, https://www.csis.org/analysis/dilemmas-deterrence-united-states-smart-new-strategy-has-six-daunting-trade-offs.

14. Michael R. Gordon and Nancy A. Youssef, "The Marines Transformed to Take On China. Will They Be Ready for Everything Else?," *The Wall Street Journal*, December 28, 2023, https://www.wsj.com/politics/national-security/the-marines-transformed-to-take-on-china-will-they-be-ready-for-everything-else-d4ea24c6.

15. William C. Greenwalt, "DOD's Replicator Program: Challenges and Opportunities," testimony before the House Committee on Armed Services, Subcommittee on Cyber, Innovative Technologies, and Information Systems, October 19, 2023, https://www.aei.org/research-products/testimony/dods-replicator-program-challenges-and-opportunities/.

10

How to Recruit and Retain the Force We Need

KORI SCHAKE AND JAMES MATTIS

Historians and national security experts agree that America faces complex and increasingly perilous threats to its existence. Yet at age 50, our modern all-volunteer force (AVF) is stumbling—failing to recruit the requisite number of qualified troops and turning to extraordinary measures to make up for the shortfalls. Hobbled by inadequate forces, our country is ill-equipped to enforce peace or prevail in war we're increasingly unlikely to deter with such a weakened military. Defining the specific obstacles to manning the force and developing timely solutions are critical in sustaining the force needed to protect the republic.

The United States military is too small for the requirements of its recent usage and stated strategy. It was clear that challenges from our adversaries were increasing by 2018, when US Defense Secretary James Mattis said,

> The negative impact on military readiness is resulting from the longest continuous stretch of combat in our nation's history and defense spending caps, because we have been operating also for nine of the last 10 years under continuing resolutions that have created an overstretched and under-resourced military.[1]

In the years since, China, Russia, North Korea, and Iran have posed an increasing danger, both individually and as an alliance working against our interests. Russia's defense spending has increased at twice the rate of the United States', and China's has increased by nearly four times the US rate.[2] While the size of these countries' conventional forces has not substantially increased, their military cooperation—and, in some cases, even integration—has.[3]

The United States' strategy is predicated on dealing with these adversaries as singular threats, not a combined alliance. Moreover, our forces have not increased: Defense spending hasn't even kept pace with inflation, technology has not substituted for people at scale, integrated whole-of-government action continues to prove elusive, allies have not proved capable of absorbing responsibilities the US wishes to shift, and we have not found new tools or a novel strategy to obviate the need for military force to underwrite American diplomacy. As a result, US forces are stretched dangerously—and, for any adversary, temptingly—thin.

The bipartisan Congressional Commission on the Strategic Posture of the United States determined in 2023 that

> the risk of conflict with [China and Russia] is increasing. It is an existential challenge for which the United States is ill-prepared. . . .
>
> The Commission reached the unanimous, non-partisan conclusion that today's strategic outlook requires an urgent national focus and a series of concerted actions not currently planned.[4]

In 2024, the bipartisan Commission on the National Defense Strategy concluded,

> The threats the United States faces are the most serious and most challenging the nation has encountered since 1945 and include the potential for near-term major war. The United States last fought a global conflict during World War II, which ended nearly 80 years ago. The nation was last prepared for such a fight during the Cold War, which ended 35 years ago. It is not prepared today.[5]

Both commissions recommended significant increases in defense spending, programs, and force structure.

The US has a well-designed system for determining how large a force it needs: The president establishes major policies, which are incorporated into a National Security Strategy to guide the Department of Defense

(DOD) in developing its National Defense Strategy and the military in developing its National Military Strategy. These strategies are then developed into plans that establish the necessary forces. Crucial considerations include the following:

- Clarity on what the US will defend,

- The capabilities of the forces America needs to defend against,

- The role of alliances in reducing requirements for US forces,

- Trade-offs between conventional force size and reliance on nuclear weapons,

- The question of whether forces should be forward deployed to engage with allies and deter adversaries, and

- Prioritization and sequencing of operations if forces are inadequate to meet all demands simultaneously.

The Inadequacy of the Current Force

Historically, US forces have not been adequate to address all threats simultaneously—even with 12 million servicemen in World War II, the US had to prioritize the European theater and swing forces subsequently to the economy of force theater in the Pacific. But the AVF was not designed to bear the burden of sustained combat. It is a credit to America's military and the young patriots who fill its ranks that it has held up so well through decades of fighting. We owe it to the men and women of our military to reduce the demands of routine operations and overall strategy or expand the force.

The international environment is unlikely to permit a constriction of US engagement without deeply disadvantageous consequences for US interests. Our diplomats are most effective and persuasive in dealing with threats when backed by a lethal and clearly capable military. Adversaries are increasingly challenging our defenses and commitments because we aren't fielding forces sufficient to deter conflict. Therefore, our country needs a larger military.

Yet even many who acknowledge that a larger force is necessary consider it unaffordable.[6] Arguments rest on comparisons between the US population (5 percent of the global population) and the preponderance of global defense spending, concerns about migrating responsibilities for defending America's allies to the US, and the costly unwieldiness of DOD procurement practices. But the central argument against the affordability of a larger US military focuses on the cost of its personnel, which has increased dramatically in recent years.

Each service member costs US taxpayers over $100,000 per year in pay and benefits, before training and arming. A major driver of cost increases is health care, paralleling the dynamic in the overall federal budget, where entitlement spending is crowding out discretionary spending. That means DOD must prioritize pay and benefits over equipment, training, research and development, operations, and maintenance. This is crucial because warfare remains a human endeavor. The initiative, grit, and inventiveness of American military personnel remain an inestimable advantage in deterring authoritarians, maintaining our allies' trust (and forces), and passing our freedoms intact to the next generation.

This chapter's fundamental argument is that defending America's interests is affordable. In 1943–44, the US managed to spend 40 percent of its gross domestic product (GDP) on defense;[7] during the Korean War, it mustered 12 percent. But after the end of the Vietnam War, US defense spending dropped to 4.2 percent. Between 1975 and 2025 it jumped around, increasing with the Reagan buildup, dropping with the end of the Cold War, and increasing back to around 4 percent after 9/11. Over the past 13 years, it has continued to decline. Although Americans are considerably wealthier than in 1974 (per capita GDP was $7,226 in 1974, compared with $81,695 in 2023), we spend a smaller percentage of our national wealth on defense.[8]

Although prewar activities deter war, money cannot buy back the time to prepare for it. By suggesting that so prosperous a country cannot afford to defend its interests, we are talking ourselves into our own demise. We currently spend just 3.2 percent of GDP on defense, significantly less than the 5 percent that President Donald Trump is calling on our allies to spend.[9] America can afford survival, and survival with our freedoms intact is our generation's responsibility to future generations.

Impediments to Recruiting

Even acknowledging that a larger force is needed and can be funded responsibly, however, there is significant skepticism that Americans would be willing to join in the numbers needed. After all, the military is struggling to meet its recruiting goals for the current force, let alone a significantly larger one. In 2023, only the Marine Corps and Space Force met their recruiting goals; the Army and Navy recruited less than 70 percent of their goals for active and reserve components, falling 41,000 recruits short of sustaining the current force.[10] The American military is shrinking not due to a policy determination about the size of the force needed but because the services cannot recruit enough Americans to defend the country.

Ineligibility and Disinterest. The military has diverged from American society in many ways, as reflected in the statistic that in 2022, 77 percent of American youth did not qualify for military service. Reasons included being overweight (11 percent), drug or alcohol use (8 percent), physical or mental health problems (7 percent and 4 percent, respectively), misconduct (1 percent), and inaptitude (1 percent).[11] An additional 44 percent were disqualified for multiple of these reasons. The military must also confront the reality that only 9 percent of Americans between age 17 and 24 (prime recruitment age) have an interest in signing up.[12]

Misperceptions of the Military. The public knows little about the military. There is a misperception, still lingering from the 1960s, that the American military disproportionately recruits from among minorities and the poor. In reality, 19 percent of the poorest quintile of our country serve, as do 17 percent of the richest quintile, while the majority of recruits are from middle-income families.[13] Our military personnel come disproportionately from those who live near military bases and come from military families.[14] Nor are their politics distinguishable from those of other Americans with equivalent education and income.

Misperceptions about what service may entail are also prevalent. According to an article published by the Army,

> The Army's own polling shows today's youth have a dispropor-
> tionate perception of their likelihood of being injured, killed,
> or suffering from post-traumatic stress disorder (PTSD) if they
> join the military. A large percentage of women believe they will
> be sexually harassed or assaulted.[15]

These misperceptions significantly inhibit Americans' propensity to serve in the military and will be difficult to overcome. They result partly from increased, even exaggerated, attention to real problems like post-traumatic stress disorder and sexual assault. But they also result from broader cultural and generational shifts that make military service less appealing.

Cultural Shifts. One legacy of the long wars of the 21st century has been the distancing of the military from broader American society. It's commonplace for military personnel to grumble that we're not a country at war; we're just a military at war.[16] And they're right. The Triangle Institute for Security Studies' 1999 study and subsequent survey research confirms that, 50 years since the end of conscription, American society has less direct stake in military service and the application of force and increasingly defers to the military on those issues.[17]

The same Army article mentioned above highlights a *Wall Street Journal*–NORC poll that found that far fewer young adults considered patriotism important in 2023 (23 percent) than did so in 1998 (70 percent). The article explains that "today's military-age adults value flexibility, self-expression, individual identity, and leisure. They are much more likely to believe that climate change is a greater existential threat than is China or Russia."[18]

Political polarization exacerbates recruitment challenges, as it drags the military into America's culture wars. The 2024 Reagan National Defense Survey indicates that after plummeting more than 20 points in three years, confidence in the US military has stabilized and is slowly trending back up—and that the military remains our public's most trusted institution.[19] But polling also reveals that a polarized American body politic remains concerned about the perceived politicization of our military: Another Reagan poll showed in 2023 that 38 percent of Republicans consider the military too focused on social issues rather than warfighting, while 47 percent of Democrats consider the balance between social issues and warfighting appropriate.[20] Apparently, those who are traditionally most likely to serve perceive the military as preoccupied with social issues rather than focused on fighting and winning the nation's wars. Civilian departmental leaders have been forcing divisive social issues onto the agenda, but they aren't being driven by manpower or warfighting necessities.[21]

Whether "wokeness" is a problem in the military is open to debate, and veterans' attitudes may not reflect the views of those currently in service because of generational differences. But what is clear is that the civilian public—and in particular the veteran community—*believe* that focus on progressive social issues and lack of mission focus are problems. The willingness of military families and veterans to encourage family members toward service has declined precipitously, and given how much recruitment draws on the military as a family business, that is a serious problem. Their concerns also affect the attitudes of school counselors and the parents of potential recruits, who are becoming hesitant to encourage military service.

Older veterans are not the only ones with concerns about military leadership. Many younger veterans and service members express disillusionment about the wars they fought and the lack of accountability among both the military and elected leaders. They especially resent that "a callous foreign policy elite in Washington unjustly asked them to fight in unwinnable wars."[22] While grumbling in the military ranks is routine, civilian leaders should not continue to place troops in harm's way without doing the political work to keep the purpose of such sacrifice evident.

How to expand the pool of recruits without alienating those who serve in greatest numbers is the challenge. In trying to expand the recruitment pool to less traditional constituencies, there is a tendency to use the success of desegregation in the military to justify other socially progressive policies. But doing so widens the civil-military divide, as many in uniform conclude that civilians neither understand the exigencies of military life nor share the burdens of policies that make service members' work even harder. Moreover, 70 percent of recruits come from the South and West, where populations tend to be more socially conservative.[23] Promoting progressive social messages runs counter to the data provided by where recruits are coming from.

Many social justice efforts are advanced without considering the practical consequences for the military. For example, Laura Miller and John Allen Williams show that civilians weigh civil rights concerns more heavily than military effectiveness in considering defense policies.[24] But civil society cannot always impose its social imperatives in the primitive environment of the battlefield, where military imperatives must take priority. For an organization whose victory or defeat will be calculated in body bags, it is crucial to recognize that unit cohesion, trust, and seemingly old-fashioned values are military imperatives—even when at odds with the societal values they're designed to protect.

For example, more than 200,000 women serve in the American military, and we want them to. In fact, if we hope to retain current end strength—let alone expand it—we need them to serve. Yet scholarly research conclusively reinforces—and military experience shows—that unit cohesion is critical for success in warfare,[25] and 82 percent of the military is male (as were 89 percent of those who deployed to the wars in Iraq and Afghanistan).[26] Close-in combat occurs in an atavistic environment, is physically demanding, and requires a level of physical intimacy that makes managing the interactions of 18- to 29-year-old men and women incredibly difficult.

We cannot wish away those difficulties. But we can make them easier to manage by reaffirming common standards for assignment to close-in combat units, focusing on equality of opportunity rather than equality of outcome. There is an important difference between policies aimed at equality of opportunity—like desegregation, which focused on applying standards fairly to expand opportunity and improved military effectiveness—and those prioritizing equality of outcome. (For example, the NFL doesn't exclude female players.) Close-in combat poses similar demands, which we must take seriously if we are to restore trust among those who serve. To allow women to serve in the infantry without requiring them to meet the same standards as men weakens the infantry.

The Trump administration is amplifying, rather than attenuating, these frictions with nominees who are focused on reversing current policies on issues like women serving in combat while threatening to fire "woke" generals. They are not wrong that the aggressive pursuit of certain social policies is alienating many in the force and merits reconsideration. But those issues are not dominating the military internally. Army surveys of 50,000 soldiers reveal that their predominant reasons for leaving military service are the effects of deployments on their families, the degree of stability in Army life, the difficulty of two-career families, and plans to have children. Only 6 percent of the soldiers cited concerns about sexual assault as an extremely important reason to leave, while only 7 percent cited diversity policies.[27] The political issues identified by outsiders don't reflect realities experienced by the vast majority serving in the ranks.

Difficult as these impediments are, workable solutions to most can be found. They lie in what brings people into the force and what keeps them there. The experiences of racially integrating the force in the 1940s and establishing a recruited military can shed light on how to affordably recruit the larger force we need.

Creating the Volunteer Force

The US ended conscription in 1973 based on a confluence of factors: political opposition to the Vietnam War, ideological opposition to involuntary service, an oversized demographic pool for conscription, the loss of the military's confidence in the quality of a conscripted force, and the judgment that a volunteer force could be recruited and retained affordably.[28] The Gates Commission, established by President Richard Nixon, made a strong economic case that, although DOD was paying less than half the market rate in salaries, the true costs of conscription were not factored in. The commission reported that considering these costs, a volunteer force was no more expensive than conscription.[29]

Concerns at the time about transitioning to a volunteer force were more than just financial, however. In defending the end of conscription, Nixon had to dispense with three arguments about who would be in the force and its effect on policymaking:

The first is that a volunteer army would be a black army, so it is a scheme to use Negroes to defend a white America. The second is that a volunteer army would actually be an army of hired mercenaries. The third is, a volunteer army would dangerously increase military influence in our society.[30]

Within the military, there was grave apprehension about whether recruiting could deliver the necessary numbers and whether it would lower standards. The Army was the service most concerned about the end of conscription, as it was both the largest service and had the greatest proportion of draftees. In debates, Army leaders, both civilian and military, worried that pay increases would prove inadequate to meet end-strength requirements, fail to bring sufficiently skilled recruits, and divert such a large proportion of the military budget to training that the force could not modernize. Their fears were initially justified: Recruits proved less committed, less skilled, poorer, and disproportionately from minority populations.[31]

Milton Friedman's and Alan Greenspan's elegant arguments in the Gates Commission dramatically underestimated the cost of recruiting and retaining a force of the quality the military wanted, and Congress did not appropriate even the amounts that the commission recommended.[32] It took a decade of experimentation and reform to shape policies and develop marketing campaigns that delivered the desired quality and quantity of recruits. The 1984 GI Bill, Ronald Reagan's pay raises, serious market research, and creative advertising (such as "Be all you can be" and "The few, the proud, the Marines") finally brought into the force the men and women the services wanted.

Transitioning from conscription to a volunteer force raises issues that remain salient for expanding the force today:

- A tendency by politicians in the executive and legislative branches to downplay the actual costs of bringing and retaining recruits with the necessary skills;

- The appeal of education and health benefits;

- The cost-effectiveness of retaining quality recruits;

- The value of nonmonetary incentives such as personal fulfillment, adventure, and commitment to a mission; and

- The fact that a volunteer force would be untenable in a large-scale war, so Selective Service registration has been retained.[33]

It is surprising the volunteer force has held up as well as it has with the demands of the past two decades. Concerns are legitimately raised about cost, capacity, and whether enough Americans are willing to serve.[34] We would add to that list the military's dissociation from broader American society, the lack of elected officials' support—including that of the commander in chief—and the civic paucity of treating military service as merely a labor commodity.[35]

Cost. The volunteer force is unquestionably expensive. Personnel costs are the largest component of defense spending, at half the total budget. The fundamental proposition of a volunteer force is that the government competes in the marketplace for labor. When the labor market is tight, the force becomes more expensive. The natural rate of unemployment in the US economy is 4.4 percent.[36] And despite a pandemic-driven spike in 2020 alone, the US unemployment rate has been below 4 percent since 2018.[37] So the force is expensive because it's competing in a tight labor market. To say the force is expensive is not to say it is unaffordable, however: Whether to buy a larger force is a choice.

Capacity. Friedman acknowledged upon the volunteer force's creation that a major conflict would break the AVF.[38] The duration of wars in Afghanistan and Iraq strained the force with repeated deployments because it was too small to meet strategic demands. As a result, the National Guard and reserves became regular parts of the rotation rather than the strategic backup they were designed to be. Thus, not only active-duty but also National Guard and reserve forces are badly strained.

Federal law requires men between age 18 and 25 to register for potential conscription into military service. We tend to think of fair conscription practices as requiring universality.[39] But there are 31,795,000 Americans age 17–24, a figure greater than the population of Texas, Florida, or

New York and more than 10 times the size of the current military.[40] It is unlikely that any form of compulsory service would find meaningful uses for so many young Americans, and the economic impact of taking 32 million potential workers from the labor force would unquestionably be negative. But it's called the *Selective* Service because it needn't be universal, and there are cohorts with specialized skills that the military has long directed funds to acquire.

Inability to serve will also dramatically narrow the service base, since 77 percent of Americans age 17–24 do not meet the mental and physical standards for enlistment. A few times since the AVF's advent, the US military has lowered its standards to expand the force; the results have validated the higher standards. When standards are relaxed to serve social purposes, they risk discrediting those the effort has been designed to assist. Racial integration was so successful in our military partially because it maintained a common standard of performance for everyone, which legitimated the success of black Americans among their military colleagues.

Conscription is best used to familiarize a broad population base with military training, increase subsequent voluntary accession into service, and expand the force leading up to war, as a political signal and to provide time to fully train the conscripts.[41] It can be a reminder that citizenship brings duties, not just rights provided by others. But the Selective Service System could not mobilize a larger force—or any force—quickly, because it hasn't been tested in more than 50 years.

Can you recall President Barack Obama, President Trump, or President Joe Biden ever saying Uncle Sam needs you in the US military? With nearly no public officials or community leaders extolling public service of any kind—much less military service in particular—the Selective Service is unquestionably unpopular. Challenges to the system have been active in Congress since 2016, even though the constitutionality of involuntary service—even in peacetime—and its applicability to only men have been upheld.

Conscription will be necessary for any major war the US has to fight. But such a war could be better deterred in the first place by demonstrating a functioning Selective Service System. This would force enemies to consider both an expanded force and an American society willing to produce that force.

Willingness to Serve. Cost and capacity are affected by propensity to serve, because if there is low willingness to join the military, more money is needed to entice and retain recruits. And if unemployment remains as low as in recent years (which it hopefully will), recruitment based on financial incentives will remain exorbitant and potentially politically controversial. So the most important question in recruiting and retaining the force that current international circumstances require is how to increase public willingness to serve. And in 2022, just 9 percent of eligible individuals expressed an openness to serving in the American military.[42] Considering that 77 percent of the young adults are unqualified to serve, the arithmetic does not favor sustaining the AVF. Fortunately, civic activism, particularly by political leaders, can increase propensity to serve.

A related question is whether Americans are willing to tolerate the casualties from a major war. The public has been remarkably unaffected by casualties in recent wars, likely due to volunteer service and the small proportion of the population represented in the force. In fact, the American public increasingly views casualties as intrinsic to the military profession, as they do with firefighting and policing. But whether that attitude would hold at the scale of casualties that a war against China would produce is unknown—although facing that question will be unavoidable if we don't have a military large enough to deter war.

The Army and Navy have recently instituted preparatory programs for recruits who cannot meet the physical or mental standards but are willing to serve. With this extraordinary measure, the services aim to correct problems prevalent in American society, particularly obesity and lack of physical fitness, reading comprehension, and English proficiency. Those programs currently supply a quarter of Army recruits and a fifth of Navy recruits.[43] Their long-term impacts, positive or negative, remain to be seen.

The prevalence of criticism of the AVF from the right and left obscures how good a fighting force it has produced. Maintaining discipline is much less of a problem than under conscription, establishing draft infrastructure and policing evasion require minimal effort, and proficiency is higher because volunteers demonstrate greater motivation and, as Nixon predicted, remain longer in service.

Also overlooked is how high retention rates are, despite the strain of frequent deployments: All the services are meeting or exceeding their goals.[44] They are, however, critically short of personnel with some demanding skill sets. That is a leading indicator of how to expand the force: Once in service, recruits' experience is positive enough that they stay. Whether the recruits we want to stay are staying is a question requiring further analysis.

Recommendations

Despite low eligibility and interest among military-age Americans, we are skeptical that the AVF is in crisis or unsustainable, either at its current end strength or with the expansion we advocate. Our confidence comes from how well the force has adapted and held up in the demands of the preceding 25 years and from the positive effect engagement by political and community leaders could make. But important adjustments are needed to increase Americans' propensity to serve and facilitate accession of those Americans willing or needed to serve.

Restore Military and Civilian Leaders' Mission Focus. The military's priority should be to fight and win the nation's wars. Political leaders should educate the public on how and why the military that guards our freedoms must be different from broader society. There are genuine trade-offs between military proficiency and many other good things our society values. Political leaders should approach with greater humility the use of the military to advance broader social change. Propensity to serve increases significantly when leaders engage with the public on these issues. The Trump administration is inclined toward public engagement but risks further alienating the military from broader society and reducing Americans' propensity to serve by prosecuting the case to dangerous excess, such as by pardoning convicted war criminals or convening extrajudicial panels of veterans to judge the "wokeness" of serving officers.

Increase Defense Spending. America must provide the pay and benefits that recruit and retain the military force. There is no escaping the fact that a volunteer force is expensive. Significant savings can be wrung from the existing budget—Elaine McCusker's work shows that one out of every seven defense dollars goes to things unrelated to fighting the nation's wars.[45] Thus, Congress is complicit in inflating the defense topline without increasing military capability by hiding funds for worthy programs like breast cancer research in the defense budget—one of the few bills that reliably passes. But more money is needed to avoid continuing to trade readiness and force structure for personnel costs.

The US should also take up President Trump's call for NATO allies to spend 5 percent of GDP on defense. That would add roughly $323 billion to the defense topline and be a solid start on repairing the damage of recent years. Sustained increases are necessary to produce the peace through strength that the president and congressional leadership are advocating.

Reform the Selective Service. The US should reform the Selective Service System to enroll all Americans, exercise the system to increase public awareness, and create functional call-ups for short-supply specialists. We now have the formalities of the Selective Service but not its practical benefits; citizens' only interaction with the system is the irritation of registering or being excluded from employment opportunities if they do not. This reinforces the service-dampening notion that citizens have rights but no responsibilities. A public campaign is needed to educate Americans about why the system exists, what is required of every citizen age 18–25, and what specialized skill sets are needed.

Moreover, the system must be exercised to be functional; call-ups will never work on short notice, but they will be essential for looming wars against major states. Political and military leaders, such as members of Congress, should welcome enrollees at exercise points, and recruiters should follow up with enrollees after exercises. We must not overlook civic education to convey the expectation of service to the republic. This is clear to every immigrant who swears in their naturalization ceremony to serve in the armed forces if needed.

Minimize Disqualifiers. Finally, the military should review disqualifiers that prevent recruits from joining but wouldn't affect their service. More accurate medical records have become a significant disqualifier of recruits seeking to join the military. While cultural and legal prohibitions have relaxed, rules against admitting those with tattoos or a history of marijuana use remain a serious barrier to service. Review by Congress and the services to scrape away the accretion of disqualifiers is overdue. Removing unnecessary impediments to service does not lower standards.

Conclusion

While the current volunteer force is not experiencing a crisis, unless we find a way to provide the surge of capable manpower that international circumstances demand, America's leaders will find themselves either facing a world that's escalating quickly toward nuclear warfare or conceding.

President Trump would be an unlikely advocate for most of our recommendations, having received medical waivers to avoid the draft himself and proclaimed mandatory service a "ridiculous idea."[46] And that's before considering the challenge of so divisive a president providing the leadership required to persuade the American public. But Trump wants a US that is powerful and respected by the world. In the first two years of his first term, he was persuaded to provide the funding and policy tools to strengthen the force. Meanwhile, congressional leaders have adopted President Reagan's mantra of peace through strength. Asserting their constitutional prerogatives to legislate defense policy will be determinative.

Restoring civil participation and shared responsibility isn't just the president's work; it is also the work of Congress and civilian and military leaders.[47] Ultimately, if we don't make progress, technical fixes that more accurately target a shrinking cohort will prove to be a failing strategy for defending our country.

Notes

1. James Mattis, "Transcript: Remarks by Secretary Mattis on the National Defense Strategy," US Department of Defense, January 19, 2018, https://www.defense.gov/News/Transcripts/Transcript/Article/1420042/remarks-by-secretary-mattis-on-the-national-defense-strategy/.

2. Russia has increased defense spending by 360 percent in constant dollars since 2000. China's defense spending has grown by 596 percent, while the United States' has increased 156 percent. Stockholm International Peace Research Institute, "SIPRI Military Expenditure Database," https://www.sipri.org/databases/milex; and

US Department of Defense, Office of the Under Secretary of Defense (Comptroller), *National Defense Budget Estimates for FY 2025*, April 2024, https://comptroller.defense. gov/Portals/45/Documents/defbudget/FY2025/fy25_Green_Book.pdf.

3. Shanshan Mei and Denis J. Blasko, "Back to Basics: How Many People Are in the People's Liberation Army?," *War on the Rocks*, July 12, 2024, https://warontherocks. com/2024/07/back-to-the-basics-how-many-people-are-in-the-peoples-liberation-army; Christopher Walker, *An Axis of Autocracy? China's Relations with Russia, Iran, and North Korea*, 119th Cong. 23–24 (2025) (statement of Christopher Walker, vice president for studies and analysis, National Endowment for Democracy), https://www.uscc. gov/hearings/axis-autocracy-chinas-relations-russia-iran-and-north-korea.

4. Madelyn R. Creedon et al., *America's Strategic Posture: The Final Report of the Congressional Commission on the Strategic Posture of the United States*, Institute for Defense Analyses, October 2023, vii, https://www.ida.org/-/media/feature/publications/a/am/ americas-strategic-posture/strategic-posture-commission-report.ashx.

5. Jane Harman et al., *Commission on the National Defense Strategy*, RAND Corporation, July 29, 2024, https://www.rand.org/nsrd/projects/NDS-commission.html.

6. Loren B. Thompson, "The All-Volunteer Force Is Becoming Unaffordable," Lexington Institute, September 22, 2009, https://lexingtoninstitute.org/the-all-volunteer-force-is-becoming-unaffordable/.

7. Guillaume Vandenbroucke, "Which War Saw the Highest Defense Spending? Depends How It's Measured," Federal Reserve Bank of St. Louis, February 4, 2020, https://www.stlouisfed.org/on-the-economy/2020/february/war-highest-defense-spending-measured.

8. Macrotrends, U.S. GDP per Capita 1960–2025, https://www.macrotrends.net/ global-metrics/countries/usa/united-states/gdp-per-capita.

9. Holly Ellyot, "Like It or Not, NATO's Hitting a 5% Defense Spending Target, U.S. Says," CNBC, June 5, 2025, https://www.cnbc.com/2025/06/05/5percent-will-happen-us-says-as-nato-defense-spend-hike-looks-likely.html.

10. US Department of Defense, "Department of Defense Announces Recruiting and Retention Numbers for Fiscal Year 2023—Thru May 2023," press release, https://prhome.defense.gov/Portals/52/Press%20Release%20May%2023%20-%20 Recruiting%20and%20Retention%20Report.pdf.

11. US Army Recruiting Command, "Recruiting Challenges," https://recruiting. army.mil/pao/facts_figures/; and Thomas Novelly, "Even More Young Americans Are Unfit to Serve, a New Study Finds. Here's Why.," *Military.com*, September 28, 2022, https://www.military.com/daily-news/2022/09/28/new-pentagon-study-shows-77-of-young-americans-are-ineligible-military-service.html.

12. Dave Philipps, "With Few Able and Fewer Willing, U.S. Military Can't Find Recruits," *The New York Times*, July 14, 2022, https://www.nytimes.com/2022/07/14/us/ us-military-recruiting-enlistment.html.

13. Brendan R. Stickles, "How the U.S. Military Became the Exception to America's Wage Stagnation Problem," Brookings Institution, November 29, 2018, https:// www.brookings.edu/articles/how-the-u-s-military-became-the-exception-to-americas-wage-stagnation-problem/.

14. *The Economist,* "Recruits to America's Armed Forces Are Not What They Used to Be," April 18, 2020, https://www.economist.com/united-states/2020/04/18/recruits-to-americas-armed-forces-are-not-what-they-used-to-be.

15. Michael Mai, "The All-Volunteer Army at 50—Does Milton Friedman's Case Still Make Sense?," US Army, June 28, 2023, https://www.army.mil/article/267984/the_all_volunteer_army_at_50_does_milton_friedmans_case_still_make_sense.

16. Another expression of this idea is "We're at war while America is at the mall." Phil Klay, "The Warrior at the Mall," *The New York Times,* April 14, 2018, https://www.nytimes.com/2018/04/14/opinion/sunday/the-warrior-at-the-mall.html.

17. Triangle Institute for Security Studies, "Project on the Gap Between the Military and Civil Society," https://tiss-nc.org/past-programs/civil-military-gap/. See also Kori Schake and James Mattis, eds., *Warriors and Citizens: American Views of Our Military* (Hoover Institution Press, 2015); and Peter Feaver, *Thanks for Your Service: The Causes and Consequences of Public Confidence in the US Military* (Oxford University Press, 2023).

18. Mai, "The All-Volunteer Army at 50—Does Milton Friedman's Case Still Make Sense?"

19. Ronald Reagan Institute, *Reagan National Defense Survey,* December 5, 2024, https://cloud.3dissue.net/28997/28913/29166/125257/index.html.

20. Ronald Reagan Institute, *Reagan National Defense Survey,* November 30, 2023, https://cloud.3dissue.net/28997/28913/29166/103650/index.html.

21. Kevin Wallsten and Owen West, "DEI Is Crushing Military Recruitment," *The Wall Street Journal,* October 24, 2024, https://www.wsj.com/opinion/dei-is-crushing-military-recruitment-family-recommendations-diversity-equity-inclusion-7be6240c.

22. Joel Schectman et al., "At the Top of Trump's Team: Angry Vets Who Want to Upend U.S. Foreign Policy," *The Wall Street Journal,* December 6, 2024, https://www.wsj.com/politics/national-security/the-angry-iraq-vets-who-want-to-upend-u-s-foreign-policy-852f9775.

23. US Department of Defense, Office of the Under Secretary of Defense, Personnel and Readiness, *Population Representation in the Military Services: Fiscal Year 2016 Summary Report,* https://www.cna.org/pop-rep/2016/summary/summary.pdf.

24. Laura L. Miller and John Allen Williams, "Do Military Policies on Gender and Sexuality Undermine Combat Effectiveness?," in *Soldiers and Civilians: The Civil-Military Gap and American National Security,* ed. Peter D. Feaver and Richard H. Kohn (MIT Press, 2001).

25. Jason Lyall, *Divided Armies: Inequality and Battlefield Performance in Modern War* (Princeton University Press, 2020).

26. US Naval Institute, "Department of Defense 2022 Demographic Profile," November 29, 2023, https://news.usni.org/2023/11/29/department-of-defense-2022-demographic-profile; and Committee on the Initial Assessment of Readjustment Needs of Military Personnel, Veterans, and Their Families, *Returning Home from Iraq and Afghanistan: Preliminary Assessment of Readjustment Needs of Veterans, Service Members, and Their Families* (National Academies Press, 2010), https://pubmed.ncbi.nlm.nih.gov/25032369/.

27. Loryana L. Vie et al., *Department of the Army Career Engagement Survey: First Annual Report*, US Department of the Army, June 2021, https://talent.army.mil/wp-content/uploads/2021/11/DACES-Annual-Report_JUNE2021.pdf.

28. Bernard D. Rostker, *The Evolution of the All-Volunteer Force*, RAND Corporation, August 28, 2006, https://www.rand.org/pubs/research_briefs/RB9195.html.

29. Thomas Gates et al., *The Report of the President's Commission on an All-Volunteer Armed Force*, February 20, 1970, https://www.nixonfoundation.org/wp-content/uploads/2012/01/The-Report-Of-The-Presidents-Commission-On-An-All-Volunteer-Armed-Force.pdf.

30. Richard Nixon, "Remarks on the CBS Radio Network: 'The All-Volunteer Armed Force,'" American Presidency Project, October 17, 1968, https://www.presidency.ucsb.edu/documents/remarks-the-cbs-radio-network-the-all-volunteer-armed-force.

31. Samuel Hubbard Hays, "A Military View of Selective Service," in *The Draft: A Handbook of Facts and Alternative*s, ed. Sol Tax (University of Chicago Press, 1967), 10.

32. Diana L. Carson and Gary A. Roulier, "The Systemic Shortcomings of the All-Volunteer Force Model That Adversely Affect America's National Security," American College of National Security Leaders, January 24, 2025, https://acnsl.net/publications-1/blog-post-title-one-7yxca-etd3s.

33. Friedman questioned the viability of market-based recruitment in a large-scale war. Mai, "The All-Volunteer Army at 50—Does Milton Friedman's Case Still Make Sense?"

34. Jason Dempsey and Gil Barndollar, "The All-Volunteer Force Is in Crisis," *The Atlantic*, July 3, 2023, https://www.theatlantic.com/ideas/archive/2023/07/all-volunteer-force-crisis/674603/.

35. This case is strongly made in Eliot A. Cohen, *Citizens and Soldiers: The Dilemmas of Military Service* (Cornell University Press, 1990).

36. Lida R. Weinstock, *Introduction to U.S. Economy: Unemployment*, Congressional Research Service, July 12, 2022, https://sgp.fas.org/crs/misc/IF10443.pdf.

37. US Bureau of Labor Statistics, Labor Force Statistics from the Current Population Survey: Unemployment Rate, 1948 to 2023, https://data.bls.gov/timeseries/LNS14000000?years_option=all_years.

38. Gates et al., *The Report of the President's Commission on an All-Volunteer Armed Force.*

39. National Commission on Military, National, and Public Service, *Inspired to Serve: The Final Report of the National Commission on Military, National, and Public Service*, March 2020, https://www.volckeralliance.org/sites/default/files/attachments/Final%20Report%20-%20National%20Commission.pdf.

40. US Census Bureau, *U.S. and World Population Clock*, https://www.census.gov/popclock/.

41. Taren Sylvester and Katherine Kuzminski, "Preparing for the Possibility of a Draft Without Panic," *War on the Rocks*, August 8, 2024, https://warontherocks.com/2024/08/preparing-for-the-possibility-of-a-draft-without-panic/.

42. Philipps, "With Few Able and Fewer Willing, U.S. Military Can't Find Recruits."

43. Dexter Filkins, "The U.S. Military's Recruiting Crisis," *The New Yorker*, February 3, 2025, https://www.newyorker.com/magazine/2025/02/10/the-us-militarys-recruiting-crisis.

44. C. Todd Lopez, "All-Volunteer Force Proves Successful for U.S. Military," US Department of Defense, March 2, 2023, https://www.defense.gov/News/News-Stories/Article/Article/3316678/all-volunteer-force-proves-successful-for-us-military/.

45. Elaine McCusker, "Reforming Defense Budgeting," in *Defense Budgeting for a Safer World: The Experts Speak*, ed. Michael J. Boskin and John Rader (Hoover Institution Press, 2023).

46. Ryan Bass, "Military Recruitment Shortfall: Should US Bring Back the Draft?," Yahoo, June 12, 2024, https://www.yahoo.com/news/military-recruitment-shortfall-us-bring-162655292.html.

47. Elliot Ackerman, "Why Bringing Back the Draft Could Stop America's Forever Wars," *Time*, October 10, 2019, https://time.com/5696950/bring-back-the-draft/.

11

The Future of War

FREDERICK W. KAGAN

The character of war is changing rapidly and profoundly. This change is most visible in Ukraine and in the Iran-Israel war, but indications of its spread are in conflicts around the world, from Syria deep into Africa. It is tempting to identify it as the unmanned systems revolution, but such a rubric is far too simplistic to capture the extent and profundity of the changes in warfare now underway. We now can see only the initial glimpses of the current transformation's full effects, and it is too early to encapsulate that transformation in words, ideas, or programs. It is already apparent, however, that the US and all major militaries must begin changing their concepts of how to wage war and all facets of their war-waging institutions to keep up with and prepare for the rapid and dynamic developments now gaining speed and momentum.

Past as Misleading Prologue

The author and Kimberly Kagan have elsewhere observed that the war in Ukraine is to the next major great-power war as the Spanish Civil War was to World War II.[1] The Spanish Civil War was a laboratory in which prototypes of most of the technologies that would make the Second World War so dramatically different from World War I were tested against one another. The Soviets and Germans provided the opposing sides with tanks, aircraft, and other systems both to achieve desired political outcomes and to observe the large-scale live-fire exercise that revealed the strengths, weaknesses, and best uses of those systems. The other great powers observed and drew their own conclusions.

But the tests were of limited value in forecasting the character of the next war because of the limitations of the combatants' capabilities. Both sides in the Spanish Civil War were far weaker than any great power, with extremely limited defense industrial bases (DIBs) of their own, and they received only relatively small numbers of early prototype weapons. One could catch glimpses of what modern airpower or tanks could do and what air defense and anti-tank systems would look like or how they would perform, but those glimpses were far from a full preview of German blitzkrieg or Soviet deep battle.

The war in Ukraine is similar to the Spanish Civil War in that Ukraine's Western backers have provided relatively small numbers of advanced weapons, though often older versions than the ones they themselves use. Ukraine, in addition, has until recently had a limited ability to use its own DIB at scale. The Russians, for their part, have used their arsenal of advanced weapons and systems and have partially mobilized their own extensive DIB. However, their ability to mobilize their industry has been affected by sanctions, and the actual "modern" characteristics of many of their systems have turned out to be overhyped.

It is easy to argue, therefore, as some have done, that the US and its allies have relatively little to learn from the fighting in Ukraine because "we wouldn't fight that way." The US and its NATO and Pacific allies and partners have extensive inventories of advanced systems that they have not shared with Ukraine but that they would certainly use in a major war. The combined DIB of the US and its allies dwarfs Ukraine's in size and capability. Russia, for its part, entered the war a relatively weak great power, at least as measured by conventional rather than nuclear capabilities. It lags far behind the People's Republic of China (PRC) in the ability to produce large numbers of modern weapons and systems at scale, and it has not been able to produce the most modern systems—true fifth-generation aircraft or hypersonic missiles, for example—at all. A war between the US and the PRC today would not look like the war in Ukraine, and it is tempting to extrapolate from that fact that one can marginalize or dismiss the lessons to be drawn from Ukraine and the Middle East.

But Russia and Ukraine are not the opposing sides in a civil war. Each is a powerful country in its own right with a serious DIB and a fully modern military. The Russian DIB can outproduce Ukraine's partners in some important areas, such as artillery and other munitions. (Russia has had to turn to North Korea for the majority of its artillery munitions and ballistic missiles, which reflects its inability to keep up with its own demands—but it still produces more than NATO does.) Ukraine has also expanded its DIB to produce NATO-standard weapons at rates similar to NATO's own production of some systems and is working to increase that capability further. The main delta between the combatants in this conflict and those who would likely fight in, say, a Taiwan scenario is in the absence of large numbers of the most advanced systems mentioned above.

The initial period of war between the US and the PRC would almost certainly look different from anything seen in the Russia-Ukraine or Iran-Israel wars. Stealth aircraft of both sides would penetrate the adversary's air defenses in ways that neither side has been able to do in Ukraine and that only Israel has been able to do in the Iran-Israel war. The naval war would see the most modern surface and subsurface vessels and munitions used against each other and against targets on land at a scale not seen in either of the current conflicts. One could list other differences.

But how long would that initial period last before the combatants ran through their arsenals of high-end systems? Stealth aircraft and hypersonic missiles are expensive and cannot be mass-produced, at least not with current technologies. Long-range strike systems are also relatively scarce and difficult to replace, as are the most advanced air and missile defense systems. A US-PRC war need not last long to wear both sides down to reliance on more traditional systems such as those dominating the current wars and to production levels not necessarily dissimilar to today's levels. We should be leery of deciding that the US will have—and be able to use—sufficient numbers of its most advanced systems for long enough to force any future war to conclusion on its terms and therefore of deciding that the current wars offer as limited a glimpse of the future as the Spanish Civil War did in its time.

Characteristics of the Current Transformation of War

The character of war changes most rapidly during large-scale protracted wars. Peacetime preparations to transform war set conditions for transformation but rarely achieve it—until war actually comes, completing the transformation and then developing it further. Desert Storm was the anomaly in this regard, not the norm. The technologies that would lead to trench warfare and then to its demise in World War I were mostly well-developed before 1914, but the urgency of war brought them to their apotheosis within about 18 months. The urgency of escaping from the horrors of trench warfare then drove the separate lines of development in Germany and among the Allied powers that broke the stalemate another 18 months or so later. Armored warfare was well-developed as a concept before 1939, but German blitzkrieg changed profoundly between the invasions of Poland and France and then again before and during the invasion of the Soviet Union. Mechanized warfare in 1945 looked little like the initial German invasion of Poland. Both technologies and the ways in which they were employed changed rapidly throughout World War II until its end, whereupon development once more slowed down. None of the weapons or systems used in World War II were invented during the war, apart from atomic bombs, but the character of those weapons and systems and the means with which they were employed were transformed repeatedly in a few years. That is the normal pattern of military transformations.

The Russia-Ukraine and Iran-Israel wars have likewise not seen the introduction of any wholly new weapons or systems. Unmanned aerial vehicles (UAVs), unmanned ground systems (UGS), unmanned surface vehicles (USVs), and unmanned underwater vehicles all existed in militaries before the full-scale Russian invasion in 2022, and most had been used in combat in one form or another. Integrated air and missile defense systems (IAMDS) have been used in war for decades, as have electronic warfare (EW), cyberattacks, and, of course, satellite-supported intelligence, surveillance, and reconnaissance and communications.

These wars, however, have been the first to see several phenomena:

- Large-scale use of IAMDS against multiple large, complex long-range strike packages composed of ballistic and cruise missiles and long-range UAVs

- Fielding of tactical UAVs for surveillance and attack on the scale of millions on each side

- Fielding of EW so extensive and intensive that it can disrupt GPS signals and communications across areas spanning scores of miles

- Development of integrative systems to extract targeting information from thousands of manned and unmanned systems simultaneously and make that information available to individuals operating tactical UAVs and other systems in near-real time

- Initial integration of machine learning (ML) algorithms to support precise geolocation without any external communications and target both identification and engagement

- Use of precise long-range attack drones to hit critical components of military and economic infrastructure

- Use of UGS at scale for tactical resupply, casualty evacuation, mining, and mine-clearing operations

- Use of USVs at scale to disable or sink naval vessels alone or in conjunction with UAV or missile attacks

This chapter will focus on the first five of these phenomena, which are the most salient for the immediate future of land warfare.

The weapons and systems used in every one of these phenomena have changed and developed over the course of the wars, but none of them were invented during the conflicts. The task confronting the American national security community is to identify the lessons to be drawn from the changes these phenomena have already wrought in warfare, forecast the future developments of these phenomena, and forecast the possibilities for entirely new capabilities not yet seen on either set of battlefields.

IAMDS. The proliferation of drones has received the most attention thus far in discussions of lessons the Ukraine war might hold for the future, and those lessons are certainly important. But the implications of the ongoing air and missile campaigns in Ukraine and the Middle East are in some respects at least as profound for the future of American military operations.

It has long been assumed that, to paraphrase UK Prime Minister Stanley Baldwin, the missile will always get through. The patchy performance and limited deployment of missile defense systems before 2022 gave no real indication of how effective they would be or could rapidly become against large-scale and prolonged missile-strike series. US national security experts generally expected that the US could rely on its own missiles getting through to their targets and striking them precisely, but the experts also assumed that PRC missiles would be able to hit their aim points without much disruption. The ongoing conflicts call both assumptions into question.

The Russia-Ukraine and Iran-Israel wars have shown that certain kinds of cruise missiles are virtually useless against modern IAMDS, except as decoys and interceptor absorbers. Israel and its allies shot down every single cruise missile Iran fired at it in April 2024 before any had reached Israeli territory, and Ukraine regularly shoots down 90–100 percent of the cruise missiles Russia fires at it. Russian and Iranian cruise missiles are simply too slow and lack sufficient stealth or other masking capabilities to defeat the IAMDS fielded by Israel and Ukraine. More advanced cruise missiles presumably could defeat those systems, at least to some degree, but ordinary missiles that are easy to mass-produce, such as the Russian Kh-101 series, cannot be relied on to penetrate such defenses.

Ballistic missiles are more reliable penetrators, but they too can be defeated. Ukrainian forces have been able to use US-produced Patriot systems to shoot down Russian ballistic missiles, but the majority of ballistic missiles the Russians fire penetrate the Ukrainian IAMDS. It is impossible to assess from available open-source information what role Ukrainian Patriot launchers and interceptors play in the Russian penetration rates, but it is certain that the Ukrainians have not nearly enough Patriot launchers or interceptors to attempt to down every ballistic missile fired at them. Thus, the true penetration rate is impossible to discern from open sources.

The October 2024 Iranian ballistic missile salvo against Israel offers good evidence that a dense and well-provisioned IAMDS can, indeed, shoot down large majorities of incoming ballistic missiles.[2] That strike consisted of 180–200 such missiles. The actual number that impacted was never publicly confirmed, but some estimates put it in the dozens. Those estimates would indicate that the combined Israel-allied IAMDS downed well over half and possibly as many as three-quarters of the ballistic missiles Iran launched.

Quasi-hypersonic missiles perform better, naturally, but not perfectly. The Russian Kinzhal aeroballistic missile, which is not a true hypersonic weapon despite the Russian hype of it, often penetrates Ukrainian defenses, but not always—Ukrainian forces regularly intercept Kinzhals. Only the truly hypersonic Russian Zircon missile, designed originally for an anti-shipping role, appears always to be able to penetrate Ukrainian defenses.

Iran has not claimed to field hypersonic missiles, but the Houthis have asserted that their Palestine 2 missile has hypersonic characteristics. The Houthis have been able to penetrate Israeli-allied IAMDS with at least one such missile, but a US Terminal High-Altitude Area Defense (THAAD) system reportedly downed at least one.

The Missile Will Only Sometimes Get Through. The lesson here is clear: Almost any missile lacking true hypersonic capabilities can be shot down, with penetration rates varying largely by the missile's speed. Denser IAMDS naturally provide much better protection than sparser ones, but even relatively sparse IAMDS can protect areas the size of central Kyiv reliably. Consistent missile penetration therefore depends on either overwhelming the IAMDS or using the most advanced (and thus scarcest, most expensive, and least replaceable) missiles.

On the flip side, the US should not assume a priori that it will be unable to defend bases in the Pacific against PRC missile salvos. Nor should it assume that its own lower-end missiles will be able to penetrate PRC IAMDS to strike heavily defended targets on the Chinese mainland.

Defense against long-range UAVs is even more effective. Ukraine regularly downs nearly 100 percent of incoming Russian long-range UAV strikes, including even Russian decoy UAVs. Such long-range UAV strikes are therefore far more useful as distractions combined with missile strikes and as reconnaissance and reconnaissance-in-force efforts to locate Ukrainian air defenses and determine their ability and willingness to engage targets.

IAMDS Optimization Lessons. Ukraine and Israel have taken different approaches to the challenge of optimizing IAMDS engagement patterns to conserve scarce and expensive interceptors. The Israeli approach has emphasized optimizing engagement against projectiles with ballistic trajectories because of the extraordinarily high number of rockets and short-range ballistic missiles the country faced before the outbreak of the October 7 war. Israel's IAMDS optimization thus reportedly relied on determining whether the incoming projectile was likely to hit desert or a valuable target and then refraining from wasting interceptors on projectiles that were going to hit only sand. However, the primary systems for engaging all incoming projectiles, from quasi-hypersonics to UAVs, appear to be the same set of antimissile systems (e.g., Iron Dome, David's Sling, and Arrow, supplemented by US THAADs and Patriots).

Ukraine faced a different problem earlier in the war that shaped its optimization strategy. Starved of the most advanced missile defense systems but confronted, by late 2023, with masses of Iranian-built Shahed long-range UAVs, the Ukrainians rapidly realized that they could not waste interceptors on such drones. They therefore fell back on much more primitive systems—shotguns and rifles fielded by what they call "mobile fire teams" that stand watch for UAVs and shoot them down. Ukrainian forces generally engage long-range UAVs with interceptors only when these more primitive systems have been unable to down them (or when the UAVs are close to sensitive targets). The Ukrainians are currently investing in their abilities to destroy or divert Russian long-range UAVs using EW before they need to engage them with rifles or shotguns, although the Russians will likely find at least some counters to this solution.

Future combatants will face the same challenges as Ukraine and must consider adjusting their own IAMDS optimization algorithms (and force fielding) accordingly. Interceptors that can down missiles will almost inevitably cost far more than long-range drones (to say nothing of tactical drones) and will be far more difficult to mass-produce. Similarly, the systems that can shoot down ballistic missiles (or hypersonics) must not be wasted shooting down cruise missiles. IAMDS usage algorithms thus must optimize for availability and cost as well as for the threat the incoming projectile poses to targets that matter, ensuring that the most expensive and rarest interceptors are used exclusively against the targets that only they can engage. The concept of an IAMDS, moreover, must be expanded to include ground-based primitive systems such as shotguns (or, when appropriate and necessary, systems like the Vulcan or other rapid-fire air defense systems) and integrate those systems into the same target engagement algorithms as the higher-end systems.

The Tactical Reconnaissance Strike Complex. The most profound innovation in the Russia-Ukraine war has been the integration of tactical UAVs; long-range rockets, missiles, and UAVs; tube artillery; and EW into a single coherent system that the author and Kimberly Kagan have described in detail elsewhere. We coined the expression "tactical reconnaissance strike complex" (TRSC) to capture the reality that this system combines the features of what the Russians called the "reconnaissance-fires complex," which operates at the tactical level, with those of the "reconnaissance-strike complex," which functions at the operational level. The TRSC combines operational-level assets with tactical assets to achieve tactical effects that can generate operational impacts.[3]

The offense-defense race between unmanned systems and EW is one of the defining characteristics of the TRSC and its implications for modern war. The author will consider that interaction in more detail below, but it must be kept in mind as the single most important factor currently driving the rapid innovation cycle occurring on the battlefields of Ukraine and Russia and as one of the most significant phenomena likely to profoundly affect future war.

Tactical UAVs. The proliferation of tactical UAVs with ranges of up to 50 kilometers is the most obvious and visible change in the character of modern war. Both sides are fielding millions of these systems annually, and tactical UAVs are becoming one of the most important combat systems on the battlefield.

UAV Characteristics in Current Conditions. A UAV, like almost any modern weapons platform, consists of three main components: the platform itself, its electronics (including sensors, avionics, and communications systems), and its software. Its communications capabilities also consist of three elements, in general: the link between controller and UAV; the data link the

UAV uses to provide video or other intelligence to the controller, some integrative system, or both; and GPS or some other passive system used for geolocation. Attack UAVs can either have explosive payloads integrated into their bodies or carry ordnance to be dropped or fired on targets. Almost all attack UAVs are designed to provide data back to their controllers and integrative systems up to the moment of their destruction.

The three components of a UAV can change at different rates. Producing a large number of UAVs with different form factors or otherwise different physical characteristics takes much longer than generating and pushing software patches or updates. Upgrading electronics—communications systems or sensors, for example—usually goes faster than redesigning the platform but more slowly than improving software.

The basic UAV form factors used in both the Russia-Ukraine and Iran-Israel wars have not changed dramatically. Tactical drones are still primarily quadcopters or hexcopters similar to those in widespread commercial use before the 2022 full-scale Russian invasion. Innovations have extended their ranges and payloads somewhat, but not in a transformative way. The transformative innovations have come in the UAVs' electronics and software and have resulted primarily from the urgent need to overcome advances in EW.

All three modes of communication used by UAVs are vulnerable to jamming, spoofing, and, sometimes, hacking. GPS jamming has become so pervasive on the battlefield that, on the whole, tactical drone operators no longer rely on GPS to geolocate their UAVs. They rely instead on knowledge of where the drone launched and imagery and familiarity with the terrain over which the UAV flies to recognize its location manually. Efforts are underway to automate this process through ML algorithms that will geolocate UAVs precisely by recognizing terrain using the drone's onboard video feed. Such capabilities could be fielded at scale in 2025, largely obviating the need for external sources of geolocation information.

EW interference with (and hacking of) UAV control and data communications also has become pervasive and is a major challenge on the battlefield. Both sides have engaged in efforts to expand the frequency ranges on which drones can communicate, use frequency-hopping algorithms, and find other ways to adjust communications frequencies and modes dynamically. The latter allows them to find open wavelengths through which to control UAVs in flight even as enemy EW operators labor to identify and close those gaps. Large EW systems can generate blanket coverage of all or almost all usable frequencies, sometimes over wide areas, depriving drone operators of any ground-based means of controlling their UAVs. But both sides have innovated with using UAV-based satellite uplink systems to circumvent such ground-based jamming, and efforts to jam those UAV-based uplinks have so far had only modest success. The Russians also have fielded drones guided through fiber-optic wires that so far are proof against EW interference but suffer from various performance degradations because of the wire.

UAV electronics and control software are therefore locked in a tight race with EW innovations—a race that can see changes ripple across the battle space in a matter of weeks. Two clear conclusions emerge thus far from this race: The UAV operator cannot rely on getting any electromagnetic signal to the drone once it has taken off, but the EW operator cannot rely on blocking all signals to enemy drones either. Communications on and near the battlefield have become highly contested and are likely to remain so.

The primary UAV innovations thus far have been oriented toward defeating or mitigating this communications challenge, and those pressures are leading to intensive efforts to integrate full autonomy into reconnaissance and attack drones. Once UAVs are equipped with ML-driven visual positioning systems that can geolocate them using their own internal video feed as well as through AI/ML-driven target identification systems, such UAVs will be able to navigate, find, and attack targets with no external communications. We will consider the implications of such lethal autonomous systems (LAS) on the battlefield in Ukraine in more detail below, but for purposes of this section, what matters is that such systems will likely be fielded in 2025.

Quantity Has a Quality All Its Own. A defining characteristic of modern tactical UAVs is that they are inexpensive. Handheld quadcopter surveillance or attack drones can cost $3,000–$5,000. Quadcopters with one-way ranges up to 40 kilometers and payloads of 20–25 kilograms can cost around $25,000. This affordability and the relatively ready availability of parts to produce UAVs have enabled Russia and Ukraine together to put more than three million drones onto the battlefield in 2024 alone. That number will increase and possibly double in 2025.

The sheer number of drones on the battlefield is powerfully shaping the character of current war. Pervasive coverage of enormous areas with visual, thermal, and electromagnetic sensing has created the partially transparent battlefield long dreamed of by airpower enthusiasts. It is impossible to conceal a large concentration of vehicles or personnel for an attack on such a battlefield, and it is difficult to conceal vehicles at all.

Tactical attack drones are now also capable of destroying most objects on the battlefield, including tanks, often using means as simple as dropping shaped-charge anti-tank munitions directly onto turret hatches or other vulnerable points. Efforts to rig slat armor or other means of protecting vehicles have been generally unsuccessful, largely because drones under human control can find and attack any exposed point of vulnerability and strike repeatedly first to destroy any such protective systems and then hit the vehicle the systems were protecting.

The close integration of all UAV feeds with traditional fires systems such as tube artillery has proved deadly to traditional mechanized maneuver. When the drones themselves cannot destroy enemy vehicles fast enough or at all, their operators can engage friendly artillery to do the job. With enough warning and enough concentration of enemy force, the defender can choose to use long-range fires systems—drones, rockets, or missiles—to devastating effect.

These factors are the primary causes of the current positional nature of the war in Ukraine. An attacker cannot mass without being observed and, when observed, struck. Surprise cannot be achieved through concealment of location, force size, or composition. Vehicles lacking integrated counter-drone systems cannot survive on the modern battlefield. Drones are so inexpensive and pervasive that even infantry squads are suitable targets.

Russian forces on the offensive throughout 2024 repeatedly proved the folly of attempting massed mechanized assaults, as they regularly lost many of the vehicles they committed to such attacks for marginal gains, if they advanced at all. They largely abandoned massed infantry assaults as well. The gains Russian forces made, largely in Donetsk region, in the last quarter of 2024 came, by contrast, through penetrations made by small groups of infantry (two to five soldiers) infiltrating defensive positions, followed by reinforcements, which were usually also brought forward in small groups.

Pervasive tactical drones, properly integrated into a TRSC, have eliminated mechanized maneuver from the battle space for now. We will consider presently some possibilities for restoring such maneuver in different ways.

EW. The urgent need to find a defense against drones has driven dramatic improvements and changes in EW systems on both sides. The Russians in particular have invested in a complex of EW systems ranging from large-scale, high-powered systems with long ranges to handheld systems intended to take down individual drones. The Ukrainians also field such systems, although theirs are generally smaller and with more limited ranges.

The Russians achieved their most noteworthy EW success during the 2023 Ukrainian counteroffensive. Russian forces massed enough EW, including long-range GPS jammers, to block even vehicle-to-vehicle communications in some cases, causing Ukrainian forces to bunch up in order to communicate and thus make themselves vulnerable to devastating artillery fire. Russian GPS jamming has rendered US-provided High-Mobility Artillery Rocket System (HIMARS) rockets effectively unusable in parts of the battle space as well. (Ukraine has received only older HIMARS rockets vulnerable to such GPS jamming, not newer US systems that are reportedly more resistant.) Both sides have deployed handheld jammers to frontline troops in the trenches that they use to defend themselves against tactical UAVs.

EW has not proved a panacea against UAVs, however. UAV communications engineers on both sides have repeatedly circumvented or otherwise overcome EW successes to restore communications and navigation to their drones. Moreover, neither side has fielded enough EW systems to cover the battle space evenly, thus creating areas of vulnerability where drones can operate. The fielding of satellite communications on larger tactical drones has so far been largely effective and difficult to block, and the use of such communications together with human or machine visual positioning helps evade GPS jamming.

Large high-powered and long-range EW systems suffer from several challenges, at least at this stage of technology. These systems tend to overheat when used for long periods, for one thing, requiring either downtime in which large areas are uncovered or the deployment of multiple scarce and expensive systems close together to maintain coverage. These systems' size also makes them vulnerable to attack. The Borisoglebsk-2 EW system, for example, is built on the chassis of an MT-LB armored personnel carrier weighing about 12 tons. But the full EW complex includes several vehicles and either generators (and fuel for them) or connections to civilian power. Ukrainian forces have managed to destroy a number of Borisoglebsk and other large EW systems. The systems can be geolocated by their emissions and targeted with tube or rocket artillery that does not rely on electronic communications of any sort. Ukrainian forces also have destroyed some of these systems with the drones they are intended to defend against, taking advantage of niche vulnerabilities I will not discuss further in this chapter.

Russian forces have thus found it necessary to keep such systems back from the lines and away from Ukrainian artillery as best they can and, more importantly, to ring them with air defense systems to defend against Ukrainian drones that somehow penetrate the EW blanket. The Russians have, in fact, created a complex of EW combined with air defense in depth, using smaller, tactical EW and air defense systems closest to the lines and larger, longer-range EW and air defense systems farther in the rear. This complex ties up many air defense assets and limits the effectiveness of the larger EW systems, although the air defense assets also provide cover to Russian forces and other installations in the area. Ukrainian forces, however, have achieved kills even against systems within such layered defenses.

Lessons for the US. The battle space in Ukraine is characterized by extremely high lethality delivered by a combination of systems, some of which rely on electromagnetic communications for terminal guidance. Anything that must be within range of tube or rocket artillery, to say nothing of tanks, mortars, or other infantry weapons, can be destroyed regardless of its EW capabilities. Surveillance has become so pervasive that any vehicle-sized system is likely to be observed (and anything emitting in the electromagnetic spectrum is almost certain to be observed). Systems that may appear "highly mobile" and "low profile" are, in fact, extremely vulnerable on the Ukrainian battlefield and require complex combined-arms protection arrays to survive.

This raises questions about the survivability of any EW or counter-drone system that relies on a continuous supply of high volumes of electricity. It also highlights the reality that any vehicle-mounted system is vulnerable. These circumstances do not mean that high-end counter-drone directed-energy or EW systems will be useless—they are, on the contrary, an important component of modern warfare. It does mean, however, that they are unlikely to clear the skies of enemy drones magically, that they will be part of the same offense-defense cycle affecting all other parts of the drone-EW complex, and that their survival will depend on their deployment within a complicated and dynamic defensive array against all the threats an adversary can bring.

Fratricide. A sizable proportion of the tactical drones lost to EW by both sides is, in fact, the result of fratricide. The fielding of individual EW systems combined with the ubiquity of drones and the impossibility of recognizing easily whether a drone is friend or foe has led to a situation in which soldiers seeing drones instinctively down them. Neither the Russians nor the Ukrainians have solved this problem. There does not appear to be a simple solution, moreover, because of the intensity of the EW contest and the unreliability of communications at the front line.

One could, in principle, kit out drones with identify-friend-foe (IFF) transponders, provide frontline troops with an intelligence picture that includes the ability to rapidly query whether a given drone is friend or foe, or otherwise attempt to use integrated data and communications to solve this problem. (Using markings or any physical characteristics can be dismissed out of hand because of the ease with which the adversary can spoof them.) Both sides are wrestling with questions about the echelons at which to place command of tactical EW and UAV operations and are considering, in part, how to optimize communications to reduce the fratricide.

But where communications are so unreliable, systems that rely on them are also unreliable. IFF transponder systems would need to be extremely sophisticated to be proof against enemy spoofing, particularly since both drones and IFF query systems will inevitably be captured quickly. Making integrated data systems fusing drone locations available for use by infantry soldiers is also likely to fail: Too many drones will be operating without reliable communications and, especially, without reliable digital geolocation that they can relay back to their controllers; the infantry soldiers will likely be without live communications a considerable part of the time; and soldiers hearing and then seeing a nearby drone will always be more inclined to down it than to leaf through a touchscreen to see if it is friend or foe. These problems will only grow as truly autonomous UAVs are fielded, since such vehicles will not need to generate electromagnetic emissions and may be designed not to do so. The "solution" for now appears to be accepting high percentages of UAV fratricide and simply fielding enough tactical UAVs to succeed nevertheless. The real solution will likely require significant changes in doctrine, training, and technology.

TOW Drones. The Russians have pioneered one mitigation to the EW problem—drones guided by fiber-optic cable they drag after them. The Ukrainians report that such drones are, in fact, generally proof against their EW systems and can be effective. Wire-guided drones suffer from obvious challenges, however, including the limitations on range, payload, or both imposed by having to carry and pay out the cable and the risk of the cable being tangled or cut. It is unclear whether such drones, which operate somewhat like the tube-launched, optically tracked, wire-guided (TOW) missile, will establish themselves on the modern battlefield or whether they are an ephemeral experiment that will be superseded by better technology.

Lethal Autonomous Systems Are Here. The more promising developments in EW-proof drones lie in the realm of autonomous systems. Both sides in Ukraine have amassed enormous datasets of manually identified military systems, soldiers, and other targets taken from drone feed. These datasets are exquisite training sets for neural nets, and both sides have used them to develop autonomous targeting systems. Neither side has yet fielded such systems at scale, but the developments appear to be far enough along that such systems will likely appear within 12 to 18 months at the outside.

Discussions in the US and allied states about LAS have hitherto turned heavily on the legal and ethical challenges involved in fielding them. How will such systems be designed to adhere to the law of armed conflict relating to collateral damage and civilian casualties? Who bears responsibility for violations of the law of armed conflict? Popular discussions continue to focus on the question of whether a machine should be allowed to kill without human oversight.

The urgent need to make systems proof against electromagnetic interference, ideally by eliminating their need to communicate at all once launched, has driven both the Russians and the Ukrainians to develop such systems. The delays in fielding them thus far are largely the result of pragmatic problems rather than ethical dilemmas, but the solutions of the pragmatic problems will likely create systems that can respond to the ethical dilemmas as well.

The problem both sides in this war face in developing fully autonomous lethal systems is that they use roughly the same kit—there are T-72s, BMPs, and other Soviet systems on both sides of the line. Close combat remains the norm, moreover, such that it is impossible to draw a neat geographical box near the front line within which any legitimate target can be identified as the enemy. The unreliability of geolocation in the current EW environment also degrades the utility of precisely drawn geofences near the front lines.

One partial solution in progress is the development of "last-mile autonomous" systems. Such systems are manually launched and human guided to a given engagement area that is deemed free of friendly forces and then set free, in what is likely the most seriously contested EW space, to find and attack legitimate targets on their own. These systems face the obvious challenge of penetrating densely EW-covered airspace to get to their free-fire zones, but careful route planning can partially alleviate this problem. The challenge of reaching the free-fire zone, nevertheless, is one of the main drivers behind the push to full autonomy—systems that can launch themselves, navigate to an appropriate area, and select and destroy targets without any human intervention.

Such systems must be able to distinguish between friendly and enemy forces on their own and without communicating back to a home station in real time. They must, in other words, ensure that they attack only enemy

T-72s and not friendly T-72s. That ability to discriminate between friend and foe T-72s is a much higher bar to meet than the ability to avoid striking, say, a Toyota Hilux when looking for a T-72. The target discrimination being built into LAS under development in Ukraine will thus need to meet any reasonable requirement relating to law of armed conflict targeting.

The reasonableness of such requirements must flow from the standards already applied to human-directed weapons, moreover, not to some arbitrary standard of perfection. LAS cannot be required *never* to kill innocent civilians or cause collateral damage, because humans fighting in war are not so required. LAS must, rather, perform at least as well as humans in this regard—and the standards they must meet to avoid fratricidal attacks in close combat will likely ensure that they can. (Note also that the conventional battlefields in Ukraine, unlike the irregular warfare battlefields of Iraq and Afghanistan, are much less densely occupied by civilians, who generally flee as enemy forces approach, greatly reducing the risks of tactical LAS engaging civilian targets.) The ethical and legal complexities of LAS are real and must remain considerations in such systems' development and employment. But discussions about LAS must consider the capabilities of the systems now being developed and proceed from the recognition that those capabilities inherently create systems that can address many of the legitimate and important legal and ethical concerns.

Kinetic Counter-Drone Systems. The limitations of EW in defending against drones highlight the importance of developing effective kinetic counter-drone systems that can be both man portable and vehicle mounted. The advent of truly EW-proof LAS will make such systems essential. Neither side has yet fielded effective kinetic counter-drone systems intended to defend against tactical UAVs at scale (the author is unaware of whether any prototypes have been tested or fielded). Both sides have fielded UAV prototypes that can attack helicopters and other UAVs using various means, from nets to ramming. But vehicle-mounted and man-portable systems have not yet appeared.

The challenges of spotting, identifying, and shooting down an attacking drone using vehicle-mounted or human-carried systems are considerable, to be sure. Such systems must avoid firing at every bird, for example, or even at every drone in order to permit friendly drones to operate.

They should presumably be able to identify and down a drone only if, through its flight pattern, it poses a clear danger to whatever they are defending—a complex challenge indeed. But even though the challenge of defeating rocket-propelled grenades using kinetic defenses was also long regarded as almost impossible to solve, the Trophy system mounted on Israeli vehicles has proved quite effective. So there is no reason to assume that the counter-drone challenge will not be amenable to an appropriate kinetic defense.

The word "kinetic" here is used to mean simply defenses that actually destroy the drone rather than interfere with its electronics. Means of destruction can be bullets, nets, directed energy, or anything else that actually physically wrecks the drone before it can strike. Systems to defend exposed infantry must destroy the drone in such a way that its debris does not cause too much damage either.

The development and fielding of such kinetic counter-drone systems capable of defending individual vehicles and squads or fire teams are essential to restoring maneuver warfare. Such systems will likely become part of the defensive requirement of any system that must operate on the modern battlefield—they will become part of a redefinition of "armor."

All such systems will be vulnerable to countermeasures. Any system can be overwhelmed by numbers, for example, or by drones designed to ensure that even their debris is lethal. The same offense-defense race will develop between drones and kinetic counter-drone systems that is now occurring between drones and EW. Such offense-defense races are inherent in warfare, however. For example, they also characterized the development of armor for tanks and tank main guns and main gun rounds. There are no panaceas in military technology. But kinetic counter-drone systems form one of the few areas of obvious technological requirement and development that has not yet seen significant advances in the Russia-Ukraine war but will likely come to prominence in the relatively near future.

Long-Range Attack Drones. Both the Russia-Ukraine and Iran-Israel wars feature the widespread use of very long-range (greater than 1,000 kilometers) one-way attack drones. The Russians (and, of course, the Iranians and their proxies) famously rely on Iranian-developed

Shaheds and some indigenous variants, while the Ukrainians have produced their own long-range one-way attack drones.

These drones are inferior to long-range precision missiles in two main ways—their speed and their payloads. Their relatively slow speed makes intercepting them considerably easier than intercepting long-range missiles, permitting even individuals with rifles to do the job in some instances, as previously noted. Their relatively small payloads restrict their ability to attack most hardened and many softer targets effectively.

These drones offset their disadvantages by being much less expensive to produce and often more reliably precise. Their slow speed, in addition, increases their ability to collect intelligence in the course of their attacks, making almost every attacking drone a sensor, even if it fails in its strike mission. Such drones are designed and built to be rapidly modifiable with different sensors, communications systems, and software. Their low cost makes rapid experimentation in the field feasible.

These drones' reliable precision offsets their limited payloads by allowing them to hit identified vulnerable components in large complexes that they could not otherwise heavily damage. They can hit control centers, critical valves, electrical junctions, or other soft but vital targets in refinery and other industrial complexes, sometimes taking them offline for weeks or months. They can take advantage of poor practices in storing ammunition or fuel to truly devastating effect, as the Ukrainians have shown on several occasions.

Their low cost also makes them suitable as decoys to distract and absorb attention and interceptors from air defense elements, thus allowing missiles to penetrate. On several occasions, the Ukrainians have used drones in such modes to permit missiles to destroy Russian advanced air defense systems (S-300 and S-400) that should have been able to down the missiles. The Russians have gone so far as to establish serial production of purely decoy drones made of Styrofoam and plywood without explosives that are intended only to distract Ukrainian air defenses and return intelligence.

Both the Russians and the Iranians have been experimenting with optimal strike packages that include long-range drones, cruise missiles, and ballistic missiles. The Russians dynamically adjust the compositions of their packages as Ukrainian defenders respond.[4]

The most important characteristic of such drones at this time is that they are cheap and plentiful, with ranges that rival Tomahawk Land Attack Missiles. The Ukrainian air force reported that it downed roughly 14,400 reconnaissance and strike drones in 2024. The Shahed-type drones reportedly have ranges in excess of 2,000 kilometers and possibly as great as 2,500 kilometers.[5] Long-range one-way attack drones are unlikely to replace missiles, which are far better suited for many critical targets, but they will continue to supplement missiles and enhance their effectiveness by drawing off air defenders' attention and resources. Such drones can and will also be used to strike targets whose value is not great enough to justify expending scarce and expensive long-range missiles to attack, potentially greatly broadening the set of vulnerable places that a defender must protect.

Implications for the US

Drones and EW. American ground forces are not currently prepared to operate effectively in an environment characterized by the phenomena described above. All US military vehicles are susceptible to destruction by the tactical drone systems being used in Ukraine; the US does not have reliable counter-drone systems, either kinetic or EW, to prevent the use of such drones; and the US does not currently field large numbers of tactical drones or the integrative software systems required to use them effectively. US forces can likely operate more effectively than Ukrainian forces in the sort of EW environment currently seen in Ukraine but are not immune to the effects of that environment.

American technological advantages in other areas will not remediate these problems. The US and its allies can likely establish air superiority or even air supremacy over any adversary other than the PRC, which will almost certainly be able to contest airspace. But air supremacy does not translate into UAV supremacy. A situation in which the US has air supremacy at the altitudes of fixed-wing aircraft but the adversary has supremacy at the altitudes of tactical UAVs is not only possible but actually likely in current circumstances.

Tactical drones are operated by small groups of individuals sprinkled throughout ground forces. Integrative control systems can function in dispersed nodes relying on cloud-based infrastructure—and it is noteworthy that the Russians have completely failed to prevent Ukraine from using such infrastructure despite Russia's much-vaunted cyber capabilities. Destroying the adversary's ability to use drones by relying on advantages resulting from air supremacy is tantamount to destroying the enemy's necessarily dispersed ground forces from the air.

Long-range precision strike systems do not solve the problem either, for similar reasons. Finding lucrative targets for expensive and rare long-range strike systems against an adversary that can and will disperse logistics systems supplying its small, lightweight drones to the front lines will be difficult. Destroying those logistics systems with precision strikes will likely prove impossible.

The development of effective kinetic and EW-based counter-drone systems suitable for point defense is an urgent requirement for the US and allied militaries. Such systems must be affordable and suitable for mass serial production as well as rapid in-the-field upgrades to platforms, electronics, and software. They must be able to defend against tactical drones on the battlefield and long-range one-way strike drones aimed at targets thousands of kilometers from the front lines. They must be able to do so inexpensively and without diverting the attention and resources of IAMDS suitable for defense against missiles and other more advanced air threats.

The US must also reconsider its basing strategy in light of the developments in long-range one-way attack drones. Such drones could be used to strike military housing, logistics support centers, and other facilities in Europe that are not and cannot be readily hardened but that would not have constituted suitable targets for long-range missile attack. Reliable counter-drone systems can reduce the requirement to transform the US basing posture, but they will not likely eliminate that requirement, since reliability will be measured in percentages of kills, not clear skies.

US forward basing near potential future front lines will likely have to become much more dispersed and will have to field reliable tactical counter-UAV systems. Swarm tactics will develop to overwhelm those defenses, making large concentrations of forces vulnerable once more, even after counter-UAV systems are fielded. (This argument assumes that the cost and challenge of using drone swarms will limit their use to relatively lucrative targets, at least initially, but that assumption is tenuous and unlikely to hold over the long term.)

The US and its allies and partners can and should also derive the benefits that drone and EW capabilities offer the defender. The Russia-Ukraine war shows that, at least at the current level of technology, the drone-EW competition gives the defender a considerable advantage. The US and its allies will be on the defensive in the most likely conflicts for which they must be prepared and should have this capability in their arsenals. Effective point-defense counter-drone systems will reduce the defender's advantage over time, to be sure, by allowing attacking forces to protect themselves while concentrating on the offensive, but the offense-defense race cycling at high speed will periodically restore it.

These technological developments will likely also demand changes in campaign design, as the author and Kimberly Kagan have argued elsewhere.[6] The near impossibility of conducting effective maneuver operations in the face of a defending TRSC will likely impel attackers to first develop ways of temporarily neutralizing the defender's TRSC and then sustain that neutralization long enough and deep enough into the defender's rear to permit attacking forces to secure operationally significant objectives. Ukrainian and Russian forces are already experimenting with this approach on limited scales. "Concentrating for the attack" will thus likely come to require concentrating (and holding back and concealing) technological advances as well as forces.

The extremely rapid offense-defense cycle has implications for the DIB and stockage policies. It is unlikely that millions of drones produced before a war breaks out will be effective for very long after hostilities begin. Such drones will, at a minimum, need to be modified rapidly, especially in their electronics and software components. It is also possible, however, that the optimum strategy will rely less on stockpiling large numbers of systems that may prove obsolete quickly and more on sustaining the DIB necessary to produce large numbers of continually modified systems on demand.

IAMDS. The principal implications of the effectiveness of IAMDS in both the Russia-Ukraine and Iran-Israel wars are nearly self-evident and have been partially laid out above. The US and its allies must devise systems that optimize for cost and availability of defensive systems as well as for effectiveness. They must ensure that expensive interceptors are not wasted on decoy drones but rather reserved for the targets only they can engage. The scale of the requirement for interceptors is also daunting. Reports of shortages of Patriot and National Advanced Surface-to-Air Missile System interceptors are ubiquitous and concerning. One need only tally the number of missiles the PRC has stockpiled and consider the defense requirements of US forces in Japan, the Japan Self-Defense Forces, and Taiwan to reflect on the need for a fundamental change in US acquisition approaches to IAMDS interceptors and launchers.

The US military should not rely comfortably on the fact that it reportedly has geolocation and other capabilities to prevent an adversary from interfering with its long-range strike systems the way the Russians have interfered with US-supplied HIMARS and Army Tactical Missile System rounds. The PRC has considerably more technological and industrial capacity than Russia has, and the main lesson of these two current conflicts is likely to hold into the future: The missile will only sometimes get through.

Caveats

The author is a long-standing skeptic of overhyped "revolutions in military affairs" and has repeatedly criticized others for exaggerating the revolutionary impact of technology on warfare. The example of J. F. C. Fuller is particularly vivid in this respect. Fuller accurately observed transformations in the character of war that World War I had generated—predominantly but not exclusively by the advent of tanks and aircraft—and then extrapolated them to absurd degrees in his Gold Medal Essay on the future of war.[7] The foregoing text reads, even to the author himself, like something of an echo of that essay, particularly in the confident and dispositive statements about what successful militaries will require in future wars. The first critical caveat to the argument above, therefore, is that changes in technology that appear for a few years to be absolutely transformative may not be so in the long run, and this chapter may be no more prescient than Fuller's. Forecasting the full impact of technological innovations early in their adoption is extremely fraught and error prone.

The counterargument to this caveat is that tanks actually did transform the character of war, in conjunction with aircraft and other technologies, when properly integrated into existing and transforming military systems. Fuller did not really foresee what that integration would look like or what the transformed war would be, but he did capture a true inflection in the character of war based on his observations of changes in war as it was being fought. The observations in this chapter, drawn from actual combat in two theaters, are surely wrong in many important respects. The likelihood that the advent of mass drone warfare and the drone-EW race will not significantly change the character of war over the long term, however, appears very small.

Old weapons systems will not lose their value on the future battlefield suddenly, if at all. The tank has not suddenly become any more obsolete than it ever was just because of drones. Neither has artillery. On the contrary, those traditional systems and many others remain critical components of the full TRSC that the Russians and Ukrainians are fielding. There have been systems capable of destroying tanks since before there were tanks. The advent of airpower, long-range strike, and, now, drones has not made even towed tube artillery obsolete or irrelevant. Shell hunger correlates directly with battlefield performance even today. It is either possible to defend against attacking drones (in which case tanks, artillery, and other "archaic" systems can continue to function at least in part as intended), or it isn't (in which case nothing will be able to survive and no movement will be possible). The loudest clarion call emerging from the current conflict is the development of such defensive systems and the integration of new technologies optimally with current capabilities, not the abolition of traditional systems.

The final caveat, however, is that success in future war will likely require significant adjustments in all aspects of military forces and their employment. Sprinkling hundreds of thousands or millions of drones onto military forces as they are currently organized, trained, and equipped will fail. It is impossible to see now what the next optimized forms of warfare and shapes of military forces will be, but we must begin to envisage and develop the next "interim" force to implement the requirements for change that we can see now, recognizing that all force constructs, in the end, are interim.

Notes

1. Frederick W. Kagan and Kimberly Kagan, *Ukraine and the Problem of Restoring Maneuver in Contemporary War*, Institute for the Study of War, August 12, 2024, https://www.understandingwar.org/backgrounder/ukraine-and-problem-restoring-maneuver-contemporary-war.

2. Alexandra Braverman et al., "Iran Update, October 1, 2024," Critical Threats Project at the American Enterprise Institute, October 1, 2024, https://www.criticalthreats.org/analysis/iran-update-october-1-2024; and Alexandra Braverman et al., "Iran Update, October 2, 2024," Critical Threats Project at the American Enterprise Institute, October 2, 2024, https://www.criticalthreats.org/analysis/iran-update-october-2-2024. See also Riley Bailey and Frederick W. Kagan, *Special Report: Russian Strikes More Effective as Ukraine Exhausts Defenses*, Institute for the Study of War, April 12, 2024, https://www.understandingwar.org/backgrounder/special-report-russian-strikes-more-effective-ukraine-exhausts-defenses; and Riley Bailey and Frederick W. Kagan, *A Defense of Taiwan with Ukrainian Characteristics: Lessons from the War in Ukraine for the Western Pacific*, Institute for the Study of War, October 30, 2024, https://www.understandingwar.org/backgrounder/defense-taiwan-ukrainian-characteristics-lessons-war-ukraine-western-pacific.

3. Kagan and Kagan, *Ukraine and the Problem of Restoring Maneuver in Contemporary War*.

4. Brian Carter and Frederick W. Kagan, "Iran's Attempt to Hit Israel with a Russian-Style Strike Package Failed . . . for Now," Critical Threats Project at the American Enterprise Institute, April 14, 2024, https://www.aei.org/articles/irans-attempt-to-h-it-israel-with-a-russian-style-strike-package-failedfor-now/; and Kagan and Bailey, *Russian Strikes More Effective as Ukraine Exhausts Defenses*.

5. Angelica Evans et al., *Russian Offensive Campaign Assessment*, Institute for the Study of War, December 31, 2024, https://understandingwar.org/backgrounder/russian-offensive-campaign-assessment-december-31-2024.

6. Kagan and Kagan, *Ukraine and the Problem of Restoring Maneuver in Contemporary War*.

7. J. F. C. Fuller, "Gold Medal (Military) Prize Essay for 1919: The Application of Recent Developments in Mechanics and Other Scientific Knowledge to Preparation and Training for Future War on Land," *Journal of the Royal United Service Institution* 65, no. 458 (1920): 239–74, https://www.tandfonline.com/doi/epdf/10.1080/03071842009421885.

12

US Land Forces: Slouching Toward Sitzkrieg

GISELLE DONNELLY

America's land forces appear to have lost their way. Beset by budget cuts, erratic strategic guidance, and uncertainty about the character of land combat, the Marine Corps and the Army have, for several decades now, lurched about in a variety of often contradictory directions. Military services that by the end of the Cold War exuded confidence in their ability to exert geopolitically significant influence through the conduct of large-scale offensive operational maneuver now seek merely to "protect Joint and Coalition forces" and, at best, "deliver long-range fires in support of joint-force maneuver."[1]

This retreat to a defensive crouch is particularly unfortunate in that a clear understanding of US national security interests, particularly in Europe and the Middle East, calls for a renewed emphasis on counter-offensive operations and securing territory. To be sure, emerging technologies are creating new battlefield problems, but US land forces must solve them if they are to meet the nation's true needs—not merely in response to emerging threats but to seize the strategic opportunities of the moment. The rollback of Russian revanche and Iran and its proxies and partners (and the continued suppression of Salafi-jihadi groups) requires a restored ability to take and secure territory and populations. In such cases, land forces must do more than provide targeting information and munitions delivery if they are to fulfill the requirements for defending US global security interests.

Land Warfare: Change and Continuity

It has seemed to many observers that the conduct of land warfare is evolving, if not undergoing some more radical change.[2] Much of this discussion results from the fact that neither the Ukraine war nor Israel's wars in Gaza and Lebanon and blunting the effects of Iranian drone and missile strikes unfolded as anticipated. This is especially true in the Ukraine case; even the most senior US military and defense officials in 2022 believed Russian forces would overwhelm the Ukrainian army in a few days.[3]

This is to say that a degree of modesty is in order in predicting the future conduct of land warfare in general and the resulting implications for the US Army, Marine Corps, and special operations forces. In parsing the recent lessons of Ukraine, Gaza, and Lebanon, it is critical not to lose sight of the particulars of each conflict: the contestants' strategic objectives; their operational, tactical, and technological capabilities and capacities; the geographical and human terrain; the character of the armed forces involved; and so on. For example, the prevalence of drones, electronic warfare, and indirect fires reflects the shortcomings of the contesting forces as well as their strengths. In studying recent conflicts, American forces must see the continuities as well as the changes.

It is further important to assess the lessons of ongoing conflicts in light of enduring American security interests. Having been slow to recognize the importance of Chinese military modernization and geopolitical ambition, the entire Department of Defense is now in danger of overreacting in at least two ways that have had deleterious effects on the Army and Marine Corps. First, an obsession with the potential invasion or blockade of Taiwan tends to reduce the strategic competition with Beijing (and American defense strategy overall) to the defense of the first island chain, the maritime littoral of the western Pacific. This may indeed be a focal point, but it narrows the US military's strategic field of view, not only in Asia but globally. Second, and relatedly, this definition of the problem reinforces the tactical and technological obsession with what Soviet doctrinal writers defined as the "reconnaissance-strike complex." The idea behind this concept was to exploit emerging technologies in sensing, computing, and precision weaponry to speed the process of finding targets, distributing target information, and attacking them. The US military has better developed the concept in practice, but when it is detached from an equal emphasis on maneuver, the result is an "attritionist" approach to warfare, leading to operational and strategic stalemate.

There are, however, at least two themes that emerge from the battle-fields of recent years. One is that control of territory remains a principal objective in war, and thus that land power retains its strategic salience. The second is that land wars are by nature protracted struggles; if the Desert Storm dream of "rapid, decisive operations" had not already become the nightmares of Iraq and Afghanistan, the evidence from the Donbas, Gaza, and Lebanon would be a final wake-up call—these are already conflicts measured in decades. American land forces must prepare for a series of "forever wars."

This has been a term associated with Afghanistan, Iraq, and the global war on terror, but in fact, it equally describes history's great-power conflicts. French hegemonic ambitions began with Louis XIV in the 1660s and did not conclude until Waterloo in 1815. The same clearly applies to Russian revanche, Iranian aspirations, and China's "rise." No conflict with such adversaries can be concluded in a single battle or campaign. And if the United States consigns itself to attrition warfare, these protracted conflicts will prove even more costly and difficult to sustain.

The Department of Defense also needs to refocus its efforts and investments on the US Army, the nation's principal land-war force. This also means, as will be discussed below, a reevaluation of the costs and benefits of the US Marine Corps and, to a lesser extent, US special operations forces, which have many of the characteristics of a separate service. Concomitant with this is a continued and, indeed, increased effort working with allies and longer-term coalition partners—without losing focus on adversaries. Long wars are team sports.

The Three-Theater Challenge

The measure of the United States' status as a global power is calculated by the relative balance of power in three regions, or theaters: Europe, the greater Middle East, and maritime East Asia. This has been the structure of the post–Cold War peace, now under assault in each theater. To secure its global interests and the international order—the military, diplomatic, and economic arrangements conducive to American security, liberty, and prosperity—America cannot afford to pivot so sharply in any one direction that it neglects the overall picture, and it is a mistake to imagine that in an age of globalization, the balance of global power can be so neatly segmented. It may be better to see these regions as composing a larger theater: Eurasia.

Nevertheless, the particulars of the three theaters demand that US land forces set certain relative priorities. This means that even if the United States' larger military strategy emphasizes the challenge from China as the "pacing challenge,"[4] the maritime and aerospace characters of the Indo-Pacific, as the Pentagon has come to describe the region, tend to diminish the requirements for land forces, although this narrow understanding of Chinese strategy is historically debatable and tends to overlook China's growing global presence. By contrast, ground troops earn their strategic keep in Europe and the greater Middle East.

The US Army especially needs to pivot back to a European focus, not simply maintaining the rotational brigades and division headquarters deployed there but building a more robust presence, in partnership with NATO allies, from the Baltic to the Black Sea. The war in Ukraine is but one manifestation of the larger conflict with Russia and its fellow travelers in China, Iran, and North Korea. This struggle is a threat to the United States' foundational international security interest: the balance of power in western Eurasia. Therefore, Europe's security is too important an American interest to be left in the hands of others, even our best traditional allies.

In Ukraine, the conflict is all but certain to continue regardless of any ceasefire—and negotiations cannot be expected to do anything more. The means of war are already quite varied, including subversion, corruption, and other forms of political and economic warfare, but the ultimate prize for Vladimir Putin and his backers is direct political control of the lands of Eastern Europe and the east of Central Europe, the fracturing of NATO, the neutralization of Western Europe, and the rollback of American influence on the Continent. A prime recent example is the cutting of communications and other cables in the Baltic, an act that may have involved not just Russian but Chinese vessels. Only a substantial US presence, including a substantial, permanent complement of US Army troops and formations, can prevent or deter further Russian revanche.

However, US forces' principal role in Europe is to improve the command structures, lethality, and overall performance of NATO coalition forces. As will be discussed below, only US participation in a leadership role can create a new "allied AirLand Battle" counteroffensive capability centered in Poland that would act as a powerful deterrent by denial and punishment. Moscow might not only fail in any attack but suffer territorial losses in Belarus, for example. Ukraine's incursion into Kursk oblast is another recent development that needs strategic and operational evaluation but has received precious little, and it has even been downplayed.[5] That it has shifted Russian military planning is now without doubt, not only diverting Russian forces but prompting the introduction of more than 10,000 North Korean troops.[6] Possession of Russian territory would, at a minimum, give Ukraine leverage in any ceasefire talks. There is a lesson for NATO here.

The need for land power is equally clear in the greater Middle East, as Israel's failure to preserve sufficient defense in depth in Gaza—and its subsequent success in reestablishing it there and in southern Lebanon—makes plain. For the Jewish state, this is as much an existential issue as an Iranian nuclear weapon would be, perhaps a lesser but a more clear and present daily danger. The record of American land forces in the region is decidedly mixed. There have been evanescent successes—the 1991 Gulf War, the initial invasions of Afghanistan in 2001 and Iraq in 2003, the surge of 2007–09, and various special operations forces raids—framed by more failures resulting from imprudent withdrawals. The most egregious by far was the Obama administration's retreat from Iraq in the wake of the surge, but the shambolic pullout from Afghanistan and the failure to provide support to the anti-Assad rebels in Syria stem from not only flagging political will but also the sheer exhaustion of land forces too small to sustain their missions.

The Israelis' term for inevitable but invariably indecisive campaigns such as these—"mowing the grass"—contrasts significantly with Americans' lament over "forever wars." Israel may have little choice, but if the past five decades are anything to go by, neither does the United States. The region's geopolitical importance has not, in fact, been diminished by the changes in energy markets or the US oil and gas boom. Moreover, the regional alliance of anti-Iran, anti-jihadist Arab states and Israel is a delicate thing, far less robust or institutionalized than NATO in Europe. In the greater Middle East, the United States has truly been an "indispensable nation," a role underscored by the ability to deploy powerful land forces. This is a role that annoys China, which, while reluctant and perhaps unable to assume to itself, is looking for ways to raise its strategic profile in the region. As Jonathan Fulton and Michael Schuman report for the Atlantic Council, Beijing is shifting from a "hedging" to a "wedging" approach to the Middle East, seeking to pry apart American strategic and military partnerships.[7]

Finally, elevating the China challenge as the Defense Department's pacing threat has distorted land force planning, particularly regarding the Marine Corps, which in turn has complicated overall, joint, allied, and coalition thinking. The Marines' desire to get in the fight, while admirable, has consequences for others. Second, the addition of the "Indo" region to what was US Pacific Command has not sparked much broader strategic thinking about how to complicate Chinese planning by trying to create and leverage land power in Southeast Asia; summoning the spirit of Orde Wingate is worth a séance or two. The Indo-Pacific contains multiple theaters, and while maritime and aerospace forces are critical everywhere, the possibilities for land power may be greater outside northeast Asia.

The Army's Role in the Three-Theater Construct

The United States Army has always been the principal measure of American land power. Even if the nation fully mobilized the National Guard and Army Reserve, it could not field a three-theater Army. Nor a two-theater Army; as the then-chairman of the Joint Chiefs of Staff, Admiral Mike Mullen, confessed to the House Committee on Armed Services in 2007, "In Iraq, we do what we must," while "in Afghanistan, we do what we can."[8] In other words, there were insufficient troops to properly conduct what by historical standards were two relatively small wars. Since Mullen's confession, the size of the active-duty Army has dropped by more than 100,000, from about 560,000 at the height of the Iraq surge to roughly 450,000 today.[9]

The Total Army also includes 350,000 National Guard soldiers and 175,000 in the Army Reserve. The small and shrinking size of the active component placed a substantial burden on the other two components through the duration of the Iraq and Afghanistan wars, although deployments to the Middle East have picked up somewhat since 2024. On average, members of the Army National Guard will be deployed every two to three years for a year in support of federal missions; reservists, about once every five years.

As the scope of Russian revanche has revealed itself—the brutal suppression of Chechnya, the invasions of Georgia and Ukraine, troublemaking in Moldova, cyberattacks on the Baltic states, the barely concealed annexation of Belarus, the attempt to improve the quality of its military and now simply to expand its army with conscripts, contract soldiers, mercenaries, and even North Koreans—the requirements for European security have increased. This, in turn, should drive the Army to increase the personnel strength of all its components.

The post–Cold War period has seen two significant reductions in US troop strength in the theater: from about 220,000 to 60,000 during the Clinton administration and then to fewer than 40,000 during the Obama years. Halfway through the second Obama term, and in response to the initial Russian invasion of Ukraine, the administration created the European Reassurance Initiative, now renamed the European Deterrence Initiative, which has rotated additional tens of thousands of soldiers to Eastern Europe, including heavy armored forces. These programs have also added pre-positioned stocks of weapons and munitions and improved the theater's logistics infrastructure to allow for quicker response across NATO's eastern front. Yet while these initiatives have been a welcome development, they are sufficient in neither capability nor capacity. Even with back-to-back unit rotations, the effect of the presence is less than what the effect of a more permanent stationing arrangement would be.

How Did We Get Here?

To understand the confusion and challenges that US land forces face, one must begin with the reductions in funding that have been accumulating since the end of the Cold War. For the Army, the decline began with the 1992 "base force" budget, which saw a whopping 19 percent reduction in the services budget; measured in constant 2025 dollars, the total outlays for the Army that year were just under $175 billion, about 1 percent of US gross domestic product. Army allocations reached their nadir in the 1998 budget, falling to less than $129 billion in 2025 dollars, or 0.7 percent of the overall economy. In 2022, the Army's expenditures totaled $201 billion in 2025 dollars, also 0.7 percent of that year's gross domestic product. In sum, over the past three decades, the service has lost trillions of dollars in purchasing power relative to what was assumed to be the minimum required force.[10]

The result of this massive reduction in funding has been a hectic series of service reorganizations. Much of the Army's effort in the 1990s went toward simply reducing the number of active-duty troops in as orderly and humane a manner as possible. The active-duty force dropped from over 610,000 soldiers to 493,000, whereas reserve-component strength—both Army National Guard and Army Reserve—has remained relatively constant at about 550,000 through the entirety of the post–Cold War period.[11]

The first reorganization, completed in 2003, was to create a "Modular Army,"[12] optimized to "better meet the challenges of the 21st century security environment and . . . fight and win the Global War on Terrorism."[13] In so doing, the Army tried to increase the number of rotationally deployable units by 50 percent, design units that would require fewer augmentations before deployment, and create a more predictable deployment schedule. As the Association of the US Army observed, this meant "moving the Army from a division-centric structure to one built around a brigade combat team."[14] That is, the service broke itself into smaller, more self-contained units, sacrificing capabilities such as divisional artillery and logistics organizations needed for larger-scale operations, to meet the needs of constant rotations to the Middle East. Even more importantly, this rearrangement was driven by the need to maintain lower personnel levels—the Army did its best to execute a mission it was unprepared for by reallocating existing personnel and assets. The reorganization consumed a substantial portion of a stagnant Army budget, with the cost of the project rising from $28 billion in 2004 to $53 billion a year later.[15]

The second drawdown-cum-reorganization began with the second Obama administration. In the last years of the George W. Bush term, with the implementation of the Iraq surge and, during Barack Obama's first presidency, the renewed effort in Afghanistan, the active Army had grown—rapidly and somewhat haphazardly—back to roughly 570,000 soldiers. But what had gone up quickly came down equally fast: The Obama Defense Department would cut end strength back to 490,000 by the end of 2017, along with 12 of the 35 newly formed brigade combat teams.[16] Packaged as part of the administration's "pivot to the Pacific" strategy, the reality was withdrawal from Iraq and Europe; in addition to terminating the US combat mission in Iraq, Obama reduced the number of brigades in Europe by half. The administration also initiated an effort to reorganize Army National Guard brigades in the "modular" fashion.[17]

The Obama administration also saw a third, smaller reorganization of Army structure in 2017 with a slight increase in personnel strength, also related to the new emphasis on the Pacific and threats from North Korea and China. About 30,000 additional soldiers were to be raised to "begin to address and reduce the capabilities gap against near-peer, high-end adversaries" such as China; "reduce modernization gaps; and improve readiness in existing units."[18] This permitted the Army to raise more units to full personnel strength, add additional training cadres, retain units in Alaska and South Korea that were to be inactivated, and convert and create additional maneuver and aviation brigades and artillery brigades.

Where Are We Now?

The Army's confusion over its structure, posture, organization, and equipment—that is, in essence, its primary purpose—seems to have only increased in recent years. In 2018, it scurried to try to align itself with a new, formal national defense strategy, which veered away from the "countering violent extremists" mission that had driven modularity and a brigade-centric force design. The Army shifted its focus back to "near-peer competitors" or "revisionist powers" and unveiled a new concept for multi-domain operations, which tried to account for new and newly emphasized technologies—the proliferation of unmanned systems, information and political warfare (particularly in the cyber realm), electronic warfare, the influence of space systems, and so on. One very positive step from this was beginning to rebuild the capacity to fight at higher echelons—divisions, corps, and theater commands—to conduct larger, campaign-level operations against these more powerful adversaries.

By 2020, the Army had developed a roadmap for implementing this shift—the AimPoint Force Structure Initiative. This continued the effort to bring "hollow" units up to designed levels of personnel and equipment, but it also added back complements of staff, specialists, and new units with new capabilities. Signally, the Army reactivated V Corps—principally headquartered at Fort Knox, Kentucky, but with a forward-stationed element; while the personnel would rotate, the headquarters organization would not—in Poznań, Poland. This welcome development reflected an overdue return of emphasis on the Eastern European theater and Poland's centrality to NATO and other coalition military operations in the region; Poland has vigorously modernized and professionalized its forces, committing more than 3 percent or more of its annual economic product to military spending.[19]

A second element of the AimPoint project was the creation of five Multi-Domain Task Forces (MDTFs) to enable land forces to penetrate adversary defenses by suppressing enemy anti-access and area-denial capabilities, disrupting targeting networks, and expanding and accelerating efforts to deliver longer-range precision fires. These task forces are to be theater-level organizations roughly the size of a brigade of four main battalions: an "intelligence, information, cyber, electronic warfare, and space" battalion; a "strategic fires" battalion, which will incorporate hypersonic weapons; an air defense battalion, which will include a counter-drone company; and a support battalion.[20] As theater-specific organizations, each MDTF will be tailored to combatant commanders' requirements: one MDTF for Europe, two aligned for the Indo-Pacific, one for the Arctic but available elsewhere, and one for global response to be stationed at Fort Liberty, North Carolina, home of XVIII Airborne Corps and the 82nd Airborne Division and next to the Air Force's hub at Pope Field.

These task forces are indicative of the Army's increasing orientation toward a defensive, fires-centric understanding of its role. Further, the design reflects an intentional reduction in overall personnel strength and a diminishment of combined-arms reconnaissance formations, notably divisional cavalry squadrons. Whether a single MDTF will have the capacity to support a large-scale counteroffensive is an open question.

Corresponding to the overall AimPoint directive, in January 2022 the Army settled on a set of near-term "Army 2030" force designs that would standardize divisions as Standard Light, Standard Heavy, Penetration, Joint Force Entry Air Assault, and Joint Force Entry Airborne. The Penetration Division is the least traditional structure and is a key to rebuilding the Army's operational counteroffensive capability. According to the original force design, it was to have additional engineer assets, an Extended Range Cannon Artillery piece with double the range of current howitzers, a powerful armored cavalry squadron instead of the previous Stryker-equipped divisional cavalry squadrons, an improved aviation brigade with a light armed reconnaissance helicopter, and a tilt-rotor Future Long-Range Assault Aircraft to replace many current UH-60 Black Hawks, capable of flying much farther and faster.

These ambitious plans have been substantially gutted. In a February 2024 white paper, the Army admitted it did not have the personnel strength to execute the designs.[21] The current active-duty force of 450,000 soldiers is far below the total of 494,000 needed under the Army 2030 force structure.[22] The planned expansion of engineer capabilities has been rolled back, and the Army will deactivate all but one of the cavalry squadrons in its Stryker and infantry brigades. Some of these capacities will be consolidated at the division level, but the overall number of engineers will be reduced. In addition, the Army is reducing the weapons companies in infantry brigades to a single platoon. Together, these force-structure changes will reduce brigades' ability to fight for information, their firepower, and their independent ability to create defensive works and penetrate adversary lines. Brigades will be extremely dependent on help from their parent divisions and the theater MDTFs.

The service's transformation plans have been further handicapped by halting modernization efforts. Also, in February 2024, the Army terminated the Future Attack Reconnaissance Aircraft (FARA), the fourth attempt to build such a helicopter since 2004. Tens of billions of dollars have been spent on the Comanche, the armed reconnaissance helicopter, the Armed Aerial Scout, and FARA efforts. Despite these failures, the importance of the air-ground littoral, the low-level airspace surrounding the tactical battlefield, has only grown—particularly with the proliferation of drones. In the announcement of the FARA termination, the Army argued that "in light of new technological developments, battlefield developments and current budget projections, . . . the increased capabilities [FARA] offered could be more affordably and effectively achieved by relying on a mix of enduring, unmanned and space-based assets."[23] This is undoubtedly a correct assessment, but it leaves the Army with much work to do to develop alternative capabilities—no easy task in a constrained budget environment. FARA's problems also raise questions about its bigger brother, the Future Long-Range Assault Aircraft.

Under the umbrella of long-range precision fires (LRPF), the Army has also thrown in the towel on its previous effort to build a longer-range artillery piece. The Extended Range Cannon Program was an experiment to examine a very long, 58-caliber gun tube, much bigger than the current standard 39-caliber models and even longer than the 52-caliber tubes on the French Caesar, German Panzerhaubitze 2000, and Korean K9 howitzers. These longer tubes are already prone to wearing out prematurely due to the stress of firing. In its search for a gun that will reach to the ranges desired on modern battlefields and necessary for its doctrine and force designs, the Army has little alternative but to turn to research on advanced propellants.

A second element of LRPF is the Precision Strike Missile, slated to replace the venerable Army Tactical Missile System, which was first employed in Operation Desert Storm and is still effective in Ukraine. The new missile has approximately double the range, to something like 250 miles, and a slimmer design that will double the number of missiles in each pod. The program appears to generally be on track, and the Army has taken delivery of a first batch of missiles. Moreover, later versions of the Precision Strike Missile will be able to hit moving targets and targets at sea, a capability demonstrated in a recent exercise.

Two final areas of Army modernization should be of concern. The first is the service's efforts to exploit the revolution in unmanned systems and the related issues of electronic warfare and rapid software development, all distinguishing elements of the Ukraine war. The Army has recognized the importance of these issues, but it is hard to discern whether it has a coherent plan to field such capabilities or is well organized to do so. Many of the Ukrainian army's innovations have come from outside, civilian developers; many are also short-lived improvements in a constantly shifting contest with the Russians. Second, the Army's chief of staff has nixed the idea of a "drone corps," or "drone branch," an idea proposed in the House of Representatives version of the fiscal year 2025 National Defense Authorization Act. "Specializing a singular drone branch to get after the operations of these capabilities," says Under Secretary of the Army Gabe Camarillo, "runs counter to what we have been focused on, which is ensuring that we are experimenting with different parts of different formations to understand how to best employ them."[24]

The Pentagon-wide Defense Innovation Unit is spearheading work on smaller drones. Two factors call this approach into question: First, the overall drone (and counter-drone) effort may fall prey to the entrenched interests of the Army's current branch system. Second, the track record of organizations such as the Defense Innovation Unit, with limited budgets, overseen by the Office of the Secretary of Defense rather than the services, and an emphasis on new technologies rather than fielded systems, is poor.

In sum, decades of declining resources, strategic uncertainty, and halting or misconceived modernization programs have left the Army whiplashed. Perhaps most importantly, these intertwined problems are eroding the service's doctrinal commitment to operational counteroffensives that are the Army's unique contribution to US national defense strategy. To be sure, attriting adversary forces from a distance is a necessary condition for land campaigns—and it is also a job for joint and coalition forces. Yet it is far from sufficient. Today's battlefields reveal new challenges, but the need to close with the enemy, drive him from occupied territory, secure the gain, and reset for follow-on operations remains the salient characteristic of victory on land.

So, what should the Army be doing, and what should it be doing differently? Here are six recommendations:

- Rethink the Army's role in the Pacific theater with a view to providing only those capabilities and capacities that are unique to the service and necessary to overall, joint-force operations.

- With the Air Force and Space Force, rapidly develop a new concept of counteroffensive operations and accompanying service doctrine, an AirLand Battle that accounts for current conditions, particularly in the European theater. Until these challenges are met, the Army lacks guidelines for investment, personnel strength, force posture, and design.

- At the division level, establish force protection organizations able to synchronize effects in the electromagnetic; cyber; air, missile, and drone defense; and other related capabilities to enable larger-scale land force maneuver. These organizations must retain the command agility to rapidly adapt to shifting battlefield conditions and integrate the talents of civilian auxiliaries.

- Quickly determine the viability of long-range, large-scale air assaults. The program cost estimate for the Future Long-Range Assault Aircraft is, at minimum, $70 billion; the Army should either accelerate or terminate the program within two years.

- Accelerate the development and fielding of the Long-Range Hypersonic Weapon (Dark Eagle) while preparing multiple lines of production. This 1,700-mile-range missile, unlike other Army capabilities, can be a cardinal Army contribution to operations in the western Pacific; while the Navy (which is jointly developing the missile) intends to mount this on its *Zumwalt*-class destroyers, the sea service has but three of these ships. The Army's program to buy just 300 Dark Eagles would be insufficient to sustain extended operations.

- Continue to modify the M1 Abrams tank and M2 Bradley infantry fighting vehicles to improve their survivability, particularly against autonomous drone attacks, and lethality. As emphasized above, these modifications must be capable of rapid production and fielding, as the Ukrainian army has done with its first-generation Leopard tanks.

Corps of Contention

If anything, the Marine Corps is undergoing even greater turmoil than the Army. The corps's new force-structure concept, Force Design 2030 (now known simply as Force Design), introduced in a surprise announcement by the then-commandant, General David H. Berger, represented a decisive move away from the Marines' previous role as a medium-weight, combined-arms maneuver force able to rapidly project a substantial amount of initial combat power from the sea onto land.

While a full explication of the issues and arguments is beyond the scope of this chapter, suffice it to say that the concept has been utterly rejected by Marine traditionalists, including former commandants Walter Boomer and James Conway. In the summer of 2024, they wrote that the Marine Corps was "no longer capable of effectively conducting combat operations across the spectrum of conflict," and that Force Design betrayed a "flawed operational concept" resulting from a "lack of operational competence in some current and recently retired senior Marine Corps leaders," a direct shot at Berger and his successor, General Eric Smith.[25] Other notable opponents of Force Design include former Secretary of Defense James Mattis, former Chairman of the Joint Chiefs of Staff Joseph Dunford, and former Secretary of Homeland Security John Kelly, all retired four-star Marine Corps generals.[26]

The critique, however, is more than a fit of personal pique on the part of retired generals. Berger's new force design was a reaction to the 2018 National Defense Strategy (a document that has caused much mischief) and its increased emphasis on rising threats from China. In critics' minds, this was a hastily conceived overreaction, and in assessing the changes made and planned for Marine structure, force design, equipment, personnel levels, and modernization, the charge rings true.

The first step toward implementing Force Design was eliminating substantial ground force units and capabilities—including all Marine tank battalions, bridging companies, and military police battalions—reducing the number of infantry battalions from 24 to 21, howitzer battalions from 21 to five, and amphibious vehicle companies from six to four. The Marines took similarly rapid reductions in aviation—an area they have invested in heavily over the past several decades (including the Navy's creation of

America-class amphibious ships that can serve as small aircraft carriers with up to 35 F-35B jump jets)—including two V-22 tilt-rotor squadrons, two attack helicopter squadrons, and an undetermined number of F-35s organized in smaller squadrons of just 10 aircraft.

Force Design's Pacific orientation is best revealed in the reorganization of higher commands, principally focused on the III Marine Expeditionary Force (III MEF), based in Okinawa, Japan. The role of the Marines' other, similar commands, based at Camp Lejeune on the East Coast and Camp Pendleton on the West Coast of the United States, serve as sources of force generation for III MEF. This inevitably will shortchange the Marines' ability to operate in Europe or the Middle East. To put it mildly, this is a big mistake. Traditional Marine capacities and capabilities can be especially useful in a number of Middle East scenarios, and if, for example, greater sustainment capabilities were incorporated in organic Marine formations, the Marines' strategic utility would be not merely restored but enhanced. The Marine Corps should be heavier, not lighter.

More broadly, the extent of changes under Force Design is unclear. To begin with, the Marines' plan creates three Marine Littoral Regiments, organized, trained, and equipped for "sea denial"—threatening adversary naval vessels—and "control within contested maritime spaces." These regiments would have three main subordinate units, a Littoral Combat Team with an infantry battalion and long-range anti-ship missiles, a Littoral Anti-Air Battalion, and a Littoral Logistics Battalion. These would operate on small islands, hopscotching from location to location.[27]

The underlying operational rationale parallels that of the Army and similarly reflects a static, attritionist view of warfare. Given the size of China's air, naval, and missile buildup, this may be the best approach to the immediate maritime dilemma in the first island chain. However, the amount of firepower such small Marine detachments could bring to bear—and the relatively short range of the anti-ship missiles that would equip the initial regiments—would be of questionable effect. The corps also plans to field three modified Marine Expeditionary Units with some traditional and some of these new capabilities—the unit design is unclear and intended to be flexible—that could deploy as part of Amphibious Ready Groups, the configuration of which is equally unclear.[28]

Finally, Force Design calls for up to 35 of the Navy's Medium Landing Ships to deliver the Littoral Regiments to their dispersed locations.[29] Sized to carry just 75 or fewer marines and their gear[30]—and to hide among the busy commercial shipping trafficking the western Pacific—the program is intended as a supplement to larger, traditional amphibious warships. Navy leaders, recently burned by the troubles of their own Littoral Combat Ship program, which was also intended as a smaller, relatively inexpensive platform for close-in brown-water operations, are skeptical of the small amphib design, believing that the Marines' advertised price tag of $100 million per ship is unrealistic and that the ship itself is not survivable.

In sum, it is hard to avoid the conclusion that the Marines jumped too quickly back in 2020 and did not anticipate the world of 2024 and beyond, where crises in Europe and the Middle East forced their way to the immediate forefront of US national security concerns. In particular, the Marines should reevaluate the virtues of their previous posture and design—an initially powerful, sea-based, combined-arms maneuver force—which is well suited to respond to Middle East crises and opportunities and to conduct larger-scale raids ashore. These would make a greater contribution to a three-theater defense strategy than the "rockets on rocks" of Force Design, a marginal element in a large-scale confrontation in the western Pacific.

Here are recommendations for reviving the Marine Corps:

- All Marine units should be redesigned to increase their firepower, mobility, and sustainability. This should apply especially to the expansibility of the Marine Expeditionary Forces—the largest organic Marine formation, commanded by a three-star general. Additional amphibious assault and logistics ships should be added to Amphibious Ready Groups, which should routinely deploy with at least five such ships rather than three, thus perhaps reducing the need for support from Navy carriers, destroyers, and submarines.

- The First Marine Expeditionary Force—the MEF stationed on the East Coast and most suitable for Mediterranean and Middle East operations—should be given precedence in this rebalancing. III MEF—already being transferred from Okinawa to Guam and thus less able to intervene rapidly in a western Pacific crisis—should be deactivated or become a mostly reserve-component organization.

- Older amphibious ships should be decommissioned or put in reserve status. It would be preferable to have two modern, fully equipped and capable Amphibious Ready Groups than three hollow ones.

- In general, the Marine land forces should be transformed into a kind of shipborne air assault unit, but with the fixed-wing support of the F-35B. Infantry units should return to their traditional size, and missile- and rocket-artillery units should be re-created.

Conclusion

The saga of American land forces over the past three decades resembles nothing so much as a children's soccer game, a frenzied scramble to follow the ball with little thought to how it got there and where it might go next. While in large measure this was the result of the Afghanistan and Iraq wars and understandable as a response to the strategic surprise of 9/11, the Army and Marine Corps had earlier traditions in counterterrorism and counterinsurgency warfare. But the mania of the Pacific pivot and the reaction to technologies creating an apparently transparent tactical battlefield have had more disorienting effects.

Ultimately, the Army and Marine Corps need to find roles commensurate with the requirements of the overall, joint-force three-theater construct outlined above. There are more things in being a global power than were dreamt of in our recent national defense philosophies, things that call for counteroffensive land power and the ability to seize and secure territory. America's land forces need to rise to these challenges, not be further paralyzed by them.

Notes

1. US Army, "Army Force Structure Transformation," February 27, 2024, 1, https://api.army.mil/e2/c/downloads/2024/02/27/091989c9/army-white-paper-army-force-structure-transformation.pdf.

2. For one example of the proliferating projects and studies exploring these changes, see Center for a New American Security, "The Future of Warfare," https://www.cnas.org/research/defense/the-future-of-warfare.

3. To understand the scope and causes of these flawed assessments, see Eliot A. Cohen and Phillips O'Brien, *The Russia-Ukraine War: A Study in Analytic Failure*, Center for Strategic and International Studies, September 24, 2024, https://www.csis.org/analysis/russia-ukraine-war-study-analytic-failure.

4. US Department of Defense, 2022 *National Defense Strategy of the United States of America*, 2022, 2, https://media.defense.gov/2022/Oct/27/2003103845/-1/-1/1/2022-NATIONAL-DEFENSE-STRATEGY-NPR-MDR.pdf.

5. Stephen Walt, "The Murky Meaning of Ukraine's Kursk Offensive," Quincy Institute for Responsible Statecraft, August 28, 2024, https://quincyinst.org/2024/08/28/the-murky-meaning-of-ukraines-kursk-offensive/.

6. David Vergun, "North Korean Troops Enter Kursk Where Ukrainians Are Fighting," US Department of Defense, November 18, 2024, https://www.defense.gov/News/News-Stories/Article/article/3968230/north-korean-troops-enter-kursk-where-ukrainians-are-fighting/.

7. Jonathan Fulton and Michael Schuman, "China's Middle East Policy Shift from 'Hedging' to 'Wedging,'" Atlantic Council, September 5, 2024, https://www.atlanticcouncil.org/in-depth-research-reports/report/chinas-middle-east-policy-shift-from-hedging-to-wedging/.

8. *Security and Stability in Afghanistan: Status of U.S. Strategy and Operations and the Way Ahead*, 110th Cong. 7 (2007) (statement of Michael Mullen, chairman of the Joint Chiefs of Staff).

9. See Stuart E. Johnson et al., *A Review of the Army's Modular Force Structure*, RAND Corporation, March 16, 2012, iii, https://www.rand.org/pubs/technical_reports/TR927-2.html.

10. US Department of Defense, Office of the Under Secretary of Defense (Comptroller), *National Defense Budget Estimates for FY 2025*, April 2024, https://comptroller.defense.gov/Portals/45/Documents/defbudget/FY2025/fy25_Green_Book.pdf.

11. US Department of Defense, Office of the Under Secretary of Defense, Personnel and Readiness, *Population Representation in the Military Services: Fiscal Year 2017 Summary Report*, Table D-39, https://www.cna.org/pop-rep/2017/appendixd/d_39.html.

12. Johnson et al., *A Review of the Army's Modular Force Structure*.

13. US Department of Defense, "Army Strategic Planning Guidance 2005," January 15, 2005, 9, https://digital.library.unt.edu/ark:/67531/metadc22343/.

14. Association of the US Army, *The U.S. Army: A Modular Force for the 21st Century*, March 15, 2005, 3, https://www.ausa.org/sites/default/files/TBNSR-2005-The-US-Army-A-Modular-Force-for-the-21st-Century.pdf.

15. Andrew Feickert, *U.S. Army's Modular Design: Issues for Congress*, Congressional Research Service, January 27, 2007, 6, https://crsreports.congress.gov/product/pdf/RL/RL32476/8.

16. See US Department of Defense, Office of the Under Secretary of Defense, Personnel and Readiness, *Population Representation in the Military Services*, Table D-39.

17. See Kenneth G. Lieberthal, "The American Pivot to Asia," Brookings Institution, December 21, 2011, https://www.brookings.edu/articles/the-american-pivot-to-asia/.

18. US Army War College, "U.S. Army Announces Force Structure Decisions for Fiscal Year 2017," June 15, 2017, https://www.armywarcollege.edu/news/Archives/13323.pdf.

19. Gergely Szakacs and Karl Badohal, "Poland Leads on Defence Spending—but Can It Afford It?," Reuters, October 23, 2024, https://www.reuters.com/world/europe/poland-leads-nato-defence-spend-can-it-afford-it-2024-10-23/.

20. US Army, "Army Force Structure Transformation," https://api.army.mil/e2/c/downloads/2024/02/27/091989c9/army-white-paper-army-force-structure-transformation.pdf.

21. US Army, "Army Force Structure Transformation."

22. Nicholas M. Munves, *FY2025 NDAA: Active Component End-Strength*, Congressional Research Service, October 21, 2024, https://crsreports.congress.gov/product/pdf/IN/IN12449/2.

23. US Army, "Army Announces Aviation Investment Rebalance," press release, February 8, 2024, https://www.army.mil/article/273594/army_announces_aviation_investment_rebalance.

24. Quoted in Courtney Albion, "Drone Corps Would Disrupt US Army Plans, Says Undersecretary," *C4ISRNet*, May 15, 2024, https://www.c4isrnet.com/unmanned/uas/2024/05/17/drone-corps-proposal-would-disrupt-us-army-plans-says-undersecretary/.

25. Walter Boomer and James Conway, "Force Design 2030: Operational Incompetence," *RealClearDefense*, June 15, 2024, https://www.realcleardefense.com/articles/2024/06/15/force_design_2030_operational_incompetence_1038257.html.

26. Andrew Feickert, *US Marine Corps Force Design Initiative: Background and Issues for Congress*, Congressional Research Service, October 3, 2024, 8, https://crsreports.congress.gov/product/pdf/R/R47614.

27. Feickert, *US Marine Corps Force Design Initiative*, 2.

28. Feickert, *US Marine Corps Force Design Initiative*.

29. US Marine Corps, *Force Design 2030: Annual Update*, June 2023, 9, https://www.marines.mil/Portals/1/Docs/Force_Design_2030_Annual_Update_June_2023.pdf.

30. Mallory Shelbourne, "Landing Ship Medium Program Stalled over Price, Navy Cancels Industry RFP," December 17, 2024, https://news.usni.org/2024/12/17/landing-ship-medium-program-stalled-over-price-navy-cancels-industry-rfp.

13

The Navy Needs a 180-Degree Pivot: Embracing Autonomy and AI for Maritime Dominance

JOHN G. FERRARI

The Congress shall have Power . . . To provide and maintain a Navy.

—US Constitution[1]

For whosoever commands the Sea, Commands the Trade: whosoever Commands the Trade of the world: Commands the Riches of the world and consequently the world it selfe.[2]

—Sir Walter Raleigh

America has been and always will be a maritime nation. Even in the early postrevolutionary days of 1801, American sailors were sent to far-off places like the coast of North Africa to protect US trade from Barbary predation.[3] Later in the 19th century and into the 20th, Alfred Thayer Mahan preached the gospel of navalism, and Theodore Roosevelt received it. While some might argue that more than a century after Mahan and Roosevelt, the air, space, and cyber domains have displaced the sea, this is not entirely true. Indeed, the sea domain will remain relevant so long as maritime trade is central to the US economy.

By some estimates, about 27 percent of the US gross domestic product (GDP) is tied to international trade (exports and imports), with about 70 percent of this trade's volume moving by sea.[4] In 2022, the value of sea trade to and from the US was about $2.2 trillion, or roughly 8.5 percent of the $25.5 trillion US GDP.[5] Losing the critical sea routes this trade flows through could plunge the United States into an economic depression of intensity not seen since the 1930s. Thus, the seas will continue to play an outsized role in the United States' security considerations even if the US adopts more protectionist measures; there will still be a need to protect maritime exports.

Although most conflicts in the world today (and in the future) are fought on land, maritime capabilities are essential for the prosperity of the global economy, which makes possessing such capabilities all the more important during war.[6] It is possible that a resurgent Russia could harass shipping off the Alaskan coast or in the Atlantic just as Iran and its proxies are currently harassing trade along the sea routes of the Middle East and while Russia's Chinese "friends without limits" threaten trade along the sea routes of the Pacific, specifically near Taiwan and its adjacent waters.[7] As Figure 1 shows, nine primary choke points and 15 secondary choke points on sea routes could, if threatened, bring the global economy to a halt. Only a strong and capable US Navy can keep these critical lanes free and open.

These choke points are clustered in three potential theaters. The primary challenge facing the US Navy today is that it possesses neither the capacity nor the capability to be active in those three theaters simultaneously.[8] Sized for one short war, the Navy lacks the depth in munitions, ships, and personnel for sustained combat operations.[9]

To make matters worse, our nation's shipyards may be permanently broken and unable to produce the warships necessary to rebuild the fleet.[10] The Navy is still using the same shipyards and concepts honed during World War II and the Cold War. It is sailing in circles trying to find a way out of its current dilemma. We could continue down the same path, but as was once said, the definition of insanity is doing the same thing repeatedly while expecting different results. It is time for a 180-degree pivot toward an affordable, efficient, effective path ahead.

This would be a 180-degree pivot away from the Navy's current taste for exquisite, large, and costly platforms and toward a future of mass production and customizability. It would manifest itself as a full embrace of autonomy in the air, a massive embrace of autonomy at sea, and a revolutionary cultural change to embrace software programmers as warfighters, who would replace aviators as the key partners for sailors. This pivot would give the US the Navy it needs at a price it can afford.

Figure 1. Maritime Shipping Routes and Strategic Locations

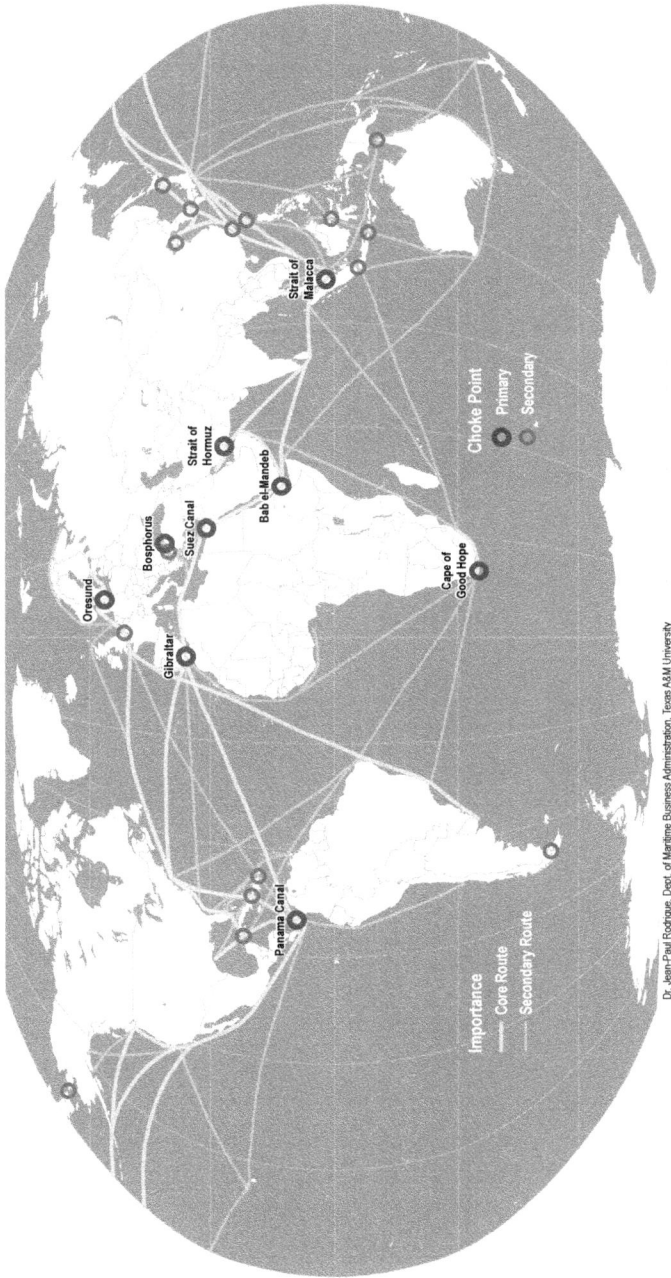

Source: Jean-Paul Rodrigue, "Main Maritime Shipping Routes and Chokepoints," Port Economics, Management and Policy, https://porteconomicsmanagement.org/wp-content/uploads/Map-Passages-with-Shipping-Routes.pdf.

Most militaries cannot fundamentally change without large-scale failure, yet that would be a national and global catastrophe. A large-scale Navy failure would decimate the US economy and the global economy along with it.[11] The US Navy has been the backbone of the global trading systems, and today's globally distributed supply chains will crumble if it fails. We don't have to look too far back to recall the COVID-19 semiconductor shortage, which affected any product that used microchips and shut down the auto sector among many others.[12] That shortage would pale in comparison to the results of a large-scale Naval failure, which would create a multiyear rather than a multi-month economic crisis.[13]

Fixing our broken Navy is therefore nonnegotiable, and, fortunately, the change needed is achievable and affordable. The US Congress, which has the constitutional authority to "provide and maintain a Navy," must furnish the funding, flexibility, and moral support required to make this fix.[14]

Why a Navy Is Needed

It's expensive. We recognize that. But it's less expensive than fighting a war with somebody who thought that we were weak enough that they could take advantage.

—Former Secretary of Defense James Mattis[15]

History teaches us that weakness invites aggression and that preventing war is cheaper than waging it. The United States is a global country. Our trade flows and other interests span the globe, and we need a strong Navy to project power wherever those interests lie. A strong Navy provides not only for our security and prosperity but for that of our allies and even many non-allies as well.

In the security domain, the Navy fulfills three key roles that cannot be replicated, each of which enables the president to fulfill their constitutional role as the commander in chief. First, the Navy is essential for deterring potential adversaries and defending the nation against threats. It provides a strategic and operational deterrent by ensuring our adversaries know that they are under constant threat. Second, the Navy maintains a global presence, which allows it to respond quickly to international crises and conflicts, enabling the president to stabilize crises and prevent wars. Third, the Navy plays a significant role in humanitarian assistance and disaster relief operations, bolstering US credibility on the world stage.

As for prosperity, the Navy's protection of sea-lanes is vital for the global economy.[16] By ensuring the free flow of goods and resources, the Navy supports international trade and economic stability. Not only do we benefit from the classic Ricardian efficiencies of trade, but we also wield enormous economic influence globally in large part due to our efforts to sustain the global economic system.

Finally, in terms of the state of the world, the United States has shifted over the past three decades from leading a post–Cold War order based on free trade and democracy to a three-theater battle with China, Iran, and Russia who each advance authoritarianism and seek to dominate their respective regions. In 2015, American Enterprise Institute scholars wrote about this in their seminal report *To Rebuild America's Military*.[17] Despite their prescience, their warnings and recommendations went unheeded, enabling a decade-long buildup of adversarial forces meant to threaten America's economic prosperity and national security. Only a strong Navy will allow us to compete and win in this new era.

China is spending more money than most realize in support of its military ambitions (Figure 2), funding a massive expansion and modernization of its navy, the People's Liberation Army Navy (PLAN).[18] Since it surpassed the US Navy in fleet size around 2020, the PLAN has become the world's largest navy by number of vessels, comprising over 370 major ships including surface combatants, submarines, and auxiliary vessels.[19] This count is expected to grow to 435 ships by 2030, underscoring China's strategic push for dominance, especially in its "near seas" region, which includes the East and South China Seas. The PLAN's expansion is bolstered by China's immense shipbuilding capacity, which outpaces the US by a significant margin.[20] This advantage allows China to sustain a rapid build rate of large warships and smaller vessels like frigates and corvettes. China is simultaneously developing and fielding modern technologies such as hypersonic missiles and advanced anti-ship systems, which pose growing challenges for US and allied forces operating in the Indo-Pacific.[21]

Figure 2. Unveiling the True Size of China's 2022 Military Budget (US Dollars, Billions)

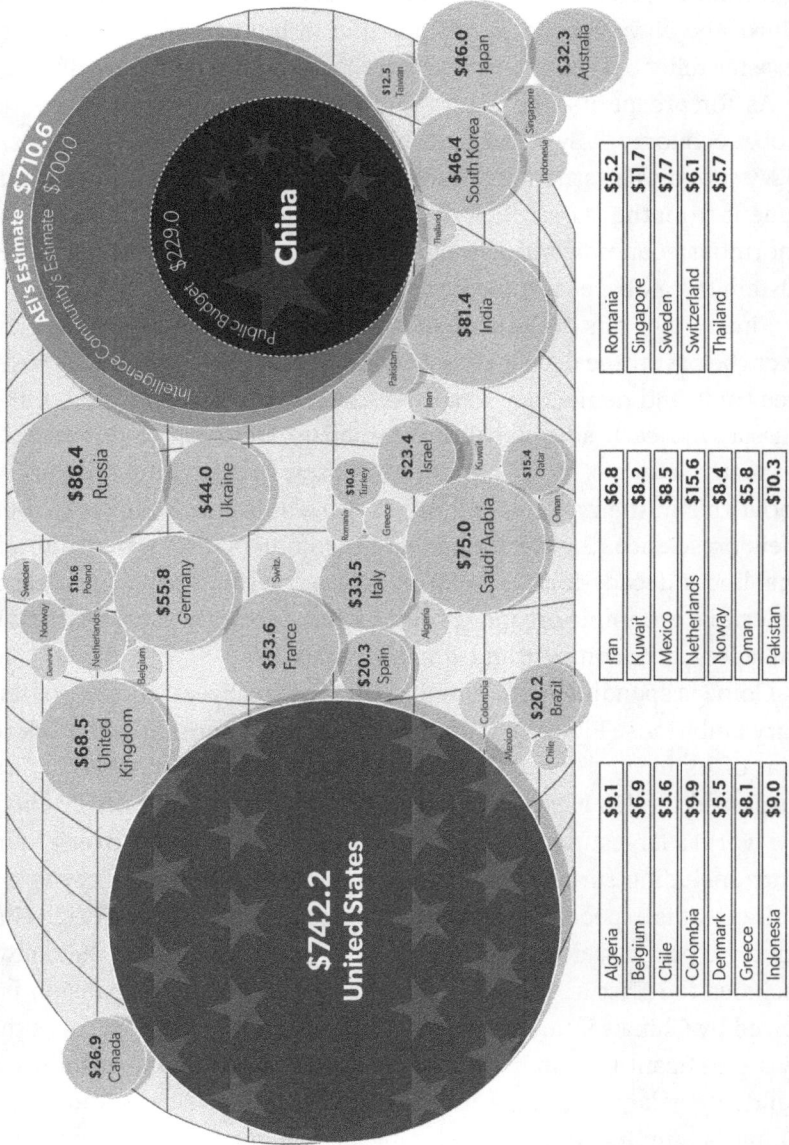

AEI's Estimate $710.6
Intelligence Community's Estimate $700.0
Public Budget $229.0

China

$86.4 Russia
$44.0 Ukraine
$81.4 India
$46.4 South Korea
$46.0 Japan
$32.3 Australia
$12.5 Taiwan
Singapore
Indonesia
Thailand
Pakistan
Iran

$742.2 United States
$68.5 United Kingdom
$26.9 Canada
$55.8 Germany
$53.6 France
$33.5 Italy
$20.3 Spain
$20.2 Brazil
$16.6 Poland
$75.0 Saudi Arabia
$23.4 Israel
$15.4 Qatar
$10.6 Turkey
Greece
Sweden
Norway
Denmark
Netherlands
Belgium
Switz.
Algeria
Colombia
Mexico
Chile
Oman
Kuwait

Algeria	$9.1		Iran	$6.8		Romania	$5.2
Belgium	$6.9		Kuwait	$8.2		Singapore	$11.7
Chile	$5.6		Mexico	$8.5		Sweden	$7.7
Colombia	$9.9		Netherlands	$15.6		Switzerland	$6.1
Denmark	$5.5		Norway	$8.4		Thailand	$5.7
Greece	$8.1		Oman	$5.8			
Indonesia	$9.0		Pakistan	$10.3			

Source: Mackenzie Eaglen, *Keeping Up with the Pacing Threat*, American Enterprise Institute, April 29, 2024, Figure 4, https://www.aei.org/research-products/report/keeping-up-with-the-pacing-threat-unveiling-the-true-size-of-beijings-military-spending/.

More important than China's naval rise is the rapid integration of emerging technologies underway by China and other adversaries including Iran and Russia.[22] Advanced weapons and autonomous systems that are produced at scale around the world essentially enable any adversary, large or small, to challenge and perhaps defeat the US Navy, if not today, then in a few years as these technologies further mature.[23]

The advent of unmanned systems, often powered by artificial intelligence, is already providing relatively unsophisticated and poorly funded enemy forces, such as the Houthis, with a virtually unlimited supply of cheap, smart, unmanned, and possibly autonomous systems that are challenging the Navy in new ways.[24]

Naval drones are maturing with extraordinary speed. Surface and subsurface unmanned systems, such as the Houthis' Toofan-1, are revolutionizing surveillance, reconnaissance, and strike capabilities.[25] These drones are cost-effective and able to operate in high-risk zones without endangering personnel, and they can conduct precision strikes. In conflicts, drone swarms have proven capable of bypassing traditional defenses, marking a shift from a reliance on larger, manned ships to a more versatile, agile naval force. The relative ease of developing these capabilities will enable many previously unconsidered groups and nations to challenge and perhaps gain the upper hand on the US Navy.[26]

We must also consider that cyber and electronic warfare are now here. New electronic warfare capabilities, available to just about any nation or terrorist group, will enable the United States' adversaries to disrupt the Navy's sensors, communications, and targeting—their entire information system.[27]

Finally, directed energy and advanced weapons are on the near-term horizon.[28] High-energy lasers and hypersonic missiles are some of the cutting-edge weaponries that China and Russia are developing. This is while US Navy leaders operating against the Houthis in the Red Sea have complained that the current Navy laser weapons are relatively ineffective and that having to fire multimillion-dollar missiles at multi-thousand-dollar drones is not efficient or sustainable. Only with larger investments and full-throated all-of-industry efforts will the Navy get the greater accuracy and power this unlimited "ammunition" could offer. Therefore, the Navy should commit to a much larger scale program of building operational prototypes and quickly iterating to put these crucial systems in the hands of warfighters.

The technological revolution that originated in the United States is enabling practically every state and terrorist group in the world to build smart weapons at scale, stealing a competitive advantage the United States once held. Not only has this technology proliferated, but since these nations and groups do not have older, less capable ships or planes, they are able to leapfrog the US Navy, which is tied down to its expensive and creaking legacy programs.

The era of uncontested US Naval primacy over the seas has come to a close. Our adversaries have shown not only that they possess dangerous capabilities but that they are willing to use them to disrupt and destroy our country's abiding interest in safeguarding the global economic system.

Why the Current Navy Is Broken

In the post–Cold War period, the Navy made two fatal mistakes. First, it prioritized building aircraft over ships. From 1991 to 2015, the Navy spent around $258 billion on aviation procurement, compared with $254.6 billion on ship procurement, creating a lost generation of 25 years for shipbuilding.[29] In the past decade, however, the Navy has wisely reversed this ratio by spending about $60 billion more on shipbuilding than on aircraft. Those gains, while in the right direction, are less impressive as they have been largely eaten up by increased shipyard costs rather than increased production of ships.

This 25-year period, which was marked by the defense peace dividend (1991–2000), the global war on terror (2001–12), and budget sequestration (2013–16) saw the Navy cannibalize itself by underinvesting in everything while maintaining an unsustainable can-do operational tempo. The results are stark, with the Navy's fleet size ever shrinking while its budget is growing.[30] The post–Cold War divergence between the budget trend and the fleet size trend can be observed in Figure 3.

The Navy has essentially rotted in place since the 1990s, while our adversaries have adopted American-origin technologies to build advanced naval capabilities at scale, jeopardizing America's security and prosperity.

Figure 3. Navy Budget and Fleet Size, 1970–2025

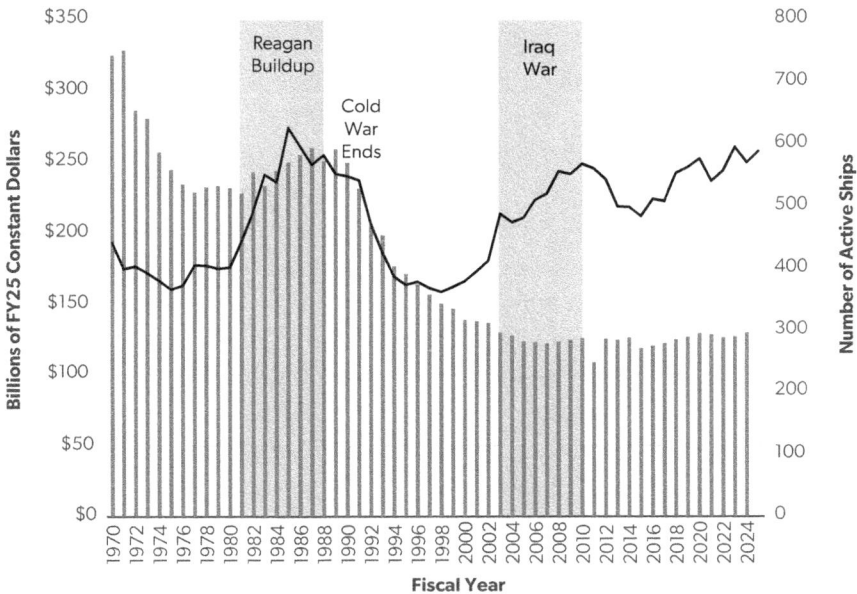

Source: Regarding the budget, see US Department of Defense, Office of the Under Secretary of Defense (Comptroller), *National Defense Budget Estimates for FY2025*, US Department of Defense, April 2024, 154–61, Table 6-10, https://comptroller.defense.gov/Portals/45/Documents/defbudget/FY2025/FY25_Green_Book.pdf. Regarding fleet size, see Ronald O'Rourke, *Navy Force Structure and Shipbuilding Plans: Background and Issues for Congress*, Congressional Research Service, November 16, 2023, https://www.congress.gov/crs-product/RL32665.

Decades of continuous budget cuts, failed modernization efforts, and maintenance backlogs have left the Navy struggling to meet its global demands.[31] The fleet is not large enough to handle day-to-day operations safely, and repeated deployments have exacerbated maintenance issues. Additionally, increased maintenance delays and parts shortages have forced crews to cannibalize parts for repairs.[32]

The Navy has insurmountable ship maintenance and readiness issues while it is in the middle of a procurement death spiral in which the unit cost of new weapons outpaces defense budgets.[33] Many vessels are unable to undergo needed maintenance due to overcrowded shipyards and outdated infrastructure, creating a backlog that has delayed deployment schedules. The result has been low ship and aircraft readiness rates and numerous vessels kept "in a non-deployable state."[34]

The Navy's fleet is rapidly aging, driven by its attempts to build exquisite ships and planes that may be better fit for the wars of the past than those of the present and future. This conundrum is leading the Navy to extend the usage of its platforms long beyond their expected service lives, causing more breakdowns and increasing maintenance costs.[35] These heightened maintenance costs result in fewer dollars available to procure more ships, further increasing upkeep costs as old ships used past their prime deteriorate ever more quickly. The cycle cannot fix itself.

Even though the Navy has been buying fewer and fewer ships, the cost of each ship keeps increasing. The increased costs for ships and aircraft mean that the Navy can buy fewer, which drives up costs as research, development, test, and evaluation spending is distributed over fewer units. Even with all the money it could receive at this point and into the future, America may now lack the industrial base it would need to build "new" World War II–vintage, scalable naval ships.

The Navy, like the other services, is hindered by personnel shortages.[36] The Navy often has difficulty maintaining fully staffed crews, especially on submarines and certain surface vessels, affecting operational capacity and increasing the workload on current personnel. Driven by a high operational tempo, the Navy continues to extend deployments without sufficient downtime, leading to burnout among sailors and, even worse, crews that are not properly trained. Coupled with high-profile scandals and ethical breaches among Navy leadership and you have a situation in which the Navy's morale and the public's trust in its Navy have eroded.[37]

We can see some of the results of the broader degradation in fatal accidents, which are the result of inadequate training, particularly in basic seamanship and navigation. Many collisions such as those involving the USS *Fitzgerald* and USS *John S. McCain* in 2017 attest to this degradation.[38] These accidents and other incidents that have been well-documented, including collisions, fires, and breakdowns, indicate systemic problems. All this is driven by an outdated doctrine and strategic vision.[39]

Finally, as warfare shifts toward software-defined weapons, the Navy has struggled to keep up, making it vulnerable to cyberattacks.[40] Several breaches have compromised critical information about naval plans and ship designs.[41] Most importantly, however, the Navy is not prepared to operate offensively with cyber, software, and electromagnetic spectrum capabilities.

The cumulative effect of these issues will lead many to conclude that the Navy's effectiveness is compromised. While individual reforms, additional funding, or modernized practices might address certain problems, the scale of these challenges suggests that more extensive structural and cultural changes are necessary.

How to Fix the Navy

If it pivots now, all is not lost for the United States and its Navy. This pivot will be difficult, but so long as the Navy receives the resources, flexibility, and support it needs, it can regain its rule of the waves over the next decade. The only solution may be a 180-degree pivot away from exquisite, large, and costly platforms and toward a future of mass production and mass customization. As mentioned above, this would manifest itself as a full embrace of autonomy in the air, a massive embrace of autonomy at sea, and a revolutionary culture change to embrace software programmers as warfighters that will displace aviators as the key partners for sailors. This change will enable the nation to have the Navy that it needs at a price that it can afford.

The guiding philosophy of this naval transformation should focus on autonomous systems and AI, cyber and electronic warfare, and distributed lethality.[42]

Autonomous naval systems integrated with AI are already here, but the Navy is still debating the adoption of these new technologies across the service, much as sailors debated moving from coal-fired engines to oil-fired engines a century ago.[43] Unmanned surface and subsurface ships are at a similar development stage as unmanned aircraft were a decade ago. However, the maturity curve and adoption of drone ships is going to proceed much more rapidly than it has for comparable aircraft. This is for two simple reasons: AI's rapid development is providing a springboard that aerial drones did not have a decade ago, and sea-drone production will benefit from the lessons learned from aerial drones.

To conduct cyber and electronic warfare at scale, the Navy must develop specialized skill sets in its human capital. For instance, sailors who maintain the engine rooms on existing ships will now need to write software in real time. Additionally, as we have seen in Ukraine, "pilots" flying aerial drones require skills in rewriting software in response to the adversary's tactical use of electronic warfare. Since many aerial drones can fly themselves with AI, coding skills will be the most important attribute for future aviators. Until the Navy adopts this core task of developing thousands of its people with the necessary skill sets, it will be unable to transition to these new technologies.

While manned vessels will never fully go away, the Navy should pivot away from its long-held 355 ship target—which is proving unrealistic from a production standpoint anyway—and instead plan for tens of thousands of mostly smaller and relatively autonomous vessels, many of which will be tailored, specialized platforms for specific mission sets. Unlike the flawed Littoral Combat Ship or the Joint Strike Fighter, which are built to be jacks-of-all-trades but masters of none, the Navy must learn to build tailored and specialized platforms for discrete and specific mission sets. It must be able to mass customize production in near-real time and at scale. With the White House announcing a wholesale overhaul of shipbuilding, this new direction will ensure that the United States becomes the global leader for producing these new ships of the future, rather than investing in rebuilding the shipyards of the past.

With these as its guiding principles, the Navy should change its ships, submarines, planes, munitions, and people. Simply put, the Navy must change everything. Of course, this will not happen overnight, and it is likely that the current inventory of around 280 naval vessels will be around for decades to come.

Still, integrating new technologies and selectively replacing some ships will be necessary, and other systems can be replaced much more rapidly. To begin revolutionizing its force, the Navy should prioritize autonomous seaborne vessels to support its manned sea fleet, eliminate its manned aviation fleet as quickly as possible in favor of several hundred thousand aerial drones, and create new industrial and software production capabilities to produce at scale in near-real time.

The Navy must also miniaturize its surface fleet. Swarms of smaller, modular vessels like patrol boats and gunboats should be deployed near coastlines, offering a deterrent and fast-response force without a major shipyard overhaul. These ships are cheaper to produce and deploy, particularly in contested or crowded areas. Thousands of drones, like the Orca, a large autonomous submarine designed for intelligence and mine hunting currently under development, could provide a persistent presence in contested waters.[44]

In addition, the era of manned Naval aircraft should end. Manned aircraft necessitate large aircraft carriers, which in turn require other ships for protection. Moving away from large ships to smaller, autonomous vessels is crucial. This shift will allow the Navy to leverage massive fleets of small and autonomous surface and subsurface drones, acting as force multipliers for surveillance, reconnaissance, and logistics support.

Cancel F/A-XX, the Navy's future sixth-generation air superiority fighter, and invest that money into unmanned systems. Large numbers of aerial drones can enhance naval operations with intelligence, surveillance, and reconnaissance capabilities, extending the Navy's eyes and ears without endangering its manned sea vessels. Combat operations in the Middle East and Europe show that swarming drones, specialized drones, and cheap, attritable drones that function as munitions dramatically reshape the battlefield.[45] While longer ranges will require larger unmanned systems due to weight and power, systems designed to operate without a pilot will still be smaller than manned fighters.

The Navy's nuclear submarine fleet is America's crown jewel, but recent accidents and an inability to rapidly manufacture and repair the fleet are leading to its decline.[46] Some may argue that if the Navy just spent more money, the production constraints would disappear. Another alternative is for the Navy to quit while it is ahead and find a new crown jewel for its portfolio. Oftentimes, large institutions fail to disrupt themselves when they are on top, so they wait for some other organization to knock them off their perch, akin to the transition between wooden ships and steel in the 1880s or the rise of tank warfare between World War I and World War II. To avoid being displaced, the Navy must rise to the occasion and develop the next generation of subsurface weapons systems that are affordable and scalable. Underwater autonomous sea vessels can be an effective partner to the Navy's submarine fleet by providing the enemy with multiple subsea challenges. These vessels can also make the submarine fleet more risk acceptant, as they could use autonomous vessels for particularly dangerous missions.

With advances in secure and rapid communication, a networked fleet of small ships and drones could be as effective as a smaller number of large vessels. Distributed lethality allows each unit to play a role in the fleet's offensive and defensive capabilities, making 35,000 interconnected nodes a powerful and resilient force.[47] This autonomous and miniaturized fleet would be serviced by manned ships that operate like aircraft carriers today but are much smaller in size and signature.

The Navy will need to build on and leverage existing technology and build human capital to take the lead in building future-use technology for 3D printing and rapid aerial drone building and shipbuilding for on-the-fly fleet and aircraft expansion.[48] Granted that this is unproven and will be difficult, portable shipbuilding facilities could add temporary ships to the fleet quickly and efficiently. This approach could be crucial to replace losses or adjust to shifting demands in wartime. Additionally, modular vessels, like floating bases or repair ships, could act as mother ships that support or refit the smaller vessels and drones, providing adaptability and resilience in the fleet without each platform requiring its own heavy support structure.

As the Navy shifts toward more AI-driven, cyber-integrated, and distributed operations, its sailors and officers must adapt to new technologies and tactics. This will require substantial investment in education and training programs and an updating of naval doctrine to reflect new warfare concepts. Traditional career paths in large ship commands may give way to positions focused on managing autonomous systems or overseeing complex networks of smaller platforms or even in writing software code.

Finally, the Navy will need pre-positioned, modular, and "just-in-case" fleets, such as large logistic stocks of unmanned assets, that operate much like the Army's pre-positioned equipment fleet. In times of crisis, the Navy could rapidly deploy these assets to act as reconnaissance, supply, or fire support.

This type of scale would demand a shift from a traditionally centralized and hierarchical Navy to a distributed, data-centric force. With tens of thousands of ships (many being drones or autonomous craft), the

Navy would prioritize information dominance, strategic autonomy, and overwhelming the adversary with a difficult-to-combat number of small, capable assets.

Challenges to This Pivot

As noted in *The Innovator's Dilemma*, changes of this magnitude are difficult because new technologies often cause great organizations to fail.[49] It is frequently the case that great militaries change only after brutal wartime losses, exactly the outcome that the United States must avoid. To make this 180-degree pivot, the Navy must overcome three challenges: bureaucratic and institutional resistance, accelerating technological innovation, and obtaining sufficient financial resources.

Like any large bureaucracy, the Navy has historically resisted significant change due to entrenched interests. Many in the Navy still favor large, traditional platforms like aircraft carriers despite calls for more agile, distributed forces.[50] Transitioning from exquisite, large, and costly platforms toward a future of mass production and mass customization may require a new generation of Navy leaders.

The Pentagon's acquisition system is notoriously slow and risk averse.[51] The long timelines for fielding new systems due to rigid procurement rules inhibit innovation. Wholesale adoption of the recommendations put forth by the Commission on Planning, Programming, Budgeting, and Execution Reform will be necessary to shift from a 1950s, Soviet-style, centralized acquisition system toward a decentralized acquisition and resourcing system.[52] Warfighting commands should have the money and talent to acquire these mass-customized systems for the very near-term tasks that they need to solve.

Overcoming the technological hurdles will be difficult but not impossible. While AI and unmanned systems promise to revolutionize naval operations, developing reliable, secure, and autonomous platforms capable of operating in complex maritime environments is still an evolving goal. Issues such as human-in-the-loop AI kill chains, secure communications, and interoperability between systems can be overcome. Additionally, as the Navy becomes increasingly reliant on autonomous systems, it will have to find a solution to the increased risks of cyberattacks. The Navy must develop its own talent, supplemented by the talent of the civilian sector to overcome these challenges.

Finally, transitioning to alternative propulsion technologies, such as electric propulsion or renewable energy, is technically complex and expensive for large vehicles. However, completing this transition for large numbers of smaller unmanned ships is nevertheless challenging but much easier overall.[53]

For the United States, enabling the Navy to advance technologies such as AI, additive manufacturing (3D printing), and new propulsion systems might drive commercial innovation and economic growth just as NASA's programs stimulated growth in the 1960s.[54]

How to Fund the Pivot

Nothing is more complicated than conducting a 180-degree pivot while supporting global operations amid two wars and facing an aggressive China that could be ready to invade Taiwan in a few years.[55] With interest payments on US debt now exceeding spending on our military, some may argue that now is not the time to spend more on defense.[56] However, for the reasons outlined above, the US can and must spend more to pivot the Navy, though the service must also do its part by terminating long-cherished programs that will in effect "co-pay" for this pivot.

Senator Roger Wicker, the chair of the Senate Armed Services Committee, recently published a strategic plan for the military that called for defense spending to rise to 5 percent of GDP by the early 2030s.[57] As of September 30, 2024, the US GDP stood at $29.35 trillion, which would yield a defense budget for this year of nearly $1.5 trillion, compared with $850 billion for the Pentagon.[58] This $500 billion increase, spread over seven years, would yield an increase of $67 billion per year. This request is probably on the upper end of the possible levels of funding. Therefore, let's assume spending might increase by about one-third of that amount, or $21 billion a year in real terms. Of that $21 billion, given the primacy of the Navy in protecting the sea-lanes and the peacetime economic well-being of the United States, the Navy would receive about one-third

Table 1. Potential Navy Budget (US Dollars, Billions)

	FY2025	FY2026	FY2027	FY2028	FY2029
Inflation Increase of 3% per Year	—	$7.7	$8.1	$8.6	$9.1
Real Growth of 2.5% per Year for 180-Degree Pivot	—	$6.4	$6.8	$7.2	$7.5
Budget Level	**$257.0**	**$271.1**	**$286.0**	**$301.8**	**$318.4**
Cumulative New Dollars for 180-Degree Pivot	—	$6.4	$13.2	$20.4	$27.9
Internal Navy Savings from Program Cancellations	—	$6.1	$7.3	$10.2	$13.9
Total Dollars Available for 180-Degree Pivot	—	**$12.5**	**$20.5**	**$30.6**	**$41.8**

Source: Author's calculations.

of the real growth increase, or about $7 billion a year in additional funding above inflation. For the Navy, this comes out to about 2.5 percent real growth per year in its budget, which is conservatively below the 3–5 percent real growth endorsed by the Commission on the National Defense Strategy's recent report.[59]

The Navy's fiscal year (FY) 2025 budget request is around $257 billion, which includes the Navy and the Marine Corps.[60] As we look for programmatic procurement reductions to "co-pay" the increased budget, this analysis does not reduce Marine Corps procurement accounts, only Navy accounts. Table 1 depicts how the Navy can have over $41 billion per year by the end of this decade to fund this 180-degree pivot while still preserving operating dollars to operate in today's high-tempo environment.

Before discussing what the Navy could procure with $42 billion per year by the end of the decade, it is important to lay out a feasible path forward to achieving $14 billion per year in savings over the same time period. To do this, the American Enterprise Institute's Defense Futures Simulator was used to estimate the quantities and cost savings. The estimates

Table 2. Examples of Items to Cut in the Navy Budget (US Dollars, Billions)

	FY2026	FY2027	FY2028	FY2029	
F-35C (Terminate)	$3.4	$3.6	$3.6	$5.1	69 Aircraft
Conventional Prompt Strike Missile (Terminate)	$1.0	$2.0	$1.5	$1.6	61 Missiles
Littoral Combat Ship (Retire Six)			$0.4	$0.7	6 Vessels
MQ-25 Stingray (Terminate)	$0.8	$0.8	$1.0	$1.4	21 Aircraft
S&T Internal Realignment			$1.0	$1.0	
SM-6 Missile (Terminate)			$1.3	$1.4	600 Missiles
F/A-XX Next-Generation Fighter (Terminate)	$1.0	$1.0	$1.0	$1.0	
EA-18G Growler Block II Upgrades (Terminate)				$1.3	
DDG(X) Future Guided Missile Destroyer (Terminate)			$0.2	$0.2	
Los Angeles-Class Submarine (Retire One)			$0.2	$0.3	1 Submarine in FY2028
	$6.1	$7.3	$10.2	$13.9	

Source: Author's calculations from American Enterprise Institute, Defense Futures Simulator, https://defensefutures.aei.org/.
Note: The rightmost column lists the number of systems currently projected for procurement from FY2026 to FY2029 that wouldn't be purchased due to termination.

in Table 2 yield the roughly $14 billion per year in savings needed by FY2029.[61]

Table 2 shows how altering only 10 Navy programs can generate almost $14 billion per year to fund this 180-degree pivot. The basis for reducing these programs is to reduce programs that are the opposite of the new strategy—in essence, programs that are enormously expensive and

produce exquisite, unscalable platforms or weapons. This strategy protects the nuclear submarine fleet from reductions other than retiring
early one *Los Angeles*–class submarine in 2028, by which time the Navy
should begin fielding undersea drone vehicles.

To start, the terminations zero in on the F-35C Joint Strike Fighter,
which epitomizes the opposite of this 180-degree pivot.[62] Similarly, the
new Conventional Prompt Strike missile produces only 61 missiles for
many billions of dollars, while the Standard Missile–6 (SM-6) will cost
$2.7 billion for only 600 missiles, or $4.5 million per missile.[63] These
reductions call for the early retirement of six Littoral Combat Ships due
to its many challenges and high operational costs.[64] With a strategy calling for tens of thousands of unmanned vessels, the Navy could take the
money from these ships and the MQ-25 aerial refueling drone and use it
for systems that can be mass-produced. Rounding out the list of 10 are
cuts to three new programs or upgrades, yielding new funds for the pivot
rather than reinforcement of the old procurement strategy.

With the additional funding from Congress plus the money from
the above terminations, the Navy would have about $10 billion in addi-
tional funding each year, resulting in $40 billion per year by FY2029. This
approach of adding $10 billion in procurement blocks per year enables the
Navy and the new defense industrial base to ramp up production capacity
at a sustainable rate. For those who believe this cannot be done at scale,
consider that the Ukrainians are producing over one million drones per
year and are ramping up to four million per year.[65] If Ukraine can essentially scale these small drones at a scale never before imagined, the United
States' industrial might should be able to take the next leap—again, with
funding, desire, and the innovative know-how of the private sector.

Mass-producing tens of thousands of sea drones and millions of aviation drones for the Navy will not be easy, but it surely will be impossible
if not started immediately. Under this funding plan, the Navy would have
about $10 billion in additional funding each year, ramping from $10 billion
in FY2026 to $40 billion per year in FY2029 and beyond to pay for this
pivot. Table 3 is an example of where the money could and should be spent.

Tranche 1 of funding for increased investment should go to con-
structing the technologies, integrations, and industrial base needed to
mass-produce these platforms and weapons. Investments in science and

technology (S&T) will enable future technological breakthroughs that will pay off in a decade or more. Investments in research and development (R&D) will be required to take existing commercial technologies and integrate them into military-capable weapons and platforms. Finally, investments in the industrial base will enable the mass production of these drones and missiles. All told, the Navy could invest $8.4 billion per year by FY2029 in developing the technology, integration, and production capacity required for this pivot.

The next batch of funding, Tranche 2, would be directed toward rapidly fielding sea drones at scale. While the Navy would not reach 35,000 sea drones in its inventory by the end of the decade, it could partially get there with over 15,000 sea drones, a start that certainly would enable future growth. This strategy funds a mix of drone sizes and functions, as each drone could be customized for specific mission sets and be considered disposable or attritable. With $21.4 billion per year in funding by FY2029, one can expect much innovation in this sector.

Next, in Tranche 3, the Navy would need to fund an aggressive counter-drone program and a program to retrofit its existing drone fleet. Finally, in Tranche 4 are the air drones, which would receive $8 billion per year by FY2029 and displace the Navy's manned aviation over time. Overall, with $41 billion per year in funding, this 180-degree pivot for the Navy would be well resourced.

The Path Forward

Our nation is at a strategic crossroads. The challenges outlined in AEI's 2015 report *To Rebuild America's Military* have arrived, and we must make a choice: Either we surrender our primacy on the world stage and our economic future along with it or we invest in and modernize our military. Luckily for America, its commercial sector is leading the world in developing the technologies that will provide our country with the edge it needs. However, those technologies will require, albeit in relatively small amounts, time and money to make them militarily capable. Right now, our adversaries are stealing this technology and militarizing it against us. This trend must be reversed.

Table 3. Potential Investment Strategy

		Unit Cost (US Dollars, Millions)	FY2026 (US Dollars, Billions)	FY2027 (US Dollars, Billions)	FY2028 (US Dollars, Billions)	FY2026 (US Dollars, Billions)	Item Quantity
Tranche 1	S&T, R&D, and Industrial Base for Sea Drones	—	$0.8	$1.6	$2.5	$2.8	—
	S&T, R&D, and Industrial Base for Aerial Drones	—	$0.8	$1.6	$2.5	$2.8	—
	S&T, R&D, and Industrial Base for Missiles	—	$0.8	$1.6	$2.5	$2.8	—
Tranche 2	Small Unmanned Surface and Undersea Drones	$0.5	$0.5	$1.0	$1.5	$4.0	14,000
	Dive-LD Underwater Drones	$25.0	$0.5	$1.0	$2.0	$4.0	3,000
	Medium Unmanned Surface Vehicles	$50.0	$1.0	$2.0	$4.0	$8.0	300
	Large Unmanned Surface Vehicles	$400.0	$1.2	$1.6	$2.4	$2.4	19
	Extra-Large Unmanned Underwater Vehicle Orca	$10.0	$0.5	$1.0	$1.5	$3.0	60
Tranche 3	Counter–Unmanned Aircraft Systems Drones	$0.5	$0.5	$1.0	$2.0	$3.0	13,000
	Retrofitting Current Fleet for Drones	—	$1.4	$1.3	$1.6	$1.0	—
Tranche 4	Small Unmanned Naval Aviation	$0.1	$1.0	$1.5	$1.5	$1.5	110,000
	Medium Unmanned Naval Aviation	$0.5	$1.0	$1.5	$1.5	$1.5	11,000
	Large Unmanned Naval Aviation	$25.0	$2.5	$3.8	$5.0	$5.0	750
Total			**$12.5**	**$20.5**	**$30.5**	**$41.8**	

Source: Author's calculations.

While not the only service requiring critical investments, the Navy is perhaps the most important because of its utility in both fighting wars and safeguarding global maritime trade. The Navy has been hollowed out after 30 years of underfunding and is now likely incapable of conducting even one long-duration war, never mind keeping the peace and fighting in three theaters.

For less than $28 billion in increased real spending per year, the Navy can achieve this transformation that will pivot it away from exquisite, large, and costly platforms and toward a future of mass production and mass customization.

The biggest hurdle to this transformation is the Navy itself. Whether it can walk away from manned aircraft and massive ships for a future of tens of thousands of smaller ships and millions of unmanned aircraft remains to be seen. If the Navy can pull this culture change off, it then must convince a skeptical Congress to fund this new vision, a difficult task given the many acquisition failures the entire defense establishment has had over the past 50 years.

Congress may nevertheless prove to be a willing partner in this effort, as defense spending often has significant multiplier effects in local and regional economies. The construction of new ships, submarines, and autonomous systems would not only directly employ thousands of workers but also indirectly support other sectors such as transportation, energy, and services. Communities near these new shipyards and defense facilities will experience economic growth, as will associated suppliers of materials and components.

Failing to fix our broken Navy is nonnegotiable. Fortunately, the change that is needed is affordable and achievable. But it is up to the US Congress, which has the constitutional duty to "provide and maintain a Navy," to supply the funding, flexibility, and moral support needed to make this fix.[66]

Notes

1. US Const. art. I, § 8.
2. Walter Raleigh, "A Discourse of the Inventions of Ships, Anchors, Compasse, &c. [...]," in *Judicious and Select Essays and Observations* [...] (London, 1650), 20.

3. US Department of State, Office of the Historian, "Barbary Wars, 1801–1805 and 1815–1816," https://history.state.gov/milestones/1801-1829/barbary-wars.

4. Macrotrends, "U.S. Trade to GDP Ratio 1970–2025," https://www.macrotrends.net/global-metrics/countries/USA/united-states/trade-gdp-ratio; and US Department of Transportation, Bureau of Transportation Statistics, U.S.-International Freight Trade by Transportation Mode, https://www.bts.gov/browse-statistical-products-and-data/freight-facts-and-figures/us-international-freight-trade.

5. US Department of Transportation, Bureau of Transportation Statistics, U.S.-International Freight Trade by Transportation Mode; and US Department of Commerce, Bureau of Economic Analysis, "Gross Domestic Product, Fourth Quarter and Year 2022 (Third Estimate), GDP by Industry, and Corporate Profits," press release, March 30, 2023, https://www.bea.gov/news/2023/gross-domestic-product-fourth-quarter-and-year-2022-third-estimate-gdp-industry-and.

6. Council on Foreign Relations, Global Conflict Tracker, website, https://www.cfr.org/global-conflict-tracker.

7. Mike Baker, "'Are We Getting Invaded?' U.S. Boats Faced Russian Aggression Near Alaska," *The New York Times*, December 1, 2020, https://www.nytimes.com/2020/11/12/us/russia-military-alaska-arctic-fishing.html; NewsinEnglish.no, "Russia Viewed as 'Harassing' Research Ship," November 2, 2023, https://www.newsinenglish.no/2023/11/02/russia-scorned-after-harassing-research-ship/; Sam LaGrone, "Video: 3 Iranian Fast Attack Craft Harass U.S. Navy Ships in Strait of Hormuz," *USNI News*, June 21, 2022, https://news.usni.org/2022/06/21/video-3-iranian-fast-attack-craft-harass-u-s-navy-ships-in-strait-of-hormuz; Dearbail Jordan, "China and Philippines Trade Blame as Ships Collide," BBC, August 31, 2024, https://www.bbc.com/news/articles/cx2erwedxz50; and Marek Jestrab, *A Maritime Blockade of Taiwan by the People's Republic of China: A Strategy to Defeat Fear and Coercion*, Atlantic Council, December 12, 2023, https://www.atlanticcouncil.org/wp-content/uploads/2023/12/strategy-paper_naval-blockade-of-Taiwan.pdf.

8. Peter Suciu, "The Incredible Shrinking U.S. Navy Is a Nightmare (Smallest Since 1917)," *The National Interest*, May 7, 2024, https://nationalinterest.org/blog/buzz/incredible-shrinking-us-navy-nightmare-smallest-1917-210926.

9. Hal Brands and Evan Braden Montgomery, "One War Is Not Enough: Strategy and Force Planning for Great-Power Competition," *Texas National Security Review* 3, no. 2 (2020): 80–92, https://tnsr.org/2020/03/one-war-is-not-enough-strategy-and-force-planning-for-great-power-competition/.

10. David Sharp, "The US Navy's Warship Production Is in Its Worst State in 25 Years. What's Behind It?," Associated Press, August 11, 2024, https://apnews.com/article/navy-frigate-shipyard-workforce-retention-318c99f2161c4284e5ddcf0c1fa2b353.

11. Ben Zweibelson, "An Inquiry into Why Militaries Are Terrible at Innovation (Part 1 of 5)," Archipelago, April 2, 2023, https://aodnetwork.ca/an-inquiry-into-why-militaries-are-terrible-at-innovation-part-1-of-5/.

12. Ian King et al., "How a Chip Shortage Snarled Everything from Phones to Cars," *Bloomberg*, March 29, 2021, https://www.bloomberg.com/graphics/2021-semiconductors-chips-shortage/; and Manpreet Singh, *Semiconductor Shortage*

Constrains Vehicle Production, Congressional Research Service, December 13, 2021, https://crsreports.congress.gov/product/pdf/IF/IF12000.

13. Robyn Klingler-Vidra, "The Microchip Industry Would Implode If China Invaded Taiwan, and It Would Affect Everyone," *The Conversation*, June 9, 2023, https://theconversation.com/the-microchip-industry-would-implode-if-china-invaded-taiwan-and-it-would-affect-everyone-206335.

14. US Const. art. 1, § 8, cl. 13.

15. James Mattis, "Remarks by Secretary Mattis on the National Defense Strategy," US Department of Defense, January 19, 2018, https://www.defense.gov/News/Transcripts/Transcript/Article/1420042/remarks-by-secretary-mattis-on-the-national-defense-strategy/.

16. Steve Cohen, "U.S. Navy's Lapse in Sea Lane Security Risks Global Trade," *The Hill*, September 9, 2024, https://thehill.com/opinion/4868313-us-navy-suez-canal-loss/.

17. Giselle Donnelly et al., *To Rebuild America's Military*, American Enterprise Institute, October 7, 2015, https://www.aei.org/research-products/report/to-rebuild-americas-military/.

18. Mackenzie Eaglen, *10 Ways the United States Is Falling Behind China in National Security*, American Enterprise Institute, September 5, 2023, https://www.aei.org/research-products/report/10-ways-the-us-is-falling-behind-china-in-national-security/.

19. Alexander Palmer et al., "Unpacking China's Naval Buildup," Center for Strategic and International Studies, June 5, 2024, https://www.csis.org/analysis/unpacking-chinas-naval-buildup.

20. Joseph Trevithick, "Alarming Navy Intel Slide Warns of China's 200 Times Greater Shipbuilding Capacity," *The War Zone*, July 11, 2023, https://www.twz.com/alarming-navy-intel-slide-warns-of-chinas-200-times-greater-shipbuilding-capacity.

21. Paul Bernstein and Dain Hancock, "China's Hypersonic Weapons," *Georgetown Journal of International Affairs*, January 27, 2021, https://gjia.georgetown.edu/2021/01/27/chinas-hypersonic-weapons/; and Dmitry Filipoff, "Fighting DMO, Pt. 8: China's Anti-Ship Firepower and Mass Firing Schemes," Center for International Maritime Security, May 1, 2023, https://cimsec.org/fighting-dmo-pt-8-chinas-anti-ship-firepower-and-mass-firing-schemes/.

22. Al Jazeera, "Iran Launches 'Domestically Developed' Imaging Satellite from Russia," February 29, 2024, https://www.aljazeera.com/news/2024/2/29/iran-launches-domestically-developed-imaging-satellite-from-russia; and David Albright and Spencer Faragasso, *Iran/Russia Military Technology Axis: Russia Showcases to Iran New and Advanced Military Technology*, Institute for Science and International Security, June 25, 2024, https://isis-online.org/isis-reports/detail/iran-russia-military-technology-axis-russia-showcases-to-iran-new-and-advan/.

23. Oded Yaron, "Gold for Drones: Massive Leak Reveals the Iranian Shahed Project in Russia," *Haaretz*, February 21, 2024, https://www.haaretz.com/israel-news/security-aviation/2024-02-21/ty-article-magazine/gold-for-drones-massive-leak-reveals-the-iranian-shahed-project-in-russia/0000018d-bb85-dd5e-a59d-ffb729890000.

24. Colin Demarest, "How Iranian Tech Empowers Houthi Drone, Missile Attacks in the Red Sea," *C4ISRNET*, January 8, 2024, https://www.c4isrnet.com/unmanned/2024/01/08/how-iranian-tech-empowers-houthi-drone-missile-attacks-in-the-red-

sea/; and Luca Nevola and Valentin d'Hauthuille, "Six Houthi Warfare Drone Strategies: How Innovation Is Shifting the Regional Balance of Power," Armed Conflict Location and Event Data, August 6, 2024, https://acleddata.com/2024/08/06/six-houthi-drone-warfare-strategies-how-innovation-is-shifting-the-regional-balance-of-power/.

25. Thomas Newdick, "Small, Agile Houthi Drone Boat Shown Obliterating Ship During Test," *The War Zone*, June 22, 2024, https://www.twz.com/news-features/small-and-agile-houthi-drone-boat-shown-obliterating-ship-during-test.

26. Bryan Clark and Dan Patt, *Hedging Bets: Rethinking Force Design for a Post-Dominance Era*, Hudson Institute, https://www.hudson.org/defense-strategy/hedging-bets-rethinking-force-design-post-dominance-era-bryan-clark-dan-patt.

27. Foundation for Defense of Democracies, "Iran Obtains Advanced Cyber Warfare Capabilities from Russia," March 28, 2023, https://www.fdd.org/analysis/2023/03/28/iran-obtains-advanced-cyber-warfare-capabilities-from-russia/; and Jeffrey Engstrom, *Systems Confrontation and System Destruction Warfare: How the Chinese People's Liberation Army Seeks to Wage Modern Warfare*, RAND Corporation, 2018, https://www.rand.org/pubs/research_reports/RR1708.html.

28. Kelley M. Sayler, *Defense Primer: Directed-Energy Weapons*, Congressional Research Service, November 4, 2024, https://sgp.fas.org/crs/natsec/IF11882.pdf.

29. Data available upon request. Data are from National Defense Authorization Acts for FY1991–FY1997 and *National Defense Budget Estimates* (green books) for FY1997–FY2025.

30. Kirkland Donald et al., "The U.S. Navy's Enduring Role in Ensuring 21st Century American Security and Prosperity," *RealClearDefense*, March 16, 2017, https://www.realcleardefense.com/articles/2017/03/16/navy_21st_century_american_security_and_prosperity__110980.html.

31. Joaquin Sapien, "A Deep Dive into US Navy's Epic Shipbuilding Failure," *gCaptain*, September 7, 2023, https://gcaptain.com/a-deep-dive-us-navy-shipbuilding-failure/; Congressional Budget Office, *The Navy's Costs to Eliminate Its Deferred Maintenance Backlog and to Renovate and Modernize Its Buildings*, November 30, 2023, https://www.cbo.gov/publication/59381; and Brandon J. Weichert, "The Decline of the U.S. Navy Is Real," *The National Interest*, August 27, 2024, https://nationalinterest.org/blog/buzz/decline-us-navy-real-212481.

32. Michael Peck, "The US Navy's Struggle to Keep Ships in Fighting Shape Is Leading Sailors to 'Cannibalize' More Parts from Other Ships," *Business Insider*, February 15, 2023, https://www.businessinsider.com/us-navy-sailors-are-cannibalizing-parts-to-keep-warships-operational-2023-2.

33. Dan Grazier, "Welcome to the Defense Death Spiral," Stimson Center, October 21, 2024, https://www.stimson.org/2024/welcome-to-the-defense-death-spiral/.

34. Ryan Pickrell, "Half the US Navy's Aircraft Carrier Fleet Can't Deploy, but the Service Says It Has What It Needs to Maintain the Fleet," *Business Insider*, October 23, 2019, https://www.businessinsider.com/half-the-us-navys-aircraft-carrier-fleet-cant-deploy-2019-10.

35. Caitlin M. Kenney, "Navy to Keep Four Aging Destroyers Beyond Their Service Lives," *Defense One*, August 3, 2023, https://www.defenseone.com/policy/2023/08/navy-keep-four-aging-destroyers-beyond-their-service-lives/389087/.

36. Holly Hobbs and Diana Maurer, "Sailor Shortages and Lack of Training May Leave Navy Ships in Disrepair," September 9, 2024, *GAO Watchdog Report*, podcast, US Government Accountability Office, https://www.gao.gov/podcast/sailor-shortages-and-lack-training-may-leave-navy-ships-disrepair.

37. Robert Prentice, "'Fat Leonard': The U.S. Navy's Moral Disaster," University of Texas at Austin, McCombs School of Business, Ethics Unwrapped, July 19, 2024, https://ethicsunwrapped.utexas.edu/fat-leonard-the-u-s-navys-moral-disaster; and Statista, "Public Confidence Levels in the United States Armed Forces from 1975 to 2024," July 2024, https://www.statista.com/statistics/239149/confidence-in-the-us-armed-forces/.

38. Sam LaGrone, "NTSB: Lack of Navy Oversight, Training Were Primary Causes of Fatal McCain Collision," *USNI News*, August 6, 2019, https://news.usni.org/2019/08/06/ntsb-lack-of-navy-oversight-training-were-primary-causes-of-fatal-mccain-collision.

39. Robert O. Work, "A Slavish Devotion to Forward Presence Has Nearly Broken the U.S. Navy," *Proceedings* 147, no. 12 (2021), https://www.usni.org/magazines/proceedings/2021/december/slavish-devotion-forward-presence-has-nearly-broken-us-navy.

40. Rohan Goswami, "Chinese State-Sponsored Hackers Infiltrated U.S. Naval Infrastructure, Secretary of the Navy Says," CNBC, May 25, 2023, https://www.cnbc.com/2023/05/25/us-navy-impacted-by-china-backed-hackers-secretary-of-the-navy.html.

41. Zachary Fryer-Biggs, "Latest Theft of Navy Data Another Sign of China Targeting Defense Companies," *US Naval Institute News*, June 11, 2018, https://news.usni.org/2018/06/11/latest-theft-navy-data-another-sign-china-targeting-defense-companies.

42. Thomas Rowden et al., "Distributed Lethality," *Proceedings* 141, no. 1 (2015), https://www.usni.org/magazines/proceedings/2015/january/distributed-lethality.

43. Erik J. Dahl, "Naval Innovation: From Coal to Oil," *Joint Forces Quarterly*, Winter 2000–01, https://apps.dtic.mil/sti/pdfs/ADA524799.pdf.

44. Rebecca Grant, "The U.S. Navy's Orca Drone Ship: A Game-Changer for Mine Warfare Against China," *The National Interest*, November 5, 2024, https://nationalinterest.org/blog/buzz/us-navy's-orca-drone-ship-game-changer-mine-warfare-against-china-213584.

45. Oleksandra Molloy, *Drones in Modern Warfare: Lessons Learnt from the War in Ukraine*, Australian Army Research Center, 2024, https://researchcentre.army.gov.au/sites/default/files/241022-Occasional-Paper-29-Lessons-Learnt-from-Ukraine_2.pdf.

46. Brad Lendon, "How Did a $3 Billion US Navy Submarine Hit an Undersea Mountain?," CNN, November 4, 2021, https://www.cnn.com/2021/11/04/asia/submarine-uss-connecticut-accident-undersea-mountain-hnk-intl-ml-dst/index.html; Alexander Grey, "The Submarine Workforce Crisis: Admitting Realities and Restructuring Long-Term Strategy," *War on the Rocks*, April 4, 2024, https://warontherocks.com/2024/04/the-submarine-workforce-crisis-admitting-realities-and-restructuring-long-term-strategy/; and Roger Wicker, "The U.S. Navy Needs More Attack Submarines," *The Wall Street Journal*, July 16, 2023, https://www.wicker.senate.gov/2023/7/the-u-s-navy-needs-more-attack-submarines.

47. Rowden et al., "Distributed Lethality."

48. Tahitianrider, "How to Design and 3D Print Your Very Own Quadcopter!!," Autodesk Instructables, https://www.instructables.com/How-to-Design-and-3D-Print-Your-Very-Own-Quadcopte/; and CPSdrone, "Build Your Own Underwater Drone," https://www.cpsdrone.com.

49. Clayton M. Christensen, *The Innovator's Dilemma: When New Technologies Cause Great Firms to Fail* (Harvard Business School Press, 1997).

50. Harrison Kass, "Medium-Aircraft Carriers: The Great U.S. Navy Mistake?," *The National Interest*, September 23, 2024, https://nationalinterest.org/blog/buzz/medium-aircraft-carriers-great-us-navy-mistake-208228.

51. US Government Accountability Office, *Weapons System Annual Assessment: DOD Is Not Yet Well-Positioned to Field Systems with Speed*, July 18, 2024, https://www.gao.gov/assets/gao-24-106831.pdf.

52. Commission on Planning, Programming, Budgeting, and Execution Reform, "Defense Resourcing for the Future," press release, March 6, 2024, https://ppbereform.senate.gov/finalreport/.

53. Jonathan Panter, "Unmanned Ships: A Fleet to Do What?," Center for International Maritime Security, October 17, 2023, https://cimsec.org/unmanned-ships-a-fleet-to-do-what/.

54. Stanford Research Institute, *Some Major Impacts of the National Space Program: V. Economic Impacts*, June 1968, https://ntrs.nasa.gov/api/citations/19680024915/downloads/19680024915.pdf.

55. Noah Robertson, "How DC Became Obsessed with a Potential 2027 Chinese Invasion of Taiwan," *Defense News*, May 7, 2024, https://www.defensenews.com/pentagon/2024/05/07/how-dc-became-obsessed-with-a-potential-2027-chinese-invasion-of-taiwan/.

56. Benn Steil and Elisabeth Harding, "For the First Time, the U.S. Is Spending More on Debt Interest Than Defense," Council on Foreign Relations, May 23, 2024, https://www.cfr.org/blog/first-time-us-spending-more-debt-interest-defense; and Bernie Sanders, "The Pentagon Doesn't Need $886bn. I Oppose This Bloated Defense Budget," *The Guardian*, July 24, 2023, https://www.sanders.senate.gov/op-eds/the-pentagon-doesnt-need-886bn-i-oppose-this-bloated-defense-budget/.

57. Roger Wicker, *21st Century Peace Through Strength: A Generational Investment in the U.S. Military*, May 2024, https://www.wicker.senate.gov/services/files/BC957888-0A93-432F-A49E-6202768A9CE0.

58. YCharts, "US GDP (I:USGDP)," 2024, https://ycharts.com/indicators/us_gdp; and US Department of Defense, Office of the Under Secretary of Defense (Comptroller), *Defense Budget Overview: United States Department of Defense: Fiscal Year 2025 Budget Request*, March 2024, https://comptroller.defense.gov/Portals/45/Documents/defbudget/FY2025/FY2025_Budget_Request.pdf.

59. Commission on the National Defense Strategy, *Report of the Commission on the National Defense Strategy*, RAND Corporation, July 29, 2024, https://www.rand.org/nsrd/projects/NDS-commission.html.

60. US Navy, "Highlights of the Department of the Navy FY25 Budget," March 2024, https://www.secnav.navy.mil/fmc/fmb/Documents/25pres/DON_Budget_Card.pdf.

61. American Enterprise Institute, Defense Futures Simulator, https://defensefutures.aei.org/.

62. US Government Accountability Office, *F-35 Joint Strike Fighter: Program Continues to Encounter Production Issues and Modernization Delays*, May 16, 2024, https://www.gao.gov/products/gao-24-106909.

63. US Government Accountability Office, *Weapons System Annual Assessment*.

64. US Government Accountability Office, *Littoral Combat Ship: Actions Needed to Address Significant Operational Challenges and Implement Planned Sustainment Approach*, February 24, 2022, https://www.gao.gov/products/gao-22-105387.

65. Kakissis and Harbage, "Ukraine Is Amping Up Drone Production to Get an Edge in the War Against Russia."

66. US Const. art. 1, § 8, cl. 13.

14

Time Is Up:
Fast Decisions for the Air Force We Need

REBECCA GRANT

The United States Air Force is older, smaller, and less modern than optimal. But it is still the single most powerful military force the world has ever known. If carefully managed, the current force can provide immediate deterrent power and a springboard to the future. The Air Force has most of what it needs to deter China, even if some of it is still conceptual. What the Air Force needs most is faster production.

With China's rise to nuclear peer status, US national security decision-makers must make the most of the existing force and programs to sustain conventional and strategic deterrence. Leaders must resist the temptation to abandon ship and terminate major programs. Fortunately, the Air Force is well aware of the challenge of ramping up to deal with threats from China, Russia, and others across domains. "The world is more dangerous now than it's been in my entire career," General Thomas Bussiere, commander of the Global Strike Command, said on December 5, 2024.[1]

The Air Force has to catch up while preparing for a multi-theater, multi-domain fight and implementing a transition to unmanned systems. As Senator Deb Fischer said, "We have to set priorities of government, and the first priority is the national defense of this country. That's where our resources should be going."[2]

Time is up. This is the Air Force, whose airmen will guard significant US national interests against a world of escalating military threats and influence. The Trump administration can make decisions about the Air Force that will strengthen air dominance and conventional and strategic deterrence. This chapter outlines several of those decisions—on the B-21 Raider bomber, the F-35, collaborative combat aircraft (CCA), intelligent data gateways for tankers and airlifters, air base defense, and more. It is by no means a comprehensive plan; the aim is rather to emphasize some of the most urgent decisions that are ripe for leadership.

America's Air Force

The Air Force's capabilities are sized around nuclear deterrence and providing a broad suite of dominant, conventional military power to combatant commanders for use in scenarios ranging from major theater war to special operations. More than any other service, the Air Force is tasked with delivering specific, mission-essential support to other branches, ranging from air mobility to aerial refueling to close air support and indirect fires. This is because airpower in all its forms has long been the global framework for America's conventional and strategic deterrence.

The United States Air Force became an independent branch in 1947 due to its combat performance in World War II. General Dwight D. Eisenhower, supreme allied commander, Europe, recognized that in order to land forces in Normandy on D-Day, the Allies would have to depend on an "overpowering air force" that would make German counter-concentration fail.[3] Thus America entered the war with a production plan and an airpower strategy that executed the great bombing campaigns to take control of the air from the Luftwaffe. In the Pacific, island bases from Guadalcanal to Iwo Jima were taken at great cost to extend the operational reach of airpower in shaping the theater. Then, as now, air superiority was the overriding goal. The US Army Air Forces, commanded by General H. H. "Hap" Arnold, operated independently to the degree that creation of a separate Air Force was widely applauded after the war.

By the early 1950s, the new Air Force had adopted jet engines, nuclear weapons, and aerial refueling; maintained occupied Berlin with an airlift; established nuclear deterrence; and provided air superiority and supporting fires in Korea. However, it was this demonstrated ability to shape war at the operational and global level—and to deliver a decisive combat punch—that made airpower the basis for the military component of America's superpower status.

The Air Force proved adept at developing and incorporating new technologies, from ICBMs to satellites and cyberspace. In its first decades, the Air Force also excelled at growing leaders for complex and innovative technology programs. For example, a P-51 Mustang pilot named Sam Phillips later worked on ICBM programs, became a lieutenant general, and was loaned to NASA to run the Apollo program culminating in the Apollo 11 landing on the Moon. Confident decision-making allowed the Air Force to push new capabilities forward rapidly.

From an operational perspective, US strategy continued to rely on air superiority and the delivery of firepower in conjunction with ground forces. This combination was at the core of the US strategy to deter the Soviet Union and was used with great effect against the forces of Iraq in Operation Desert Storm in 1991. Conflicts in Afghanistan, Iraq, and Syria again saw airpower set the terms of the fight. The war to defeat the ISIS caliphate consumed 90,991 strike sorties alone; another 56,198 sorties in intelligence, surveillance, and reconnaissance; and many more for air refueling and mobility. The "well-tuned integration of U.S. and coalition airpower [was] the lead player in [Operation Inherent Resolve's] effort against ISIS."[4]

The Air Force is a global force, and there is no going back on this commitment. At the moment, Air Force fighters of all types have been deployed to the Middle East to deter Iran, bolster Israel's air defenses, and boost protection for US forces deployed to the region. Unlike the Cold War, today's top adversaries, China and Russia, are export powerhouses, one in goods and technology and the other in oil and mayhem.[5] With the global information economy, protection of NATO members like the Netherlands and partners like Taiwan is a prerequisite for keeping America's place in the artificial intelligence revolution unfolding at breakneck speed.

The New Decision Matrix: Airpower and Conventional Deterrence

At this tense geopolitical juncture, the United States Air Force is launching the most significant transition to its basic force structure since the development of jet engines and nuclear weapons. This is the transition toward unmanned systems with artificial intelligence integrated tightly with forces for executing major combat operations. Success will ensure the dominance of American military power in the crucial decades to come.

Several variables are in play. The most crucial is the F-35 program, which provides both the mass for lethality and the springboard to more unmanned teaming. Other factors shaping the fighter force for conventional deterrence include the retirement of older fighters while balancing the force for different threat environments, preparing for mission partnering with CCAs, and ensuring next-generation air dominance.

The F-35

The transition toward unmanned systems is taking place while conventional airpower remains in high demand for military operations. The first phase of the transition toward unmanned systems centers on enhancing today's fighter and bomber force. The new core of this force is the F-35. By now, the Air Force was expected to have restocked with F-35s and retired most of its A-10s and F-15s and many of its F-16s, but this has not happened. By law, the Air Force must maintain 1,800 fighters in the inventory, with 1,145 in combat-ready status. The Air Force has a total force of 2,093 fighters, with just 1,452 in the active component, 536 in the Air National Guard, and 105 in the Air Force Reserve for a total of 2,093 fighters, averaging 26 years of age. The newest F-35s tally 408 aircraft as of 2024.[6]

The history of this joint program, managed by an outside Joint Program Office, has long attracted criticism. The F-35 is the only major weapons system run in this manner. The creation of a joint program during the Clinton administration's early years has contributed to the program's escalating costs and schedule delays. For example, the Joint Program Office has frequently revised cost and schedule goals, and in 2024, the Government Accountability Office found that the Joint Program Office had failed to award contracts related to engine improvements and thermal management subsystems.[7]

The Trump administration should consider disbanding the F-35 Joint Program Office to return authority to the Air Force and Navy. The Air Force should take over management of the F-35A variant, including those flown by most allies and international partners, while the US Navy should assume responsibility for the F-35B vertical takeoff and landing and F-35C carrier landing variants flown by the Navy, the Marine Corps, and the United Kingdom's armed forces.

Despite the Joint Strike Fighter program's mediocre acquisition history, the F-35 is a highly capable and combat-tested jet that has become the centerpiece of tactical airpower. As older aircraft retire, the F-35, along with some F-15EXs, will deliver the mass of combat striking power in conflict with China or other adversaries. The F-35 capabilities surpass those of the older F-15 and F-16 because the F-35 was designed from the outset to combine radar-evading stealth and reduced infrared signature management, with significant offensive and defensive electronic warfare capabilities integrating target detection, threat warning, countermeasures, and a 360-degree view. Sophisticated datalinks enable the F-35 to grab targeting tracks compiled by off-board platforms. The F-35 stealth fighter carries weapons internally and includes advanced mission systems that maximize offensive strike capabilities. Its powerful radar is also optimized to detect and engage cruise missiles, as an Israeli F-35 demonstrated in late 2023. These capabilities also make the F-35 the primary manned platform for working with drones and CCA.

The F-35 is also battle-tested. As the war against ISIS wound down, the F-35 flew in and around the Russian integrated air defenses in Syria, performing well in the contested environment. The Air Force deployed F-35s for a consecutive 18-month period, with 42 F-35s flying more than 1,300 sorties averaging five hours in duration. The F-35s dropped 350 weapons, expended 3,700 cannon gun rounds, and maintained a mission-capable rate of 70 percent.[8] In its most recent combat applications with Israel, F-35s destroyed most of Iran's air defenses in October, and they have intercepted Houthi-launched cruise missiles.[9] With this track record, the F-35 remains the right fighter for carrying out missions and growing unmanned, collaborative capabilities.

However, the F-35 needs the highest level of attention to increase production rates and streamline upgrades and investment. For example, the Air Force requested 42 F-35s to be purchased in fiscal year 2025, but Congress authorized 30. This rate is too slow to replace the more than 500 Air Force F-16Cs and F-16Ds in the active component with an average age of over 32 years. The Air Force must also take a wartime attitude and make decisions on priority requirements for the Block 4 upgrade, including cutting some requirements and selecting benchmarks for others. The Block 4 upgrade program started with over 80 requirements, some dating back years. The upgrades are not mere options; they include systems essential to networked air warfare and exploiting information dominance and autonomy. In some cases, as with thermal management, solutions cannot progress until the Block 4 requirements are set.

The Air Force has also committed to improvements to its F135 engine and a separate, upgraded power and cooling system to handle the spiking thermal management of new avionics and mission systems. (The F-35 was designed for about 14 kilowatts of heat dissipation but must now achieve 80 kilowatts or better.) The Air Force has funded programs for both but must execute them.

The F-35 list of international partners grew to 20 nations when Romania committed to fly F-35s in November 2024. The F-35 has become a bastion of airpower and security for NATO. For example, on December 1, 2024, four Norwegian F-35s rotated to Rzeszow Airport in Poland, near Ukraine, as part of the NATO mission for air sovereignty.[10]

Finally, the F-35 is also the mainstay for extended nuclear deterrence: the deployment of nuclear-armed tactical aircraft to reinforce allies. Certain other US Air Force fighters are nuclear certified, but the F-35 is the only advanced stealth fighter that carries nuclear weapons. The F-35 completed nuclear certification in October 2023 after 10 years of testing—and ahead of a pledge to NATO allies that certification would be in place by January 2024.[11] The F-35 carries the B61-12 gravity bomb. The B61-12 has an 825-pound, 12-foot-long bomb body with an accuracy of 30 meters and fusing options for a variable yield of 0.3, 1.5, 10, or 50 kilotons.[12] The dual-capable F-35 thus occupies a unique role in conventional and strategic deterrence—and it cannot be replaced by unmanned platforms.

For these reasons, the F-35 is nonnegotiable; it will form the bedrock of the US Air Force and allies for the next three decades. First, sinking mission-capable rates signal that the Air Force must be permitted to retire older fighters immediately, beginning with the A-10, F-15C, and F-15D. Next, the Air Force should revise its target of 1,763 F-35s and build a program with a higher ramp rate to acquire a force totaling at least 1,200 F-35s much faster, completing procurement within 10 years.

Mission Partnering with CCA

Retiring older aircraft will also speed the introduction of unmanned aircraft. The Air Force has started down the road toward unmanned "loyal wingmen" that work with crewed fighter planes and enhance their effectiveness. The Air Force made its first selection of designs for the CCA, but CCAs will not enter the force in numbers until after 2030. These early awards to General Atomics and Anduril represented designs only; CCAs may be manufactured by other companies after a downselect in 2026, and a second tranche of designs will be selected.

The Air Force is keeping its options open with a plan to buy approximately 100 CCAs by 2029 and a total of 1,000–2,000 by 2040. The budget request is for about $9 billion. The intent is to provide "a fairly transformative change to going away from the individual fighter pilots all out there at risk together, to giving our fighter pilots a wingman," according to Secretary of the Air Force Frank Kendall.[13] The CCAs build on an established trend of off-loading some mission capabilities to pods and drones. For example, the ALE-55-towed fiber-optic decoy, sometimes called the "flying zucchini," is linked by a cable to a manned plane and functions as an electronic countermeasure against continuous-wave or pulsed threats. It is not much of a stretch to picture a CCA carrying out similar missions, sans cable, and expanding to sensing, jamming, communications and data linkage, and additional weapons employment. Spectrum dominance—fending off adversaries and exploiting the electromagnetic spectrum—describes the overarching mission. Some CCAs may carry small amounts of fuel for aerial refueling at the battle's edge.

However, the primary missions of the CCAs will start by teaming with manned fighters and bombers (and perhaps other aircraft). To this end, the Viper Experimentation and Next-Gen Operations Model and other experiments had F-16s with autonomy routines stand in for the CCAs paired with manned fighters to explore attributes and tactics.[14] CCAs should be pursued and funded as vital complements to the F-35, B-21, and other systems but not yet as replacements for all missions carried out by manned aircraft.

Next Generation Air Dominance. Since 2014, the Air Force has been at work on a next-generation platform to replace the F-22 and take on other air superiority and attack roles. The overall program includes the CCA and other elements in the "family of systems." The crewed component of the Next Generation Air Dominance (NGAD) has been an Air Force priority for well over a decade. Surfacing occasionally under different names, such as Penetrating Combat Aircraft, the mission has remained about the same—to penetrate at longer range using all possible stealth, speed, and altitude to hold the most difficult targets at risk. Demonstrator aircraft have flown, and a decision was expected in 2024. However, Secretary of the Air Force Kendall delayed the decision in order to reevaluate mission capabilities and cost.

The Trump administration should continue with a contract award for NGAD to begin engineering and manufacturing development. Without NGAD, the operational risks multiply, as no other platform is designed specifically for penetrating attacks against enemy air defenses and aircraft. For example, the Air Force has not made the case that CCAs without an NGAD can take on all the repeat penetration attacks required for some target sets. Targets in the enemy interior may require repeated restrike— be that space launch sites on Hainan Island, China's five ground-based laser weapon bases, or some menace lurking in the mountains of North Korea or Iran.[15] However, until the NGAD is fielded, the Air Force must continue to upgrade the combat-coded F-22s and accelerate any systems upgrades and enhancements.

Rated Aircrew. Stronger conventional deterrence requires proficient pilots, and the Air Force should invest in operations and maintenance funding to beef up flying hours for combat pilots. Even with unmanned combat aircraft in development, the Air Force is still reliant on its pilot force. However, the Air Force is short of pilots and has cut back training hours. The Air Force said it was short 1,142 fighter pilots in 2024.[16] For the fighter force, monthly active duty flying hours improved from 5.7 hours in 2019 to 10.7 hours in 2022.[17] That figure is still far below previous proficiency levels. In the 1980s and 1990s, pilots flew over 16 hours per month, a mark that set them apart from adversaries and allies. Per month, 12 hours sustain capability, while 16 hours—about four sorties per week—allows pilots to "get better at everything."[18]

Rated aircrew are also the source for complex mission planning and the integration of spectrum warfare. With the systems and techniques for accomplishing air superiority changing so fast, the Air Force needs pilots skilled in the complexities of air operations for its own combat operations and as senior leaders making procurement and force-sizing decisions. Plus, it will take at least another generation of highly trained, skilled pilots to shepherd the transition to greater reliance on unmanned collaborative aircraft. The Air Force should increase its flying hour program. In addition, the Air Force must resolve delays affecting the T-7 undergraduate training aircraft, now in development but scheduled to deliver ultimately about 350 aircraft.

Two Legs of the Triad for Nuclear Deterrence

The Air Force is in the early phases of a major modernization of its two legs of the nuclear triad: the bomber force and the ICBMs. The B-21 Raider stealth bomber will replace the 19 remaining B-2 Spirits in the bomber leg of the triad, while a completely new Sentinel missile will replace the Minuteman III. Modernization of the nuclear triad also includes the Navy's *Columbia*-class submarines. The *Columbia* class will carry 16 missiles, with the first ship scheduled for operations in 2031.[19] A former Air Force vice chief of staff said,

> Each leg brings unique complementary attributes which are mutually supporting and key to signaling and establishing deterrence amidst an increasingly complex and dynamic security environment which, for the first time, includes the People's Republic of China as a major nuclear armed power and strategic competitor.[20]

The 2017–21 Trump administration was fully supportive of triad modernization. Since then, risk has grown due to China's nuclear acceleration and hiccups with *Columbia*-class submarines and the Sentinel missiles. The key components are schedule and adroit management.

Hedging against risk is part of nuclear strategy,[21] and one of the most efficient hedge measures is to procure more B-21s. The *Columbia*-class submarines have experienced delays that will constrain the program. In contrast, flight-testing of the B-21 is proceeding swiftly. The Trump administration should double production of the B-21 bomber, aiming to produce a total fleet of between 200 and 400 B-21s. To do this, the program should open a second manufacturing site for resilience and to speed up production.

The B-21 made its first flight on November 10, 2023, and three aircraft are now in testing, with flights occurring several times per month. Officially, the Air Force buy is 80–100 aircraft, but the consensus from the strategic posture review is that at least 200 are needed. Former National Security Adviser Robert C. O'Brien has advocated for between 300 and 400 B-21s.[22] The B-21 could also be a prime focus for CCAs. The design of the B-21 has intentionally preserved a path for integrating CCAs into the bomber's air dominance mission set. Given the additional crew and space on the B-21, the new bomber could handle a wide range of assignments alongside CCAs.

The B-21 has benefited from industry lessons learned from the F-117, B-2, F-22, and F-35 programs and from having the program run by the Air Force's Rapid Capabilities Office (RCO). The program is coming in below the inflation-adjusted unit cost target of about $700 million per aircraft. The F-117 stealth fighter program of the early 1980s had a compressed acquisition cycle configured for steady-rate production, and the B-21 should follow suit and set a new production target and revise the production rate. Former RCO Director Randall Walden has stated that production could be increased quickly with funding for additional tooling.[23] The Air Force should also authorize a second site for production, perhaps at or near Oklahoma City Air Logistics Center or a similar location. Given increasing threats to the US homeland, a second site might be prudent.

Also vital for the triad's bomber leg is the Long Range Stand Off weapon (LRSO), the successor to the AGM-86B air-launched cruise missile, to be deployed on the B-52J. The AGM-181 LRSO is vital to the triad because it can be launched from longer ranges, and its stealthy characteristics will make it the most survivable and flexible of the bomber munitions.

Next is the mammoth project known as Sentinel, which will replace the triad's land-based leg. The Air Force's Minuteman III was first deployed in 1970. At nearly 80,000 pounds, this missile can be launched in minutes from its unmanned silo. At 50 years old, Minuteman is already operating years beyond its planned service life and can no longer be effectively upgraded.

The case for the triad's ICBM leg rests on its deterrent role. ICBMs are the fastest nuclear-strike weapon, able to reach targets in about an hour. The concept is that a force of 400 ICBMs thus forces an adversary to assign at least 400 weapons to target the ICBM force, all while facing assured second-strike retaliation from submarines and the bomber force. This raises costs and deters a nuclear strike. The case has been made for a road-mobile version of the Sentinel to complicate adversary targeting and enhance survivability.[24] While the idea may have merit, the rise of space surveillance, drones, and other forms of tracking could affect those advantages.

Sentinel is an entirely new design intended to last through 2075. The program will build 400 missiles and refurbish 450 silos along with updating more than 600 facilities located in eight states. Missiles are on alert 24-7, and the swap out will occur without changing the alert status. United States Strategic Command has set a deadline of September 2030 for the initial operational capability for Sentinel. Sentinel missile technical data will be purchased by the Air Force to allow multiple contractors to compete on maintenance projects over the Sentinel's 50-year lifespan.[25] Milestone B, the go-ahead for engineering and manufacturing development, was passed in 2020; however, that milestone was rescinded in 2024 pending further review of requirements and restructuring of the program. The development of the missile is on pace, but costs and requirements associated with the launch facilities and other components of the vast infrastructure have grown, exacerbated by inflation.

The Sentinel program needs a champion. The Trump administration should appoint a single "nuclear czar" empowered to make decisions to streamline requirements and produce a new schedule. Modernizing the triad's land-based leg is something that has not been done for 60 years. Early Air Force ICBMs had a single architect, General Bernard Schriever, who began the programs in 1954 and oversaw Thor, Atlas, Titan, and Minuteman (and cultivated leaders such as his aforementioned protégé, Phillips). Then as now, leadership required close contact with industry and ruthless decisions on requirements. Schriever was fortunate to have President Eisenhower's personal attention in the missile programs' formative years.

Finally, credible nuclear deterrence starts with command and control. The rise of a two-peer threat has sped up the Air Force's requirement to modernize nuclear command and control.[26] The Air Force's E-4B Nightwatch aircraft (which are militarized 747-200s) were all delivered before 1985. A key program is the new Survivable Airborne Operations Center (SAOC), a group of wide-body jets that will be modified with communications for airborne command of nuclear forces and hardened to withstand a nuclear attack environment. SAOC is the top priority for nuclear C3 modernization, and the Trump administration should fully support it.

Intelligent Mobility Under Fire

The US Air Force's global reach depends on air refueling tankers and mobility aircraft. Protecting these high-value assets is crucial to air dominance. Unlike in past decades, the Air Force is now training its mobility forces to face contested airspace, bases under attack, and cyber blackouts that impair logistics. To cope with these threats, the Trump administration should urgently fund digital and AI upgrades to the mobility and tanker fleet that will incorporate them more fully into the networked battle space and allow them to function as data links and communications nodes. This is essential for their own defense and agility and to maintain the flow of fuel, parts, people, and aeromedical evacuation.

During an air campaign, tankers are set up to fly tracks in 30-by-70 nautical mile boxes where thirsty fighters can find them fast.[27] Tankers can put additional distributed command and control and beyond-line-of-sight data flows "near the fight and fighter aircraft who need the fuel," said Lieutenant Colonel Curtis Andersen of the 513th Operations Support Squadron, who led the team in testing the Platform Agnostic Command and Control concept. Fighter intercepts like those of the Russian "Bear" bombers flying with a pair of Chinese H-6N nuclear-capable bombers in the high north depend on tanker support and typically take place beyond the line of sight, for example.[28]

These upgrades are ready to go and should be procured as if on a wartime basis. Intelligent gateways with advanced, AI-enabled communications have been tested aboard mobility aircraft at exercises such as Northern Edge.[29] Tanker and mobility crews and command centers must also be given opportunities to train to proficiency in a high-data environment; simulated and live virtual constructive training, contracted out if necessary, can make a big difference in execution during a crisis.

KC-46 production should continue, as it provides the most direct path to recapitalizing the fleet. The increased fuel off-load and carrying capacity for cargo pallets, passengers, and medical evacuations are also valuable. Manned tankers will continue to dominate the future Air Force fleet and will be necessary for supporting the B-2, B-21, and B-52J in their nuclear deterrence missions due to the missions' urgency. Deterring multiple nuclear competitors will stretch the global reactions of the bombers, which must be supported by tankers, including tankers able to stay on station near hostile areas as bombers penetrate. However, the Air Force is also evaluating potential unmanned tanker options as it pursues the Next Generation Air Refueling System, a design for a survivable, low-observable tanker. Research into this design should continue to be a high priority for the Air Force.

Fighting Under Attack: Defending Bases and Airspace

Air base defense has likewise become a key part of air superiority. Air bases operated under threats in the past, as examples from Balad in Iraq to Bien Hoa in Vietnam demonstrate. But the problem has grown much more severe with the rise of drones and cruise missiles and the soaring threat posed by Russia in Europe and China's ballistic missiles in the Pacific.

The Trump administration should order an immediate "red team" review of base defense covering forward operating bases and bases on US territory. The administration should also encourage Congress to amend statutes to allow the Air Force to acquire and operate its own medium- and long-range systems. Since 1947, the Army has held statutory responsibility for air base defense. This is highly unusual. For example, the US

Army operates the Patriot air defense system. Guam, with its two major runways, is receiving major upgrades to its layered defenses. Andersen Air Force Base is defended by a 48-missile Terminal High Altitude Area Defense battery on the island but controlled by the Army from Hawaii, with assistance from Navy Aegis destroyers.[30] Nearly every other military in the world, including NATO partners, assigns air defense to its air force for reasons of efficiency. The Air Force has much to contribute and much to lose. For example, the F-35 may be able to take on incoming ballistic and cruise missiles.[31]

Special Operations

The Air Force operates nearly a dozen types of aircraft for special operations, ranging from gunships to the tilt-rotor CV-22 Osprey. The AC-130J Ghostrider featured prominently in US Central Command operations during the fall of the Assad regime in Syria. While it most often flies behind the scenes, this branch of airpower is essential to conventional deterrence.

The evolving gray-area strategy of opposing China with small-force packages at multiple points in the Pacific will rely heavily on Air Force special operations. Fortunately, the Air Force did recapitalize with the 55 MC-130J Commando IIs and 30 AC-130J Ghostriders, all of which are less than seven years old. In future years, the Trump administration should consider acquiring the Army Future Long Range Assault Aircraft and advanced tilt-rotor aircraft, with open systems architecture developed from the successful V-280 Valor demonstrator aircraft.

Conclusion

The United States Air Force came into being due to advances in technology that changed the way wars were fought. The airplane's development and combat employment took the United States military from the days of balloons and mounted cavalry into the reaches of space. The Air Force has long embraced innovation and is actively seeking to retain its edge in a time of new technologies, from drones and spectrum dominance to artificial intelligence.

What the Air Force needs is rapid decisions and actions on its key priorities. Eisenhower's expectations for airpower were formed when "the planes we needed did not yet exist," but his group of planners took the role of airpower "almost as faith," and American industry built the force to execute it.[32] As this chapter has highlighted, new Air Force leadership has an opportunity to make bold and nimble decisions that strengthen deterrence and turn innovation into combat capability.

In the words of former Air Force Chief of Staff General John Jumper, "For those who have gone before us, who have given their lives so that we could have the greatest Air Force on Earth, so that we could enjoy the wonders of freedom and liberty, we pledge our best."[33]

Notes

1. Thomas A. Bussiere, *Aerospace Nation*, podcast, "Aerospace Nation: Interview with Gen. Thomas A. Bussiere," Mitchell Institute for Aerospace Studies, December 5, 2024, https://mitchellaerospacepower.org/event/an-gen-thomas-a-bussiere/.

2. *Breaking Defense*, "RNDF 2024: An Interview with U.S. Senator Deb Fischer," YouTube, December 9, 2024, https://www.youtube.com/watch?v=6G6ksmIRZMc.

3. Dwight D. Eisenhower, *Crusade in Europe* (Doubleday, 1948), 46–47.

4. Benjamin S. Lambeth, *Airpower Against the Islamic State: A Diagnostic Assessment of Operation Inherent Resolve*, Mitchell Institute for Aerospace Studies, April 2021, 23, https://www.mitchellaerospacepower.org/app/uploads/2021/05/a2dd91_90f2ae9b8d564dde976fddb295d0fcc6.pdf.

5. See Peter Morici, "The Stock Market Is Expecting More Interest Rate Cuts Than the Fed Can Give," *MarketWatch*, November 9, 2024, https://www.marketwatch.com/story/the-stock-market-is-expecting-more-interest-rate-cuts-than-the-fed-can-give-a05c9428?mod=mw_latestnews.

6. Air & Space Forces Association, *Air and Space Forces Almanac 2024*, May 2024, 56, https://www.airandspaceforces.com/app/uploads/2024/06/Almanac2024_Fullissue_V11.pdf.

7. US Government Accountability Office, *F-35 Joint Strike Fighter: Program Continues to Encounter Production Issues and Modernization Delays*, May 16, 2024, https://www.gao.gov/assets/gao-24-106909.pdf.

8. John A. Tirpak, "Make-or-Break Time for the F-35," *Air & Space Forces Magazine*, April 23, 2021, https://www.airandspaceforces.com/article/make-or-break-time-for-the-f-35/.

9. Jake Epstein, "Israel Showed the 'Power' of F-35s in Destroying Nearly All of Iran's Air Defenses Without a Loss, UK Admiral Says," *Business Insider*, December 4, 2024, https://www.businessinsider.com/israel-showed-power-of-f-35s-iran-strikes-uk-admiral-2024-12.

10. Yahoo News, "Norway Sends F-35s, 100 Soldiers to Guard Polish Airport near Ukraine," December 3, 2024, https://www.yahoo.com/news/norway-sends-f-35s-100-051232355.html.

11. Michael Marrow, "Exclusive: F-35A Officially Certified to Carry Nuclear Bomb," *Breaking Defense*, March 8, 2024, https://breakingdefense.com/2024/03/exclusive-f-35a-officially-certified-to-carry-nuclear-bomb/.

12. Airforce Technology, "B61-12 Nuclear Bomb," November 6, 2020, https://www.airforce-technology.com/projects/b61-12-nuclear-bomb/.

13. John A. Tirpak, "Kendall Expects 100 CCAs by 2030," *Air & Space Forces Magazine*, June 7, 2024, https://www.airandspaceforces.com/article/world-modernization-5/.

14. John A. Tirpak, "USAF Wants $5.8 Billion for CCAs over Five Years. First Up: A Spectral Warfare Platform," *Air & Space Forces Magazine*, March 22, 2023, https://www.airandspaceforces.com/usaf-5-8-billion-ccas-five-years-spectral-warfare/.

15. Brian G. Chow and Henry Sokolski, "U.S. Satellites Increasingly Vulnerable to China's Ground-Based Lasers," *SpaceNews*, July 10, 2023, https://spacenews.com/op-ed-u-s-satellites-increasingly-vulnerable-to-chinas-ground-based-lasers/.

16. Thomas Novelly and Rachel Cohen, "Newly Trained Air Force Pilots May Take On Jobs Outside Fighters and Bombers," Military Officers Association of America, September 11, 2024, https://www.moaa.org/content/publications-and-media/news-articles/2024-news-articles/recommended-reads/newly-trained-air-force-pilots-may-take-on-jobs-outside-fighters-and-bombers/.

17. Air & Space Forces Association, *Air and Space Forces Almanac 2024*, 60.

18. John Venable, "Fighter Pilots Aren't Flying Enough to Hone the Skills of Full-Spectrum War," *Defense One*, November 21, 2016, https://www.defenseone.com/ideas/2016/11/fighter-pilots-arent-flying-enough-hone-skills-full-spectrum-war/133328/?oref=d1-author-river.

19. William A. LaPlante, "Department of Defense Acquisition Programs," testimony before the Senate Committee on Appropriations, Subcommittee on Defense, May 15, 2024, https://www.appropriations.senate.gov/imo/media/doc/download_testimony60.pdf.

20. C. Todd Lopez, "Sentinel Land-Based Nuclear Modernization Program Will Continue, with Changes," US Department of Defense, July 10, 2024, https://www.defense.gov/News/News-Stories/Article/Article/3834502/sentinel-land-based-nuclear-modernization-program-will-continue-with-changes/.

21. Madelyn R. Creedon et al., *America's Strategic Posture Report*, Senate Committee on Armed Services, October 2023, 27, https://www.armed-services.senate.gov/imo/media/doc/americas_strategic_posture_the_final_report_of_the_congressional_commission_on_the_strategic_posture_of_the_united_states.pdf.

22. Harry Kazianis, "Robert O'Brien: Air Force Needs 300–400 B-21 Raiders," *RealClearDefense*, October 2, 2023, https://www.realcleardefense.com/2023/10/02/robert_obrien_air_force_needs_300-400_b-21_raiders_983176.html.

23. See Rebeccah Heinrichs et al., *America's B-21 Raiders: Deterring and Assuring in the New Cold War*, Hudson Institute, December 2023, 27, https://s3.amazonaws.com/media.hudson.org/America%E2%80%99s+B-21+Raiders+(1).pdf.

24. See Robert Peters, *It Is Time to Make the Next Generation of America's ICBMs Road-Mobile*, Heritage Foundation, January 11, 2024, https://www.heritage.org/sites/default/files/2024-01/IB5337.pdf.

25. Aaliyah Beverly, "Sentinel: The History of the DAF Modernizing the Backbone of the Triad," Tinker Air Force Base, August 16, 2024, https://www.tinker.af.mil/News/Article-Display/Article/3877691/sentinel-the-history-of-the-daf-modernizing-the-backbone-of-americas-national-s/.

26. Jason Armagost, "Air-Based Leg of US Strategic Nuclear Deterrent," Advanced Nuclear Weapons Alliance Deterrence Center Virtual Forum, December 5, 2024, https://anwadeter.org/2024-forums.

27. See, for example, Alexander Wathen, "The Miracle of Operation Iraqi Freedom Airspace Management," *Air and Space Power Journal* 19, no. 4 (2005), https://www.airuniversity.af.edu/Portals/10/ASPJ/journals/Chronicles/wathen.pdf.

28. Air National Guard, "Tanker Modernization Enhances Battlefield Communication," August 2, 2023, https://www.ang.af.mil/Media/Article-Display/Article/3480132/tanker-modernization-enhances-battlefield-communication/.

29. Peter Felstead, "Collins Aerospace Connects New Platforms to Serve as Battlefield Nodes," *European Security & Defense*, August 4, 2023, https://euro-sd.com/2023/08/news/33315/collins-aerospace-connects-new-platforms-to-serve-as-battlefield-nodes/.

30. Josh Taylor, "Operation Noble Eagle—Pacific: Integrated Air and Missile Defense for America's Pacific Homeland," *Journal of Indo-Pacific Affairs* 7, no. 4 (2024), https://media.defense.gov/2024/Jun/28/2003493999/-1/-1/1/VIEW%20-%20TAYLOR.PDF/VIEW%20-%20TAYLOR.PDF.

31. Tom Burbage et al., *F-35: The Inside Story of the Lightning II* (Skyhorse Publishing, 2023), 383.

32. Eisenhower, *Crusade in Europe*.

33. US Air Force, *2003 Annual Financial Statement*, January 2004, 7, https://comptroller.defense.gov/Portals/45/documents/cfs/fy2003/Fiscal_Year_2003_Department_of_the_Air_Force_Financial_Statements.pdf.

15

Embracing Space Force Exceptionalism

TODD HARRISON

Congress created the Space Force in 2019 to restore the US military's focus on space and accelerate efforts to counter the threats China and Russia pose in space. In the years since, overall funding for space in the Department of Defense (DOD) budget has more than doubled from $12.6 billion in fiscal year (FY) 2018 to $32.9 billion in FY2024 (in then-year dollars), and the Space Force has begun building a new space architecture that is more resilient to attack.[1] For the first time, military space forces and programs are aligned under a unified chain of command, and the space cadre of military and civilian guardians has the independence it needs to develop a new warfighting culture.

The hard work of building the Space Force, however, is far from complete. This chapter offers a vision for the Space Force with a more expansive mandate than it currently has. It explores alternative force-planning constructs for space, identifies new mission areas the Space Force should pursue, recommends reforms to the Space Force's personnel and readiness systems, and analyzes the budgetary resources needed to implement these changes. A recurring theme is that the Space Force is fundamentally different from the other services, and it should not settle for being bound by the same rules, processes, and constraints. The Space Force should embrace its uniqueness and the opportunity it has over the coming years to fully realize its destiny as the exceptional service.

Force Sizing for Space

One of the Space Force's distinctive characteristics relative to the other military services is how its capabilities scale under different force-planning assumptions. The military's force-planning construct describes the force size and capabilities necessary to execute its strategy. At the end of the Cold War, the United States adopted a two-theater planning construct based on the idea that the US military should be able to fight two major theater wars nearly simultaneously.[2] However, this has evolved over the past three decades to become what is effectively a "one-plus" construct—a military sized to defeat one adversary while reserving enough forces to deter (but not necessarily defeat) a second aggressor.[3] The Commission on the National Defense Strategy concluded in its 2024 final report that "the current force-sizing construct is inadequate for today's needs and tomorrow's challenges" and instead proposes a "multiple theater force construct."[4]

Forces in other domains tend to scale roughly linearly with the number of theaters they need to support simultaneously, meaning a two-theater planning construct requires about twice the forces as a one-theater planning construct (depending on the scale and simultaneity of the wars assumed). Space capabilities, in contrast, tend to be global and therefore highly nonlinear in how they scale. For many space missions, a two-theater construct requires significantly less than double the forces (i.e., satellites and operators) of a one-theater construct.[5]

One reason for this is the absenteeism problem—the fact that satellites in orbits that constantly move over the Earth's surface (i.e., nongeostationary orbits) spend most of their time over areas other than the theater of interest. Designers must account for absenteeism when sizing satellite constellations, which means more satellites are needed in a constellation to maintain continuous coverage over one theater.[6] The absenteeism problem becomes an advantage in a multiple theater force-planning construct because a satellite constellation large enough to support one theater inherently provides coverage and capacity for other theaters. As satellites orbit the Earth and pass out of range for one theater, they pass over a different theater.[7] GPS, for example, needs only four satellites over a given point on Earth to enable precision positioning, navigation, and timing (PNT). Because GPS satellites are in constant motion, orbiting the Earth every 12 hours, the GPS constellation needs at least 24 satellites in total to ensure at least four are always visible at any given point on the surface. But this also means that a GPS constellation sized for one theater inherently covers all theaters.

Another example of the differences in how space capabilities scale compared to other domains is the ground moving target indication (GMTI) mission that the Air Force has supported for decades using the E-8 Joint Surveillance Target Attack Radar System (JSTARS) aircraft. To have a sufficient fleet of aircraft to simultaneously perform this mission in two theaters requires roughly twice the aircraft (and supporting systems, crews, and other assets) as a one-theater force.[8] When the GMTI mission is moved to space, however, the satellites needed to cover one theater can also cover other theaters because they are constantly moving relative to the Earth's surface. As a satellite in the constellation passes over the Indo-Pacific, for example, it covers that region. Minutes later that same satellite may be over Europe while other satellites in the constellation are now over the Indo-Pacific region. Moving the GMTI mission to space makes it inherently multi-theater—and unlike aircraft, satellites provide continuous coverage that is indefinitely sustainable.

Other important force-planning characteristics for space, such as the need to be resilient against different forms of attack and maintain a high degree of space situational awareness, are also not closely correlated with how many theaters can be supported simultaneously. The level of protection required, for example, is based on the worst anticipated threats in any theater, and all satellites of a given type and the system as a whole (including ground stations) need the same protection regardless of how many theaters they support. Additional capacity and attrition reserves may be needed for certain capabilities, and additional space situational awareness sensors and processing may be needed to track more adversary actions simultaneously. But these increases are relatively small in magnitude relative to the overall force—and they are arguably needed regardless of the force-planning construct assumed.

A multiple theater force-planning construct is therefore much easier to implement for the Space Force than for the other services. Moreover, a multiple theater force becomes more achievable if additional missions are moved to space (when possible). While the other services struggle to scale in size, the Space Force can focus its resources on improving its capabilities and resilience and expanding into more missions.

New Space Force Missions

This leads to a second factor that sets the Space Force apart from the other services: It is better positioned to take on new missions in a multiple theater force-planning construct. This includes relatively new missions for the military—such as offensive and defensive counterspace—and existing missions that can be better performed from space than from other domains. Like GMTI, the airborne warning and control mission has traditionally been conducted from the air, but advances in adversary air defenses make these aircraft increasingly vulnerable. Conducting this mission from space has the added advantage of covering all of an adversary's territory, even during peacetime. Unlike in the air, land, and maritime domains, the right of free overflight in space is well established and is a defining characteristic of space operations.

Whether to move a mission to space or keep it in another domain is not always a binary decision. Sometimes the best choice may be to do both. Competition for missions among the services and with the intelligence community is not always a bad thing. Competition can stimulate innovation and incentivize the services to be more responsive to warfighter demands. It also creates an additional layer of resiliency, ensuring if one service's capability is defeated or degraded, a competing capability from another part of the joint force may still be able to accomplish the mission. The Space Force should pursue and, where necessary, compete vigorously and unapologetically for new and expanded missions in several key areas, including tactical surveillance, reconnaissance, and targeting; rapid transportation of cargo and personnel (i.e., spacelift); and offensive and defensive counterspace.

Tactical Surveillance, Reconnaissance, and Targeting. Other than missile warning, the US military has not traditionally conducted surveillance and reconnaissance of the Earth from space. Space-based surveillance and reconnaissance has been the National Reconnaissance Office's (NRO's) job, and its focus has been on providing national-level capabilities using highly capable satellites, often referred to as "national technical means." While the NRO should be credited with fielding a new, more resilient proliferated architecture faster than the Space Force—having launched a new constellation of over 100 satellites between May and December 2024—the intelligence community should not be granted a monopoly on conducting surveillance from space.[9] The Space Force has an important role in providing a more tactically responsive capability for the warfighter, but bureaucratic infighting with the intelligence community has hamstrung these efforts. As then–Space Force Acquisition Chief Frank Calvelli noted in public remarks, "I think if we drive tactical ISR [intelligence, surveillance, and reconnaissance] in space to be more like national technical means, the country will lose, the warfighter will lose."[10]

The Space Force announced its intention to begin developing a space-based radar system for GMTI in May 2021.[11] After years of wrangling over roles and authorities with the intelligence community, the program did not pass Milestone B—the official start of an acquisition program—until August 2024.[12] Taking over three years to *start* a program is not moving at the speed of innovation; it is moving at the speed of bureaucracy.

The Space Force should part ways with the intelligence community on this program and make moving target indication (to include ground, maritime, and airborne targets) part of the custody layer of the Proliferated Warfighter Space Architecture (PWSA) called for in one of President Donald Trump's executive orders.[13] The custody layer is intended to provide commanders the ability to maintain "custody of time-sensitive targets to support engagement by advanced weapons."[14] The Space Development Agency (SDA) should build a tactically responsive system that allows users at lower echelons in all domains to directly task the system to scan the battle space and downlink processed (but not necessarily analyzed) data in real time directly to forces and weapons systems in any theater. In the interim, the Space Force should begin using commercial synthetic aperture radar systems to experiment and provide an interim capability for the warfighter. Using commercially owned and operated systems will help refine requirements for a military-owned and -operated system and assess the trade-offs between cost and performance.

Spacelift. Another new mission area for the Space Force is cargo delivery to remote and inaccessible locations via space—sometimes referred to as spacelift. Just as airlift revolutionized military logistics and enabled new operational concepts for ground forces, spacelift may also prove revolutionary for the joint force. While at first it may be a niche capability due to the cost per pound delivered and the total payload capacity, spacelift can still be highly advantageous in certain situations. For example, it could rapidly deliver ammunition and supplies directly to forward operating forces or an embassy under attack when those areas are otherwise unreachable in a timely manner.

The Space Force's paltry $4 million request in the FY2025 budget, however, is hardly a strong start.[15] It needs the funding and authority to accelerate work with commercial launch providers and begin flying test missions as soon as possible. The aim should be to reach an initial operating capability for cargo transport to ships at sea and remote airfields within two years and crew transport by 2030.

Offensive and Defensive Counterspace. Chief of Space Operations General Chance Saltzman has called space superiority "the reason the Space Force exists."[16] As he defines it, space superiority has two components: employing space capabilities to support US and allied military operations and preventing an adversary from using their space capabilities against US and allied forces. The second component—the ability to degrade or disrupt adversary space and counterspace capabilities—is often referred to as offensive and defensive counterspace. While some capabilities may be classified, the Space Force has not publicly revealed or demonstrated many of the basic capabilities needed for this mission area, such as bodyguard satellites capable of disrupting or disabling adversary space and counterspace assets.

In Saltzman's theory of success, he calls on the Space Force to "be prepared to undertake responsible counterspace campaigning," which he defines as "confronting malign activity in the domain through protracted, day-to-day competition."[17] Adversaries, particularly Russia in its war against Ukraine, routinely attack and interfere with the operation of US military space systems, including the widespread use of GPS jamming and spoofing.[18] Yet the Space Force has not directly confronted these malign activities.

This lack of action suggests that the United States does not have either the will or the capability to respond. Either way, it undermines the Space Force's credibility to achieve space superiority in a conflict. The new administration must ensure that the Space Force has the right suite of capabilities for offensive and defensive counterspace operations and that it uses these capabilities to confront bad actors by conducting responsible counterspace campaigning in peacetime.

Updated Roles and Missions. To facilitate the addition of new Space Force missions and a broader understanding within DOD of the Space Force's role in the joint force, the new administration should update Department of Defense Directive (DODD) 5100.01, *Functions of the Department of Defense and Its Major Components.* The hasty update, made after the Space Force was created, lists five vague and overlapping functions for the service that are inconsistent with subsequent doctrine and terms of reference.[19] For example, DODD 5100.01 does not mention key Space Force functions, including space superiority, PNT, missile warning, and satellite communications (SATCOM).

In contrast, it is much more specific about other services' key functions. For example, one of the Air Force's key functions is to "conduct offensive and defensive operations . . . to gain and maintain air superiority, and air supremacy as required," and one of the Navy's key functions is to "conduct offensive and defensive operations associated with the maritime domain including achieving and maintaining sea control."[20] DODD 5100.01 is a foundational document for the US military, and it is critical to get this foundation right because it is the basis on which all Space Force missions are established and defended.

Personnel and Readiness Reform

A third factor that makes the Space Force exceptional is its people and the way it trains and maintains a ready force. While it may be easy to think of the Space Force as a microcosm of the overall military, this is an overly simplistic and misleading comparison. The Space Force's composition and force posture are necessarily different from the other services. As a result, the personnel and readiness systems inherited from the Air Force and the practices and processes used by all of the other military services create serious challenges for the Space Force and its ability to attract, train, and retain the people it needs. The Space Force's small size, however, also presents a unique opportunity. Unlike the other services, the Space Force can experiment with new policies and processes faster and with less political resistance. It must evolve its culture and internal processes to better fit the missions it supports and its role in the joint force—beginning with a concerted effort to rethink its rank structure and career paths, readiness model, and internal organization.

Rank Structure and Career Paths. Figure 1 shows that the rank distribution of personnel in the Space Force is distinct from the other services. The Space Force has a larger share of officers than the other services by far—48 percent of the Space Force's active-duty personnel are officers compared to 19 percent in the Air Force, 17 percent in the Army, 16 percent in the Navy, and 11 percent in the Marine Corps (not including warrant officers). And within the officer and enlisted ranks, the Space Force is more heavily weighted toward the higher ranks.[21] Guardians are also more educated than their peers in the other services: 20 percent of enlisted personnel in the Space Force have a bachelor's degree or higher, and 56 percent of officers have an advanced degree. In the other services, only 10 percent of enlisted personnel have a bachelor's degree or higher and only 39 percent of officers have an advanced degree.[22]

This does not mean, however, that the Space Force is too top-heavy or educated. Rather, it reflects the divergent needs of the Space Force because the systems it acquires and the way it operates are fundamentally different from the other services. The Space Force is perhaps the polar opposite of the Marine Corps, which needs a large pipeline of young people to fill its battalions. Over 65 percent of marines are age 25 or younger, and a high turnover rate in the lower ranks is desirable to keep the Marine Corps young and physically strong.[23] In contrast, the Space Force needs people with a higher level of intellectual expertise in a narrow set of disciplines who are increasingly in high demand in the private sector. A high turnover rate may be desirable for the Marine Corps, but it is highly undesirable for the Space Force. Therefore, the personnel systems and policies that may work for the other services are not well suited for the Space Force. While the quantity of people may have a quality of its own for the other services, quality is the quantity that matters most for guardians.

Figure 1. Rank Distribution Across the Military Services

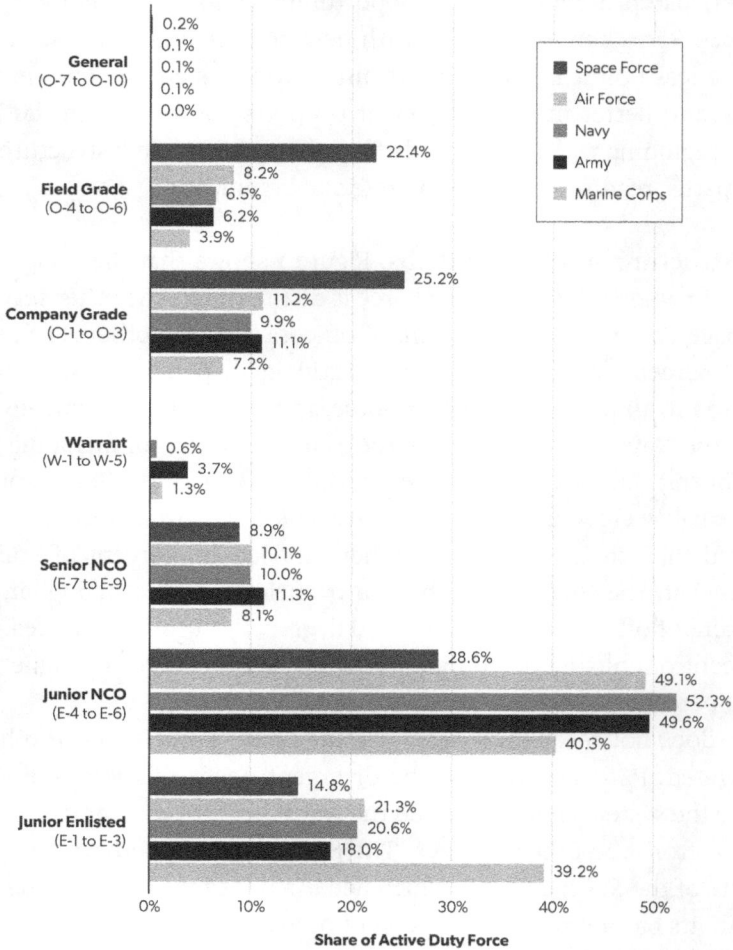

General
(O-7 to O-10)
- 0.2%
- 0.1%
- 0.1%
- 0.1%
- 0.0%

Legend:
- Space Force
- Air Force
- Navy
- Army
- Marine Corps

Field Grade
(O-4 to O-6)
- 22.4%
- 8.2%
- 6.5%
- 6.2%
- 3.9%

Company Grade
(O-1 to O-3)
- 25.2%
- 11.2%
- 9.9%
- 11.1%
- 7.2%

Warrant
(W-1 to W-5)
- 0.6%
- 3.7%
- 1.3%

Senior NCO
(E-7 to E-9)
- 8.9%
- 10.1%
- 10.0%
- 11.3%
- 8.1%

Junior NCO
(E-4 to E-6)
- 28.6%
- 49.1%
- 52.3%
- 49.6%
- 40.3%

Junior Enlisted
(E-1 to E-3)
- 14.8%
- 21.3%
- 20.6%
- 18.0%
- 39.2%

Share of Active Duty Force

Source: Author's analysis of data compiled in Military OneSource, 2023 Demographics: Interactive Profile of the Military Community, Chapter 2: Active-Duty Members, Education, September 2023, https://demographics.militaryonesource.mil/chapter-2-education.
Note: NCO stands for noncommissioned officer.

The Space Force should work with Congress to rethink the Space Force's rank structure, accession paths, and career tracks to better fit a space-centric workforce's needs. Specifically, Congress and the Space Force should consider making the following changes:

- Eliminate the officer-enlisted divide by creating a single, continuous rank system. For example, it could adopt a unified rank system that spans from G-1 to G-10 for all guardians rather than E-1 to E-9 for enlisted and O-1 to O-10 for officers, and it could combine some ranks where the service has few billets. Table 1 provides a hypothetical example of how this could be accomplished as a starting point for debate.[24]

- Make lateral entry the norm rather than the exception so that all guardians enter the service at a rank commensurate with their education and work experience. Using the example provided in Table 1, someone right out of high school would enter as a G-1, someone with a two-year associate degree would enter as a G-2, someone with a four-year bachelor's degree would enter as a G-4, and someone with an advanced degree would enter as a G-5. All accessions would still go through a basic training course commensurate with their experience to familiarize them with the service and how it functions.

- Adopt a merit-based promotion system based on education, experience, performance, and service needs, and eliminate time in grade, peer groups, and up-or-out as factors in the promotion process.

- Make reentry simple and commonplace by allowing guardians that separate from the service to return at a rank commensurate with their education and work experience. Using Table 1 again as an example, a person that leaves as a G-5 with a four-year degree and five years of experience and returns after obtaining an advanced degree and two additional years of work experience would rejoin as a G-6.

- Create separate technical and leadership tracks, allowing personnel in technical tracks to remain in jobs longer and become more specialized in their respective disciplines. This will help reduce the number of unnecessary permanent change of station moves, improving family stability, retention, and subject matter expertise.

Table 1. Notional Space Force Unified Rank Structure

Category	Grade	Rank	Education and Experience Guidelines	Equivalent Legacy Rank(s)
General Officer	G-10	General	Advanced degree and over 26 years of experience	O-9 or O-10
General Officer	G-9	Lieutenant General	Advanced degree and over 22 years of experience	O-7 or O-8
Field Grade Officer	G-8	Colonel	Advanced degree and over 18 years of experience	O-6
Field Grade Officer	G-7	Lieutenant Colonel	Advanced degree and over two years of experience or four-year degree and over 16 years of experience	O-5
Company Grade Officer	G-6	Major	Advanced degree and over six years of experience or four-year degree and over 10 years of experience	O-4
Company Grade Officer	G-5	Captain	Advanced degree and no experience, four-year degree and over four years of experience, or two-year degree and over 12 years of experience	O-3
Company Grade Officer	G-4	Lieutenant	Four-year degree and no experience, two-year degree and over six years of experience, or high school or GED and over eight years of experience	O-1 or O-2
Noncom-missioned Officer	G-3	Sergeant	Two-year degree and two years of experience or high school or GED and over four years of experience	E-5 or E-6
Junior Enlisted	G-2	Specialist	Two-year degree and no experience or high school or GED and over two years of experience	E-3 or E-4
Junior Enlisted	G-1	Specialist Basic	High school or GED and no experience	E-1 or E-2

Source: Author.

- Eliminate the categorization of guardians by specialty codes (e.g., 13S Space Operator and 63A Acquisitions Manager). These designations exacerbate the divide between acquirers and operators (and other subcommunities in the workforce) and should be viewed more like special skills or certifications that each guardian can earn rather than separate career tracks.

Changes to rank structure, accessions, promotions, lateral entry, and overall career management should not be made in isolation or without considering the many interdependent effects involved in each decision. Congress should create a commission to study changes to the personnel system and recommend an integrated package of reforms. It should be careful, however, to limit the number of retired general officers on the commission to ensure adequate representation of other points of view. General officers tend to strongly favor the status quo because by definition the current system worked well for them—a system the Space Force inherited that was designed and managed by the Air Force. Members of the commission should include former junior officers, junior enlisted personnel, and—since the private sector is where the Space Force must compete most vigorously for talent—individuals with private sector experience.

Major changes such as combining ranks and eliminating the officer-enlisted divide would likely evoke a strong response at first. One of the main arguments against a different rank structure for the Space Force is that personnel would not be easily aligned with their peers in the other services for the purposes of protocol and precedence in joint meetings and operations. This can be remedied in the same way the military currently translates between civilian and military ranks. DOD publishes equivalency tables in which each civilian rank (GS-1 through SES) has a corresponding military rank, and DOD Instruction 1000.01 identifies Geneva Conventions categories and their equivalent military and civilian grades.[25] DOD could merely add a column to these tables including the equivalent guardian rank. While it would take time for people to learn the new system, it would soon become as natural and commonly understood as the fact that a Navy captain outranks an Air Force captain.

While the military itself can make some of the changes needed to the personnel system, other changes will require Congress to create exceptions, pilot programs, or entirely new authorities specific to the Space Force. Congress has already signaled that, with sufficient justification, it is open to making significant exceptions for the Space Force. The FY2024 National Defense Authorization Act, for example, included a section known as the Space Force Personnel Management Act, which allowed the Space Force to create a single component for active and reserve guardians.[26] The Space Force should build on this legislative success to enact broader reforms, and Congress should avoid taking actions that compel the Space Force to become more like the other services.

Readiness Model. The Space Force also requires a separate and distinct readiness model for training, operations, and sustainment. The service is already implementing what it calls the Space Force Generation (SPAFORGEN) model, which includes three phases: prepare, ready, and commit. This bears some similarities to the Air Force Force Generation (AFFORGEN) model, which uses four phases: prepare, ready, available to commit, and reset. One significant difference is that the AFFORGEN model spans 24 months per cycle (approximately six months per phase) while the SPAFORGEN model spans 24 weeks (three weeks for the prepare phase, six weeks for the ready phase, and 15 weeks for the commit phase).[27] This rotational schedule means that people will be non-deployed 37.5 percent of the time, requiring some increase in end strength.

Studies have shown that forces that are continuously employed in place, such as drone operators, can experience burnout and low retention. It can be difficult for these personnel to balance the demands of continuous operations (including night shifts) with the expectations of family life.[28] Continuous operations also limit time for professional and personal development. SPAFORGEN is intended to give guardians dedicated time and greater certainty in their schedule to plan for vacations, training, and professional military education. However, some guardians have expressed concerns about the rigid schedules the SPAFORGEN rotational model imposes and instead recommend a data-driven, human-centric approach that provides more flexibility for leaders and individuals to get the support they need.[29]

With this new approach, the Space Force should avoid attempting to follow the other services' readiness practices. It should not blindly assume personnel requirements scale linearly with the number of satellites it operates and use this as an excuse for personnel bloat. Some growth in end strength will be necessary to accommodate new mission areas and the fraction of the force allocated for the prepare and ready phases of the SPAFORGEN model, but this growth should not be used as a justification for increasing headquarters staff and overhead.

With the new SPAFORGEN model, the Space Force must also be clear-eyed about the trade-offs and interdependencies among operational readiness, modernization, and force size. For a given level of resources, improvements in one of these must necessarily come at the expense of one or both of the others.[30] The Space Force, however, needs to increase all three at once, and it can only accomplish this by increasing its over-all budget. But if Congress does not provide sufficient funding, it will be forced to make trade-offs. Representative Mike Rogers, chairman of the House Armed Services Committee, recently warned that the Space Force should not sacrifice modernization for the sake of operational readiness.[31] Modernizing capabilities to keep pace with threats should remain the Space Force's top priority.

Internal Organization. The Space Force has already taken steps to flatten its organization by reducing the number of echelons in its force structure. Soon after its formation, it changed from the Air Force's wing, group, and squadron model to a delta structure.[32] However, in some areas it continues to mirror its parent service in inefficient and ineffective ways. For example, the Space Force has maintained separate field commands for acquisition (Space Systems Command, or SSC) and operations (Space Operations Command, or SPOC) and is establishing a new organization known as Space Futures Command. Having separate commands for acquisition, operations, and future concept development is counterproductive to innovation. It separates personnel in different chains of command based on their function (e.g., acquisition and operations) rather than the mission they support (PNT, SATCOM, missile warning, etc.), and this limits their ability to interact and solve cross-functional problems within each mission area.

More than any other service, the Space Force competes with adversaries based on how quickly it innovates and brings new capabilities to the fight. The innovation cycle is accelerated when engineers, acquirers, intelligence analysts, and operators all work closely together within a mission area. This enables faster feedback and a deeper understanding of what operators need now and in the future. It also helps operators understand the opportunities new technologies present and the threats adversary developments pose. Proactive innovation happens when engineers, acquirers, and analysts find solutions to problems operators don't yet know they need to solve.

The Space Force should immediately halt the establishment of Space Futures Command and combine SSC and SPOC into a new organizational structure aligned around mission areas. A notional concept for realignment around mission areas is shown in Figure 2 as a starting point for debate. Once units are transferred from SSC and SPOC, each mission commander should combine and reshape all deltas and program offices under their command to best suit their mission area's unique needs. Mission commanders should be appointed for terms of at least five years and report directly to the chief of space operations, while the acquisition functions in each mission area would also report to the assistant secretary for space acquisition and integration. In each mission area, operators, analysts, acquirers, and engineers should be physically co-located to maximize opportunities for innovation and the development of deep subject matter expertise. Integration across mission areas would occur through the secondary alignment of personnel by functional certifications, allowing them to share best practices and explore opportunities for collaboration. Integration would also occur through the cross-mission area deltas under Space Training and Readiness Command.

The Department of the Air Force also needs a dedicated senior civilian position for space. The Trump administration's original legislative proposal for the Space Force included an undersecretary of the Air Force for space, but in pursuing efficiency, Congress neglected to create this position.[33] Without it, the senior-most civilian position exclusively focused on space in the Department of the Air Force is the assistant secretary for space acquisition and integration, which only has purview over space acquisitions. A dedicated undersecretary position for space would ensure proper civilian oversight and authority for all aspects of the Space Force, including strategy, training, readiness, and force development. As in the

Figure 2. Concept of a New Organizational Approach

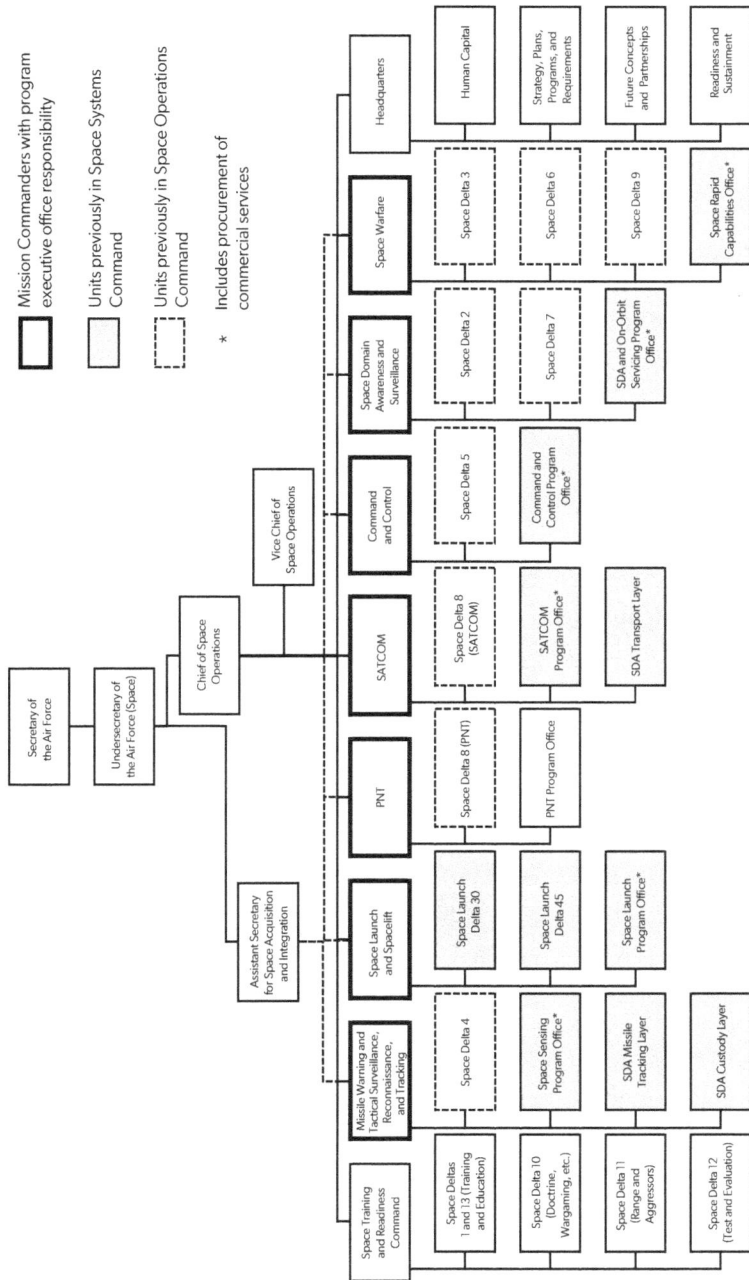

Source: Author.

past, such an undersecretary position could also be dual hatted as director of the National Reconnaissance Office to ensure better coordination and integration between military and intelligence space activities.[34]

Specific Recommendations and Resources Required

Perhaps the Space Force's most exceptional characteristic is how much capability it brings to the joint force relative to its budget. For only 3.5 percent of the DOD budget, the Space Force provides precision positioning, navigation and timing for the entire world, missile warning and tracking that protects the homeland and forward-deployed forces, satellite communications that support nuclear command and control and conventional forces, space domain awareness and collision avoidance for all space operators (civilian and military), and many other capabilities. The Space Force is a critical enabler for forces in all other domains and for the global economy—it is the foundation of the US military's global power projection capabilities.

Given the increasingly pivotal role the Space Force plays in US national security, it must embrace change and reform itself to remain the world's preeminent space power. This will require a partnership between the Space Force and Congress that engenders trust and cooperation. Congress needs to provide more funding and new authorities, but that must be matched by improved transparency, communication, and accountability from the Space Force and its senior leaders. Failures and mistakes along the way should be expected. What matters most for maintaining trust is how quickly they are disclosed and corrected. In this respect, the Space Force should aim to become the exceptional service in how closely it works with Congress.

One of the most important changes that trust between the Space Force and Congress could enable is the restructuring of appropriations accounts around mission areas, as Congress's Commission on Planning, Programming, Budgeting, and Execution Reform recommended for all of DOD. The current system structures the budget around life cycle phases (i.e., development, procurement, operations, etc.), which is an industrial age approach that does not work well in the Information Age.[35] While a wholesale change in budget structure for all of DOD at once would be difficult to accomplish, the Space Force is an ideal test case, allowing appropriators to get more comfortable with the idea and see how well it works in practice. A mission-centric budget structure would align appropriations in the same way the Space Force should organize itself internally and, as a recent Aerospace Corporation report notes, would give Congress increased insight into how funding is being used by mission area.[36] Most importantly, it would align budget authority with operational responsibility so that Congress can hold the Space Force's mission commanders accountable for their performance. It would also give the service more flexibility to respond to new threats and opportunities that arise within the budget cycle—a key to accelerating the pace of innovation.

The lists below give specific recommendations in rough priority order for what Congress, the new administration, and the Space Force should and should not do over the coming years. The net budget impact of these recommendations is estimated to be roughly $31 billion more over the next five years than planned in the FY2025 budget request—an average increase of approximately $6 billion above the currently planned annual funding level.[37] While many of these recommendations will incur additional costs, some do not have a meaningful budget impact, and others will save money by eliminating or preventing the creation of wasteful programs, organizations, and activities.

To-Do List

- Create a Commission on Reforming the Space Force Personnel System tasked to study the following:
  - Combining enlisted and officer ranks into a single guardian rank structure;
  - Normalizing lateral entry and reentry by making the rank for new and returning guardians a function of education and work experience;
  - Reforming the promotion process by eliminating up or out, time in grade, and other non-merit-based requirements;
  - Creating separate technical and leadership career tracks;

- o Reducing the number of unnecessary permanent change of station moves; and
- o Eliminating the categorization of guardians by specialty codes.

- Combine SSC and SPOC into a new organizational structure aligned around mission areas.

- Halt the establishment of Space Futures Command.

- Restructure the Space Force budget around mission areas rather than life cycle phases.

- Ensure operators, analysts, engineers, and acquirers are physically located together within mission areas.

- Update DOD 5100.01 to better articulate the Space Force's roles and missions.

- Create an undersecretary of the Air Force for space to serve as the senior civilian for the service.

- Stop worrying about competing with the intelligence community and the other services for missions.

- Develop a tactically responsive moving target indication system separate from the intelligence community as part of the PWSA custody layer.

- Fully fund the development of GPS M-Code Increment 2 receivers.

- Accelerate future tranches of the PWSA missile tracking and data transport layers.

- Prioritize the offensive and defensive counterspace mission area and begin using capabilities such as electronic warfare and bodyguard satellites to confront malign activities in space.

- Create a separate budget line and five-year funding projection for commercial space intelligence, surveillance, and reconnaissance (ISR) and make the Space Force the central buyer of commercial space ISR for the combatant commands (as it already is for SATCOM).

- Increase funding and the five-year funding projection for commercial SATCOM.

- Stop buying new "legacy" satellites, such as Wideband Global SATCOM and Mobile User Objective System.

- Make spacelift a new mission area for the Space Force and fully fund accelerated testing of cargo delivery via space.

- Accelerate protected SATCOM disaggregation by increasing funding for Evolved Strategic SATCOM and Protected Tactical SATCOM.

- Fund additional launch range modernization to support a higher volume of launches and improve existing facilities' resiliency.

- Increase Space Force operations and maintenance funding and end strength to support the addition of new mission areas.

- Do not assume personnel requirements scale linearly with the overall number of satellites on orbit.

- Do not create a Space National Guard.[38]

Conclusion

Due to its small size and the strategic priority of the domain in which it operates, the Space Force is—in many ways—the exception among the military services. It is exceptional in the critical enabling capabilities it provides for the other services, the way it conducts operations and employs forces across the spectrum of conflict, the skills and deep expertise of its people, and the unique role it plays in global commerce and the lives of every American. The Space Force is the foundation of US power projection—it provides the reach and strategic endurance the US military relies on across the spectrum of conflict.

The Space Force should not assume it is constrained by the old ways of doing business or the rules and regulations designed for the other services. Rather than trying to normalize itself and conform to the mold set by others, the Space Force should embrace its exceptionalism and be more aggressive and forward leaning in the missions, reforms, and policies it pursues. Recent history has shown that both Congress and the Trump administration are more open to disruptive ideas from the Space Force than from any other part of DOD. Congress and the White House recognize that the Space Force is different, and the public assumes it is different, but the Space Force itself has not fully accepted its uniqueness. The Space Force is the exceptional service, and Space Force exceptionalism should be the heart of its culture, values, and vision.

Notes

1. US Department of Defense, Office of the Under Secretary of Defense (Comptroller), "Table 6–4: Department of Defense TOA by Major Force Program Current Dollars (Dollars in Millions)," https://comptroller.defense.gov/Portals/45/Documents/defbudget/FY2025/fy25_Green_Book.pdf.

2. Les Aspin, *The Bottom-Up Review: Forces for a New Era*, US Department of Defense, September 1, 1993, https://www.history.navy.mil/content/dam/nhhc/research/library/online-reading-room/history-surveys/needs-opportunities-modern-history-us-navy/bottom-up-review-aspin-sept-1993.pdf.

3. US Department of Defense, 2022 *National Defense Strategy of the United States of America*, October 27, 2022, https://media.defense.gov/2022/Oct/27/2003103845/-1/-1/1/2022-NATIONAL-DEFENSE-STRATEGY-NPR-MDR.pdf.

4. Jane Harman et al., *Report of the Commission on the National Defense Strategy*, RAND Corporation, July 29, 2024, 37, https://www.rand.org/nsrd/projects/NDS-commission.html.

5. Notable exceptions to this are using space-based kinetic weapons to strike targets on Earth—a concept also known as "Rods from God"—and using space-based kinetic missile interceptors for missile defense. Neither of these space missions scale favorably when compared to traditional alternatives, such as ground-based long-range

missiles and missile interceptors. See Todd Harrison et al., *Implications of Ultra-Low-Cost Access to Space*, Center for Strategic and International Studies, March 21, 2017, https://www.csis.org/analysis/implications-ultra-low-cost-access-space.

6. David Wright et al., *The Physics of Space Security: A Reference Manual*, American Academy of Arts and Sciences, January 2005, 15, https://www.amacad.org/publication/physics-space-security-reference-manual.

7. Exceptions to this are satellites in geostationary orbits with coverage over only part of the Earth or satellites in non-geostationary orbits that have power or other operating limitations that prevent them from performing their mission continuously throughout their orbit (i.e., satellites with a low duty cycle).

8. The number of aircraft could be slightly more or less than double depending on how spares, reserve aircraft, and training aircraft are allocated and the specific geography, basing, and operational demands in each theater.

9. Will Robinson-Smith, "SpaceX Launches Starshield Satellites on Falcon 9 Rocket from California for the NRO," *Spaceflight Now*, December 17, 2024, https://spaceflightnow.com/2024/12/17/live-coverage-spacex-to-launch-starshield-satellites-on-falcon-9-rocket-from-california-for-the-nro/.

10. Theresa Hitchens, "'Tactical ISR' from Space Requires DoD, NRO Policy Changes: Calvelli," *Breaking Defense*, February 26, 2024, https://breakingdefense.com/2024/02/tactical-isr-from-space-requires-dod-nro-policy-changes-calvelli/.

11. Theresa Hitchens, "Raymond Unveils Classified Target Tracking Space Radar Effort," *Breaking Defense*, May 12, 2021, https://breakingdefense.com/2021/05/raymond-unveils-classified-target-tracking-space-radar-effort/.

12. RA Editorial Desk, "Baseline for New NRO–Space Force Satellites to Track Ground Targets Certified by US Air Force," *Raksha Anirveda*, September 1, 2024, https://raksha-anirveda.com/baseline-for-new-nro-space-force-satellites-to-track-ground-targets-certified-by-us-air-force/.

13. Exec. Order No. 14186, 90 Fed. Reg. 8767 (February 3, 2025), https://www.govinfo.gov/content/pkg/FR-2025-02-03/pdf/FR-2025-02-03.pdf.

14. Space Development Agency, "Custody," https://www.sda.mil/custody/.

15. US Department of Defense, Department of the Air Force, "Department of the Air Force President's Budget Request FY25," March 2024, https://www.saffm.hq.af.mil/FM-Resources/Budget/Air-Force-Presidents-Budget-FY25/.

16. Office of the Chief of Space Operations, Strategic Initiatives Group, "White Paper on Competitive Endurance: A Proposed Theory of Success for the U.S. Space Force" (working paper, US Space Force, January 11, 2024), 1, https://www.spaceforce.mil/Portals/2/Documents/White_Paper_Summary_of_Competitive_Endurance.pdf.

17. Office of the Chief of Space Operations, Strategic Initiatives Group, "White Paper on Competitive Endurance: A Proposed Theory of Success for the U.S. Space Force," 4.

18. Shaun Waterman, "Russian Jamming Is Wreaking Havoc on GPS in Eastern Europe. But Is It Hybrid Warfare?," *Air & Space Forces Magazine*, July 10, 2024, https://www.airandspaceforces.com/russian-gps-jamming-nato-ukraine/.

19. Chief of Space Operations, "CSO Notice to Guardians (C-Note #32)," October 25, 2024, https://www.spaceforce.mil/Portals/2/cso-library/C_Note_32_25_Oct_24_

Our_Words_Have_Meaning.pdf; and US Space Force, *Space Doctrine Publication (SDP)* 3-0, *Operations: Doctrine for Space Forces,* July 19, 2023, https://www.starcom.spaceforce.mil/Portals/2/SDP%203-0%20Operations%20(19%20July%202023).pdf.

20. US Department of Defense, "Functions of the Department of Defense and Its Major Components," December 21, 2010, https://www.esd.whs.mil/Portals/54/Documents/DD/issuances/dodd/510001p.pdf.

21. Data are for FY2025 requested authorization, as detailed in the services' military personnel budget justification books. See US Department of the Army, *Fiscal Year (FY) 2025 Budget Estimates: Military Personnel, Army Justification Book,* March 2024, https://www.asafm.army.mil/Portals/72/Documents/BudgetMaterial/2025/Base%20Budget/Military%20Personnel/Military%20Personnel%20Army%20Volume%201.pdf; US Department of the Air Force, *Fiscal Year (FY) 2025 Budget Estimates: Military Personnel Appropriation,* March 2024, https://www.saffm.hq.af.mil/Portals/84/documents/FY25/FY25%20Air%20Force%20Military%20Personnel.pdf?ver=LIVcoFWwyr9iwf7x VNoQaA%3d%3d; US Department of the Air Force, *Fiscal Year (FY) 2025 Budget Estimates: Military Personnel, Space Force,* March 2024, https://www.saffm.hq.af.mil/Portals/84/documents/FY25/FY25%20Space%20Force%20Military%20Personnel.pdf?ver=k-yb1vS-gA29nZKx4Y8frw%3d%3d; US Department of the Navy, *Fiscal Year (FY) 2025 Budget Estimates: Justification of Estimates—Military Personnel, Navy,* March 2024, https://www.secnav.navy.mil/fmc/fmb/Documents/25pres/MPN_Book.pdf; and US Department of the Navy, *Fiscal Year (FY) 2025 Budget Estimates: Justification of Estimates—Military Personnel, Marine Corps (MPMC),* March 2024, https://www.secnav.navy.mil/fmc/fmb/Documents/25pres/MPMC_Book.pdf.

22. Author's analysis of data compiled in Military OneSource, 2023 Demographics: Interactive Profile of the Military Community, Chapter 2: Active-Duty Members, Education, September 2023, https://demographics.militaryonesource.mil/chapter-2-education.

23. Military OneSource, 2023 Demographics: Interactive Profile of the Military Community, Chapter 2: Active-Duty Members, Age, September 2023, https://demographics.militaryonesource.mil/chapter-2-age.

24. For additional thoughts on eliminating the officer-enlisted divide, see Nicholas Wood, "Bad Idea: The Officer-Enlisted Divide," Center for Strategic and International Studies, January 7, 2022, https://defense360.csis.org/bad-idea-the-officer-enlisted-divide/.

25. US Department of Defense, "Identification (ID) Cards Required by the Geneva Conventions," April 16, 2012, https://www.esd.whs.mil/Portals/54/Documents/DD/issuances/dodi/100001p.pdf.

26. National Defense Authorization Act for Fiscal Year 2024, H.R. 2670, §§ 1701–42, https://www.congress.gov/118/crpt/hrpt301/CRPT-118hrpt301.pdf.

27. Chris Gordon, "VCSAF Slife: New Force Generation Model Better Explains 'Capacity, Risk, and Readiness,'" *Air & Space Forces Magazine,* January 12, 2024, https://www.airandspaceforces.com/vcasf-slife-new-force-generation-model/; and SpOC Public Affairs, "Space Force Generation Model," US Space Force, Space Force Operations Command, April 19, 2024, https://www.spoc.spaceforce.mil/About-Us/Fact-Sheets/Display/Article/3752539/space-force-generation-model-infographic.

28. Jamal M. Campbell, "Psychological Effects on UAV Operators and Proposed Mitigation Strategies to Combat PTSD" (master's thesis, Naval Postgraduate School, June 2021), https://apps.dtic.mil/sti/trecms/pdf/AD1150884.pdf.

29. Will P., "SPAFORGEN: A Call to Action to Prevent a Possible Crisis of Retention, Mission Readiness, and Guardian Well-Being," LinkedIn, January 11, 2025, https://www.linkedin.com/pulse/spaforgen-call-action-prevent-possible-crisis-mission-will-paulson-dhiee/?trackingId=prXg8DtC711Baan5Zl17rA%3D%3D.

30. Kathleen Hicks, "Defense Strategy and the Iron Triangle of Painful Tradeoffs," Center for Strategic and International Studies, June 21, 2017, https://defense360.csis.org/defense-strategy-and-the-iron-triangle-of-painful-tradeoffs/.

31. Sam Cestari, "Celebrating the U.S. Space Force and Charting Its Future," Center for Strategic and International Studies, December 17, 2024, https://www.csis.org/events/celebrating-us-space-force-and-charting-its-future.

32. Space Force Public Affairs, "Space Force Begins to Transition into Field Organizational Structure," US Space Force, July 24, 2020, https://www.spaceforce.mil/News/Article/2287005/space-force-begins-transition-into-field-organizational-structure/.

33. US Department of Defense, *United States Space Force*, February 2019, https://media.defense.gov/2019/Mar/01/2002095012/-1/-1/1/UNITED-STATES-SPACE-FORCE-STRATEGIC-OVERVIEW.PDF/.

34. *Air & Space Forces Magazine*, "Former NRO Chief, USAF Undersecretary Peter Teets: 1942–2020," https://www.airandspaceforces.com/former-nro-chief-usaf-undersecretary-peter-teets-1942-2020/.

35. Commission on Planning, Programming, Budgeting, and Execution Reform, *Defense Resourcing for the Future: Final Report*, March 6, 2024, https://ppbereform.senate.gov/wp-content/uploads/2024/03/Commission-on-PPBE-Reform_Full-Report_6-March-2024_FINAL.pdf.

36. Robert S. Wilson et al., *Why Transforming the Budget Structure Would Benefit Defense Space*, Center for Space Policy and Strategy, October 2024, https://csps.aerospace.org/papers/why-transforming-budget-structure-would-benefit-defense-space.

37. Budget estimates were made using the AEI Defense Futures Simulator, available at American Enterprise Institute, Defense Futures Simulator, November 2024, https://defensefutures.aei.org/.

38. Todd Harrison, "Kill the Zombie Space National Guard Idea," *Defense One*, May 16, 2024, https://www.defenseone.com/ideas/2024/05/kill-zombie-space-national-guard-idea/396626/.

16

To Deter and Assure: A US Nuclear Posture Tailored for Three Theaters

KYLE BALZER

The United States confronts an unprecedented—and unexpected—geopolitical challenge. For the first time in the nuclear age, America faces not one but two nuclear-armed peer adversaries in China and Russia. Beijing has shocked Washington by undertaking a massive nuclear buildup and will soon join Moscow as a nuclear power of equal standing with Washington. The Kremlin, meanwhile, has defied America's expectations by violating arms control agreements, growing a large theater nuclear force, and launching brutal wars against its neighbors. And this is to say nothing of a nuclear-armed North Korea conducting provocative flight tests of ballistic missiles and an Iran poised to cross the nuclear threshold. Put simply, when US planners established nuclear force requirements more than a decade ago, they did not anticipate the threats confronting the United States today.

Flawed assumptions have thus saddled the United States with a nuclear arsenal lacking the capacity and capability to compete against two nuclear peers and lesser regional threats. This "two-peer-plus" security environment demands a US nuclear posture that can deter across multiple theaters and, should deterrence fail in one or more of them, achieve wartime objectives while dissuading opportunistic aggression elsewhere. Washington can no longer afford to wish away mounting nuclear threats in the Asia-Pacific, Europe, and the Middle East—especially since these threats have coalesced into an autocratic axis bent on breaking the US-led liberal order. Fortunately, Washington *can* afford a nuclear deterrent that underwrites a multi-theater posture and assures far-flung allies of the US security guarantee. And it can do so without weakening America's overall deterrence and turning the conventional posture into the bill payer for nuclear modernization.

Deterring adversaries and assuring allies across geographically dispersed regions is by no means a novel challenge for US defense planners. But the emerging two-peer-plus threat environment undoubtedly intensifies this dilemma and calls for tailored adjustments to the US nuclear posture. While the nature of deterrence transcends time, space, and the number of adversaries—peer or otherwise—its character must reflect the particular players; their distinctive values, theories of victory, and geographic orientations; and the balance of resolve and military capability among them.

This chapter develops a US nuclear posture fit for the unique attributes of today's evolving security environment. First, I examine how flawed planning assumptions caused the strategy-resource mismatch the US nuclear posture finds itself in today. Second, to close the gap between US nuclear strategy and the resources available to execute it, I establish new force requirements tailored to the distinctive coercive attributes of America's adversaries. Finally, I lay out a US nuclear posture fit to deter threats and assure allies across three theaters. Meeting the security challenges of today and tomorrow will require a nuclear posture with enhanced strike capacity, selectivity, and flexibility.

Misreading the Room

Flawed assumptions and misguided expectations have left the United States ill prepared for today's rapidly changing nuclear threat environment. In 2010, the Obama administration's Nuclear Posture Review identified "nuclear terrorism" as the "most immediate and extreme danger" facing the United States—and forecast that it would remain so in the long run.[1] This assessment appeared eminently sensible at the time, with the country devoting enormous resources to the global war on terror. It also aligned with a long-standing bipartisan push to adjust the US military posture to the reality that the Soviet Union, America's only nuclear-peer adversary, had collapsed. The immediate post–Cold War security landscape was thus a far cry from that of the 1980s, when the United States confronted a hostile superpower armed to the teeth with some 33,000 nuclear weapons. Accordingly, Washington treated the relatively benign security environment of the early 21st century as an opportunity to reduce reliance on nuclear deterrence.

This optimistic threat forecast, however, proved more fantasy than reality. Even as the United States slashed its nuclear arsenal, other states refused to act in good faith and follow suit. Consequently, the existing US nuclear posture—and the ongoing modernization program and weapons industrial base that supports it—now finds itself behind the curve of a threat environment that more closely resembles the 1980s Cold War than what planners had anticipated and set force requirements to address.

Nuclear Fantasy. In the Obama administration's early years, America's only nuclear peer, Russia, was deemed a reliable partner on a host of security initiatives, including President Barack Obama's "commitment to seek the peace and security of a world without nuclear weapons."[2] US defense planners designated China as a lesser-included nuclear power that harbored no ambition to join the United States and Russia as a nuclear equal. And though North Korea had successfully tested an atomic device in 2006 and Iran was researching and developing the technical means to follow suit, Washington treated both states as problems to be managed. US officials believed a robust diplomatic campaign, in partnership with Moscow and Beijing, would roll back or tame Pyongyang's and Tehran's nuclear ambitions.

Senior Obama administration officials thus anticipated—and set force requirements for—a relatively benign nuclear threat environment for the 2010s and beyond. Terrorism and proliferation would remain the defining challenges of the era. And great-power nuclear relations would remain a matter of arms control and disarmament—not nuclear deterrence. Having perceived "fundamental changes" in security affairs and the "easing of Cold War rivalries," US defense planners moved confidently to reduce reliance on nuclear weapons and concentrate instead on America's "unrivaled" precision strike conventional capabilities.[3] And all the better for it, since Obama had challenged the planners "to put an end to Cold War thinking" and set an example for Russia and China to follow.[4]

The Obama administration believed its superior conventional strike capabilities would allow the United States, in partnership with Russia, to slash strategic nuclear force levels dramatically. In April 2010,

Obama signed the New Strategic Arms Reduction Treaty (New START) with Moscow, which limited both signatories to 1,550 deployed strategic warheads carried on no more than 700 delivery systems.[5] This marked a 30 percent reduction in accountable warheads from the force ceiling of 2,200 warheads the George W. Bush administration had established with Russia in 2002.[6] Indeed, New START represented the logical next step in a long-standing bipartisan campaign to pull down America's deployed warheads from the heights of a strategic posture that had, in the late 1980s, peaked at some 13,600 weapons. As Bush declared in a 2001 address at National Defense University, the United States would "change the size, the composition, the character of [its] nuclear forces in a way that reflects the reality that the Cold War is over." "Today's Russia is not yesterday's Soviet Union," he explained. And his administration was "committed to achieving a credible deterrent with the lowest possible number of nuclear weapons."[7]

For the Obama administration, New START established that number— or at least the lowest possible number acceptable to Congress. But in exchange for Senate ratification of the treaty, the administration acceded to calls for recapitalizing all three legs of the nuclear triad. It established a modest program to replace America's Cold War–era strategic bombers, air-launched cruise missiles (ALCMs), land-based intercontinental ballistic missiles (ICBMs), and ballistic missile submarines (SSBNs) with modernized versions of themselves. The United States would also pursue life-extension programs for its suite of aging warheads. Though this like-for-like modernization effort was not one of capacity (next-generation *Columbia*-class submarines, for example, are set to come online in fewer numbers and with markedly fewer missile launchers than today's *Ohio*-class boats),[8] it was deemed sufficient for a tranquil environment in which the only nuclear peer in sight was considered a reliable partner.

Indeed, the Obama administration's decision to extend the life of America's aging warheads rather than develop new ones was taken in part to perpetuate the benign security environment of the early 21st century. Every post–Cold War US administration had feared that developing novel nuclear weapons might provoke minor powers like China to undertake what Secretary of Defense Donald Rumsfeld had characterized as a "sprint toward parity" with the United States.[9] Thus, with no acute nuclear-peer adversary on the horizon, successive administrations had deferred or canceled the modernization of nuclear weapons and delivery systems that were decades past their service life.

As a result, the US nuclear weapons industrial base atrophied to such an extent that it was ill prepared to service Obama's modernization program.[10] Nevertheless, America's decayed nuclear production infrastructure—and its modernization program quickly falling behind schedule—hardly seemed cause for concern in such a benign setting. These were, after all, the heady days of Obama's Prague Agenda, when many believed a nuclear-free world was within reach—if only Washington could muster the courage and discipline to lead the world down the path to disarmament.

Nuclear Reality. Alas, China, North Korea, and Russia were unwilling to follow the United States anywhere—least of all to nuclear zero. For these three despotic regimes harboring revisionist intentions, Cold War–style thinking about nuclear weapons remained very much alive.

Vladimir Putin's Russia proved immune to Bush's vision of a democratic post-Soviet state "at peace with itself and its neighbors."[11] And following its 2008 invasion of Georgia, the Kremlin exploited Obama's attempted "reset" by launching a brutal war in Ukraine that continues to this day.[12] As of this writing, Russia has built up a massive theater-range nuclear arsenal that dwarfs its American counterpart, and it has nearly completed a generational effort to modernize all three legs of its nuclear triad while developing a suite of "exotic" delivery systems.[13] Together, these new force capabilities have shielded Russia's ongoing war in Ukraine from a more forward-leaning American response. The Kremlin's incessant nuclear saber-rattling has successfully constrained Western assistance to Kyiv and, in effect, transformed the Russian homeland into a sanctuary.

China, for its part, refused to oblige the United States and instead embarked on Rumsfeld's feared "sprint" toward parity (which the US intelligence community projects to be on pace to match, if not exceed, America's deployed nuclear arsenal by 2035).[14] Analogous to Russia's nuclear-backed aggression in Europe, China's stunning nuclear breakout has provided cover for Beijing's ongoing "short-of-war coercion" campaign in the western Pacific, which seeks to dissolve America's forward position in East Asia.[15] China now boasts vastly more land-based, nuclear-capable intercontinental and theater-range missile launchers than the United States.[16] And America's Asia-Pacific allies and partners are increasingly concerned that, as the US homeland grows more vulnerable to nuclear coercion, Washington will become risk averse in defending the regional status quo. That the United States retired its only regional nuclear response option—the Tomahawk Land Attack Missile–Nuclear (TLAM-N)—even as China fielded a massive theater capability of its own has exacerbated allied concerns about the US nuclear umbrella.[17]

As for North Korea, Pyongyang skirted—and with Russian and Chinese assistance, eventually wiggled its way out from under—an international sanctions regime to develop some 50 warheads and counting and a suite of nuclear-capable missile systems in various stages of development.[18] And as Pyongyang's arsenal and the reach of its missiles have grown, so has its willingness to conduct aggressive provocations along its frontier.[19] South Korea in turn is increasingly anxious about America's extended deterrence guarantee. Seoul's anxiety is such that it has even floated the idea of developing an independent nuclear arsenal to hedge against an American retreat from the Korean Peninsula.[20]

Iran, meanwhile, has been knocking on the door of this nuclear-armed autocratic club—no doubt perceiving security benefits in defying Washington and gaining membership. Though it has so far refrained from crossing the nuclear threshold, Iran's recent missile exchanges with Israel and the collapse of its Axis of Resistance have exposed the glaring weakness of Tehran's regional position—and therefore might incentivize it to bolt for the bomb. Iran is already coordinating with China, North Korea, and Russia to undermine the US-led liberal order through conventional means.[21] Tehran may soon calculate that membership in this deepening axis of aggression lends it cover to safely cross the nuclear finish line and shore up its weakened deterrence.

The United States thus finds itself in a growing mismatch between its deterrence strategy and the resources available to execute it. Its updated 2024 nuclear weapons employment policy calls for a strategic posture "able to deter Russia, the PRC [People's Republic of China], *and* the DPRK [Democratic People's Republic of Korea] simultaneously in peacetime, crisis, and conflict." (Emphasis added.) And to fulfill this mission, it set a requirement for a strike capacity and capability "to hold at risk what [these] adversaries value most"—including, to the extent practicable, their expanding nuclear forces.[22] But America's existing force posture (featuring 400 Minuteman III ICBMs, 14 *Ohio*-class SSBNs carrying 240 Trident D5 sea-launched ballistic missiles, 19 B-2 stealth bombers, 46 B-52H standoff bombers, and 528 ALCMs) was not sized and shaped to carry out this job. Nor was its like-for-like replacement program (featuring 400 Sentinel ICBMs, 12 *Columbia*-class SSBNs, 100 B-21 stealth bombers, and 1,087 Long-Range Standoff cruise missiles) designed to hold at risk multiple peer adversaries simultaneously. A simple quantitative assessment of the changing threat environment thus makes plain that the current program of record cannot sufficiently cover rapidly expanding target sets in Asia and Europe.

Targeting arithmetic alone, however, constitutes an incomplete force-sizing and force-shaping construct. To deter adversaries and assure allies across multiple theaters, the United States must do more than simply narrow the widening gap between strike capability and target sets. It must also tailor capability more closely to its adversaries' distinctive approaches to nuclear weapons and its allies' growing concerns. Thus, to establish an adequate force-planning construct that redresses America's strategy-resource mismatch, the United States should first appraise its adversaries' "national styles" in nuclear strategy—and their impact on US and allied security interests and capabilities.[23]

Setting Requirements

China, North Korea, and Russia have coercive national styles in nuclear strategy. They have demonstrated a willingness to exploit America's mistaken planning assumptions by expanding their arsenals *and* employing nuclear-backed coercion to support their revisionist agendas. And they are all leveraging America's comparative restraint at the strategic and theater nuclear levels, at which Moscow especially has rattled the nuclear saber to paralyze NATO.

Thus, to adjust the US nuclear posture to the two-peer-plus environment, planners must tailor force requirements to distinctive adversaries and their coercive impact on American interests and allied concerns. Since deterrence threats and assurance pledges are a state of mind more than a rational science, US planners must calibrate force requirements to the peculiar adversary and allied styles of deterrence.

"Deterrence *à la Russe*." The Russian way of nuclear deterrence is more forward leaning than the American national style. It encompasses the US conception of deterrence (threats to dissuade an adversary from taking a particular course of action) and what American strategic thought treats distinctly as "compellence" (threatening or actually employing nuclear weapons to compel a change in adversary behavior).[24] "Deterrence *à la Russe*" thus spans activities in peacetime competition and extends through all phases of armed conflict.[25] And it has profound implications for US nuclear planning.

The Kremlin, for instance, believes its way of deterrence has succeeded in Ukraine, forestalling direct NATO intervention and slowing—in select cases, even preventing—Western arms deliveries to Kyiv. Thus, US force planners would be wise to assume that even if the Russo-Ukraine war stops, Russian threats to employ nuclear weapons will not. As the security analyst Dmitry Adamsky makes clear, nuclear coercion embodies Russia's new normal. And it will likely remain a central feature of Kremlin statecraft in the long run, given the decimation of Russia's professional military in Ukraine.[26]

US nuclear planners should set force requirements on the basis that the Kremlin to a great extent considers its war against Ukraine a deterrence success. They should also recognize that Russia's new normal means the Kremlin might consider limited nuclear employment an asymmetric advantage in a future conflict with NATO. Deterrence *à la Russe* certainly lends itself to that kind of thinking. Moreover, Russia's conventional power has received a thrashing in Ukraine. And its massive theater nuclear buildup vis-à-vis America's one-sided nuclear restraint represents one of the few areas—if not the only area—of the NATO-Russia military balance in which the Kremlin holds a clear advantage. In the years ahead, then, Russia might be tempted to run risks at lower levels of conflict for two reasons: The Kremlin believes Russia's geographic proximity to NATO's central region or northern flank opens up an opportunity to snatch territory in a conventional fait accompli, and the Kremlin believes that even if NATO mobilizes in time to stymie such a conventional assault, Russia could still escalate its way to victory via theater nuclear employment.

NATO allies like Poland and Finland are sensitive to Russia's theater nuclear advantage—so much so that both have expressed interest in playing a greater role in the alliance's nuclear mission.[27] Indeed, the Poles' fervor to join NATO's nuclear-sharing program betrays how the alliance has failed to adjust to Russia's theater buildup *and* NATO's changing post–Cold War geography. For frontline members like Poland and Finland, which joined NATO following the Warsaw Pact's demise, a future in which Russia attempts to escalate its way to victory is very real. Accordingly, they value forward-deployed US nuclear weapons far more than do Washington and the other NATO members whose borders do not rim the Russian threat. And they are increasingly unsatisfied with the hundred or so US gravity bombs—and the dual-capable fighter aircraft certified to carry them—that are based farther afield in Belgium, Germany, Italy, the Netherlands, and Turkey. Thus, to reassure anxious allies and deter Russia from exploiting its theater nuclear advantage, Washington must diversify its regional nuclear options and reconsider its basing arrangements. Poland represents NATO's new center of gravity, and US officials should lead the alliance in integrating Warsaw (and, if interested, Helsinki) into its nuclear mission.

US planners should also reset force requirements on the assumption that Russia will be tempted to run risks at the theater level if the Kremlin senses Washington is vulnerable to coercion at the *strategic* nuclear level. Russian preparations to bring online the new "superheavy" RS-28 Sarmat ICBM, capable of carrying up to 10 warheads and threatening America's geographically dispersed missile silos, are certainly an unwelcome development. However, the Sarmat alone will be insufficient to overturn the strategic balance. Alongside the US triad's land-based ICBMs, the United States maintains a highly survivable fleet of 14 *Ohio*-class strategic missile submarines—set to be replaced by 12 next-generation *Columbia*-class boats starting in 2030. And America's airborne leg of 19 B-2 stealth bombers and 46 B-52H standoff bombers provides further insurance.

But the existing US triad and modernization program was designed to maintain strategic- and theater-level deterrence with only the Russian threat in mind. US planners did not anticipate China ditching its long-held minimum deterrent—to say nothing of a peer nuclear China with a coercive national style on par with Russia's.

Deterrence with Chinese Characteristics. China's national style in nuclear strategy diverges sharply from that of the United States. The Chinese way of deterrence, or *weishe*, entails dissuading the adversary from taking actions harmful to Beijing *and* compelling actions beneficial to Beijing.[28] Leading Chinese defense intellectuals now routinely depict China's expanding nuclear arsenal as a trump card to forestall or reverse US intervention in the western Pacific.[29] And Chinese military writings frequently treat the modernization of nuclear weaponry as "an important guarantee for achieving control of the enemy without fighting."[30]

Perhaps it is unsurprising, then, that China's massive nuclear buildup over the past five years has coincided with Beijing ramping up its short-of-war coercion campaign to drive a wedge between Washington and its allies in the Asia-Pacific. Almost daily, China's air and naval forces encroach on the airspace and territorial waters of America's regional partners in a bid to revise the regional order. Correlation, of course, is not causation. But prudence calls for US planners to assume Beijing views its expanding nuclear arsenal as a coercive shield under which it can transform the western Pacific into a Chinese lake. Consider that even as a weak nuclear power in the immediate post–Cold War era, Beijing was willing to engage in nuclear coercion during the Third Taiwan Strait Crisis in 1996. At the height of that crisis, Chinese officials reportedly threatened to annihilate Los Angeles in a futile bid to deter US carrier strike groups from entering the region in support of Taipei.[31] That Beijing is no longer a lesser-included nuclear power will impose new demands on US force requirements—at the strategic and theater levels—to maintain America's forward position in the Asia-Pacific.

At the theater level, US planners should set force requirements on the assumption that China is already leveraging its improved regional nuclear capabilities to break America's alliances. To deter and assure against this threat, the US theater nuclear posture must signal to Beijing *and* America's allies that China cannot revise the regional status quo via nuclear-backed coercion or the limited employment of nuclear arms. Given China's rapid buildup of theater nuclear delivery systems, this force requirement will present an imposing challenge to US planners.

Beijing now has in spades what it lacked for theater striking power in 1996—a problem exacerbated by America's decision to retire the TLAM-N in 2010. Beijing boasts a suite of nuclear-capable ballistic missile systems that can hold targets at risk across the entire western Pacific. The US military hub on Guam, which enables the projection of power into the Asia-Pacific rimland, is particularly vulnerable to nuclear attack by the intermediate-range DF-26 ballistic missile. And as in Europe, America's Asian allies are apprehensive about the dramatic shift in the theater nuclear balance. No less than Japan's prime minister, Shigeru Ishiba, has expressed concern that the two-peer-plus threat will make "the US extended deterrence in the region . . . no longer function."[32]

American planners should reintroduce a theater-range nuclear system that has an enduring presence and the survivability to signal to allies and Beijing that US nuclear forces remain coupled to the region. Given the two-peer threat, the United States does not have the option to swing dual-capable fighter aircraft from Europe. And given the politics surrounding nuclear weapons in the western Pacific—Japan in particular—the US basing system in the region lacks the infrastructure to host nuclear weapons. A seaborne nuclear option thus offers a promising alternative to ground-based systems—all the more so because the Asia-Pacific is primarily a maritime theater.

At the strategic level, US planners should set force requirements on the assumption that a weak American triad would tempt China to run risks at the theater level. Washington must convince Beijing that if it attempts to escalate its way out of a failing regional war by employing strategic nuclear forces, America's triad has the capacity to absorb a large-scale attack and still inflict unacceptable damage in retaliation. This planning criterion is what makes Russia's Sarmat ICBM, in combination with China's strategic breakout, a challenge for US nuclear planning. China's rapid buildup of intercontinental missile launchers alone has blown past America's 400 operational ICBM silos. And Beijing's estimated 550 ICBM launchers, split between silos and more survivable road-mobile platforms, will soon house missiles carrying multiple warheads that can hold America's dispersed missile silos at risk.[33]

Thus, between China's and Russia's ICBM capabilities, the existing and planned US ICBM fleet will fall under increasing strain over the next 10 years—especially if Beijing and Moscow engage in a coordinated attack. The prospect that any war with China—whether on its own or in combination with Russia—will be protracted only adds to this burden.[34] Prudence calls for US planners to assume strategic submarines and bombers will suffer losses and technical failures in an extended fight.

At the strategic level of deterrence, then, the US requires more capacity and capability to absorb a massive Sino-Russian attack and then inflict catastrophic damage on targets the offending parties value most. Yet America's program of record was sized and shaped to hold at risk just a single nuclear peer. Though the probability of Beijing and Moscow coordinating with each other to cripple the US ICBM fleet is low, strategic deterrence is of such importance to America's global military posture that planners must prepare for this worst-case scenario. The projection of US conventional military power into the Asia-Pacific, Europe, and the Middle East depends entirely on strategic deterrence holding. And above all else, the only existential military threat to the US homeland is that of a large-scale nuclear attack.

Given the stakes and Russia's and China's coercive national styles, the strategic level of deterrence would be an unwise place for US planners to tolerate greater risk. Moreover, an assessment of the threats emerging in northeast Asia and the Middle East makes clear the United States should shore up its strategic deterrence so it can project power into these regions.

Deterrence of the Lesser Included. Though North Korea—and Iran, if it goes nuclear—will remain a lesser-included threat, Pyongyang's habits of coercion will stress the mismatch between America's nuclear strategy, strike capability, and assurance guarantees. If Washington hopes to deter North Korea *and* keep South Korea under its nuclear umbrella, US force planners need to reintroduce flexible and selective attack options to northeast Asia.

In January 2021, Kim Jong Un unveiled plans to develop both "ultralarge" and "smaller and lighter" tactical nuclear weapons. Pyongyang has since conducted a seemingly endless parade of test flights of short-range ballistic missiles capable of delivering such tactical weaponry.[35] The US Defense Intelligence Agency recently assessed that these developments signal the regime's shift from focusing entirely on deterrence to a nuclear posture capable of managing escalation and terminating hostilities quickly should a conflict break out on the Korean Peninsula.[36]

Pyongyang has also paired its development of more advanced tactical nuclear weapons with incendiary rhetoric about its ability to hold the US homeland at risk of nuclear attack. North Korea's growing intercontinental missile arsenal has raised understandable alarm in South Korea that Pyongyang has weakened, if not neutralized, the United States' extended deterrence guarantee.[37] South Korea's president, Yoon Suk Yeol, has warned that if the situation "gets worse . . . our country will introduce tactical nuclear weapons or build them on our own."[38] That Pyongyang and Beijing have lent critical technical assistance to Tehran's ballistic missile program has raised similar concerns in the Middle East about Washington's staying power in the Persian Gulf—in no small part due to the specter of a nuclear-armed Iran that looms on the horizon.[39]

Thus, US defense planners must tailor nuclear force requirements to growing allied concerns about the US extended deterrence guarantee in northeast Asia. Moreover, since the decisions made today will determine the US nuclear posture of the 2080s (given the long lead times and lifespans of such weapons systems), planners should also factor in the prospect of a nuclear-armed Iran. Pyongyang and Tehran will, in all likelihood, remain lesser-included threats. But their respective positions on Russia's and China's peripheries reinforce that the US nuclear posture requires more selective and flexible response options.

For example, responding to a large-scale North Korean nuclear attack on South Korea with even a limited ICBM or submarine-launched ballistic missile (SLBM) strike would raise concerns in Moscow and Beijing about Washington's intended target. This is especially the case because the United States might find itself engaged in simultaneous conflicts with North Korea and one or both of America's great-power rivals. Washington thus requires a menu of more selective and flexible options, with flight profiles and azimuths that Moscow and Beijing can clearly distinguish from the ballistic trajectories of strategic missiles. This demand suggests that reintroducing a theater-range cruise missile to the Asia-Pacific would pay dividends for reasons beyond deterring China and Russia. Similarly, US planners should ensure that America's strategic bomber fleet—the most selective and flexible attack option in the existing US arsenal—has enough slack to penetrate the vast Eurasian periphery. To deter and assure against coercion in multiple theaters, the US nuclear posture will require greater strike capacity, selectivity, and flexibility.

Conclusion: A Three-Theater Nuclear Posture

The discussion thus far has demonstrated that the existing US nuclear posture and modernization program are tailored to a benign threat environment that no longer exists. Russia has reverted to Soviet form, engaging in nuclear coercion and violating arms control agreements by building up a massive theater-range arsenal and denying Washington its right to inspect Russian nuclear sites under the New START provisions. China, meanwhile, has unexpectedly ditched its minimum deterrent and joined Russia as a peer nuclear adversary, building up at both the strategic and theater levels. And although North Korea (and possibly Iran) will remain a lesser-included nuclear threat, Pyongyang has sown doubt about America's credibility as a security partner.

The United States therefore finds itself in a mismatch between its nuclear strategy and the resources available to execute it. The analysis so far has treated America's existing nuclear weapons employment policy—targeting what the adversary values most (i.e., its political leadership, selected portions of its nuclear and conventional forces, and its war-supporting industries)—as entirely appropriate for the two-peer-plus environment. The analysis has also recognized that US planners must close the strategy-resource gap in such a way as to address the coercive national styles of America's adversaries. Here, it is worth noting that for the United States to fulfill existing policy, its nuclear force posture does *not* require a strike capacity that equals the combined arsenals of its nuclear-armed peer competitors.

Matching China and Russia on a weapon-for-weapon basis would be irresponsible and entirely unnecessary. US planners should instead tailor nuclear forces to adversary coercive styles rather than narrowly focus on target sets alone. If the United States were to engage in a quantitative arms race, it would cede the initiative to its great-power rivals and steer vital resources away from rebuilding the Navy and other critical conventional capabilities. There is, after all, a certain synergy between nuclear and conventional deterrence. One cannot operate effectively without the other. And if one became the bill payer for the other's reinforcement, America's overall deterrence would be weakened. Defense planners must ensure that growing and diversifying the nuclear force structure does not starve the conventional posture of precious resources.

The preceding analysis also suggests two force-planning objectives that will resolve the strategy-resource mismatch in a coercive two-peer-plus threat environment. These planning objectives entail (1) sizing and shaping regional nuclear forces to convey to adversaries that any attempt to escalate their way to victory at the theater level is futile and (2) sizing and shaping strategic nuclear forces to convince peer adversaries that they cannot escalate their way out of a failing theater-level war by coercing Washington into submission at the strategic level. These planning objectives also dovetail with the imperative to reassure allies that US nuclear forces remain coupled to their defense.

To assess the extent to which these planning objectives have been met, the analysis has suggested looking for three areas of improvement: (1) increased strike *capacity* at the strategic and theater levels in Europe and Asia, (2) greater *selectivity* in the form of an expanded strategic bomber fleet and an expanded theater nuclear arsenal in Europe and Asia, and (3) greater *flexibility* in the form of more diverse and enduring regional response options in Europe and Asia.

Expanding the nuclear force structure in certain areas (e.g., the airborne and sea-based legs of the triad) will be costly. These are highly complex delivery systems, and the atrophied state of the weapons production complex throws an additional hurdle into the equation. Nevertheless, as many of the chapters in this volume demonstrate, the US economy can ramp up and sustain higher levels of defense spending to support a modest nuclear expansion that does not starve conventional capabilities. Given the mounting threats the country faces, the nuclear balance would be an unwise place for Washington to accept greater risks.

What follows, then, is a proposal for a nuclear posture sized and shaped to meet the above force-planning standards and, ultimately, strengthen the country's overall deterrence. The first part concentrates on the immediate steps that can be taken at the strategic level and the longer-term measures that should be adopted or studied. The next part treats the theater-level of deterrence in a similar fashion, prescribing steps that should be taken or studied in both the near and long term.

Strategic Nuclear Posture. Given US strategic forces' vulnerability to a coordinated Sino-Russian attack in a protracted war, the US nuclear triad requires an expanded strike capacity across the board. Each leg of the triad provides unique and complementary attributes that make the whole greater than the sum of its parts. ICBMs are America's most responsive and prompt strategic attack option—and impose disproportionate costs on adversaries by forcing them to assign as many as four warheads to every US missile silo to ensure a "kill."[40] SLBMs, meanwhile, are the most survivable. And bombers are the most flexible option—to say nothing of their added value in forcing adversaries to pour enormous resources into costly air defenses. Together, all three legs enhance each other's survivability and complicate adversary planning. All three, then, should be reinforced to convince Beijing and Moscow that they cannot coerce Washington into submission at the strategic level of deterrence.

In terms of immediate next steps, the United States should prepare to upload warheads from the ready reserve stockpile on the existing 400 Minuteman III ICBMs and the 240 Trident D5 SLBMs carried on the *Ohio*-class fleet. US strategic force levels are, at this time, constrained by New START until February 4, 2026. But Russia has been in flagrant violation of the agreement since February 2023.[41] Though the political costs of withdrawing from New START may be too high, the United States should ready itself to begin uploading warheads after the treaty expires. A max loadout of the land- and sea-based legs would increase Minuteman strike capacity from 400 to at least 980 deployed warheads and Trident strike capacity from 968 to 1,626. This upload option represents the most expeditious and cost-effective way to expand strike capacity in the near term. The Trident fleet, for example, could begin uploading within months.[42] And the cost of uploading ICBMs and SLBMs would derive mostly from transporting and installing existing warheads from the reserve stockpile—a onetime cost of millions rather than billions of dollars.[43]

The United States should also restore the 30 standoff B-52H bombers that were removed from the nuclear mission in 2015. Expanding the airborne leg's strike capacity would lessen the operational strain on a dual-capable bomber force that, if deterrence fails, will be in high demand for conventional missions. It would also provide greater selectivity and flexibility at the theater level, as B-52H bombers—carrying ALCMs with non-ballistic trajectories—can operate from forward bases on the Eurasian periphery.

In the long run, the United States should swap out the existing Minuteman fleet for 400 Sentinel ICBMs (loaded with two or three warheads), examine the feasibility of a more survivable road-mobile Sentinel launcher, and expand the planned *Columbia*-class submarine fleet from 12 to 14. The United States will also need more from its B-21 stealth bomber program. The B-21 is set to replace the B-2 as America's only dual-capable bomber capable of penetrating sophisticated integrated air defenses. Yet current planning calls for just 100 of these stealthy delivery vehicles. US planners should expand the program to at least 200 bombers to ensure that the airborne leg has enough slack to conduct conventional and nuclear missions across three theaters. To further alleviate the operational strain on the dual-capable bomber force, the United States should also expand the planned long-range standoff weapon program (currently set for 1,087 missiles) to have a long-range cruise missile for every mounting point in the B-52H and B-21 fleets.

Theater Nuclear Posture. In the near term, the United States should open discussions with its Asian and European allies about forward deploying nuclear forces in their respective theaters. Frontline states are increasingly anxious about the credibility of America's extended deterrence guarantee. South Korea and Poland in particular deserve special consideration to be brought into a nuclear-sharing arrangement in which Washington maintains custody of forward-stationed nuclear weapons that in moments of crisis or conflict would be carried by South Korean and Polish dual-capable aircraft. To hedge against these allied consultations failing to produce tangible results, the United States should simultaneously explore the feasibility of redeploying an interim seaborne cruise missile that places a W-80 warhead into the Block V variant of the TLAM. This emergency measure would help offset Russia and China and provide a stopgap until the planned nuclear-armed sea-launched cruise missile (SLCM-N) enters service in the mid-to-late 2030s.

In the longer term, the United States should prepare to bring online SLCM-Ns on attack submarines. If the promise of this enduring, regional nuclear option fails to reassure South Korea and Japan, Washington may need to broach the idea of a NATO-like nuclear-sharing arrangement that suits Asia's unique political dynamics. And, in Europe, if the forward-basing option falls through and the SLCM-N fails to assuage fears in Poland, Washington may need to consider the return of theater-range, road-mobile missile launchers. Above all, the United States requires more prompt, diverse, and survivable regional nuclear options. Dual-capable fighters stationed far from the Russian border are necessary but insufficient, given their vulnerability on the ground and in the air, the Kremlin's demonstrated risk tolerance, and Poland's growing fears. And neither bombers generated from the continental United States nor port visits of ballistic missile submarines have quelled allied concerns that Beijing has decoupled America's strategic forces from their defense.

US planners' failure to anticipate the emerging two-peer-plus threat environment has placed the American nuclear posture in a severe strategy-resource mismatch. Washington can no longer treat today's deterrence landscape as if it is business as usual. To redress the widening gap between strike capability and target sets, US planners must tailor force requirements to *both* the distinctive coercive styles of its adversaries *and* the growing fears of far-flung allies.

Deterring and assuring across three theaters will ultimately depend on injecting greater strike capacity, selectivity, and flexibility into the US nuclear force structure. Implementing these adjustments will undoubtedly impose resource-intensive demands on the broader defense program. And given the synergy between conventional and nuclear deterrence, defense planners must ensure that reinforcing the latter does not come at the expense of the former, and vice versa. As the other chapters in this book demonstrate, however, America can afford to reinforce both its conventional and nuclear forces and thereby strengthen its overall deterrence.

Thus, given the singular importance of nuclear weapons to the nation's security, Washington should field a larger and more diverse nuclear posture that addresses today's unprecedented threat environment.

Notes

1. US Department of Defense, *Nuclear Posture Review Report*, April 2010, https://dod.defense.gov/portals/1/features/defensereviews/npr/2010_nuclear_posture_review_report.pdf.

2. Barack Obama, "Remarks by President Barack Obama in Prague as Delivered," speech, Hradčany Square, Prague, Czech Republic, April 5, 2009, https://obamawhitehouse.archives.gov/the-press-office/remarks-president-barack-obama-prague-delivered.

3. US Department of Defense, *Nuclear Posture Review Report*, 6.

4. Obama, "Remarks by President Barack Obama in Prague as Delivered."

5. *The New START Treaty (Treaty Doc. 111-5): Hearings Before the Committee on Foreign Relations, United States Senate*, 111th Cong. (2010).

6. US Department of State, Bureau of Verification, Compliance, and Implementation, "Comparison of START Treaty, Moscow Treaty, and New START Treaty," April 8, 2010, https://2009-2017.state.gov/t/avc/rls/139901.htm.

7. George W. Bush, "Remarks by the President to Students and Faculty at National Defense University," speech, National Defense University, Washington, DC, May 1, 2001, https://georgewbush-whitehouse.archives.gov/news/releases/2001/05/20010501-10.html.

8. Madelyn R. Creedon et al., *America's Strategic Posture: The Final Report of the Congressional Commission on the Strategic Posture of the United States*, October 2023, 43, https://www.ida.org/-/media/feature/publications/a/am/americas-strategic-posture/strategic-posture-commission-report.ashx.

9. Donald Rumsfeld, "Statement of Hon. Donald H. Rumsfeld, Secretary of Defense," testimony before the Senate Committee on Foreign Relations, July 17, 2002, https://www.congress.gov/107/chrg/CHRG-107shrg81339/CHRG-107shrg81339.pdf.

10. For an assessment of the nuclear production infrastructure, see Brad Roberts and William Tobey, eds., *The Inflection Point and the U.S. Nuclear Security Enterprise* (Lawrence Livermore National Laboratory, Center for Global Security Research, 2023).

11. Bush, "Remarks by the President to Students and Faculty at National Defense University."

12. White House, Office of the Press Secretary, "U.S.-Russia Relations: 'Reset' Fact Sheet," June 24, 2010, https://obamawhitehouse.archives.gov/the-press-office/us-russia-relations-reset-fact-sheet.

13. Anya L. Fink, *Russia's Nuclear Weapons*, Congressional Research Service, November 22, 2024, https://crsreports.congress.gov/product/pdf/IF/IF12672.

14. US Department of Defense, *Military and Security Developments Involving the People's Republic of China 2022*, 98, https://media.defense.gov/2022/Nov/29/2003122279/-1/-1/1/2022-MILITARY-AND-SECURITY-DEVELOPMENTS-INVOLVING-THE-PEOPLES-REPUBLIC-OF-CHINA.PDF.

15. Dan Blumenthal et al., *From Coercion to Capitulation: How China Can Take Taiwan Without a War*, American Enterprise Institute, May 13, 2024, https://www.aei.org/research-products/report/from-coercion-to-capitulation-how-china-can-take-taiwan-without-a-war/.

16. US Department of Defense, *Military and Security Developments Involving the People's Republic of China 2024*, 66, https://media.defense.gov/2024/Dec/18/2003615520/-1/-1/0/MILITARY-AND-SECURITY-DEVELOPMENTS-INVOLVING-THE-PEOPLES-REPUBLIC-OF-CHINA-2024.PDF; and Greg Hadley, "China Now Has More ICBM Launchers Than the US," *Air & Space Forces Magazine*, February 7, 2023, https://www.airandspaceforces.com/stratcom-china-more-icbm-launchers-than-us-not-more-missiles-warheads/.

17. Before the 2010 decision to retire TLAM-N, the 2009 Strategic Posture Commission, following extensive discussions with Asia-Pacific allies, assessed, "In Asia, extended deterrence relies heavily on the deployment of nuclear cruise missiles on some Los Angeles class attack submarines. . . . In our work as a Commission it has become clear to us that some U.S. allies in Asia would be very concerned by TLAM/N retirement." William J. Perry et al., *America's Strategic Posture: The Final Report of the Congressional Commission on the Strategic Posture of the United States* (United States Institute of Peace, 2009), 26, https://www.usip.org/sites/default/files/America's_Strategic_Posture_Auth_Ed.pdf.

18. Mary Beth D. Nikitin, *North Korea's Nuclear Weapons and Missile Programs*, Congressional Research Service, December 19, 2023, https://crsreports.congress.gov/product/pdf/IF/IF10472.

19. Mitch Shin, "North Korea Steps Up Its Hostile Moves Against South Korea," *The Diplomat*, October 16, 2024, https://thediplomat.com/2024/10/north-korea-steps-up-its-hostile-moves-against-south-korea/.

20. Dasl Yoon, "South Korean President Says Country Could Develop Nuclear Weapons," *The Wall Street Journal*, January 12, 2023, https://www.wsj.com/articles/south-korean-president-says-country-could-develop-nuclear-weapons-11673544196.

21. American Enterprise Institute, "Axis of Aggression: September 2024 Update," September 18, 2024, https://www.aei.org/research-products/one-pager/axis-of-aggression-september-2024/.

22. US Department of Defense, *Report on the Nuclear Employment Strategy of the United States*, November 7, 2024, 2–3, https://media.defense.gov/2024/Nov/15/2003584623/-1/-1/1/REPORT-ON-THE-NUCLEAR-EMPLOYMENT-STRATEGY-OF-THE-UNITED-STATES.PDF.

23. The idea that states possess distinctive "national styles," informed by their respective strategic cultures, is drawn from Colin S. Gray, *Nuclear Strategy and National Style* (Hamilton Press, 1986); and Ken Booth, *Strategy and Ethnocentrism* (Croom Helm, 1979), especially 82–85.

24. For the important distinction between "deterrence" and "compellence" in American strategic thought, see Thomas C. Schelling, *Arms and Influence* (Yale University Press, 1966), 69–86.

25. Dmitry (Dima) Adamsky, *The Russian Way of Deterrence: Strategic Culture, Coercion, and War* (Stanford University Press, 2023), 23–39, 104–8.

26. Dmitry Adamsky, "Russia's New Nuclear Normal," *Foreign Affairs*, May 19, 2023, https://www.foreignaffairs.com/russian-federation/russias-new-nuclear-normal. For a fuller treatment of Russia's steady progression to this new normal, see Dmitry Adamsky, *Russian Nuclear Orthodoxy: Religion, Politics, and Strategy* (Stanford University Press, 2019).

27. Claudia Chiappa, "Poland: We're Ready to Host Nuclear Weapons," *Politico*, April 22, 2024, https://www.politico.eu/article/poland-ready-host-nuclear-weapons-andrzej-duda-nato/; and Anne Kauranen, "NATO's Nuclear Deterrent Must Be Real for Finland, Says New President," Reuters, March 1, 2024, https://www.yahoo.com/news/finland-inaugurates-alexander-stubb-president-103310657.html.

28. Dean Cheng, "An Overview of Chinese Thinking About Deterrence," in *NL ARMS Netherlands Annual Review of Military Studies 2020: Deterrence in the 21st Century—Insights from Theory and Practice*, ed. Frans Osinga and Tim Sweijs (T.M.C. Asser Press, 2021), 178–85.

29. See, for example, Ge Tengfei, "Dazao qiangda de guojia zhanlue weisheliliang tixi" [Build a Strong National Strategic Deterrent Force System], *People's Forum*, November 21, 2022, http://paper.people.com.cn/rmlt/html/2022-11/01/content_25950663.htm.

30. Chen Jiaqi, "Wei lai zhan zheng dui wu qi zhuang bei jian she fa zhan de xin xu qiu" [New Demands for the Development of Weapons and Equipment in Future Wars], *Defence Industry Conversion in China*, no. 6 (2021), https://m.fx361.com/news/2021/0910/9359436.html.

31. Kristen Gunness and Phillip C. Saunders, *Averting Escalation and Avoiding War: Lessons from the 1995–1996 Taiwan Strait Crisis* (National Defense University Press, 2022), 36; and Barton Gellman, "U.S. and China Nearly Came to Blows in '96," *The Washington Post*, June 20, 1998, https://www.washingtonpost.com/archive/politics/1998/06/21/us-and-china-nearly-came-to-blows-in-96/926d105f-1fd8-404c-9995-90984f86a613/.

32. Shigeru Ishiba, "The Future of Japan's Foreign Policy," Hudson Institute, September 25, 2024, https://www.hudson.org/politics-government/shigeru-ishiba-japans-new-security-era-future-japans-foreign-policy.

33. US Department of Defense, *Military and Security Developments Involving the People's Republic of China 2024*, 66.

34. Iskander Rehman, *Planning for Protraction: A Historically Informed Approach to Great-Power War and Sino-US Competition* (International Institute for Strategic Studies, 2023), 9–31, 73–132; and Hal Brands and Michael Beckley, "Getting Ready for a Long War: Why a US-China Fight in the Western Pacific Won't End Quickly," in *Defending Taiwan: Essays on Deterrence, Alliances, and War*, ed. Kori Schake and Allison Schwartz (AEI Press, 2023).

35. US Defense Intelligence Agency, *Nuclear Challenges: The Growing Capabilities of Strategic Competitors and Regional Rivals*, 2024, 21, https://web.archive.org/web/

20250104010242/https://www.dia.mil/Portals/110/Images/News/Military_Powers_
Publications/Nuclear-Challenges-2024.pdf.

36. US Defense Intelligence Agency, *Nuclear Challenges*, 21.

37. In 2024, Victor Cha demonstrated that if an America First foreign policy
returned to Washington, South Korean security elites' support for an independent
nuclear arsenal "would grow exponentially." Victor Cha, *Breaking Bad: South Korea's
Nuclear Option*, Center for Strategic and International Studies, April 2024, 2–3, https://
csis-website-prod.s3.amazonaws.com/s3fs-public/2024-04/240429_Cha_Breaking_
Bad.pdf.

38. Choe Sang-Hun, "In a First, South Korea Declares Nuclear Weapons a Policy
Option," *The New York Times*, January 12, 2023, https://www.nytimes.com/2023/01/12/
world/asia/south-korea-nuclear-weapons.html.

39. American Enterprise Institute, "Axis of Aggression."

40. During his confirmation hearing to serve as secretary of defense, Mattis stated
that "any enemy that wants to take us on is going to have to commit two, three, four
weapons to make certain they take each [missile silo] out." See James N. Mattis,
"Statement of James N. Mattis, to Be Secretary of Defense," testimony before the Senate Committee on Armed Services, January 12, 2017, https://www.armed-services.sen-
ate.gov/imo/media/doc/17-03_01-12-17.pdf.

41. Shannon Bugos, "Russia Suspends New START," Arms Control Association,
March 2023, https://www.armscontrol.org/act/2023-03/news/russia-suspends-new-start.

42. Keith B. Payne and Mark B. Schneider, *US Nuclear Deterrence: What Went Wrong
and What Can Be Done?*, National Institute for Public Policy, October 7, 2024, 6, https://
nipp.org/wp-content/uploads/2024/10/IS-601.pdf.

43. The Congressional Budget Office estimates that uploading the land, sea, *and*
airborne legs of the triad to START II levels (3,000–3,500 warheads) would cost
$100 million. See Congressional Budget Office, *The Potential Costs of Expanding U.S.
Strategic Nuclear Forces If the New START Treaty Expires*, August 2020, https://www.cbo.
gov/publication/56524.

About the Authors

Kyle Balzer is a Jeane Kirkpatrick Fellow at the American Enterprise Institute, where he focuses on great-power competition, US grand strategy, long-term strategic competition, US nuclear strategy and policy, and arms control. He specializes in Cold War nuclear strategy and the evolution of American deterrence theory.

Dan Blumenthal is a senior fellow at the American Enterprise Institute and the author of *The China Nightmare: The Grand Ambitions of a Decaying State* (2020).

Hal Brands is a senior fellow at the American Enterprise Institute, where he studies US foreign policy and defense strategy. Concurrently, he is the Henry A. Kissinger Distinguished Professor of Global Affairs at the Johns Hopkins School of Advanced International Studies. He is also a columnist for *Bloomberg Opinion*.

James C. Capretta is a senior fellow and holds the Milton Friedman Chair at the American Enterprise Institute, where he studies health care, entitlement programs, and fiscal trends in advanced economies.

Zack Cooper is a senior fellow at the American Enterprise Institute, where he studies US defense strategy and allies in Asia. He also teaches at Princeton University and is the author of *Tides of Fortune: The Rise and Decline of Great Militaries* (2025).

Giselle Donnelly is a senior fellow at the American Enterprise Institute and the author of *Empire Imagined: The Personality of American Power* (2022) and *The Fourth Kingdom* (forthcoming), the first two books in a four-volume series on the personality of American power.

Mackenzie Eaglen is a senior fellow at the American Enterprise Institute, where she works on defense strategy, defense budgets, and military readiness. She is the cochairman of the National Commission on the Future of the Navy and sits on both the Army Science Board and the Army War College Board of Visitors.

John G. Ferrari is a nonresident senior fellow at the American Enterprise Institute, where his work focuses on the defense budget, defense reform and acquisition, and the US military. He is a retired major general and former director of program analysis and evaluation for the Army.

Rebecca Grant is a national security analyst based in Washington, DC, and vice president of the Lexington Institute. She graduated from Wellesley College and earned a PhD in international relations from the London School of Economics at the University of London.

Todd Harrison is a senior fellow at the American Enterprise Institute, where he focuses on defense strategy and budgeting, the defense industrial base, and space policy and security.

Frederick W. Kagan is a senior fellow and the director of the Critical Threats Project at the American Enterprise Institute.

James Mattis is a retired US Marine Corps general and former secretary of defense.

Elaine McCusker is the former acting under secretary of defense for comptroller. She is now a senior fellow at the American Enterprise Institute, where she focuses on defense strategy, budget, and innovation; the United States military; and national security. Her background is in defense planning and budgeting, military campaign assessments, defense data analytics, contingency operations, and science and technology. She has substantial experience in resolving complex strategic and tactical-level challenges, including those with international dimensions.

Kori Schake is a senior fellow and the director of Foreign and Defense Policy Studies at the American Enterprise Institute.

Michael R. Strain is the Arthur F. Burns Scholar in Political Economy at the American Enterprise Institute.

Dustin Walker is a nonresident fellow at the American Enterprise Institute. In addition to his private-sector work at Anduril Industries, he recently served on the staff of the Commission on the National Defense Strategy. Before joining the American Enterprise Institute, he was a professional staff member on the Senate Armed Services Committee and an adviser to Senator John McCain.

RESEARCH STAFF